# Death Ritual
# in Late Imperial
# and Modern China

This volume was sponsored by the Joint Committee on Chinese Studies of the American Council of Learned Societies and the Social Science Research Council, with funds provided by the National Endowment for the Humanities and the Ford Foundation.

# Death Ritual in Late Imperial and Modern China

EDITED BY

## James L. Watson
## Evelyn S. Rawski

UNIVERSITY OF CALIFORNIA PRESS
Berkeley • Los Angeles • London

University of California Press
Berkeley and Los Angeles, California
University of California Press, Ltd.
Oxford, England
© 1988 by
The Regents of the University of California
First Paperback Printing 1990

**Library of Congress Cataloging-in-Publication Data**
Death ritual in late imperial and modern China.

(Studies on China; 8)
Rev. versions of papers presented at a conference
held at the Sun Space Ranch Conference Center in
Oracle, Ariz., Jan. 2–7, 1985, and sponsored by the
Joint Committee on Chinese Studies of the American
Council of Learned Societies and Social Science
Research Council.
Includes bibliographies and index.
1. Funeral rites and ceremonies—China.
I. Watson, James L.  II. Rawski, Evelyn Sakakida.
III. Joint Committee on Chinese Studies (U.S.)
IV. Series.
GT3283.D43  1988    393'.0951    87-5982
ISBN 0-520-07129-8 (alk. paper)

Printed in the United States of America

2 3 4 5 6 7 8 9

The paper used in this publication meets the minimum requirements of
American National Standard for Information Sciences—Permanence of Paper
for Printed Library Materials, ANSI Z39.48–1984. ∞

STUDIES ON CHINA

A series of conference volumes sponsored by
the Joint Committee on Chinese Studies of the
American Council of Learned Societies and the
Social Science Research Council.

1. Origins of Chinese Civilization
*edited by David N. Keightley,*
*University of California Press, 1982*

2. Popular Chinese Literature and Performing Arts
in the People's Republic of China, 1949–1979
*edited by Bonnie S. McDougall,*
*University of California Press, 1984*

3. Class and Social Stratification in
Post-Revolution China
*edited by James L. Watson,*
*Cambridge University Press, 1984*

4. Popular Culture in Late Imperial China
*edited by David Johnson, Andrew J. Nathan, and Evelyn S. Rawski,*
*University of California Press, 1985*

5. Kinship Organization in Late Imperial China, 1000–1940
*edited by Patricia Buckley Ebrey and James L. Watson,*
*University of California Press, 1986*

6. The Vitality of the Lyric Voice:
*Shih* Poetry from the Late Han to the T'ang
*edited by Shuen-fu Lin and Stephen Owen,*
*Princeton University Press, 1986*

# CONTENTS

# PREFACE

Our interest in systematic analysis of Chinese death ritual began in conversations in 1981 at a conference on popular culture in late imperial China which was held in Honolulu, Hawaii. As we wrestled at that conference with the question of how to study the behavior and values of ordinary Chinese who did not leave extensive written materials, it became evident that focusing on ritual would permit historians to explore nonelite culture in greater depth than heretofore. As is argued in the essays that follow, the rituals performed at marriage and at death were central to definitions of Chinese cultural identity. They affected people of every social stratum. Given the Chinese preoccupation with funerals, we chose to study death ritual. Ritual, of course, has long been the focus of attention by anthropologists and specialists on religion; we felt this would be an ideal topic for interdisciplinary exchange. A conference on Chinese death ritual, held at the Sun Space Ranch Conference Center in Oracle, Arizona, January 2–7, 1985, was sponsored by the Joint Committee on Chinese Studies of the American Council of Learned Societies and Social Science Research Council. The essays included in this volume are revised versions of papers presented at the conference. They have profited from the comments of Patricia Ebrey, Thomas Laqueur, Jonathan Parry, and Chün-fang Yü, who served as discussants. Two of the conference essays are being published separately in the *Harvard Journal of Asiatic Studies* (1987); these are Ying-shih Yü, "O Soul, Come Back! The Ritual of *fu* ('Recall') and Conceptions of the Afterlife in Han China," and Anthony Yu, "Rest, Rest, Perturbed Spirit! Ghosts in Traditional Chinese Prose Fiction." David Keightley's conference paper, "Dead But Not Gone: Cultural Implications of Mortuary Practices in Neolithic and Early Bronze Age China," will be published as a chapter in the author's forthcoming monograph on early Chinese culture and society.

Six of the ten chapters in this volume are written by anthropologists, largely on the basis of fieldwork in Hong Kong's New Territories and in Taiwan over the last twenty years. Two of the anthropological essays are based on fieldwork among Cantonese in the New Territories, two focus on Hokkien groups in northern Taiwan, and two on Hakka groups in Taiwan and Hong Kong. Three chapters are by historians, and one by a sociologist. The different disciplinary perspectives of the authors form part of a subtext, most evident in the two introductory essays but present in many of the other essays as well.

All of the essays emphasize the late imperial (Ch'ing) and modern eras. In designing the conference with a heavy bias toward the twentieth century, we followed the stratagem of "beginning at the end," when and where fieldwork observations could be tapped. We concentrated on identifying some of the underlying uniformities and ritual variations in contemporary Chinese communities living relatively close together. We have deliberately eschewed a historical survey. The actual evolution of practices associated with death ritual from ancient times to the present, with a few notable exceptions, remains largely unstudied, although the reader of this volume is directed to the papers, presented at the conference, that were cited earlier.

The conference papers and discussions touched intimately and frequently on the question of what held Chinese culture together. How was it possible for diverse and indeed widely divergent ritual practices, found in different localities and among different social groups, to coexist with the notion that there was a unified culture in China? We concluded that an underlying structure is evident in Chinese funeral ritual; this structure is reflected in rites associated with settling the soul after death. James Watson's introductory essay explores this topic in detail. Watson declares that the Chinese put less emphasis on burial and postburial rituals than on funeral rites as such. The sequence of funeral rites displays impressive uniformity; the burial customs vary significantly in different regions, although, as Martin Whyte notes, most Chinese are united in rejecting cremation as an alternative to burial.

The chapters in this volume treat both funeral and burial rites. If funerary ritual demonstrates the unity of Chinese culture, the rites associated with the grave express the accompanying marking of ethnic, status, and gender boundaries that were an equally important part of the social repertoire. One could not exist without the other; put another way, the existence of an agreed-upon normative sequence of funeral rituals, which were identified as central to Chinese identity, left room for variation and localization through changes in burial practices. Deliberate ambiguity, in part the product of the absence of a unified liturgy, permitted ethnic groups practicing a wide variety of burial customs to identify their own practices as "Chinese."

Here and in his own essay Watson argues that the integration of Chinese culture was only possible because the state enforced orthopraxy and did not try to instill uniform beliefs among its citizens. The debate concerning the importance of belief versus practice runs through the various papers and is explicitly discussed in Evelyn Rawski's introductory essay. Rawski argues that China's rulers—its emperors, officials, and educated informal elites— saw belief and practice as part of a duality. Belief could stimulate proper action, but proper action (behavior, or ritual) was an approved means of inculcating desired beliefs or values as well.

The normative structure of ritual that existed in late imperial China was the product of complex interactions between actual practice and the codification (in written form) of earlier customs recorded by literate elites. Once ritual texts were created in early China, they became in themselves a major element influencing ritual practice. Officials and informal elites promoted standardization and increasing conformity by following the ritual canon. The interaction of this purposive activity with the response of Chinese to their own environmental needs and ethnic preferences forms the background for the rituals discussed by the authors of the chapters in this volume.

In the first chapter of part 2, Susan Naquin uses information gleaned from local histories (gazetteers) for north China to describe a ritual sequence that was common to the region. This survey leads her to conclude that "most Chinese appear to have assumed that these rites should not vary widely from place to place nor should they change over time." Although the ideal sequence could be modified by the age, marital condition, sex, socioeconomic status, ethnicity, and religion of the deceased person, the overall structure remained essentially the same. The striking similarity of the north China rituals to funerary rituals reported for the lower Yangtze, and even to rites performed in southeast China and the Canton delta, supports the argument that a standardized Chinese "way of death" did indeed exist during the nineteenth and early twentieth centuries. Naquin ascribes the integration of death ritual in the Ch'ing dynasty to the activities of ritual specialists, who relied on religious and Confucian texts that gave specific instructions concerning mortuary rites. She suggests that the difference between the uniform funeral and divergent burial practices is tied to differences in the training and textual base of the priests presiding at the funeral, on the one hand, and the geomantic specialists who supervised grave selection and burial, on the other. The ritual specialists transmitted not only precise ritual formats but also notions about salvation and the efficacy of geomantic manipulation. Underlying conceptions about the dead help shape the ritual structure.

The symbolic language of food prestations at different stages of the mortuary sequence is analyzed by Stuart Thompson. He shows how food offerings, and especially the offerings of rice and pork, play key roles in the transformation of a corpse into an ancestor. This is done by providing exchanges between the living and the dead whereby death can be converted into fertility and regeneration. The presentation of pork, in Thompson's view, can be seen as a way to enable the deceased to replenish the corrupting flesh and cloak the bones with new substance. The nature of the offerings, which contrast and combine (male) rice with (female) pork, expresses Chinese conceptions of duality in the cosmic as well as the social universe.

The rituals associated with settling the soul reflect in some way the ambivalent feelings of mourners as well as the dread arising from fear of the corpse. James Watson's essay, "Funeral Specialists in Cantonese Society: Pollution, Performance, and Social Hierarchy," examines this problem among people who live in dominant lineages along the Canton delta. Cantonese villagers respond to the overpowering dread of death by ostracizing funeral specialists and ensuring, through payment, that these professionals bear a large part of the "killing airs" released by the corpse. In doing so, they minimize the pollution that they themselves must accept. There is a hierarchy of professional ritual specialists ranging from corpse handlers at the very bottom to geomancers at the top. It is interesting that corpse handlers and coffin bearers are also found at the bottom of the social order in other localities, including Hui-chou.[1] Watson concludes that the actions of professionals are a formal part of the structure of funerary rites; their *performance*, in other words, is a critical feature of what makes Chinese funerals "Chinese."

Two chapters deal specifically with gender issues. Elizabeth Johnson's "Grieving for the Dead, Grieving for the Living," demonstrates the use to which Hakka women put funeral laments. The wake becomes one of the few times when women can publicly voice their grievances and aggressively enunciate their own stance in the tangled relations among relatives. Death, which frequently elicits rituals of solidarity among the survivors, here gives rise to a potentially divisive form of expression. The laments deal with personal relations within the family. They show a belief in equality and fair treatment in the family realm. Individual in form, they contrast sharply with the male-oriented grave rites analyzed by Rubie Watson. The wake is, in essence, a ritual of social inversion. Johnson's essay is one of the few studies of Chinese mortuary rites that focus on the role of women. It also deals with a domain of ritual, laments and wailing, that is extremely difficult to investigate and yet is found throughout China.

Emily Martin's "Gender and Ideological Differences in Representations of Life and Death" is an ambitious attempt to map out a woman's perspec-

---

1. Hsien-en Yeh 叶显恩, *Ming Ch'ing Hui-chou nung-ts'un she-hui yü tien-p'u chih* 明清徽州农村社会与佃仆制 [The agricultural society of Hui-chou in the Ming and Ch'ing and the system of servile tenancy] (Anhwei: People's Press, 1983).

tive of life and death in Chinese society. Martin argues that this view contrasts sharply with the dominant male perception. Marriage, seen by men as a celebration of new life, is expressed by young brides in marriage laments as a death—a cutting of the affectionate natal bond that ties a daughter to her parents and siblings. The marriage dress, by this logic, can also be seen as the shroud of the corpse. The reversal of male symbols is also found in death: for women the rituals linked with death express fertility, the completion of a cycle that will bring birth out of death. Martin argues that women see life and death in terms of the unity of opposites, whereas men try to separate opposites and resist cyclical change by striving to attain permanence in status, even in the afterlife.

Myron Cohen's essay raises the interesting question of why Chinese popular religion did not place more emphasis on salvation. Cohen points out that although the notion of rebirth in a Western Heaven was hinted at in funerary ritual, it was not stressed as a major ideological force. If salvation had been highlighted, it would have contradicted fundamental tenets bolstering ancestral worship and other major elements in popular religion, namely, belief in multiple souls, reincarnation, and the close interaction of the living with the dead. Cohen notes that the interpenetration of elite and popular religious orthodoxy, characteristic of late imperial China, could not have been achieved through state fiat alone; it rested instead on a consensus that emphasized social rather than individual identity. Salvation creeds thus failed to take deep root in the society and instead attracted people who were by Chinese definitions "socially incomplete."

With Rubie Watson's essay we shift our focus to grave ritual, which was also very widely practiced in many regions of China over long periods of time. Although burial and funeral rites intended to settle the spirit after death are universal, not all graves become sites for collective worship. In the Canton delta, for example, only the affluent could afford to establish graves for their deceased kin; it was an elaborate and costly procedure. In contrast to funerary ritual, where the spirit of the deceased is potent and unpredictable, the ancestor in the grave is no longer individualized. At this point the deceased becomes a pawn to be manipulated for the benefit of descendants. Grave rites may unite agnates, but they can also be used to separate and distinguish competing branches, assert the claims of some branches over others, and help redefine political alignments within the lineage. In short, worship at ancestral graves can be a creative and sometimes a vigorously political act.

Evelyn Rawski's "The Imperial Way of Death" focuses on court ritual in the Ming and Ch'ing periods and on the ways in which the Ch'ing dynasty's modification of Chinese laws of succession influenced new emperors to use the observance of mourning as a means of claiming legitimation. A comparison of the rituals outlined for emperors and empresses with commoner ritual in north China, as presented in Naquin's essay, shows that the ritual sequence from death to grave worship remained essentially the same. But because imperial ancestral worship overlapped with state ritual, it was also separate and distinct from the general Chinese pattern. Burial transformed a dead emperor into an ancestor who became part of the state religion.

Imperial death was a state event that never led to the formation of popular cults or pilgrimage centers for the masses. Instead, the power of the imperial ancestors was the special monopoly of the ruling house. Frederic Wakeman, Jr., looks at state ritual in the People's Republic of China and in Taiwan, by comparing the mortuary observances of Mao Tse-tung and Chiang Kai-shek. Despite the opposed political ideologies in these two contexts, there are remarkable similarities in the modern rites surrounding the deaths of China's latter-day "emperors." These hark back to Sun Yat-sen's funeral in 1925 and, even more fundamentally, to the twentieth-century attempt to use dead leaders to legitimize a regime and to strengthen its popular base (e.g., as with Lenin in the Soviet Union). The glorification of Mao's thought, an alternative to worship of his embalmed corpse, also created political problems. Mao's current successors finally decided to put Mao into history.[2] In contrast to the dynastic era, the new Chinese governments have sponsored the formation of cults around the dead leader and encouraged pilgrimages to his tomb-shrine. The corpse has become public property—indeed, a national asset. As Wakeman notes, the rituals surrounding these new shrines are not yet fully formed and are still being negotiated between the party and the people.

The discontinuity between traditional Chinese mortuary ritual and the rituals promoted by the state in the People's Republic of China is the subject of Martin K. Whyte's "Death in the People's Republic of China." State and party efforts to simplify funerals, reduce expenditures, and substitute cremation for burial have been most successful in the cities. Intellectual and socioeconomic changes that began in China's urban centers in the 1920s and 1930s also encouraged funerary reform. In the countryside, Communist efforts to alter traditional practice were less successful. Whyte argues that peasants continue to adhere to traditional norms of mortuary ritual, in spite of repeated "anti-superstition" campaigns. Prerevolutionary burial practices, in particular, have made a very strong recovery in recent years—an unplanned consequence, perhaps, of Teng's policies in the countryside. The result is a growing gap between rural and urban mortuary customs. Whyte concludes his essay with a provocative discussion of the issue of belief versus practice. He argues that despite a radical break in ritual forms, China's

2. For an analysis of the implications of the two alternatives, see Richard Madsen, *Morality and Power in a Chinese Village* (Berkeley and Los Angeles: University of California Press, 1984), chap. 1, and his discussion of "ceremonies of innocence" and "rituals of struggle."

urban dwellers continue to adhere to important elements of the traditional ideology regarding death and the world beyond. Orthodoxy is more important than orthopraxy in China today.

In this volume we have tried to sketch out some of the key issues associated with mortuary rites in Chinese society. The essays have explicitly studied both ritual practice and belief structures as they relate to death rites—the performance of required acts, variations in form, and attitudes underpinning practice. As was noted above, it is no coincidence that we have chosen to concentrate on the rituals of death; in our view they provide one of the clearest windows on Chinese society. We could equally well have focused on wedding rites and the shared set of beliefs surrounding marriage. But that is a theme for another project at another time. The point we wish to make, however, is that the materials and techniques employed in this volume for the "unpacking" of death rites and beliefs may prove to be of value in an examination of other domains of Chinese culture.

# PART I

# Introductory Perspectives

# ONE

# The Structure of Chinese Funerary Rites: Elementary Forms, Ritual Sequence, and the Primacy of Performance

*James L. Watson*

In one important respect this collection of essays is the sequel to an earlier volume entitled *Popular Culture in Late Imperial China*.[1] The popular-culture conference (held in 1980) considered the general theme of Chinese cultural diversity and uniformity, looking specifically at the question What held Chinese society together? There were, of course, many institutions and social processes that led to the creation of a unified, centrally organized culture in late imperial China. One of the most obvious was control over the written word as expressed in literature and religious texts;[2] equally important was the subtle manipulation of oral performing arts, notably opera and public storytelling.[3] The authors of *Popular Culture* approached the problem of diversity within unity from many angles, but conference discussions made it clear that one important dimension was missing, namely, ritual.

If anything is central to the creation and maintenance of a unified Chinese culture, it is the standardization of ritual. To be Chinese is to understand, and accept the view, that there is a correct way to perform rites associated with the life-cycle, the most important being weddings and funerals. By following accepted ritual routines ordinary citizens participated in the process of cultural unification. In most cases they did so voluntarily,

1. David Johnson, Andrew Nathan, and Evelyn Rawski, eds., *Popular Culture in Late Imperial China* (Berkeley and Los Angeles: University of California Press, 1985).

2. David Johnson, "Communication, Class, and Consciousness in Late Imperial China," in Johnson et al., *Popular Culture*, pp. 34–72; James Hayes, "Specialists and Written Materials in the Village World," in Johnson et al., *Popular Culture*, pp. 75–111.

3. Tanaka Issei, "The Social and Historical Context of Ming-Ch'ing Local Drama," in Johnson et al., *Popular Culture*, pp. 143–160; Barbara E. Ward, "Regional Operas and Their Audiences," in Johnson et al., *Popular Culture*, pp. 161–187; and "Not Merely Players: Drama, Act, and Ritual in Traditional China," *Man* n.s. 14 (1979): 18–39.

without the necessity of enforcement by state authorities. What we accept today as "Chinese" is in large part the product of a centuries-long process of ritual standardization.

This volume, therefore, is more than a set of essays about death and mortuary ritual: It is a study in cultural homogenization as expressed in performance, practice, and beliefs regarding the dead. The essays that follow demonstrate that there was a uniform structure of funerary rites in late imperial China. The elements of this structure are outlined below. It is my contention that the proper performance of the rites, in the accepted sequence, was of paramount importance in determining who was and who was not deemed to be fully "Chinese." Performance, in other words, took precedence over belief—it mattered little what one believed about death or the afterlife as long as the rites were performed properly. The polemical tone of this essay is deliberate. It is hoped that others will take up the cause of belief, thereby leading to an exchange of views regarding the role of ritual in Chinese society.

## RITUAL: THE TRANSFORMATIVE ASPECT

Given that this volume focuses on funeral rites and mortuary practices, it seems appropriate to begin with a general discussion of ritual. There is, of course, a vast literature on this problem, and I do not propose to review all aspects of the topic here. Suffice it to note that anthropologists have long debated the meaning and definition of ritual; unfortunately, little agreement has been reached among contending schools, and there is still no generally accepted definition.[4] However, in all studies of the subject it is generally assumed that ritual is about transformation—in particular it relates to the transformation of one being or state into another, changed being or state. Most anthropologists would agree that it is this transformative aspect that sets ritual apart from other social actions. That which is merely repeated is not necessarily ritual. Rather, rituals are repeated because they are expected to have transformative powers.[5] Rituals change people and things; the ritual process is active, not merely passive.

4. Victor Turner, *The Ritual Process* (Chicago: Aldine, 1969); Jean La Fontaine, ed., *The Interpretation of Ritual* (London: Tavistock, 1972); Clyde Kluckhohn, "Myths and Rituals: A General Theory," *Harvard Theological Review* 35 (1942): 45–79; S. J. Tambiah, "A Performative Approach to Ritual" (Radcliffe-Brown Lecture, 1979), *Proceedings of the British Academy* 65 (1979): 113–169; Sally Falk Moore and Barbara Myerhoff, eds., *Secular Ritual* (Assen, Netherlands: Van Gorcum, 1977); Edmund Leach, *Culture and Communication* (Cambridge: Cambridge University Press, 1976); Ronald Grimes, "Ritual Studies: Two Models," *Religious Studies Review* 2, no. 4 (1976): 13–24.

5. Fred W. Clothey, *Rhythm and Intent: Ritual Studies from South India* (Bombay: Blackie and Son, 1983), pp. 1–5.

One of the most insightful studies of ritual to appear in recent years is Gilbert Lewis's *Day of Shining Red*.[6] This study is a minute "unpacking" of a puberty rite practiced by New Guinea villagers. The author works his way through the received definitions of ritual only to find them wanting. He concludes: "What is clear and explicit about ritual is how to do it—rather than its meaning."[7] The people he worked among knew how to perform rites, and they knew when something was performed incorrectly, but they could not provide ready explanations (in words) for what was being expressed, communicated, or symbolized. This, of course, is a familiar problem to all fieldworkers, not just those who work in New Guinea.

Lewis raises a fundamental question that, at one time or another, has haunted most scholars who attempt to analyze rituals: How can we go beyond what we are told by informants, texts, or documentary sources?[8] Many anthropologists try to create meaning by reassembling symbols, metaphors, and actions into a coherent set of messages—thereby engaging in structural analyses of various types. Lewis is not alone in questioning such procedures.[9] Whose meaning are we constructing when rituals are interpreted: our informants' or our own? Nor is it possible, as some have suggested, to present "value free" or "pure" descriptions of ritual, devoid of contaminating interpretations by the observer. The very act of description involves multiple judgments regarding the behavior being performed. Even the most detailed description demands that one isolate certain actions as being more significant than others.

Films and photographs of ritual present equally complicated problems of analysis. During the conference that preceded this volume participants observed nearly twenty hours of slides and films dealing with Chinese funerary ritual. It was fascinating, and enlightening, to learn that everyone present "saw" something different in the visual records of Chinese rites. Historians and anthropologists, in particular, did not even appear to be witnessing the same events, to judge from their comments (the historians were preoccupied with written messages and texts evident in the slides or films, whereas anthropologists tended to treat these messages as peripheral or at least secondary to the actions of ritual specialists; see Evelyn Rawski's observations on this matter, chapter 2). I might add that such variation in interpretation is also true for those who actually participate in funerals and perform the rites portrayed in ethnographic films or slides. Among Cantonese villagers in rural Hong Kong, for instance, there is no generally

6. Gilbert Lewis, *Day of Shining Red: An Essay on Understanding Ritual* (Cambridge: Cambridge University Press, 1982).

7. Ibid., p. 19.

8. Ibid., p. 24.

9. See, e.g., Roger M. Keesing, *Kwaio Religion: The Living and the Dead in a Solomon Island Society* (New York: Columbia University Press, 1982), pp. 3–5, 181–187.

accepted agreement regarding the signification or symbolism of rituals. When I asked about the meaning of an act or a symbol I was usually told, "I'm not clear about that. We do it this way because that's how it has always been done."

Rituals must be routinized and conventionalized before they can be accepted as part of the standard repertoire at a Chinese funeral. But this does not mean that they are immutable. In fact, several chapters in this volume focus on cases of ritual variability and modification to suit changing political circumstances (see especially chapters by Rawski, Wakeman, R. Watson, and Whyte). These changes are always made, however, within a recognizable framework of cultural convention; modifications are never arbitrary, given that they must conform to general notions of "Chineseness."

Closely associated with the problem of convention are notions of performance and audience. All rituals must have an audience to judge the quality and conventionality of the performance. When considering Chinese funerary ritual the question of audience becomes very complex. Who judges, and thereby validates, the performance? the deceased? the community? the gods, ancestors, and guardians of hell? or the performers of the rites themselves? Among rural Cantonese all of these interested parties represent the audience or separate audiences. But most villagers make it clear by their actions that the general community, represented by neighbors and kin, constitutes the most important audience. It is the community that determines convention and affirms that a funeral has been performed properly (a botched funeral can have disastrous consequences for everyone involved; see chapter 5). As with Lewis's informants, Cantonese villagers know what is correct and what is not; they represent a hypercritical audience even though they may not be able to articulate the reasons for their strongly held views about ritual propriety. Lewis nicely summarizes these issues: "In ritual as in art, he who devises or creates or performs is also spectator of what he does; and he who beholds it is also active in the sense that he interprets the performance. The value of ritual lies partly in this ambiguity of the active and passive for creator, performer and beholder."[10]

At Chinese funerals the general audience plays an active role, together with paid professionals, in creating a ritual performance. Community members are both the observed and the observers; they play a leading part in performing the rites while at the same time acting as audience. It is the proper performance of the rites—by specialists, mourners, and community members—that matters most to everyone concerned. As I shall argue below, the internal state of the participants, their personal beliefs and predispositions, are largely irrelevant.

10. Lewis, *Day of Shining Red*, p. 38.

## THE STRUCTURE OF RITES, I: THE IDEOLOGICAL DOMAIN

One of the central themes emerging from this study, as was noted earlier, is the view that there was a uniform structure of funeral rites in China during the late imperial era. This structure is still very much alive in Taiwan, Hong Kong, and some overseas Chinese areas, but it no longer dominates the ritual life of modern China as it did in the past. This is particularly true of Chinese cities, although it is evident that traditional rites are reemerging in many parts of rural China (see Whyte's discussion in chapter 12).[11] Pre-revolution burial practices are evident throughout rural Kwangtung, and in 1985 the ritual paraphernalia for traditional funerals were readily available in rural markets.[12] However, in comparison with Taiwan and Hong Kong, contemporary China seems peculiarly devoid of *public* rituals that have a religious content (i.e., festivals and collective displays of devotion). There is, of course, a great deal of public ritual activity in China, but it is strictly controlled by the party and is directly related to the political goals of the central administration.[13] The deritualization, and possible reritualization, of Chinese religious life is a subject that deserves a full-scale, interdisciplinary study by a team of scholars familiar with the traditional system. It is difficult to determine whether China, in the late 1980s, now has a uniform structure of funerary rites. Whyte suggests (chapter 12) that there is a growing dichotomy between rural and urban sectors in the People's Republic, with different rites emerging in city and countryside. The implications of this will be discussed below.

During the late imperial era (approximately 1750 to 1920)[14] rituals associated with marriage and death constituted a kind of "cultural cement" that helped hold this vastly complex and diversified society together. There are several ways to approach the problem of structural uniformity: It is not a simple matter of assembling a check list of ritual acts and routines, nor is it of particular concern that elements of the structure may be found in other societies. Rather, it is the unique *configuration* of ritual elements that makes a funeral acceptably Chinese. It was, in other words, a coherent package of

11. See also William L. Parish and Martin K. Whyte, *Village and Family in Contemporary China* (Chicago: University of Chicago Press, 1978), pp. 260–266.

12. Author's field investigations, Kwangtung province, summer 1985.

13. Martin King Whyte, *Small Groups and Political Rituals in China* (Berkeley and Los Angeles: University of California Press, 1974); Richard Madsen, *Morality and Power in a Chinese Village* (Berkeley and Los Angeles: University of California Press, 1984).

14. The year 1920 might be accepted as a rough "cutoff" date for the late imperial era, although for certain features of cultural life (e.g., lineage organization, ancestor worship, folk religion) 1940 or even 1950 may serve as well. This is a matter of some debate among anthropologists.

actions, routines, and performances which constituted the structure of
Chinese rites.

There are two domains within which the processes of ritual standardization can be analyzed. The first might be called the ideological domain, given
that it is concerned with abstract notions regarding the relationship between
life and death. Many of the essays in this volume deal specifically with the
ideological aspects of mortuary rites (see chapters by Cohen and Martin).
Among Chinese, there was a strong belief in the continuity between this
world (life) and the next (death). Both worlds were governed by bureaucratic principles that mirrored the imperial bureaucracy.[15] There was, as
Thomas Laqueur pointed out during conference discussions, no radical
dualism in Chinese thought—separating body from soul—similar to the
central concern that governed European notions of life and death. In other
words, the "moment of death," whereby body and soul were forever parted,
did not have the same meaning among Chinese as it had among Euro-
peans.[16] One of the primary goals of Chinese funeral rites, in fact, was to
keep corpse and spirit together during the initial stages of death; separation
prior to the ritualized expulsion from the community was thought to bring
disaster (see chapter 5).

Another key feature of Chinese ideology regarding the afterlife was the
belief that one's social status remained largely unaffected by death. In particular, both worlds were dominated by kinship, and it was believed that
death did not terminate the relationships between agnatic kinsmen (the
status of women is more problematic and deserves further study).[17] It is
important to note that, for most Chinese, it was patrilineal kinship that
survived beyond death; matrilateral ties (through one's mother) and affinal
links (through marriage) were generally terminated upon death. Ancestor
worship was the concrete expression of this preoccupation with the patriline.

The ideological domain of late imperial China was also dominated by the
notion that the soul, or spirit, was composed of several parts. There is considerable debate regarding the exact configuration of the soul,[18] but most
observers accept a dual (*hun* versus *p'o*) or a tripartite (grave, domestic

15. Arthur P. Wolf, "Gods, Ghosts, and Ancestors," in *Religion and Ritual in Chinese
Society*, ed. Arthur P. Wolf (Stanford: Stanford University Press, 1974), pp. 131–182; Emily
Martin Ahern, *Chinese Ritual and Politics* (Cambridge: Cambridge University Press, 1981).

16. Philippe Ariès, *The Hour of Our Death* (New York: Knopf, 1981).

17. On the ambiguous status of women in the afterlife, see James L. Watson, "Of Flesh and
Bones: The Management of Death Pollution in Cantonese Society," in *Death and the Regen-
eration of Life*, eds. Maurice Bloch and Jonathan Parry (Cambridge: Cambridge University
Press, 1982), pp. 178–180.

18. Stevan Harrell, "The Concept of Soul in Chinese Folk Religion," *Journal of Asian
Studies* 38 (1979): 519–528.

shrine, hall tablet) division.[19] The origin of the *hun/p'o* dichotomy is the subject of an important essay by Ying-shih Yü.[20] Associated with this ideological complex was a preoccupation with controlling, managing, and placating the dangerous aspects of the spirit of the deceased. Much of the ritual at funerals is aimed specifically at settling the volatile and disoriented spirit of the recently dead. There is, in other words, a need for social control in the nether world; ideally no one should be allowed to wander at will, outside the constraints of kinship and community, in life or in death. To bury a person without proper attention to ritual details is to create a hungry ghost who will return to plague the living. The analogy between ghosts and bandits is a conscious one in Chinese society.[21] Both exist outside the constraints of family, kinship, and community.

Another uniform feature of the ideological domain is obvious to those who are familiar with Chinese mortuary practices. This is the idea that there must always be a balance between the sexes, even in death. The notion of gender, a cultural construction, survives in the Chinese afterlife (this is not the case in all societies). If it is at all possible, married people are reconstituted as couples in death, usually by burial in close proximity. Posthumous unions, often referred to as "ghost marriages,"[22] are sometimes arranged for unmarried people, for it is considered unnatural, in life and in death, to be without a spouse.

Closely associated with these ideas of social continuity is the final, and some might say the most important, feature of the Chinese ideological domain: the idea of *exchange* between living and dead. Death does not terminate relationships of reciprocity among Chinese, it simply transforms these ties and often makes them stronger. A central feature of Chinese funerals and postburial mortuary practices is the transfer of food, money, and goods to the deceased (see Thompson's discussion in chapter 4). In return the living expect to receive certain material benefits, including luck, wealth, and progeny.

This notion of continued exchange between living and dead is the foundation of late imperial China's ideological domain. In other words, all rituals associated with death are performed *as if* there were a continued relationship between living and dead. It is irrelevant whether or not participants actually *believe* that the spirit survives or that the presentation of offerings

19. See e.g., Maurice Freedman, "Ancestor Worship: Two Facets of the Chinese Case," in *Social Organization: Essays Presented to Raymond Firth*, ed. Maurice Freedman (London: Frank Cass, 1967), pp. 85–103.

20. Ying-shih Yü, "O Soul, Come Back: A Study of the Changing Conceptions of the Soul and Afterlife in Pre-Buddhist China," *Harvard Journal of Asiatic Studies* 47 (1987): 363–395.

21. Robert Weller, "Bandits, Beggars, and Ghosts: The Failure of State Control over Religious Interpretation in Taiwan," *American Ethnologist* 12 (1985): 46–61.

22. Wolf, "Gods, Ghosts, and Ancestors," pp. 150–152.

has an effect on the deceased. What matters is that the rites are performed according to accepted procedure.

The ideological domain in China, in other words, does not assume universal belief or unquestioned acceptance of "truth."[23] Here is where China may have been unique among centralized societies. There was, of course, a close relationship between the ideological domain and what I shall call the performative domain (i.e., ritual; see below) in late imperial China. But, unlike the common pattern one finds in Christian Europe and Hindu India, the two Chinese domains do not seem to be totally dependent upon each other. There was a noticeable disjuncture between the requirements of ritual standardization (which were absolute) and the maintenance of a centralized belief system (loosely organized at best and rarely enforced).

In dealing with religious cults among peasants, Chinese imperial authorities were content to control and legislate actions, not beliefs.[24] Much the same was true for funerary ritual. As long as the rites were performed according to standardized and generally accepted sequence, it was of little consequence what people actually thought about the efficacy of those rites. As Jonathan Parry and Thomas Laqueur (Indianist and Europeanist respectively) noted in conference discussions, a radical distinction between belief and practice was never a central feature of Hindu or Christian social orders. In early Christendom, for instance, it was belief that carried more weight than practice, and in later eras debates regarding the proper performance of the Eucharist focused on ideological concerns underpinning practice.[25]

It is my contention that this was not the case in late imperial China. The standardization of ritual practice almost always took precedence over efforts to legislate or control beliefs. This, I would argue, had profound consequences for the creation of a unified cultural system. By enforcing orthopraxy (correct practice)[26] rather than orthodoxy (correct belief) state officials made it possible to incorporate people from many different ethnic or regional backgrounds, with varying beliefs and attitudes, into an over-

23. The concept of belief, its definition and cross-cultural applicability, has been the subject of considerable debate among anthropologists; see, for example, Rodney Needham, *Belief, Language, and Experience* (Oxford: Basil Blackwell, 1972).

24. James L. Watson, "Standardizing the Gods: The Promotion of T'ien Hou (Empress of Heaven) Along the South China Coast, 960–1960," in Johnson et al., *Popular Culture in Late Imperial China*, pp. 292–324.

25. Charles Gore, *The Body of Christ: An Inquiry into the Institution and Doctrine of Holy Communion* (London: Murray, 1901); A. M. O'Neill, *The Mystery of the Eucharist* (Dublin: M. H. Gill, 1933); Rudolf Bultmann, *Theology of the New Testament*, vol. 1 (London: SCM Press, 1952); Richard A. Watson, "Transubstantiation among the Cartesians," in *Problems of Cartesianism*, eds. Thomas Lennon, John Nicholas, and John Davis (Montreal: McGill-Queen's University Press, 1982), pp. 127–148.

26. Judith A. Berling, "Orthopraxy," in *Encyclopedia of Religion*, vol. 11, ed. Mircea Eliade (New York: Macmillan, 1987), pp. 129–132.

arching social system we now call China. Had this not been the strategy (conscious or unconscious) of state officials, Chinese culture could never have reached such heights of uniformity and coherence as it did during the late imperial era.

Before moving to a consideration of the performative domain, a clarification seems in order. I am *not* suggesting that belief and ideology are somehow irrelevant to the processes of cultural integration in China. Given the obvious uniformity of beliefs just surveyed, it would be absurd to make such a contention. Rather, I would argue that the Chinese state had no effective means of controlling beliefs regarding the afterlife in the absence of a unified church. There was, in other words, no centralized hierarchy of specialists charged with the responsibility of dispensing religious truth, as in Christendom. The closest equivalents would have been imperial bureaucrats, but these were relatively few in number,[27] and they were concerned primarily with good governance, not religious beliefs. What is truly intriguing about the Chinese case, therefore, is the fact that there *was* such a high level of uniformity in beliefs, attitudes, and conceptions regarding the dead. The creation of a unified culture obviously involved more than the conscious manipulation of the ideological domain by agents of the state, as some scholars have suggested.[28] I shall return to this point in the conclusion of this essay.

## THE STRUCTURE OF RITES, II: THE PERFORMATIVE DOMAIN

A survey of ethnographic sources on Chinese funerals,[29] together with conference discussion, films, photographs, and the results of my own field research, leads me to conclude that there was indeed a prescribed set of ritual

27. On this point, see G. William Skinner, "Rural Marketing in China: Revival and Reappraisal," in *Markets and Marketing*, ed. Stuart Plattner (Lanham, Maryland: University Press of America for the Society of Economic Anthropology, 1985), pp. 7–8.

28. See, e.g., Kung-chuan Hsiao, *Rural China: Imperial Control in the Nineteenth Century* (Seattle: University of Washington Press, 1960), p. 225.

29. The Cantonese sequence is outlined in J. Watson, "Of Flesh and Bones." On ritual sequences in other parts of China, see Emily Ahern, *Cult of the Dead in a Chinese Village* (Stanford: Stanford University Press, 1973); J. J. M. de Groot, *The Religious System of China*, vol. 1 (Leiden: Brill, 1892); Henry Doré, *Researches into Chinese Superstitions* (Shanghai: T'usewei, 1914); Bernard Gallin, *Hsin Hsing, Taiwan: A Chinese Village in Change* (Berkeley and Los Angeles: University of California Press, 1966), pp. 219–230; Sidney D. Gamble, *Ting Hsien: A North China Rural Community* (Stanford: Stanford University Press, 1954), pp. 386–393; Francis L. K. Hsu, *Under the Ancestors' Shadow* (Garden City, N.Y.: Anchor Books, 1967), pp. 154–166; and Arthur P. Wolf, "Chinese Kinship and Mourning Dress," in *Family and Kinship in Chinese Society*, ed. Maurice Freedman (Stanford: Stanford University Press, 1970), pp. 189–207.

actions that had to be performed before a corpse could be expelled from the community and buried. These actions are perhaps best referred to as the elementary structure of funeral rites, in the sense that they were performed, with minor variations, throughout China during the late imperial era, irrespective of class, status, or material circumstance. It is important to distinguish between *funerary rites* and *rites of disposal*.[30] The former involve actions undertaken from the moment of death to the formal expulsion of the deceased (in a sealed coffin) from the community. Rites of disposal are distinct from funeral rites in that the procedures of burial, cremation, or coffin storage are not governed by universally accepted norms. In fact, once the corpse is removed from the community almost any form of disposal is permitted. More will be said below about variations in burial practices.

What were the main features of funeral ritual in late imperial China? It appears that by Ming and Ch'ing a uniform structure had emerged, based roughly on classical models outlined in the *Li chi* and later simplified by Chu Hsi and others (see Rawski's account in chapter 2). The standardized rites required the following actions:

(1) Public notification of death by wailing and other expressions of grief. Women of the household, in particular, announced the death to neighbors by high-pitched, stereotyped wailing. Such actions were required by survivors; they were not voluntary. Formal notification of death was also given by pasting white banners on the house of the deceased and hanging blue lanterns from the eaves (these actions were optional in some parts of China, whereas the wailing was not).

(2) Donning of white clothing, shoes, and hoods (made of sackcloth or hemp) by mourners. The degree of kinship between the deceased and the mourner was often coded in the style of dress.[31] There were, of course, many regional variations in color symbolism and garment ensemble, but the use of white as an unambiguous symbol of mourning was a key feature of Chinese funerary ritual.

(3) Ritualized bathing of the corpse. This act was often accompanied by a final change of clothing deemed to be suitable for the journey to the otherworld. The provision of new or special clothing was optional and may not have been common among the poor, but the bathing of the corpse was an essential feature of the rites. In south China the water was often purchased (for a token sum of real money) from the deity of a well

30. Rubie S. Watson (chapter 9) notes that there is also a fundamental distinction between *funeral rites* (which are prescribed) and *grave rites* (which are fluid and subject to political manipulation).
31. Wolf, "Chinese Kinship and Mourning Dress."

or a stream; this rite is called *mai-shui* (lit. "buying water").[32] The bathing of the corpse varied from a full, vigorous scrubbing to a ritualized daubing of the forehead.

(4) The transfer of food, money, and goods from the living to the dead. Mock money and paper models of items to be used in the afterlife (e.g., houses, furniture, servants, vehicles, etc.) were transmitted by burning. Food was presented in the form of offerings, whereby the essence of the gift was consumed by the deceased while the remnants were often eaten by the mourners. It appears that there was an element of symbolic communication implicit in these prestations, with pork and rice being the irreducible food gifts (see chapter 4 by Thompson). In addition to food, the basic set of material offerings to the deceased included mock money and incense[33]—all other offerings were thus optional. This elementary feature of the rites was a concrete expression of the continuing relationship between living and dead.

(5) The preparation and installation of a soul tablet for the dead. All deceased Chinese, save those who died as infants or as wandering strangers, had to have a written tablet to serve as a repository for one aspect of their soul. This feature of the rites required the services of a literate person, usually a ritual specialist. The finished tablet of most married people was installed in the domestic altar of the deceased's household (tablets in ancestral halls—outside the home—were not an essential part of the rites but an option few could afford).[34] Unmarried women and other people who were not deemed to be members of households sometimes had their tablets placed in temples, convents, or institutions that provided such services for a fee. In considering funerary ritual as a mechanism of cultural standardization it is highly significant that the soul was represented as a written name (usually a posthumous *hao*) on a tablet; the repository of the soul did not take the form of icons, statues, or pictures.[35] It is surely no coincidence that the written script, a primary instrument of Chinese cultural unification, played a central role in the formal structure

32. J. Watson, "Of Flesh and Bones," pp. 161–162.

33. Strict codes govern the number of incense sticks offered; see, e.g., Stephan Feuchtwang, "Domestic and Communal Worship in Taiwan," in *Religion and Ritual in Chinese Society*, ed. Arthur P. Wolf (Stanford: Stanford University Press, 1974), p. 107.

34. Rubie S. Watson, *Inequality Among Brothers: Class and Kinship in South China* (Cambridge: Cambridge University Press, 1985), p. 41.

35. Among Hong Kong boatpeople small wooden statues of ancestors were sometimes kept on boat altars. It is significant, however, that the boat people (mostly illiterate) also maintained written ancestral tablets; see Eugene N. Anderson, Jr., *The Floating World of Castle Peak Bay*, Anthropological Studies no. 4 (Washington: American Anthropological Association, 1970), pp. 149–150.

of funerary rites. In order to follow the prescribed rites one had to have a Chinese written name—irrespective of social background,[36] education, or general level of cultural assimilation (for those of non-Han origin).

(6) The ritualized use of money and the employment of professionals. The proper conduct of Chinese funerary rites required the services of specialists who performed ritual acts in exchange for money. It was not possible, given the complex structure of rites, for mourners or untrained neighbors to perform all of these essential services. The payment of money to specialists was more than a simple monetary exchange; it was a required feature of the rites (see chapter 5). Someone, in other words, had to accept money from the mourners (or the deceased's estate or a public charity) before the corpse could be safely expelled from the community. The implications of this exchange have yet to be thoroughly analyzed, but it is evident that monetary exchange, in numerous forms, permeates Chinese funerary ritual.[37] This is testimony, perhaps, to the extent that money—as a universal medium of exchange—had penetrated into the cultural domain of late imperial China. Even in death one continued to engage in monetary exchange.[38]

(7) Music to accompany the corpse and settle the spirit. Two forms of music seem to have played a key role in the structure of funerary rites: high-pitched piping (from an oboe-like instrument) and percussion (particularly drumming). The sound of piping and drumming accompanied the corpse during critical transitions in the ritual, most notably when physical movement was required.

(8) Sealing the corpse in an airtight coffin. This action was considered by many Chinese to be the most important feature of the traditional funerary ritual. The use of coffins, usually constructed of wood, has

36. There are some interesting gender distinctions that might be pursued in future research. For instance, a deceased Cantonese woman is represented in writing by the surname of her father—not her own, personal name. Males, on the other hand, have their full posthumous names on soul tablets, tombstones, and funeral banners. This symbolic negation of female names suggests that Cantonese women are not perceived as complete human beings, at least in the context of mortuary ritual; see Rubie S. Watson, "The Named and the Nameless: Gender and Person in Chinese Society," *American Ethnologist* 13 (1986): 619–631.

37. Discussed in chapter 5; see also Hill Gates, "Money for the Gods: The Commoditization of the Spirit," *Modern China* 13 (1987): 259–277.

38. Among Cantonese in the Hong Kong New Territories, the dead sometimes continue to make annual prestations to popular deities. The offerings are made possible by the profits of the benefactor's ancestral estate, established during his lifetime. The offerings are often elaborate, and the benefits are said to accrue to the spirit of the deceased. In one case the benefactor has been dead for over four hundred years, but he continues to worship T'ien Hou (Empress of Heaven) every year on the occasion of her "birthday."

been common in China since at least the Neolithic.[39] Settling the corpse in the coffin and packing it so no movement was possible were tasks often assigned to paid specialists. Securing the lid, with nails and caulking compounds, ensured that the coffin was airtight. The ceremonial hammering of nails to seal the coffin was a centerpiece of the ritual sequence; this act was usually performed by the chief mourner or by an invited guest (i.e., someone of high social status relative to the mourners).

(9) Expulsion of the coffin from the community. When the coffin had been sealed, it was ready for removal from the village, town, or neighborhood of the deceased. This expulsion was the last formal act in the sequence of funerary rites,[40] but it need not be accomplished immediately. In fact, high-status families (including the imperial household; see Rawski's discussion in chapter 10) often kept the coffin in the domestic realm for months—even years—as a mark of respect for the deceased. But, in the end, the coffin must be expelled from the domain of the living.

As was noted earlier, there were no generally accepted guidelines—applicable everywhere in China—for the conduct of burials, cremations, and other means of disposal. In contrast, the formal expulsion of the coffin was orchestrated with considerable uniformity. At a precise moment chosen in advance by a specialist, the coffin was carried quickly out of the community by a team of pallbearers (often paid professionals). A procession of mourners and neighbors was formed to accompany the coffin to the point of disposal. When the procession had passed beyond the boundaries of the deceased's village, town, or city (often symbolized by walls and gates), the formal sequence of funeral rites had been completed.


VARIATION AND UNIFORMITY: RITES OF DISPOSAL

By isolating these nine acts as the elementary features of Chinese funerary ritual I do not mean to imply that there was no variation in performance. So long as the acts were accomplished in the approved sequence, there was room for infinite variety in ritual expression. For instance, the bathing of the corpse and the sealing of the coffin were performed differently in almost

39. David N. Keightley, "Dead But Not Gone: Cultural Implications of Mortuary Practices in Neolithic and Early Bronze Age China," paper presented at the conference on Ritual and the Social Significance of Death in Chinese Society, Oracle, Arizona, January 1985.

40. The implication of this act is that the deceased can no longer be treated (in ritual) as a member of the community once the coffin has been formally expelled. The dead retain their membership in (patrilineal) kinship organizations, but neighbors and other non-kin cease engaging in exchange with the dead at this point. The funeral, therefore, also serves as a rite of severance from the community.

every Chinese community. In my own experience of two closely related Cantonese villages (only six miles apart) there were striking contrasts in the conduct and organization of funerals, but the overall structure of the rites was similar.[41]

Herein lies the genius of the Chinese approach to cultural standardization: The system allowed for a high degree of variation within an overarching structure of unity. The rites of disposal constitute an excellent example of this principle (variation within unity). As long as the sealed coffin was removed from the community in the accepted fashion, mourners were free to dispose of the corpse according to local custom. Research on Chinese burial customs (as opposed to funerary rites) is surprisingly underdeveloped; there are whole regions of China for which we have little information on final disposal of the dead.

Most of our data derive from the south, notably Fukien, Kwangtung, Hong Kong, and Taiwan. Secondary burial is practiced in these areas, and it is intriguing to see how local people have accommodated to the standardized rites. Briefly summarized, Chinese secondary burial involves an initial burial of the coffin for approximately seven to ten years, followed by an exhumation of bones, which are placed in a large pot and eventually reburied in a permanent tomb (see R. Watson's discussion in chapter 9 for details). As was outlined above, one of the fundamental features of Chinese funerary ritual is the evacuation of the corpse in an airtight coffin. This procedure is diametrically opposed to the requirements of secondary burial, which puts a premium on the rapid decomposition of the flesh (thereby allowing for the retrieval and reburial of bones).

Peasants in south China had no difficulty following the standard rites, given that the prescribed actions of a proper funeral ended when the coffin left the community. In Taiwan, Hokkien villagers sometimes bash in one end of the coffin with an axe just prior to burial; in another part of Taiwan a specialist is hired to drill holes in the coffin.[42] Among Cantonese the seal around the coffin lid is often broken before interment. All of these practices, of course, are designed to hasten the decomposition of the flesh.

In north China, secondary burial is not practiced, and in fact northerners are often revolted when they first learn about southern customs. But northerners do things that shock southerners, such as storing coffins above ground, sometimes for decades, until the death of a spouse or a parent—thereby allowing family reconstitution by simultaneous burial (see Naquin's summary in chapter 3).

41. For instance, in one village attendance at funerals depends upon neighborhood (hamlet) affiliation, whereas in the other funerals are organized by voluntary associations.

42. Photographic slides presented at the 1985 Death Ritual Conference by Emily Martin and Stuart Thompson respectively.

In the borderlands of Szechwan where Han and non-Han have interacted for centuries, many who consider themselves Han do not bury their dead at all; instead, coffins are left in hillside caves that serve as family sepulchers.[43] And finally, when considering methods of disposal, we must not forget that cremation was practiced in many parts of China, even though it was condemned by Neo-Confucian scholars and regularly banned by the state.

What is significant about these diverse practices is that they could all be accepted as "Chinese" customs. By excluding disposal from the standard set of funeral rites, state officials implicitly condoned the cultural expression of ethnic and regional differences. This may have been the consequence of a conscious policy, given that any attempt to control burial practices would have been disastrously expensive and impossible to enforce (as Communist authorities were to discover during the 1950s and 1960s). Following the standard funeral sequence, on the other hand, did not impinge very deeply into regional sensitivities, and it was a small price to pay for the privilege of being accepted as proper Chinese. Those who chose not to perform funerals according to standard procedure were marked as non-Chinese or, worse yet, as dangerous sectarians.[44] This is why it was in everyone's interest to embrace the funeral rites as an expression of cultural identity and as an affirmation of loyalty to the imperial state.

The Chinese cultural system thus allowed for the free expression of what outsiders might perceive to be chaotic local diversity. The performative domain of ritual, in particular, gave great scope for regional and subethnic cultural displays. The system was so flexible that those who called themselves Chinese could have their cake and eat it too: They participated in a unified, centrally organized culture and at the same time celebrated their local or regional distinctiveness.

The imperial state, of course, was intimately involved in the standardization of funerary ritual, but it would never have been possible to *impose* a uniform structure of rites on a society of such vast size and complexity. More subtle means were required. There is good evidence that imperial officials were engaged in the promotion of a standardized set of funeral and mourning customs throughout the empire. These norms were enshrined in county gazetteers and in ritual manuals,[45] available throughout the empire (see Naquin's discussion in chapter 3). Given what we know about the distribution of power in late imperial China, it is probable that local elites

43. See, e.g., Shih Chung-chien 石鐘健, "Ssu-ch'uan hsuan-kuan tsang" 四川懸棺葬 [Szechwan hanging burials], Min-tsu hsueh yen-chiu 民族學研究 [Ethnological Research] 4 (1982): 100–118.

44. J. J. M. de Groot, *Sectarianism and Religious Persecution in China* (Taipei: Ch'eng-wen Reprints, 1976 [original 1901]), pp. 231–241.

45. Manuals (printed from wood blocks) outlining the sequence of funeral ritual, with crude illustrations, can still be found in Cantonese villages, Hong Kong New Territories.

subscribed to the accepted customs and enforced a kind of ritual orthopraxy in the communities under their control. Unacceptable rites were gradually suppressed or modified to conform to centralized models.

This may well have been the mechanism for the superimposition of a standard ritual structure, but we still know little about the process of acceptance. Is the standardization we now perceive a consequence of state-sponsored social engineering carried out over a period of many centuries? Or is it the result of voluntary adoption by the general populace? Need we assume that these processes are mutually exclusive? It is obvious that there must have been some strong incentives for people of all classes and regional backgrounds to cooperate in the cultural construction of a standarized set of rites. Much more work needs to be done before we can even begin to answer these questions. What is clear, however, is that the preoccupation with performance—rather than belief—made it possible for imperial authorities, local elites, and ordinary peasants to agree on the proper *form* for the conduct of funerals.

The fact that all Chinese, irrespective of personal circumstance, appear to have been subject to the same basic set of rites is an interesting commentary on the traditional Chinese class system. This uniformity of ritual structure is not found in all class-based societies. In nineteenth-century England, for instance, paupers were treated very differently from property-owning citizens. As Laqueur notes, England was changing rapidly during this period, and notions of what constituted a minimally acceptable funeral (i.e., the basic ritual form) were changing as well.[46] Ariès, in his now classic study, *The Hour of Our Death,* documents similar changes in European mortuary customs and attitudes toward death.[47]

It is probable that China has also undergone transformations in funerary ritual over the centuries. There is some evidence, for instance, that a major change in mortuary customs occurred during the T'ang–Sung transition, corresponding to changes in the Chinese kinship system.[48] Furthermore, we may be witnessing a radical transformation in China's ritual structure today, with a new sequence of rites inspired by socialist ideology replacing the old (see Whyte's survey in chapter 12). Can we expect to find something characteristically "Chinese" in these emerging rites, or are they basically

---

46. Thomas Laqueur, "Bodies, Death, and Pauper Funerals," *Representations* 1 (1983): 109–131.

47. Ariès, *The Hour of Our Death*, pp. 559–588.

48. See, e.g., David G. Johnson, *The Medieval Chinese Oligarchy* (Boulder, Colo.: Westview Press, 1977), pp. 94, 108; Patricia B. Ebrey, *The Aristocratic Families of Early Imperial China* (Cambridge: Cambridge University Press, 1978), p. 91; and Patricia Ebrey, "The Early Stages in the Development of Chinese Descent Groups," in *Kinship Organization in Late Imperial China, 1000–1940*, eds. Patricia B. Ebrey and James L. Watson (Berkeley and Los Angeles: University of California Press, 1986), pp. 20–29.

indistinguishable from socialist forms practiced in other parts of the world?[49] Whyte's account makes it clear that the ritual structure that helped hold China together as a coherent culture for so many centuries no longer has meaning to millions of Chinese (particularly in the cities). One wonders whether a new set of rites, together with new categories of ritual specialists, will emerge to fill the void.

49. Christel Lane, *The Rites of Rulers: Ritual in Industrial Society, the Soviet Union* (Cambridge: Cambridge University Press, 1981); Christopher A. Binns, "The Changing Face of Power: Revolution and Accommodation in the Development of the Soviet Ceremonial System, Parts 1 & 2," *Man* n.s. 14 (1979): 585–601 , and 15 (1980): 170–187.

# TWO

# A Historian's Approach to Chinese Death Ritual

*Evelyn S. Rawski*

There are several reasons why a historian's overview of Chinese death ritual is different from an anthropologist's. Anthropologists have made it their business to look closely at death ritual performance "on the ground"; they rarely do diachronic analysis. The cultural "givens" of the anthropologist are all variables in the perspective of historians, who want to trace the evolution of death ritual over long periods of time and analyze how and why ritual may have changed. Most anthropologists work with peasant communities and underplay, indeed often ignore, the existence of a written, literate tradition in Chinese culture that reaches down to and encompasses the peasant village. The historian's understanding of death ritual by contrast is dominated by the texts that are constantly cited in writings on ritual, beginning with the *Li chi* (Treatises on ceremonial usages), a work from the fourth to the third century B.C., which was one of the "Five Canons" (*wu-ching*), and the *I li* (Rites and ceremonial usages), dating from the same period.[1] These texts were the reference points for subsequent compilations of ritual into the late Ch'ing period, and for historians one major question is To what extent were these texts the guide to actual ritual practice?

The differences produced by disciplinary outlooks and training were very evident during the conference that preceded this volume. One of the most revealing events of the conference came at the nightly presentation of slides of funerary and grave ritual taken by anthropologists at their field sites. It was startling for a historian to discover that the six anthropologists present, who had been acquainted with one another for many years, had not pre-

---

1. De Groot's detailed analysis of death ritual faithfully reflected the Chinese tradition in its frequent reference to these texts: J. J. M. de Groot, *The Religious System of China: Its Ancient Forms, Evolution, History and Present Aspect, Manners, Customs and Social Institutions Connected Therewith*. 6 vols. (1892–1910 ed.; reprinted Taipei: Ch'eng-wen, 1969).

viously seen each other's slides. Since the anthropologist's "text" (the village studied) is for all intents and purposes inaccessible to other researchers, whose occasional visits cannot provide them with real access to the site, this discovery underlined the latent problem of verification. Without a counterpart to the historian's primary sources, which can be read and checked by others, how are anthropologists to defend themselves against charges that their analysis is a personal and arbitrary creation?

The methodological issue raised above, which is recognized as an important problem by anthropologists, lies outside the scope of our conference volume. More directly relevant were the dichotomous perspectives of the two disciplines, revealed at many points as we viewed hundreds of slides. The historians unanimously clamored for information on the many pieces of writing displayed on the mourning altar and elsewhere; the anthropologists showed clearly in their response that they regarded these writings as peripheral to the inquiry (frequently the anthropologists could not explain them). Indeed, some anthropologists seem to have adopted the attitude that their peasant informants are the standard of evaluation of cultural information—if something cannot be explained by the peasant, then it is not central to the research enterprise. This stance, of course, ignores the ways in which Chinese peasant culture was embedded in a complex literate civilization with a long historical tradition. It precludes an attack on the broader problem of how to link a very specific culture found in one village, in one region, in one historical period, to the larger abstract entity we call "China," and to analyze the changes in Chinese culture over time.

What does a historical perspective contribute to our understanding of death ritual? I would contend that the historian's primary source materials and perspective necessarily raise questions and produce hypotheses (if not answers) that are different from and perhaps complementary to the anthropologist's. The theme raised in James Watson's introductory essay concerning the primacy of performance over belief in Chinese ritual is a specific case illustrating this point.

## BELIEF AND PERFORMANCE

Watson's introductory essay asserts the central role of standardized ritual in the maintenance of a unified Chinese culture. The agents of cultural uniformity are the imperial state, officials, and educated local elites, who tried to disseminate a standard ritual structure. The success of this effort also rested in part on the receptivity of Chinese of all strata and regional backgrounds to this kind of homogenization. But a key element in successful ritual standardization, Watson argues, is that "the preoccupation with performance—rather than belief—made it possible for imperial authorities, local elites, and ordinary peasants to agree on the proper *form* for the conduct of funerals." Earlier in his essay Watson states, "Performance . . . took precedence over belief—it mattered little what one believed about death or the afterlife as long as the rites were performed properly."

While many historians might agree that the Confucian state emphasized orthopraxy, they would not agree with Watson's conclusion that the state did not link orthopraxy with orthodoxy. Watson's thesis, an elaboration of a statement he made in an earlier essay on the subject of imperially sanctioned cults,[2] takes issue with one of the assumptions concerning Chinese culture most widely held by historians, namely that the Chinese state, its officials, and its local elites attempted to propagate approved values and beliefs. Most historians would assert that despite obvious variations, Chinese culture in the late imperial period (the sixteenth through nineteenth centuries) had achieved important commonalities in belief that cut across the boundaries of regions and social strata.

That Watson's argument is directly based on the nature of the fieldwork experience is made clear in the opening pages of his essay, which cite Gilbert Lewis's Day of Shining Red. Watson quotes Lewis's argument that the villagers' understanding of ritual is "how to do it—rather than its meaning." Like Lewis, Watson rejects structuralist interpretations of ritual because of their subjectivity, even though he admits that all observation is selective and therefore to some extent subjective. Because variations in perception attend every human event, Watson concludes that we can have no accepted agreement regarding the meaning of ritual acts.

The fact that participants and observers of ritual performance may be unable to articulate signification, and that their interpretations of the meaning of the ritual may vary, should not be surprising. This phenomenon has been frequently observed in all kinds of performances. Literary critics studying theatrical performances accept the notion of multivalence; different individuals will read different meanings into a given play, and these differences will vary with personality, gender, age, life experience, and education.[3] Similarly, participants in a culture frequently only partially comprehend many cultural events, but that does not mean that a complex structure of meaning does not exist.

The fact is that belief and performance are very difficult to separate. Indeed, the chapters in this volume both by anthropologists and by historians

2. See James L. Watson, "Standardizing the Gods: The Promotion of T'ien Hou ('Empress of Heaven') Along the South China Coast, 960–1960 ," in Popular Culture in Late Imperial China, ed. David Johnson, Andrew J. Nathan, and Evelyn S. Rawski (Berkeley and Los Angeles: University of California Press, 1985), pp. 323–324, and the "Preface," x–xiii in the same work.

3. For one attempt to systematize this phenomenon, see David Johnson, "Communication, Class, and Consciousness in Late Imperial China," in Johnson et al., Popular Culture in Late Imperial China, pp. 34–72.

refer to beliefs as well as to ritual performance. Myron Cohen's examination of why salvation beliefs did not take greater hold among Chinese, and Emily Martin's discussion of a female ideology in representations of life and death, are only the two most conspicuous examples of essays that assume that it is important, when studying ritualized action, to understand what people believe. Elizabeth Johnson's study of Hakka death laments sung by women notes their value as windows into women's grievances and values. Stuart Thompson's structuralist analysis of food prestations—a mode of analysis that aims to arrive at content from a close scrutiny of form—also proceeds on the assumption that belief matters, in this case the belief (widely held, not just among peasants but among China's elite) that beings in the other world require nourishment from the living. Rubie Watson's paper on the politics of grave ritual in south China notes the centrality of peasant beliefs about geomancy, or *feng-shui*, itself linked to the notion of multiple souls in Chinese eschatology. Even James Watson's own analysis of funeral specialists refers to underlying *emic* views and interpretations that override individual differences—for example, the Cantonese notions of death pollution and the male/female realms. The inclusion of a discussion of "ideology" in Watson's introductory essay contradicts his argument rejecting "beliefs" as an important element shaping ritual, for Watson's "ideology" turns out to be the historian's "beliefs," that is, the overarching fundamental assumptions concerning the world held by Chinese of varying social strata across China's diverse regions.

There is thus no basic disagreement on the thesis that important notions or beliefs, cutting across class and region, were held by Chinese in the late imperial and contemporary periods. What are these basic elements of the belief system? Some have already been cited, and the reader is referred to Myron Cohen's essay in this volume for another explication of this subject. Many were present in Chinese culture from the earliest periods for which we have information, in the components of "ancestor worship," which has been recently described by Benjamin Schwartz as "omnipresent" and "central" to "the entire development of Chinese civilization" from ancient times.[4]

Ancestor worship—the emphasis on the continuity of kinship links between the living and the dead, the belief that ancestors could intercede with deities on behalf of their living descendants—was an essential stimulus for the evolution of the elaborate death ritual practiced by the Chinese. Belief in ancestor worship cannot be separated from death ritual performance. From

4. Benjamin I. Schwartz, *The World of Thought in Ancient China* (Cambridge: Harvard University Press, 1985), pp. 20–21 and chap. 1 generally. See David Keightley, "Dead But Not Gone: Cultural Implications of Mortuary Practice in Neolithic and Early Bronze Age China, ca. 8000 to 1000 B.C.," paper presented at the conference on Ritual and the Social Significance of Death in Chinese Society, Oracle, Arizona, January 1985.

the Bronze Age, Chinese have asserted a continuity of ties (what Watson calls "exchange") between the living and their dead ancestors. The lack of a radical dualism between body and soul, which Watson notes, is in fact characteristic of Chinese culture from at least the Bronze Age. And the notion of multiple souls had been elaborated by Han times.[5] The historian would argue that the early date of these beliefs and their ubiquity through subsequent periods of Chinese history must be taken seriously. What is most impressive is that the first enunciations of these notions appear in written elite texts of the classical period. When the same ideas are expressed by the twentieth-century peasants of the Canton delta and New Territories, the historian argues that the Chinese were remarkably successful in disseminating and perpetuating belief systems and not simply standardized ritual. From the perspective of what Braudel called the *longue durée*, belief did shape ritual performance—in short, rituals expressed beliefs.

Not only did specific beliefs concerning the afterlife influence China's ritual structure. We can also discern the influence of some fundamental notions about the cosmic order on Chinese ritual. In his analysis of Cantonese death ritual Watson notes the *emic* view of his informants that bones are male in essence (*yang*), and flesh is female (*yin*).[6] The *yin-yang* dualism pervades Chinese culture at many different levels and helps shape the way in which people think about their world. Its own history illustrates the complex interaction between levels of culture and ritual. Historically, *yin-yang* theory developed along with the theory of the Five Phases in a system of "correlative cosmology," systematized by Tsou Yen in the fourth to third centuries B.C.[7] Tsou Yen's correlation of the Five Phases with the cycles of dynastic rule was elaborated in the Han dynasty by the scholar Tung Chung-shu (ca. 179–104 B.C.), who incorporated numerological, anatomical, psychological, and moral correspondences between human and cosmic affairs.

Like notions of the ancestors, *yin-yang* and Five Phases theory must have originated in concepts that were widely shared among Chinese people; once these concepts were articulated in written form, they became products of

---

5. See Ying-shih Yü, "O Soul, Come Back!—A Study of the Changing Conceptions of the Soul and Afterlife in Pre-Buddhist China," *Harvard Journal of Asiatic Studies* 47 (1987): 363–395.

6. For a full exposition of this analysis, see James L. Watson, "Of Flesh and Bones: The Management of Death Pollution in Cantonese Society," in *Death and the Regeneration of Life*, ed. Maurice Bloch and Jonathan Parry (Cambridge: Cambridge University Press, 1982), pp. 155–186.

7. See Benjamin Schwartz, *The World of Thought in Ancient China*, chap. 9, pp. 203, 221, 356–369 ; John Henderson, *The Development and Decline of Chinese Cosmology* (New York: Columbia University Press, 1984), chap. 1. See also Stephan D. R. Feuchtwang, *An Anthropological Analysis of Chinese Geomancy* (1974: reprinted Taipei; Southern Materials Center, 1982).

"high culture," the culture of China's creative thinkers, then were re-introduced into the belief systems of Chinese of all social strata. Geomancy (*feng-shui*), the proto- or pseudo-science of harnessing the topographical forces of nature for the benefit of man (reported among Cantonese peasants by the Watsons and other anthropologists) developed out of correlative cosmology. Most of the major modes of correlative cosmology were embedded in geomantic theory and literally incorporated into the geomancer's compass; Henderson has in fact suggested that geomancy may have been one of the major channels for the transmission of correlative thought from high culture to popular culture.[8] But it was not just peasants who believed in *feng-shui*. Geomancy became the essential guide for the auspicious siting of houses and of graves, of emperors and of peasants. Graves, houses, temples, and the emperor faced south, the *yang* direction. The placement of the seat of honor in the east, to the left hand of the ruler or deity, influenced the assignment of hierarchical ranking in the ancestral halls of commoners as well as in the chambers of the court.

Correlative thought assumed that the actions of humans (led by the ruler) should "resonate" with the cosmos. Elaborate systems were devised by thinkers for harmonizing the ritual acts of the ruler with the cyclical rhythms of nature, and recorded in books like the *Yueh ling* (Monthly ordinances), a third-century text that became part of the Book of Rites (*Li chi*) from Han times. The notion of "cosmic resonance" percolated down to China's masses, who in the Ming and Ch'ing periods consulted their almanacs, as they do even today, for a guide to "lucky" and "unlucky" days for travel, setting up a business, marrying, and burying the dead. In diet, in their analysis of sickness, and as we have seen, in their *emic* view of death ritual, the peasants of south China continue to adhere to a world view that is profoundly influenced by *yin-yang* theory. When James Watson's villagers talk about *yang* bones and *yin* flesh, discuss marriage and death as a *yang-yin* pair of events, and when they nonetheless try to break the dualism by exorcism or expulsion of *yin* (as Watson asserts they do by the preservation of the bones and elimination of the flesh), the villagers are working within a cultural vocabulary that was embraced by all traditional Chinese.[9] The vocabulary is not individualized or idiosyncratic, and it does not suffer from

8. Henderson, *The Development of Chinese Cosmology*, p. 49.

9. Ibid., pp. 20–21. On almanacs, see C. K. Yang, *Religion in Chinese Society* (Berkeley and Los Angeles: University of California Press, 1967), pp. 17–136. Manfred Porkert, "The Intellectual and Social Impulses Behind the Evolution of Traditional Chinese Medicine," in *Asian Medical Systems: A Comparative Study*, ed. Charles Leslie (Berkeley and Los Angeles: University of California Press, 1976), pp. 65–66; Angela Leung, "Autour de la Naissance: La Mère et l'Enfant en Chine aux XVIe and XVIIe Siècles," *Cahiers Internationaux de Sociologie* 76 (1984): 51–69; E. N. Anderson and Marja L. Anderson, "Modern China: South," in *Food in Chinese Culture*, ed. K. C. Chang (New Haven: Yale University Press, 1977), pp. 368–370.

the flaws Watson describes in his introductory essay. A historian would say that Watson's own and other anthropological fieldwork observations reinforce rather than detract from the argument that there are important shared cultural orientations, call them beliefs or ideologies, that bind Chinese together.

## BELIEF AND PERFORMANCE: THE ELITE VIEW

Watson, in his introductory essay, argues that it was orthopraxy and not orthodoxy that the state promoted. Most historians, surveying recent work on the subject, will agree with the first half of this statement but dispute the second. The Chinese officials and local elites did indeed try to disseminate approved values as well as behaviors; but they frequently chose to disseminate values through enforcement of orthopraxy. This is evident in the Confucian discussions concerning filial piety.

Watson stresses the importance of funerary ritual for settling the soul of the dead and smoothing the transition from corpse to ancestor. For Confucians, the social value of death was to educate individuals in filial piety, a cardinal value in the family-oriented Chinese state of the Ming and Ch'ing periods. "The root of the state is the family"; this notion, found in a Confucian text of the fourth century B.C.,[10] was reiterated and elaborated by emperors and officials in subsequent dynasties. Just as the family became the metaphor for the state, filial piety, the central expression of familial relations (which of course supported a hierarchical order), was from the time of Confucius identified with the observance of mourning. By the late imperial period, the state's promotion of filiality was spelled out in the legal code, which punished infringements of mourning observance.[11]

The importance of filial piety in reinforcing the legitimacy of the emperor is detailed in my study of Ming and Ch'ing imperial death ritual, included in this volume, and the reader is referred to that chapter. Here I will simply sketch in the ideological underpinnings of that development.

Filial piety was well articulated as a central Chinese value by Confucius's day. Filial piety, as explained by Confucius (551–479 B.C.), was the natural repayment for the care bestowed by parents: three years was the appropriate length of the mourning period because it was the interval in which a child did not leave the arms of its parents. In the *Analects*, which records conversations of the master with his disciples, we find frequent references to filial piety, and expression of this sentiment is linked with death ritual. Asked to define filial piety, Confucius answered: "That parents, when alive,

---

10. *Mencius*, IV.i.5.; the translation used is James Legge's *The Chinese Classics*, 3d ed. (Hong Kong: University Press, 1960), 2:295.
11. De Groot, *The Religious System*, 2:568–569.

should be served according to *li*; that, when dead, they should be buried according to *li*; and that offerings should be made according to *li*."[12]

We see here another central element in the Chinese cultural order, the emphasis on *li*, translated as "ritual" but also meaning "proper behavior." *Li*, which has been described as the "cement of the entire normative sociopolitical order," refers in early Confucianism to all behavioral prescriptions, "involving rites, ceremony, manners, or general deportment, that bind human beings and the spirits together in networks of interacting roles within the family, within human society, and with the numinous realm beyond."[13] Initially *li* seems to have referred to religious ritual, and even in its more generalized usage in Confucian thought it retains a religious or sacred dimension. In the *Analects*, the repository of early Confucian thought, *li* (performance) is paired with *jen* (perfect virtue). *Li* without the proper spirit is meaningless: "*Li* performed without reverence, the forms of mourning observed without grief—how can I bear to look on these things?" *Jen*, the "inner" goal of the realized man, could only be achieved through *li*, the performance of one's appropriate role. When Confucius was asked, "What is *jen*?" he replied, "Curb your ego and submit to *li*."[14]

Early Confucianism thus conceived of *li*, the performance of one's role, and "inner spirit" as an integrally linked dualism. In Confucian theory, *li*, both in this broader sense and in the specific sense of ritual, was a means of ordering the state and creating a stable hierarchical society. Confucians emphasized ritual as a promoter of order and a preventive for disorder. *Luan*, a problem frequently raised in Confucian discussions, meant internal confusion and chaos, to be feared perhaps more than the external invading army. *Luan* was also the direct outcome of death. Stuart Thompson in his essay analyzes death ritual, *li*, as the means of restoring a proper moral order after the disorder (*luan*) of death. In the process of restoring order through *li*, *yang* overrides *yin*, men affirm symbolic superiority over women, agnates over affines, rice over pork, purity over lewdness, structure over *communitas*.

*Luan* in a broader context was the disorder arising within the household, community, or state when ethical norms and social roles were subverted. The desire to promote order and prevent *luan* was held by persons all through the society. For the elite, one way to prevent *luan* was to inculcate proper values and behavior in the populace.

Rituals expressed the asymmetrical relations between superior and inferior, parent and child, husband and wife, senior and junior, and at the

12. *Analects*, XVII.xxi.1–6; also XIV.xliii.1–2; II.v.3. Modified quotation from *The Chinese Classics*, trans. James Legge, 3d ed. (Hong Kong: University Press, 1960), 1: 147.

13. Benjamin Schwartz, *The World of Thought*, p. 67.

14. See ibid., pp. 67–75, 77. The quotes, discussed by Schwartz, are from *Analects*, Book 3, chap. 26, and Book 12, chap. 1, respectively.

same time they taught, through performance, core values such as filial piety. Confucians did not assume that belief preceded and was the stimulus for performance; they also understood that *performance* could lead to inculcation of belief. Rather than making a sharp distinction between belief and practice, therefore, Chinese ruling elites tended to see belief and practice as organically linked to one another, each influencing the other. For children, as for the illiterate mass of the populace, Confucians might put primary stress on practice; for advanced students seeking Confucian cultivation, the stress would be differently placed, on the degree to which one's internal state could be translated into morally perfect action; but that the two were always necessarily part of a unity was not in doubt.

The Confucian ideas of education or moral transformation elucidated by Donald Munro help us understand better exactly why Confucians began with concrete performance when they sought to inculcate values. Confucians assumed that people were attracted to and learned to cultivate the mind through the imitation of (virtuous) role models: "Teaching by example surpasses teaching by words."[15] The Confucian texts, from the elementary primers on to advanced texts, were full of exemplars from the past; Confucians themselves were aware of their obligation to serve as good models for others to emulate. The Confucian form of learning emphasized the presentation of abstract moral principles through their concrete embodiment in an individual's life, but both elements, the specific biographical detail and the abstract principles, were present. As Munro notes, "Models manifest the link between knowledge of principles and action in accordance with them and help to make this link habitual in the learner. They stand for principle in action."[16]

The adoption of Confucianism as an approved doctrine by the state in the second century B.C. and its central position in state doctrine for the past millennium ensured that the early texts were not neglected or forgotten. Subsequent developments in Neo-Confucianism, most notably the development of the Wang Yang-ming school from the sixteenth century, also stressed the unity of knowledge and action. Ch'ing officials writing about the expansion of education to peasants stressed that schooling would help promote cultural orthodoxy as well as "ritualized perfection," and thus stabilize the society.[17] Historians would thus argue that the primary agents of cultural integration cited by Watson—the state, officials, and local elites—did intend to promote orthodoxy through orthopraxy.

15. Donald J. Munro, *The Concept of Man in Contemporary China* (Ann Arbor: University of Michigan Press, 1977), p. 136.

16. Ibid., p. 138.

17. Alexander Woodside, "Some Mid-Qing Theorists of Popular Schools," *Modern China* 9, no. 1 (1983): 3–35.

Before ending this discussion, let us turn again to the main issue of belief versus practice. In his introductory essay, Watson argues for the primacy of orthopraxy in the Chinese state by contrasting China with Christian Europe. "In early Christendom," he notes, "it was belief that carried more weight than practice, and in later eras debates regarding the proper performance of the Eucharist focused on ideological concerns underpinning practice." The contrast between Christian Europe and Ch'ing China is a telling one, for Confucian ritual was never so sharply doctrinal. One could argue that China before Mao never required the levels of commitment to a specified dogma that were demanded by the Catholic and later the Protestant church. The contrast between Chinese and Christian practice is identical to the contrast made by Richard Madsen between the pre-Maoist "ceremonies of innocence" and the Maoist "rituals of struggle" in post-1949 China.[18] "Ceremonies of innocence" are the traditional village life-cycle and seasonal rituals, which unite participants "in a common experience that is drenched with meaning but cannot be expressed by any single set of discursive ideas." By contrast, "rituals of struggle" celebrate one set of doctrines: "Ritual becomes the expression of sharply focused sacred doctrine," and aims to separate believers from heretics.[19] Chinese orthodoxy in the late imperial era never possessed this quality; but that there was an identifiable orthodoxy cannot be denied.

## THE PROPAGATION OF DEATH RITUAL

The Chinese state played an enormous role in shaping belief systems. The reader is directed to chapter 8 in this volume, where Myron Cohen looks very broadly at this subject. This essay will limit itself to a brief survey of the standardization of rites by the state, officials, and local elites. The purposive propagation of ritual to the commoner population is relatively late in China; its success owed much to underlying social and economic changes that began in the Sung but were most marked in the late Ming and early Ch'ing periods.

Until the Sung (960–1279 A.D.), ancestral ritual (and hence death ritual) was the preserve of rulers and the *shih-ta-fu*, or gentleman-official class, a hereditary ruling elite which had dominated affairs for centuries. Sumptuary restrictions on ritual performance demarcated the ruler from officials, and officials from commoners. Ancestral rites were largely the preserve of the privileged: legally, the erection of ancestral shrines (*chia miao*) was forbidden to commoners, and in ritual texts commoners were denied the right to

18. Richard Madsen, *Morality and Power in a Chinese Village* (Berkeley and Los Angeles: University of California Press, 1984), chap. 1.
    19. Ibid., p. 22.

make offerings to ancestors earlier than their grandparents.[20] This (largely unsuccessful) attempt to limit ancestor worship was a natural concomitant of the strong historical link between political authority and access to the gods, manifested already in the Late Shang state (ca. 1200–1045 B.C.).[21]

The effect of limiting the audience for classical ritual prescriptions to the ruling elite was to permit other belief systems, notably Buddhism and Taoism, to dominate popular practice, and many Sung officials complained of uncanonical (i.e., non-Confucian) marriage and funeral practices. The great philosopher Chu Hsi, while a prefect at Chang-chou, Fukien, in 1190, issued a proclamation to the citizens expressing his shock at meeting a degree-holder who had ignored the rules for mourning dress. Chu Hsi explained why one should mourn one's parents, by citing passages from the *Analects*; henceforth, those mourning the death of parents must wear mourning clothes and abstain from liquor, meat, and sex for three years, thus repaying the labors of one's parents. Chu Hsi warned that those who disobeyed would be punished. Elsewhere, Chu Hsi proclaimed that households should "never" employ "Buddhist monks, offer sacrifice to the Buddha, or make extravagant display at funerals" and stipulated punishments for citizens who violated the rules.[22] The Neo-Confucian philosophical attack on Buddhism and Taoism thus simultaneously sought to replace errant practices among commoners with approved classical rites and signaled an important reorientation toward the propagation of standards that would cover commoners as well as the gentleman-official.

In the eleventh and twelfth centuries a newly vigorous Confucian officialdom began to look closely at and to correct popular mores through reform

20. See J. Friedman and M. J. Rowlands, "Notes towards an Epigenetic Model of the Evolution of 'Civilisation,'" in *The Evolution of Social Systems*, ed. J. Friedman and M. J. Rowlands (London: Duckworth, 1977), pp. 201–276, which presents a scheme of historical evolution of societies in which monopoly over the supernatural through ancestors was the means by which a royal line emerged to form an "asiatic state." The authors use examples from Chinese history as support for their construct and note the hierarchical nature of ritual for pre-Ch'in China. Our discussions indicate that many elements echoing their descriptions of the "asiatic state" of Shang times could still be found in the late imperial era. On the Sung situation, see Patricia B. Ebrey, "Early Stages of Descent Group Organization," in *Kinship Organization in Late Imperial China, 1000–1940* (Berkeley and Los Angeles: University of California Press, 1986), pp. 16–61, and Patricia Ebrey, "The Formulation of Family Rituals during the Sung Period," paper presented at the Conference on Neo-Confucian Education, August–September 1984. On Chu Hsi's magisterial actions, see Ron-guey Chu, "Chu Hsi and Public Instruction," paper presented at the same conference.

21. The sharp break in the imperial tradition comes with the T'ang dynasty; see Howard J. Wechsler, *Offerings of Jade and Silk: Ritual and Symbol in the Legitimation of the T'ang Dynasty* (New Haven: Yale University Press, 1985). Wechsler argues that with the T'ang, there was an attempt to shift the emphasis in state ritual from worship of the imperial ancestors to more "public" worship of Heaven.

22. Ron-guey Chu, "Chu Hsi and Public Instruction," Appendices 3, 5.

of marriage and mourning customs. The impact of the Neo-Confucian concern with the social transformation of commoners and not merely the ruling elite was heightened by the many fundamental changes occurring in Sung society. The development of printing, for example, enabled wide dissemination of books, and Confucians were quick to seize on this medium to spread their ideas: indeed, a central impulse promoting the advance of printing was the urge to standardize Confucian texts. From this period, the written medium was to become, more and more, a common tool for transmission of norms.

By the late twelfth and thirteenth centuries, the Chinese state was recruiting more than half of its new officials through the system of civil service examinations that had begun in the sixth century and developed gradually thereafter. This shift to recruitment through examination spelled the end of the old *shih-ta-fu* class and heralded the beginning of a more mobile society. The Ming and Ch'ing dynasties refined the system of granting degrees by establishing regional quotas to ensure representation from every province in the empire; the result was a group of degree-holders educated in the Confucian curriculum, committed to the dynasty, and strategically placed throughout China. As the ability of the central government to intervene directly in local affairs waned (the average population in the lowest administrative unit, a county, increased consistently from the ninth century on), the central authorities began to place more and more emphasis on indirect means of social control and to rely on the informal leadership of the degree-holding elite to maintain local stability and order.

The late imperial government's reliance on indirect modes of local control emphasized broadly educational efforts, such as the rural lectures, presented twice monthly in localities by officials and notables, which featured the Sacred Edict successively promulgated by Ming and Ch'ing emperors. Early Ch'ing officials and educated men wrote handbooks presenting the normative rituals, culled from earlier compendia, to the population at large. The eighth-century compendium, the *K'ai-yuan li*, and Chu Hsi's *Chia li* (Rituals for family life) set the standard followed by the *Collected Statutes* of the Ming and Ch'ing. Chu Hsi's Family Rituals continued to enjoy wide influence. The "Family Rituals," according to de Groot, explaining how the practices he observed in late nineteenth-century Amoy replicated classical usage, "has ever since circulated throughout the empire as a standard authority," cited in numerous genealogies, encyclopedias, and in legal codes. As Patricia Ebrey notes, of all of Chu Hsi's writings, this work may have been most often consulted by persons with little schooling.[23]

The continuous transmission of ritual texts, promoted by the centralized

---

23. See Patricia Ebrey, "The Formulation of Family Rituals"; de Groot, *The Religious System*, 1:235–240.

state, was thus an important factor in the uniformity of death ritual. Private efforts to promote social reform through correction of marriage and funeral customs among the people paralleled official action. Concerted public and private efforts to transmit normative values and behavior relied on the increased ease of communication from urban to rural areas and between regions, a consequence of the sixteenth-century commercial expansion, which produced a highly developed, increasingly integrated market hierarchy. As a result, orthodox norms were disseminated more broadly than ever before.

The ritual system also changed subtly in its symbolic dimensions and its social significance. The sumptuary regulations that had limited ancestral rites to the elite were replaced by simplified rituals that thus narrowed the social distance between different strata. By the Ch'ing, one could truly say that the mourning observances for an emperor were in their essentials the same as the mourning observances for commoners; this was certainly not the case in the Sung and earlier periods. So ritual hierarchical distinctions decreased sharply over time; the society also became more mobile, not only because of the erosion of elite privilege produced by the examination system, but also because wealth became a factor of more and more importance in high status, apart from degrees. As old social boundaries dissolved, proper performance of ritual became more and more a symbol of status in its own right. Conspicuous consumption in ritual observance was now an important social reality, precisely because social structure was more fluid; in this perspective, the increased wealth spent on funerals was an investment in social climbing.

Ritual could also, in the *longue durée*, help shape social organization. This is the argument presented by Patricia Ebrey, who notes that grave worship was not commonly practiced until the mid-T'ang period, when collective worship at *ch'ing-ming* became an important addition to kin-group activities. Ebrey argues that the custom of grave worship originated, not with the Confucian elite, but among commoners, influenced by Buddhism. T'ang agnates who worshipped together at graves were thus able to express reverence for distant ancestors; this was otherwise difficult for commoners, who were prohibited (in law but not in reality) from erecting ancestral shrines. The practice of worshipping early ancestors together on one day helped foster kin-group consciousness among local agnates and may well have stimulated the formation of lineages.[24]

The symbolic significance of correct ritual performance attained additional meaning as a consequence of China's repeated involvement with other cultures. Rites, properly performed, were an essential component of Chinese identity in the late imperial period, and probably for a long time before. Originally spurred by the desire to differentiate the agrarian Han Chinese

24. See Ebrey, "Early Stages of Descent Group Organization," pp. 20–29.

from their nomadic neighbors to the north, Chineseness became defined by dietary habits (the Chinese did not eat dairy products), by clothing styles, and especially by traditions concerning marriage and death. Over the centuries, as China was repeatedly conquered by tribes from the steppe (China was ruled in whole or in part by non-Han dynasties for over five hundred of the last thousand years), the Chinese emphasis on culture over ethnicity increased. Anyone could become "Chinese" by adopting Chinese customs and behavior. During the eighteenth century, the expansion of Han Chinese settlement into southwest China, Taiwan, west China beyond the Kansu corridor, Tibet, Inner Mongolia, and Manchuria brought intensified interaction between Chinese and the aboriginal and non-Han tribes residing there, and undoubtedly contributed to underlining the concept of Chinese identity. Acculturation was expressed by Chinese as the transformation of "raw," or "uncooked," people into "ripe," or "cooked" (*shu*, meaning civilized) Chinese.[25] In the Ch'ing period, as the empire expanded to its largest extent in history, incorporating many non-Han tribes, adoption of Chinese surname exogamy, mourning observances, and correct performance of ritual had become crucial markers of membership in the Chinese cultural community.

The death rituals of the Ch'ing and later years must thus be seen as the product of the state and its Confucian elite, sustained by widespread, regionally dispersed literacy that was itself in part the consequence of the examination system. As Susan Naquin demonstrates in chapter 3 of this volume, information from texts that were available to the fully literate and highly educated members of the literati stratum was also transmitted to more humble households by religious and other mortuary specialists who were employed by all but the poorest families. In addition to the geomancer, found in all parts of China, the funeral priest, who could be a Buddhist, a Taoist, or an adherent of the numerous popular religious sects that flourished in the late imperial period, was most likely to have access to written texts of some kind. Even peasant death rituals used a wide variety of written materials. The presence of written texts signifies direct ties to the elite tradition, but as James Watson suggests in citing illiterate old women specializing in "checking" the correctness of ritual practice, there was

25. For a historical survey of the expansion of Han Chinese settlement, see Harold J. Wiens, *China's March Toward the Tropics* (Hamden: Shoe String Press, 1954), and Hisayuki Miyakawa, "The Confucianization of South China," in Arthur Wright, ed., *The Confucian Persuasion* (Stanford: Stanford University Press, 1960), pp. 21–46. On the cultural interaction of Han Chinese and Inner Asian tribes, see Owen Lattimore's *Inner Asian Frontiers of China* (New York: American Geographical Society, 1940). For a discussion of the problems of incorporation of large numbers of non-Han peoples into the Ch'ing empire, see Susan Naquin and Evelyn S. Rawski, *Chinese Society in the Eighteenth Century* (New Haven: Yale University Press, 1987).

always a living oral tradition with which the textual tradition interacted. A work by James Hayes in another context demonstrates the efficacy with which written and oral modes of communication were combined through the ubiquitous village specialists who were called upon for many and varied services.[26] The activities of these specialists provided the final link between the written traditions of the elite and the villager. They helped ensure a remarkable degree of uniformity—in ritual performance, but also in the underlying belief system—in late imperial and contemporary China.

26. James Hayes, "Specialists and Written Materials in the Village World," in Johnson et al., *Popular Culture in Late Imperial China*, pp. 75–111.

# PART II

PART II

# THREE

# Funerals in North China: Uniformity and Variation

*Susan Naquin*

More than a decade ago in a provocative essay, Maurice Freedman asked whether, despite considerable diversity, one Chinese religion did not exist. He called upon others to find ways of demonstrating that there was "some order—of a kind that should allow us (if we take the trouble) to trace the ruling principles of ideas across a vast field of apparently heterogenous beliefs, and ruling principles of form and organization in an equally enormous terrain of varied action and association."[1] He criticized recent work in Chinese anthropology for being too close to its informants and thus having a fragmented, peasant's-eye view of Chinese religion that emphasized diversity and variation. He could easily have taken Chinese historians to task (as he did one generation of sociologists) for a similar dependence on their sources and a resulting preference for seeing China through the unifying vision of its elites, a vision in which differences were minimized and deviations deplored.

Despite growing interest in the last decade in the relationship between class and culture in China, not a great deal of progress has been made in developing a method for studying uniformity and variation in ideas and organization.[2] A consideration of the role of funeral ritual seems a suitable

I wish to thank the conference participants, and especially the editors, as well as members of the Ethnohistory Workshop at the University of Pennsylvania and the Traditional China Seminar at Columbia University for their comments and suggestions. The much longer conference-paper version of this article contains a more detailed text, many illustrations, a full glossary, and far more extensive footnotes.

1. Maurice Freedman, "On the Sociological Study of Chinese Religion," in Arthur P. Wolf, ed., *Religion and Ritual in Chinese Society* (Stanford: Stanford University Press, 1974), p. 20.

2. See D. Johnson, A. J. Nathan, and E. S. Rawski, eds., *Popular Culture in Late Imperial China* (Berkeley and Los Angeles: University of California Press, 1985).

occasion for raising these issues once more. As in other cultures, ideas about
death are central to Chinese religion (or religions), while rituals are carriers
of important cultural information, especially in a peasant society. Moreover, we have reason to believe at the outset that there was considerable
uniformity combined with bewildering diversity in Chinese funeral practices extending across the geographic range of China, up and down the social
scale, and far back in time. I hope to use an investigation of uniformity and
variation in funeral ritual in one area (north China) and one period (the
nineteenth and early twentieth centuries) to analyze this larger issue: the
existence of common elements in Chinese culture and their perpetuation in
the face of entropic pressures toward cultural diversity and change.

The most detailed studies of Chinese funeral practices in the modern
period in Western languages are ethnographies done in south and central
China. Although sketches of funeral rituals in north China were left by
twentieth-century visitors, and other accounts can be found in Chinese local
histories of the late Ch'ing and Republican periods, a general description of
the ritual sequence for the north, presented so as to make possible comparisons with other regions and times, does not, to my knowledge, exist. This
chapter will begin with such an account and then turn to the problems of
variation and uniformity.

The description that follows is based on Chinese gazetteer (that is, local
history) accounts mostly written in the period 1870–1940 from a pie-
shaped wedge of north China (see the Appendix to this chapter). I have tried
to present the fullest set of those common funeral rituals that together constituted the repertory from which individual families could select.[3] I will
attempt to encompass all of the rituals, from imminent death to encoffining,
funeral, and burial, through the third-year anniversary of the deathday. The
most elaborate (and, in a sense, ideal) funeral was performed at the death of
an elderly parent, and I will occasionally follow Chinese practice in describing the ritual in terms of a son mourning his father. Abbreviations of and
variations on these rituals will then be discussed in more detail. Let us first
turn to the funeral rituals themselves.

## THE RITUAL SEQUENCE

Although preparations for a funeral (buying a coffin, locating a burial site,
readying grave clothes) might be made well in advance, the rituals them-

3. The accounts on which my study is based have several obvious biases: toward presentation of the unchanging, normative, elite, "Confucian" view of funeral ritual, and against
more varied, popular, "superstitious," local practices. I have tried to correct this bias by relying
on a large number of accounts to reconstruct the full ritual, eliminating the disparaging comments sometimes made by the authors, and drawing on foreign observers for underrecorded
aspects of the ritual.

selves began (if circumstances permitted) just before death. It was unlucky for anyone to die on the communal *k'ang* (the brick platform, heated in winter, that served as both living area and bed in north China), and so when the delicate decision was made that recovery was impossible and death imminent ("only one breath left"), the dying person had to be transferred to a special bed. This bed (a flat board) was then moved into the main ceremonial room of the house. Family members, who were expected to assemble as speedily as possible, stood around the bed, and at the moment the dying person breathed his last, the formal expression of grief began. They knelt and began the wailing indicative of mourning (the "death howl," J. J. M. de Groot calls it) and, following practices of considerable longevity, beat their breasts and stamped their feet in grief. The characteristic appearance of mourning was supposed to include loosened hair, unwashed face, plain clothing, and the absence of all ornaments. Family members might kowtow to the corpse as they keened, embracing it, praising the deceased, and lamenting their loss.

The corpse was immediately prepared for eventual encoffining, a process called *hsiao-lien* (dressing the corpse). An unpadded quilt served as a shroud and, together with a pillow, was placed under the body. Sometimes the children or spouse washed the face or body. The corpse was dressed in special "long-life" clothing, which could be, depending on his class, official robes and embroidered gowns or new but plain cotton clothes, shoes, and hat. Special objects were usually placed in the mouth of the deceased (e.g., pearls, coins) and some on the body (e.g., jewelry, mirrors); the face was covered with a piece of cloth or paper, and the feet were tied with colored string. A makeshift altar table was set up near the body at this time. A temporary spirit-tablet (*ling-p'ai*) and lighted lamp were placed on it; there paper spirit-money (currency in the otherworld) was burned as an offering. Sometimes relatives beyond the immediate family were present for these procedures.

Public notice of the death was made immediately by pasting white paper streamers on the main gate of the house. These strips of paper were hung on the left side of the gate if the deceased was a man, on the right for a woman; sometimes the number of strips represented the age of the deceased. (A paper pennant on a pole or pieces of spirit-money might be used instead of the paper streamers.) The red auspicious couplets that were pasted on many doors at New Year's were covered over with white paper.

The all-purpose diviner used as a consultant on most aspects of funerals (known in this part of China as a "yin-yang master") was promptly called in. He not only took measures to protect the family against the harmful and inauspicious influences of an unburied body and calculated the auspicious times for key events (encoffining, moving the coffin, burial), but determined the geomantic siting of the grave. When the schedule of ritual events had been determined, the deceased's family's relatives and acquaintances were formally notified (*pao-sang*). Messengers (relatives, servants) were sent out to tell close relations; a written announcement could be placed on the gate; handwritten or printed notices (*fu-wen*) might be sent out. The dates of the deceased's birth and death, an account of his career, the schedule of funeral rituals, and the names of close surviving relatives might be given on these announcements.

It was essential that the local gods be quickly notified as well. The immediate family of the deceased reported the death at the nearest shrine of the earth-god (or city-god) who was responsible for the local community. Taking candles and spirit-money, the family went to the temple, wailing all the way, made an offering, announced the death, and returned home. (In some places this ritual—called *pao-miao*—was repeated three times.)

Close relatives began coming to pay their condolences soon after the death, but the encoffining (*ta-lien*) was a more public event, involving not only more distant agnates but affinal relatives as well. Monks or a diviner might be present. Ideally, this ceremony took place on the third day. A sturdy coffin would hold the corpse. Certain objects were placed in it first (e.g., ashes, copper coins, lime), and then close relatives lifted and lowered in the body. The eldest son or the wife would personally wipe the eyes of the deceased with cotton floss (*k'ai-kuang*). Other objects were placed on or around the body, and cakes and sticks made of dough, intended for feeding and beating vicious dogs believed to lie in wait in the otherworld, were sometimes placed near the hands of the corpse. When the body was packed in the quilt, the coffin was then closed, to the accompaniment of wailing and calling to the dead ("Avoid the nails! Fear the nails!"). Offerings of real food were now made every day at mealtimes on a nearby altar.

The encoffining was followed immediately by a set of rituals collectively referred to in this region as the "third-day reception" (*chieh-san*), but sometimes known as "calling back the soul" (*chao-hun*) or "sending off [the deceased]" (*sung-lu*). Although there was considerable local diversity in these practices, two general activities usually took place: making sure that the spirit of the deceased remained with the body in the coffin, and sending useful objects to accompany the deceased in the otherworld. First, family, relatives, and sometimes Buddhist monks went again to the earth-god temple to call for the soul (then in the custody of the local god) and, returning with it, secured the soul to the encoffined body. This ritual involved different quasi-magical procedures for bringing the soul back home and was sometimes accompanied by sutra chanting. In a connected ceremony, paper representations of a variety of objects that would be useful to the deceased's journey in the otherworld—carts, attendants, horses, chests, clothing, money, and other items—were burned that evening in a public place outside the house, usually at the intersection of two lanes.

For the more formal and more public rituals that accompanied and followed the encoffining, a ceremonial area would have been set up within or beside the house. Near the coffin was the table for offerings to the spirit of the deceased; a plain-colored curtain screened the coffin from general view. An adjacent courtyard or open space was covered with a straw-mat awning and then decorated with gifts brought by friends and relations (spirit-world objects, and commemorative odes and couplets written on large paper or cloth scrolls); a small room with a desk was reserved for financial transactions and the recording of gifts. If a feast was planned, tables and chairs were set up and a separate cooking area was established. Shops that specialized in funerals usually provided the necessary equipment and services.

After the encoffining, most families engaged Buddhist monks (or Taoist priests) to come and "do the sevens" (*tso-ch'i*). Scriptures were supposed to be chanted every seventh day (from the death) until the seventh seven (the forty-ninth day), although three sevens or five sevens (twenty-one or thirty-five days) were sometimes deemed quite sufficient. This chanting was intended to see the soul of the deceased through the underworld to its next rebirth. As the monks and priests chanted to the accompaniment of music, relatives and friends came again to pay their condolences, the family wailed by the coffin, offerings of food and spirit-money were made, and the guests were feasted. Procedures for the funeral and burial proceeded independently of the seven sevens and usually took place before those rituals were completed.

Because the immediate relatives not only were assumed to be absorbed in their grief but also were expected to be principal actors in the funeral rituals, an experienced senior relation or acquaintance was usually asked to come and help manage the funeral. He saw to it that all relatives and friends within the family's social circle were invited, hired the necessary professionals, paid the bills, made sure that accurate financial records were kept, and orchestrated most of the funeral activities.

The cluster of rituals that I am terming the funeral proper took place either on the day before or the day of the removal of the coffin from the home. They included the formal offerings to the coffin in full ceremonial mourning attire, the receiving of more condolences, the feasting and entertainment of guests, the wake, and the farewell to the soul.

The receiving of condolences (*k'ai-tiao*) could be a very elaborate ceremony. All relatives and acquaintances were expected to attend and bring gifts; these usually included offerings (food, spirit-money), ceremonial objects (candles, incense, spirit-world objects, elegiac scrolls), or simply money to assist the bereaved family with expenses. Gifts were displayed in the courtyard and during the burial procession. It was during these rituals that ceremonial mourning clothes had to be worn (*ch'eng-fu*). Each of the five grades of mourning (*wu-fu*) had its special clothing or marker so that the status of every relative was immediately apparent. The chief mourner wore a coarse, loosely fitting, unbleached cloth outfit and plain hat and carried a staff. Guests were expected to wear seemly clothing and to put on a white sash when approaching the coffin.

Several (usually four) men who were distinguished friends of the family were invited to serve as masters of ceremony (*hsiang-pin*) during the funeral. Formal offerings were made by the mourners at the altar, and an invocation was read, and then, as the family knelt beside the coffin, the arrival of each guest was announced by musicians at the gate. During these *t'ang-chi* (also called *chia-chi*) rites, the condoler was brought in by the master of ceremonies, given a sash or a marker of mourning, and then led to the coffin. After the guest had wailed and made an offering there, the chief mourner kowtowed to thank him, and the guest then retired to the courtyard where he might stay and chat with friends and await the feast.

The ritual of "completing the tablet" (*ch'eng-chu*) usually took place at this time. The wooden tablet that would become one home for the soul of the deceased after burial was prepared in advance, leaving only the single dot in the character *chu* 主 (host, owner) to be filled in. The most distinguished literary acquaintance of the family would be invited to mark with a brush, perhaps in red ink or even blood and often with considerable pomp, the finishing dot that gave life to the tablet. He was known as "inscriber of the tablet" (*tien-chu* or *t'i-chu*). This ritual had the effect of transferring the deceased's spirit to the tablet and was sometimes called "saying goodbye to the spirit" (*tz'u-ling*) and was accompanied by wailing and offerings to the tablet. It was sometimes followed by the more cheerful rite of placing the tablet on the altar (*an-chu*) and thus reincorporating it into the family.

If these rituals took place on the afternoon before the departure of the coffin for burial, members of the family kept the deceased company during the night (*pan-su* or *tso-yeh*). This wake could be the occasion for storytelling and operas performed for the deceased, the guests, and the neighborhood.

The coffin was not always put in the ground immediately after the funeral, and the burial itself might occur long after the death. In order to bury a husband and wife in the same grave, the coffin of the one to die first would often be put in storage. Some families waited for months or years for a suitable grave site or auspicious date, and apparently the sight of coffins awaiting burial was a common one. Coffins were housed temporarily in temples, on vacant land, or in out-of-the-way spots, sometimes covered with makeshift roofs, sometimes exposed to the elements.

The initial movement of the coffin from the home—a dangerous moment of transition when the spirit was liable to drift away from the coffin and the tablet—was accompanied by a number of rituals, and monks or a diviner were often present. The chief mourner broke a pottery bowl (variously explained, but indicative at one level of the symbolic transformation of the child-parent relationship), and offerings were made to the coffin, to the catafalque on which it would be carried, and to the pennant that led the spirit in the procession. As soon as the coffin left the house, firecrackers were set off, and measures were taken to protect the residents against its residual inauspicious influences. (Some of the objects that had been in contact with the corpse were thought to have regenerative power for women and young children and were saved by them—dust and coins from the coffin, a piece of the shroud, earth from the grave.)

The funeral procession (*fa-yin* or *ch'u-pin*) itself could be of immense size in its fullest form, involve large numbers of people hired for the occasion, and cost a great deal of money. Most processions included the following elements in roughly this order: men who scattered spirit-money along the road; displays of mourning couplets, written testimonials to the deceased, and plaques with his titles or official posts; a testimonial banner (*ming-ching*), sometimes of enormous size on which the name, ranks, dates, and survivors of the deceased were written; spirit-world objects to be burned at the grave; musicians; monks and priests in ceremonial robes; the chief mourner, carrying the spirit-pennant; other close male relatives; the coffin itself borne in a large wooden catafalque carried by hired pallbearers or by men close to the deceased; women and children riding in carts; other guests.

Acquaintances, friends, and neighbors set up small roadside altars along the route to the grave (a practice known as *lu-chi*). The funeral procession moved slowly, stopping at each altar (and at bridges and intersections) for offerings to be made, mourners to kowtow their thanks, and musicians to play. The socially relevant portion of the funeral ended at this point. Most of those who set off with the procession turned back at the suburbs or edge of the village. Long delays could ensue, and whether the coffin was taken directly to the grave or to another place for storage was largely a private affair. If burial was taking place immediately, only close relatives went all the way to the cemetery.

The grave site itself, always distant from human dwellings, would ideally be a plot within a family cemetery selected by a yin-yang master with close attention to its alignment in the natural setting. Burial (*tsang*) in a coffin was the preferred way of disposing of a body; cremation was appropriate only under unusual and unnatural circumstances. When the procession reached the grave and the forecast auspicious moment arrived, the coffin was lowered into the ground. With it were placed a crock containing food (which had been carried to the grave by a close relative), sometimes a lamp, and usually the testimonial banner folded on top. The chief mourner was the first to put dirt on the coffin. When the grave was filled, offerings were made to the newly housed ancestor, and more spirit-world objects were burned and sent to the deceased. Offerings were also made at this time to the spirit of the soil (*hou-t'u*) who protected the grave, preferably by a respected person with some military experience, someone who could scare off evil spirits.

Dirt was piled up to make the cone-shaped mound characteristic of graves in north China. The spirit-pennant was temporarily planted in front of the grave, and sometimes a stone slab was later set up in front of the mound. In family plots where many generations had already been buried, the preferred pattern of burial was to place the founding ancestor under a larger mound at the apex of a triangle, with subsequent generations placed to each side in descending order, sometimes alternating generations (see illustration). Wives and concubines who had produced heirs were interred together with their husbands.

It appears that in north China, bodies once interred were rarely exhumed and reburied. Sometimes, in search of a more auspicious site or in order to open up a new burial ground, bones would be dug up and moved, but these were not common practices, and a small empty coffin could substitute symbolically for bones.[4]

The ancestral tablet was returned by the chief mourner with some fanfare to the family altar (*hui-ling*). Ceremonial mourning attire was removed, and the *yü* sacrifice was performed at home to formalize and celebrate the relocation of the soul in the tablet and of the tablet on the altar.

After the burial, the more extreme forms of mourning behavior were terminated, though a few rituals remained. It was important to make sure that all lingering inauspicious auras associated with the dead were exorcized from the home, and a diviner was often hired to write charms and chant spells to this end. It was also necessary for the chief mourner to thank those who had come to pay condolences, by going to their homes personally or sending symbolic gifts.

On the third day after the interment, the immediate family returned to the grave to "round it off" (*yuan-fen*)—piling up earth to make it a proper size and shape, burning incense and spirit-money and sometimes the spirit-pennant, and wailing for the last time. Care of the ancestral tablet and of the grave followed special procedures for several years, until which time the deceased had become a routinized ancestor. Offerings were made on the sixtieth and the hundredth day and on the first *ch'ing-ming* (the sweeping of the graves in the spring). Moreover, on the first, second, and third anniversaries of the deathday, special ceremonies were performed. The longest mourning (e.g., a son for his father) was supposed to last twenty-seven months, although some stopped on the second anniversary of the death. By this time, the soul of the deceased had been relocated in three places: to rebirth in another form, to the ancestral tablet, and to the grave.

---

4. Only a few sources even mention reburial. For a discussion in English, see Sidney D. Gamble, *Ting Hsien*, p. 393.

Relationships within the family had been redefined and the social networks of the family reinvigorated.

The practice of routine "ancestor worship" has been adequately described in the secondary literature. It should be sufficient to note here that such "worship" consisted of the making of special offerings (*chi*) (food, wine) on an altar usually located in the central hall of the home. Gazetteers from north China often note the lack of ancestral halls (*chia-tz'u, chia-miao*) relative to other parts of China. The ancestors were generally represented by wooden tablets, although the poor might use paper and the rich add portrait scrolls above the altar. Offerings were made before the ancestors collectively at least bimonthly (on the first and the fifteenth of the lunar month), as well as on holidays, whereas individual ancestors were remembered on the anniversaries of their births and deaths.

Offerings at the grave were made on a few key occasions during the year. On New Year's eve, the family might go to the graveyard to invite the ancestors home for the holiday or else burn spirit-money and set off firecrackers at the grave on New Year's day. A visit to the graves of recent ancestors was mandatory on *ch'ing-ming*, the solar holiday that generally fell in the third or fourth lunar month. The entire family was expected to participate, taking wine and special delicacies for their offerings. These were presented at the grave, and spirit-money was burned. Family members made clear their ownership of the grave (especially important when burial was not in a private cemetery) by building up the mound, removing weeds, and sweeping clear the area around the grave. A family or lineage feast might follow at home. The family returned to the cemetery to make fresh offerings on the fifteenth day of the seventh lunar month as part of the rituals directed toward spirits in general during that month, and came again on the first day of the tenth month for the ceremony of "sending winter clothes" (*sung han-i*) (spirit-clothes made of colored paper and burned at the side of the grave). It was rare that the grave became the focus of worship by anyone except the immediate descendants of the deceased. Although the graves of prominent individuals were often preserved, they were still private sites.[5]

The rituals described here are presented in their most common sequence, but the timing of each segment could vary considerably. Generally speaking, the two fixed events around which the others were organized were the encoffining and the removal of the coffin from the home. Ideally, encoffining took place on the third day, and saying goodbye to the soul, that evening;

5. Ch'ing rulers took responsibility for maintaining and making offerings at the tombs of emperors of their own and previous dynasties but did not permit their development as pilgrimage sites. The impressive public mausoleum built by the Republican government for Sun Yat-sen, discussed by Wakeman in chapter 11 in this volume, thus represented a significant break with tradition.

sutra chanting lasted seven, twenty-one, thirty-five, or forty-nine days; the funeral immediately preceded the moving of the coffin and ideally occurred within the seven sevens. In real life, the sequence could be and often was both compressed and simplified. The corpse could be dressed and placed in the coffin by the second day, the rituals of reporting to the temple and calling back the soul (both of which required a temple visit) could be performed together that evening, and on the third day monks came in to chant sutras, condolences were received, and the coffin was interred. Hot weather and a lack of resources were probably the two factors most likely to promote the performance of rituals in a speedy and simple fashion.

## VARIATIONS

The rituals so far discussed were, as I have indicated, generally performed at the deaths of elderly parents; for those who died childless or unmarried, modifications were made. When infants died, the bodies could be buried perfunctorily in shallow graves or simply abandoned. The older the child, the more elaborate the ceremony. Within private graveyards, certain (less desirable) areas were apparently reserved for infants and children. Families sometimes tried to arrange posthumous marriages for unwed children with a ceremony that combined a wedding and a funeral.

The religious community served as a surrogate family when Buddhist monks and nuns died. Following centuries-old practices, the corpses of these religious professionals were cremated. When a monk died, his fellow monks washed and dressed his corpse, chanted sutras over the body through the night, and then moved it (on a board or in a box or an urn) to the funeral pyre or crematorium, where it was burned the following day. Sutras were of course chanted on each of the seven sevens, at which times members of the deceased's family (who may have contributed money for the funeral masses) might attend. The ashes were most often placed in collective graves or preserved in urns that were stored in nearby pagodas. Tablets for deceased brethren were housed in a hall of the monastery, and offerings were made to them there. It was the responsibility of a disciple of the deceased to make offerings to the paper spirit-tablet that was used during the funeral and then to the wooden "ancestral" tablet itself.[6] The corpses of ascetics or exceptionally devout monks were sometimes preserved miraculously in a dried form and, lacquered and dressed, treated as sacred relics; sometimes,

6. J. J. M. de Groot, Le Code du Mahayana en Chine (Amsterdam: Johannes Müller, 1893), pp. 144–146; J. Prip-Moller, Chinese Buddhist Monasteries (Copenhagen, 1937; reprinted. Hong Kong: Hong Kong University Press, 1967), pp. 163–179. These descriptions are based on these authors' experiences in south and central China, but appear to reflect common practice throughout China.

despite government discouragement, they became objects of veneration and pilgrimage.[7]

There were, of course, a great many people who died alone and without family, especially those who were poor, single, and far from home. What happened to them? Although public services in China were far from systematically developed, some public and private charities attempted to cope with these problems. Government and community leaders were most likely to step in when many people died during large-scale disasters. Shallow pits might be dug and the bodies hurled in; if possible, however, men and women were interred separately. If many people had died by fire, leaving no bodies, the ashes were collected and carefully buried. The rules of one Tientsin association make clear several basic (and more generally applicable) principles of burial: if possible, rebury on the spot without moving the remains; keep separate the bodies of men and women who were not husbands and wives; build a mound over the grave so that others will not disturb it.[8]

Local leaders also periodically donated money or income-producing property to endow funds that could provide the needy with the essentials for funerals on a more routine basis. Such funds, often administered through local temples, appear to have had a natural life-cycle of several generations before the money was exhausted and new endowment needed. In nineteenth-century Tientsin, for example, there were a number of charity organizations (probably funded by wealthy merchants) that undertook to bury abandoned bodies. These bureaus variously gave out straw mats for the simplest form of burial, hired people to cover over or rebury unclaimed bodies or exposed coffins, buried the corpses that floated down the rivers into the city, paid to ship bodies back to their home communities, gave away coffins to people "who had died on the road or were so poor that they couldn't afford a coffin," and even helped manage funerals.[9] It is well known that native-place associations also provided a place for the temporary storage of coffins (and sometimes burial grounds) and funds for shipping bodies home.

There was generally a pervasive concern with the dangerous power of the spirits of those who had died by violence, especially those who had left no descendants. It was not in the interest of any community to be vulnerable to the vengeful acts of the unhappy spirits of the dead. In every county, the Ch'ing state had altars to untended spirits and maintained shrines for heroes, martyrs, and other people of virtue whose lives were cut short unnaturally. Many communities in north China had public graveyards for

7. P. W. Yetts, "The Disposal of the Buddhist Dead in China," *Journal of the Royal Asiatic Society*, July 1911, pp. 709–712.

8. T'ien-chin gazetteer (1870) 8.10.

9. Ibid. 8.9–10.

those who did not own private plots. Most of these "charitable burying grounds" (*i-chung*) were under ten *mou* in size (although some were as large as a hundred or more) and were located on land unsuitable for other uses. Orderly family interments were difficult to maintain in these "chaotic burial hills."

In general, the rituals performed for those Chinese who were not adults, not married, not parents, or without kin were essentially truncated versions of the full-fledged funeral rituals, explicitly adjusted for individuals who were in some sense not complete. These "variations" were in fact formal and purposeful differentiations in ritual.

It was not only the family status of an individual that could affect the degree to which he was buried according to the standard funeral-ritual procedure, but also his resources. Indeed, the variations most frequently noted in my sources were those resulting from different levels of expenditure. It is clear from the detail provided by Chinese and Western observers that a wide range of options was available.

At the most general level, the quality of the objects employed during the funeral (and often provided by specialty stores) could—and was expected to—vary with cost. The deathbed could be a wooden-plank door removed from its hinges or a brightly painted rented bed. The shroud itself could be a thin cotton sheet or a piece of fine silk with sutras printed on it in Sanskrit. A fine cedar coffin had thick planks, was heavily lacquered, and could weigh up to five hundred pounds. The spirit-world objects made of paper glued on straw or bamboo splints varied in volume and quality depending on the money expended. The most lavish procedure was to order big, brightly colored, well-made objects in large numbers. "It is an easy matter to make a dead person a millionaire in the next world."

Resources governed the amount of feasting provided, the number of guests, and the quality and quantity of the food at a funeral. One could hire a great many musicians, monks, or pallbearers, or only a few. Ordinary or special masses could be chanted once, at intervals, or for the full forty-nine days. Entertainment on the evening of the funeral seems to have ranged from nothing at all to blind storytellers, acrobats, and professional opera performers.

The size of the procession out of the community in particular was a reflection of the expenditures of the bereaved family. An ordinary family could have a simple procession that included relatives, the family, and the coffin; for the very poor, a putrifying body on a door, covered with a mat, carried by the son and two pallbearers; for the rich, a huge entourage several miles long, including dozens of monks and priests, several bands, plaques and colorful spirit-world objects carried by hired men, and newly garbed professional mourners.

Differential resources made the ceremony simpler or more complex.

Burial in less than seven days was a clear sign of poverty. Even families of moderate means who had an available site waited until at least the seventh day before transporting the coffin to the grave. The rich, on the other hand, had many acquaintances to notify and flaunted their resources by waiting past the first or third seven, even until the full forty-nine days had elapsed and an auspicious moment had arrived, not fearing the expense and inconvenience of a long period when visitors had to be entertained and the coffin kept in the home.

In short, from beginning to end, it was very easy for an observer with a fair knowledge of costs to tell just how much money had been spent on a funeral. In fact, an observer was *supposed* to be able to tell. Because a parent's funeral was seen as an expression of the son's filial devotion, he was expected to spare no expense. "The stingy are mocked"; "Those who exhaust their resources are happy." After all, the funeral created concrete benefits for the deceased: greater comfort in the next world, through the foods and objects offered, and salvation from hell, through the good auspices of the religious professionals engaged to pray for the soul. This association between filial devotion and funeral expenses created a deeply embedded encouragement of extravagance that was undeterred by protests from Ch'ing and Republican governments alike, protests that decried the unnecessary social pressure and waste of resources.

The lavishness of a funeral did more, of course, than reflect the sentiments of a child for a parent; it reflected the aspirations of a family for higher social status. It was expected that a funeral would demonstrate the limits of a family's resources, and because funerals were therefore occasions to display one's credit and financial reserves, "families in mourning competed to be new and extravagant and had no thought for those who spent on a grand scale and thus went into debt."[10] Among elite families of a locality, such ritual display was probably only one manifestation of multifaceted competition for status. There is some evidence, moreover, that from the perspective of the entire community, an expensive funeral was considered a social obligation of the rich, a time when resources were redistributed and the community could benefit from the public display and entertainment. The Kao-ch'eng county gazetteer notes that "whenever a rich person loses a parent, the country people regard it as a lucky chance to eat, a blessed thing."

The overall effect of wealth on variation in funeral ritual was direct and public. The rites almost seem designed to highlight different levels of expenditure. Funerals did, thus, vary with social status and wealth and thus offered many possibilities for defining publicly one's status with regard to both condolence-offering friends and relatives and the public more gener-

10. Fang-shan gazetteer.

ally. (Evelyn Rawski illustrates in chapter 10 in this volume the further variation introduced in imperial funeral ritual.) Because people felt these variations to be significant, virtually all of my sources note them; they too were purposeful differentiations, not deviations from a norm.

There were both religious and ethnic minorities in north China, and the variations in funeral rituals that we see among them reveal both the strong influence of the normative ideal and an acknowledgment of legitimate grounds for differences. Although bannermen (including Manchus, Mongols, and Han Chinese) had initially constituted a powerful minority group in the early Ch'ing, legal, ethnic, and cultural differences had steadily disappeared over time. By the turn of the twentieth century, differences in funeral ritual were not very great. The clothing worn by corpses and mourners at a bannerman funeral was distinctive, as was the use of a flagpole rather than a paper pennant at the front gate, and the occasional display (by the rich) of hunting animals in funeral processions.

In the funeral customs of the less sinicized Mongols, the influence of Central Asian culture is clearer. They relied, as did other Central Asian peoples, on shamans for many matters dealing with the dead, but called in priests of Tibetan Lamaist Buddhism to chant sutras as a person died, and to pray, ideally for forty-nine days, for a speedy and improved rebirth for the deceased. The bodies of Mongols were sometimes buried, following Chinese practice, but they were also sometimes cremated or even (among tribes beyond the wall) left exposed to the elements in a deserted spot.[11]

The Muslims of north China shared more customs with their non-Muslim neighbors than did Muslims of the northwest or Central Asia. Nonetheless, the chief mourner went to wail not at the earth-god shrine but in the mosque; the body of the deceased was wrapped naked in a white cloth, carried to the grave in a special box with a sliding bottom provided by the mosque, and buried facing Mecca without a coffin; the local *a-hung* (akhund or mullah) came and read from Islamic scriptures at the time of the interment; the grave was square, not round, in shape.[12] Sinicized Muslims adopted such practices as dressing the corpse in burial clothing, using a coffin, not inviting a mullah, and making subsequent offerings to an ancestral tablet. "But there are those," the Ts'ang gazetteer notes, "who have been using wooden tablets for a dozen generations, but their grave mounds are still square."[13]

We can see another example of the way in which a different set of religious beliefs professed by individuals set in the larger web of Chinese culture

---

11. See Ts'ang gazetteer 12.48–49, and Ivan A. Lopatin, *The Cult of the Dead Among the Natives of the Amur Basin* (Paris: Mouton, 1960) (data collected in 1913–18), chap. 4.

12. Muslim practices are described in the gazetteers of Hsiang-ho, Ts'ang, and Luan; also Takeda Masao, *Man-Han li-su*, pp. 336–338.

13. Ts'ang gazetteer 10.2. There is a photograph of a Muslim grave opposite p. 309 in Sidney D. Gamble, *How Chinese Families Live in Peiping* (New York: Funk & Wagnalls, 1933).

affected practices surrounding the dead if we look at the funeral practices of White Lotus sectarians. Although they may initially have been more radical,[14] because their sectarian religion drew heavily on mainstream Chinese popular culture, White Lotus sects did not differ in their funeral practices even as much as the Muslims. Their religious community supplemented the family, and pupils provided the expenses or the land for the burial of their teachers or fellow believers. De Groot describes how members of a Lung-hua sect in Amoy in the 1880s dressed the body of a deceased fellow believer in special clothing, encoffined the corpse, chanted sutras over it, and escorted it to the grave.[15]

Because they saw themselves as being among the elect children of the Eternal Mother (the chief deity of their religion), sectarians viewed with optimism the passage of the soul through the underworld. They assumed that they would go immediately to the paradise described in their scriptures without enduring the trials of hell or another incarnation. To identify themselves readily in the otherworld, believers therefore acquired (from their teachers) paper "passports" (lu-yin) on which their names would be written; these would be burned at death and the ashes placed on the body. These passports were, one believer said, "like a map to take you on the right road so that you could reach the good place"; anyone who had a passport, said another, "would be met and led through hell by a god and would not have to suffer hell's bitterness."[16]

Some sectarians developed into religious professionals themselves, chanting scriptures for a variety of occasions (including funerals), as monks and Taoist priests did. Said one eighteenth-century Hung-yang sect member, "Whenever there was a funeral for a poor person who did not have the resources to invite a monk or a priest, they asked [us] to chant sutras and escort [the coffin to the grave]."[17] Believers recited their own scriptures as

---

14. Richard Shek, citing the work of Sawada Mizuho, notes several late Ming claims that followers of Lo sects refused to perform the usual funeral ritual or make offerings to ancestors ("Religion and Society in Late Ming: Sectarianism and Popular Thought in Sixteenth and Seventeenth Century China," Ph.D. dissertation, University of California at Berkeley, 1980, pp. 228–229). I have not seen similar charges or evidence of such practices in subsequent centuries.

15. J. J. M. de Groot, Sectarianism and Religious Persecution in China (Amsterdam: Johannes Müller, 1903–4), pp. 231–241.

16. For the two quotations: Kung-chung-tang 宮中檔 [Palace memorial archive] (National Palace Museum, Taiwan) no. 48013, Ch'ien-lung (hereafter CL) 49/5/4, and no. 24036, CL 34/1/22 (this case did not come from north China). More extensive citations may be found in the conference version of this article. See also Naquin, "The Transmission of White Lotus Sectarianism in Late Imperial China," in Johnson et al., Popular Culture in Late Imperial China.

17. Kung-chung-tang, secret society category (Ming-Ch'ing Archives, Peking) 490.1, CL 34/2/12. Most of my evidence of professional chanting comes from Hung-yang sects of the Peking area circa 1800. See sources cited in Naquin, "Transmission."

well as orthodox ones, sometimes played musical instruments and wore "Taoist" robes, and relied on their piety to make their performances of penances efficacious.

In this religion there was a tendency to treat the graves of past teachers, and particularly the late Ming patriarchs of the religion, as places of pilgrimage. Not only were these graves maintained over many generations by families of believers who resided nearby, but they received regular visits from sect members. These graves had, variously, stone stele in front, pagodas nearby, and images or tablets in a temple or a hall.[18] As the line between teacher, ancestor, and deity was rather blurred in a number of these cases, it is not surprising that grave sites generated temple complexes, government disapproval notwithstanding.

Variations in funeral ritual according to family status, class, and religion were deliberate variations encouraged by the society to mark what people saw as significant social differences. They were, in Freedman's terms, "religious similarities expressed as though they were religious differences."[19] The variations in ritual that occurred across time and geographic distances may have been of a quite different order.

Because funeral rituals expressed core values and were derived from religious traditions of enduring relevance, most Chinese appear to have assumed that these rites should not vary widely from place to place nor should they change over time. The sources I have consulted unfortunately make it difficult to see much regional or temporal variation within the parts of north China in the late Ch'ing and Republican period on which this article concentrates. The Chinese preference for describing the ideal ritual, together with the limited number of sources consulted here and their relatively shallow time depth, give the strong (but false) impression that funeral rituals were similar from county to county and unchanging from the nineteenth to the twentieth century. Comparisons with other parts of China are, fortunately, much easier and, together with the model set forth by James Watson in chapter 1, may help highlight what was regionally specific about the rites here described.

Although studies of funeral ritual in parts of China besides the north are not abundant, there are more than enough to make possible some general comparisons with other regions. The classic works are the observations of Justus Doolittle on Foochow (1865), Henri Doré on the lower Yangtze (1911), and of course the voluminous work of J. J. M. de Groot on Amoy

---

18. The best known of these graves in north China were those of Patriarch Lo in Mi-yun county, Patriarch P'u-ming in Wan-ch'üan, Patriarch Mi (a woman) in Kao-ch'eng, the Ching-k'ung Patriarch in the Peking suburbs, and the Wang family ancestral hall in Luan-chou—all in Chihli province.

19. Freedman, "On the Sociological Study of Chinese Religion," p. 38.

(1892–1910).[20] These can be supplemented, with careful attention to temporal change, by the fieldwork of Arthur Wolf, Emily Martin (Ahern), and others, in Taiwan, and of Maurice Freedman, James Watson, and others, in Hong Kong.

At one level, the similarities between funeral rituals in all of these areas are striking, especially if a non-Chinese model is kept in mind. As the chapters in this volume indicate, a set of Chinese ideas about funeral ritual is certainly identifiable. Although different in many minor ways, components of the ritual sequence described by Doré (for Kiangsu and Anhwei) and Walshe (for Chekiang) replicate those I have set forth. The pattern for Fukien (Amoy and Foochow, and recent Taiwan) diverges a bit more. There, the "report to the temple" was absent, and a rite involving "buying water" with which to wash the corpse was present (both are also present in Chekiang); the specific procedures for the same actions (e.g., dressing the corpse, putting it in the coffin) are more markedly different; and the layout of the grave is quite dissimilar. Data from Hong Kong (all recent) are divergent in similar ways, but more dramatically so, and the preference in southeast China for a two- or three-stage burial process presents the most striking contrast with northern customs. (Delayed burial in north China, like secondary burial in the south, however, meant that only a comparatively small number of people would actually have formal graves.) By separating funeral rites from rites of disposal, James Watson, in chapter 1 of this volume, accommodates this diversity in burial practice to the existence of a set of standard rites. All of his nine core procedures are in fact present in north China, although bathing the corpse is not reported consistently and, like the "buying of water" (never mentioned in my sources), may not have been the essential feature of "dressing the corpse."[21]

Consideration of these sorts of variations, while enriching our knowledge of north China funerals, does not allow us much insight into why and how these differences occurred, how the ritual actually came to be standardized, and what sources of control existed. To answer these questions, another sort of approach is needed.

## RITUAL SPECIALISTS

As we have seen, funeral rituals dealt with the soul and the body of the deceased, on the one hand, and with the mourners themselves, the bereaved

20. Justus Doolittle, *Social Life of the Chinese* (New York: Harper, 1865), pp. 168–235; Henri Doré, *Researches into Chinese Superstitions*, trans. M. Kennelly, vol. 1 (Shanghai, 1911), pp. 41–87; J. J. M. de Groot, *The Religious System of China* (Leiden: Brill, 1892–1910), vol. 1; W. Gilbert Walshe, "Some Chinese Funeral Customs," *Journal of the North China Branch of the Royal Asiatic Society* 35 (1903–4): 26–64.

21. Much more attention is given in my sources to clothing the corpse than to washing it.

family and friends of the deceased, on the other. In the course of the ritual, a number of different specialists were called in to deal with these different interwoven concerns. It is my hypothesis that these ritual specialists and the manuals on which they relied were an important key to uniformity in death rites. A look at the professionals whose expertise was crucial to the performance of these different components of the ritual will, I believe, help explain how variation in ritual practice was, to different degrees, controlled.

At the simplest level, a bereaved family simply needed extra manpower to manage both the funeral and ongoing chores, and most people turned to friends and relatives for assistance. This help was given informally and formally. The 1934 Pa county gazetteer noted that sometimes neighbors would help out with manual labor; sometimes they would organize themselves into teams under a leader: "No one demands compensation, it is just an expression of mutual aid." Sometimes a family assured themselves of aid by joining a Marriage and Funeral Association (*hung-pai hui, lao-jen hui*). These small-scale savings organizations not only created a fund to which families contributed and from which they borrowed, but provided a group whose members would also come to give a hand during the funeral.

For ritual matters generally, most people surely drew for expertise, although my sources do not mention it, on the experience of older men and women in the community, people who had seen many funerals in their time and knew how things were supposed to be done. (See E. Johnson in chapter 6 in this volume for illustrations of this.)[22]

For some of the more demanding or dangerous tasks, unskilled labor could be hired (some landlords could demand that tenants provide these and other services).[23] In north China, bereaved families employed pallbearers (*kang-fu*) and gravediggers (*t'u-kung*), but apparently not the corpse handlers common in the south. Often contracted through the shops that rented funeral equipment, these men did the heavy work of preparing the grave, loading the coffin onto the frame of the catafalque, and carrying it to the graveyard.[24]

People could also rely on those men who ran the specialty shops that

22. Such knowledge was acquired throughout a lifetime. In the 1920s, Westerners picnicking in a graveyard near Peking saw a group of children who were "playing at funerals, burying crickets who died with the morning glories, and pretending to repeat Buddhist 'sutras' over the graves" (Juliet Bredon, *Peking*, 2d ed., Shanghai: Kelley and Walsh [1922], p. 252).

23. E.g., *Agrarian China*, Institute of Pacific Relations, ed. (Chicago: University of Chicago Press, 1939), pp. 16, 19, describing Wei county in Shantung and Fo-p'ing in Hopei.

24. Pallbearer organizations apparently frequently established monopolies that allowed them to charge very high rates (in T'ung, for example, the city was divided into quarters, each of which had one firm). Government measures to break these monopolies, set ceilings on rates, and provide services for the poor met with only sporadic success. See "An Account of the Establishment of a Charity Bier-Carrier Bureau" in the 1879 T'ung gazetteer. There were similar problems with both musicians and pallbearers in Tientsin (T'ien-chin gazetteer, 1739).

catered to funerals. In cities and towns, many of the objects used in funerals were rented or bought from these shops: the deathbed itself, shrouds and pillows, coffins, spirit-world items, banners and pennants, mat awnings, tables and chairs, ceremonial mourning outfits, spirit-money and food for offerings, the catafalque, grave markers. Caterers and pallbearers could also be provided for a fee. The managers of the various shops that handled such goods and services (who probably inherited their businesses from their fathers) must have known how to answer their clients' questions: what the ceremonial layout should be, which mourning outfit was appropriate for which relationship, what offerings were appropriate for which ritual, and so forth. They had no acknowledged standing as experts, and their answers may not have accorded with orthodox practices, but for many families they may have been as authoritative. In the countryside, such services were probably decreasingly available as one moved down the central place hierarchy. It would be interesting to know if regional specialization in such goods and services made for some degree of uniformity in ritual practice or equipment.

The most all-purpose expert at a funeral in north China was the yin-yang master (*yin-yang hsien-sheng* or *yin-yang shih*). His services were immediately engaged when there was a death in the family. He decided on an auspicious moment for the encoffining, procession, and burial. He also determined (by birthdates) who outside the immediate family was too vulnerable or astrologically unsuitable to be allowed near the corpse, wrote charms to "stabilize malevolent forces," oversaw the placement of paper streamers at the gate, cut out the spirit-pennant, supervised the encoffining, helped with the rite of breaking the bowl, and chanted spells every time the corpse was moved. He used charms to purify the places in the house where the coffin had been and to protect those who had been in close contact with it; he determined the time when the final remnants of the spirit would vacate the home; and he came on that day to see that the departure was without incident. In addition to harmonizing the events of the funeral with temporal rhythms, the same diviner oriented the location of the corpse in space. The placement of the body on the deathbed and of the coffin in the hall, and particularly the siting of the grave and the arrangement of the coffin within it—all were his responsibility. (Only a few of my sources referred to the services of a geomancer as distinct from a diviner.)[25]

The diviners' sphere obviously involved many rites that dealt with the body and the lingering powers of the deceased. Chinese believed that when someone died, his *hun*, which I am translating "soul," traveled first to the underworld to be judged and then was released for rebirth (in a form appropriate to its merits) or paradise. Although some connections were maintained between the *hun* in its various incarnations, they were few and

25. Terming him a *feng-shui hsien-sheng*, *feng-chien hsien-sheng*, or *hsing-chia* 形家.

tenuous. Other aspects of the deceased survived independent of this soul; these I have translated "spirit"; the technical term (not used in my sources) seems to be p'o, but compounds of the term *ling* were used here.[26] Unlike the soul, which departed speedily, this transitional spirit was closely attached to its once-living body and would ultimately find its home in the grave and in the ancestral tablet. And unlike the soul, which was only the temporary and passive recipient of the deceased's rewards and punishments, the spirit remembered its family and had considerable long-lasting potential for actively harming or helping human beings, especially if it became detached and was left to wander, homeless and hungry. Failure to settle this potentially malevolent spirit of the deceased in a satisfactory grave and identifiable ancestral tablet could lead to illness, infertility, and even death. For this reason, correct procedures were very important. These powers of the corpse and the spirit were the concerns of the yin-yang master.

Information about yin-yang masters and diviners in this period is not easy to come by. They were unlicensed during the Ch'ing and thus not controlled (or documented) by the bureaucracy, and few sources describe them. In the Republican period, at least in Peking, they were required to have permits from the police (and given the task of determining cause of death).[27] Although these men were usually literate and dependent on manuals that may have been of considerable antiquity, their social status appears to have been low, quite in contrast to the southern geomancer, who was said to be "a kind of a gentleman" in Cantonese society.[28] H. Y. Lowe's fictitious Mr. Chang, the *yin-yang-sheng*, had a small office with an auspicious (and somewhat pretentious) name, and relied on a "dog-eared almanac, almost worn out from constant handling."[29]

These men had considerable experience with funerals, and for their work they turned to various calendrical and astrological charts, wrote charms and pronounced spells (orally transmitted or copied from books of diagrams and formulae), and used a geomancer's compass and perhaps manual to interpret configurations at the grave site. Generally, they were very diverse in their training and expertise and relied on oral traditions that were rarely written down.[30]

26. Nathan Sivin has suggested the terms *yang* soul and *yin* soul to describe these two entities, and "transitional soul" for *ling* (personal communication, 1985).

27. H. Y. Lowe, *The Adventures of Wu*, 2:90; the Nan-ho gazetteer lists the names of eight diviners in the county (6.30).

28. *The Study of Chinese Society: Essays by Maurice Freedman* (Stanford: Stanford University Press, 1979), p. 322.

29. Lowe, *The Adventures of Wu*, 2:89–90. For almanacs, see de Groot, *The Religious System*, 2:99.

30. Apparently because these rituals drew principally on folk tradition, compilers of local histories noted them infrequently and with condescension. For example, one (Wan county) account that is unusually specific says, apropos of the encoffining, that "there are all kinds of

There seems to have been no systematic training for such men besides apprenticeship, no set canon of their books, and no fixed set of responsibilities. Geomantic tasks were the more clearly defined and had pretensions to being a kind of science. There were theoretically two major schools of geomancy and an informal canon of texts a millennium old; geomancers apparently drew on these in an unsystematic way.[31] An imperially issued almanac was printed every year, and a yin-yang master could rely on it, and on many other manuals of charms and formulae, more ordinary almanacs, and a variety of orally transmitted methods. He may have learned from several teachers and probably created his own eclectic system by choosing from a large pool of diverse practices.

Under these circumstances, we should not be surprised by the variety of rites and procedures exhibited in aspects of the funeral dealing with the spirit and the corpse and the confusing and contradictory accounts of what seem to be regionally specific variants on bits of the ritual sequence. For example, the breaking of a bowl by the chief mourner under the direction of a diviner just before the coffin was moved from the house was described and explained in these north China gazetteers in many different ways. Sometimes it was preceded by the snapping of a mulberry branch provided by the diviner; sometimes it was followed by the breaking of a second bowl; sometimes the bowl was smashed up against a brick. Sometimes these actions were explained as "putting an end to formal mourning," sometimes as signifying that, alas, "one can no longer make offerings to one's parents"; sometimes the bowl was filled with wood chips, sometimes with paper money. Some said that the deceased had to use the bowl to drink all the water he had wasted in his lifetime, and therefore the bowl was broken or a hole knocked in it by the chief mourner to make this task easier; others said that the hole was to keep the deceased from drinking all of the "drugging-the-soul soup" fed to him in hell to make him forget this incarnation.[32]

These actions and explanations may have drawn on a common repertory of belief, but they nevertheless show considerable diversity and probably also were influenced by local oral traditions almost out of the reach of the historian. This sphere of folk belief, although often decried by Confucian-

---

taboos (*pi-chi*) observed; there is no point in describing them." This bias of the sources on which I have so overwhelmingly relied has constricted my access to the minor variations in ritual that are the stuff of fieldwork. Takeda Masao, *Man-Han li-su*, is probably the single best source because of his lack of prejudice and relative wealth of such detail.

31. See de Groot, *The Religious System*, 3:994–1008, and Stephan Feuchtwang, *An Anthropological Analysis of Chinese Geomancy* (Vientiane: Vithagna, 1974), especially pp. 17–18 and Part 4. De Groot saw (in Amoy) "popular expositions" of geomantic theory "on sale in every bookstore, mostly of considerable bulk, and illustrated with woodcuts" (p. 1009).

32. See accounts from Shu-lu; Ting; Kao-i; Han-tan; Lowe, *The Adventures of Wu*, 2:122; Gamble, *North China Villages*, p. 260, and *Ting Hsien*, pp. 389–390; Takeda Masao, *Man-Han li-su*, p. 276. The terms used to refer to this ritual are equally varied.

trained elites, had never been systematized by them. Informally transmitted ideas about the power of a dead body and a lost spirit were certainly to be found everywhere in China, and probably can be studied today, but for earlier periods we know very little about either regional diversity or changes over time. We do know, however, that out of fear of the consequences, most people wanted professional help in dealing with these problems. Because the dangers associated with the corpse were considerable, and because the relevant professionals were unencumbered by a set of orthodox procedures, improvisation and variety in practice are certainly to be expected.

To say that the aspects of funeral rites handled by the yin-yang masters were unsystematic is not to say that there was no underlying order. As outsiders to the culture, we can see how similar ideas were the underpinnings of many of these rituals, even though these principles were nowhere written down and explicitly stated as such, and even though we still do not understand how they came to be held in common: the continuity and easy communication between the world of the living and that of the dead, for example, or the power of *yang* objects to offset the *yin* of the corpse.[33] Perhaps a study of the implicit beliefs expressed in these kinds of ritual can further illuminate this body of orally transmitted shared assumptions.

Nevertheless, a number of the most dramatic differences between the regions of China were, in fact, associated with the corpse and the grave. In the Canton delta (where the contrast with north China seems most dramatic), extremely different ideas about the corpse seem to exist. There, burial of the body in a coffin was followed by a later unearthing, scraping of the bones, temporary storage of the bones in an urn, and later reburial of the urn in a geomantically suitable setting. J. L. Watson and others have noted that this custom is related to ideas about the power of bones and the dangers of the flesh—ideas that inform the strong aversion seen in Cantonese society to those who handle corpses.[34] Another striking difference between these regions is that in the north the preferred form of burial for an individual was with his family, whereas in the Canton area family and lineage graves were dispersed and each person was sited separately. Although ideas about the corpse may be related to deep-seated beliefs (and Malayo-Polynesian culture?), these different burial patterns may be more directly connected with social structure. It seems possible, as Freedman has suggested, that the Cantonese burial pattern reflects the commonplace competition inside lineages;[35] stress within the tightly knit lineages of this region may be being

---

33. J. Watson also discusses these common assumptions in chapter 1 of this volume.

34. See Watson, "Of Flesh and Bones: The Management of Death Pollution in Cantonese Society," in Maurice Bloch and Jonathan Parry, eds., *Death and the Regeneration of Life* (Cambridge: Cambridge University Press, 1982), pp. 155–186.

35. Freedman, *The Study of Chinese Society*, p. 318.

displaced into competition over the *feng-shui* of individual graves. In the north, by contrast, burial in groups may have been an easier act of family unity for kin groups that, although they rarely had joint endeavors, competed primarily with other kin groups.

Ethnic and religious minorities were also noticeably different in their burial practices. Indeed, because they were detachable parts of the ritual sequence and managed by diverse specialists, the rituals for handling the corpse and grave may have been most responsive to local conditions. Certainly, differences in folklore might generate special clusters of interrelated taboos. A thorough study of the ideas about and measures taken toward the corpse for any historical period may, however, be very difficult. Most written sources, as we have noted, ignore this aspect of funeral ritual, and the historian will never have data of the sort gathered through interactions with informants by an anthropologist.

The rituals concerned with the salvation of the soul (*hun*) were orchestrated by other professionals who promoted a much greater degree of ritual consistency than did the yin-yang masters. These specialists were monks and priests with accumulated spiritual merit and authority on such matters who were hired to relieve the soul's sufferings and guide it through hell. The most elaborate versions of "doing the sevens" (*tso fo-shih*, "doing Buddhist things," is the Confucian term) involved building a platform in the ceremonial area on which noisy and colorful rituals were staged.

There Buddhist monks in dark robes (and sometimes nuns) set up scroll paintings of Buddhas, burned petitions to the bodhisattva Ti-tsang, and chanted sutras and penances in order to transfer merit to the soul of the deceased. Taoist priests (*tao-shih*), in distinctive robes (showed off by frequent changes), hung paintings of the Three Pure Ones and read aloud the communiqués and petitions that would secure good treatment in the underworld.[36] In the Peking area, Mongol lamas would also be invited. According to one informant, they put on the most dramatic show: displaying "hair-raising" tanka scrolls of Tibetan gods and demons, wearing bright yellow robes, and chanting in very low voices to the accompaniment of impressive drums and trumpets.[37]

The progression of the soul toward salvation (*ch'ao-tu*) was reflected in the pieces of a set ritual sequence (each with its own texts) performed by these professionals: feeding other hungry spirits (*fang-yen-k'ou*), breaking out of hell (*p'o-yü*), seeing the lantern (*kuan-teng*), and crossing the bridge

36. Doré, *Researches*, has examples (illustrations and translations) of petitions read and burned by Taoist priests (1:70–71, 74, 92–93). See also Kristofer M. Schipper, "The Written Memorial in Taoist Ceremonies," in *Religion and Ritual in Chinese Society*, ed. A. P. Wolf (Stanford: Stanford University Press, 1974), pp. 309–324.

37. Lowe, *The Adventures of Wu*, 2:112–113.

to rebirth (*tu-ch'iao*). If the deceased was a woman, special rituals were added to release her from the pool of blood in hell (*hsueh-hu* or *hsueh-p'en*). All of these rituals could involve an actual performance by the monks or priests, and sometimes the mourners themselves, in which these efforts on behalf of the soul in its journey in the otherworld were acted out. The use of music, gestures, and sometimes elaborate props could create quite dramatic effects. On the evening before the removal of the coffin, opera troupes, acrobats, or storytellers were sometimes also invited to perform, ostensibly to tell a pious story with an appropriate moral message. The tale of Mu-lien, who through his piety saved his mother from the torments of hell, could be enjoyed in the knowledge that it was also uplifting and suitable for the occasion. Monks, priests, and musicians were often hired for the funeral procession as well, although their presence here (as well as at the encoffining) may have been generally prophylactic rather than specific to the soul's progress.

Although the scale of the ritual varied widely with the money expended and depended somewhat on the age of the deceased, everyone wanted the soul looked after by a professional if possible. As we have seen, minorities substituted a mullah or a shaman or a lama or a sect member for the more normal Buddhist or Taoist priest in accordance with their different ideas about the fate of the soul after death. Not everyone was able to afford such a show or lengthy performances, however, and some chose instead a few rounds of sutra chanting. "As for ordinary people, some use monks and not priests, some use priests and not monks."[38] If these professionals were not available nearby, people turned to *huo-chü* (living-in-the-world) Taoists, lay Buddhists, or sectarians. The poor might be unable to hire any clergy at all.[39] Musicians who specialized in funerals could be brought in cheaply to supplement or even substitute for some of the clerics.

The ordinary person already had, after all, considerable familiarity with the basic ideas about life, death, and reincarnation presented in these rituals. Over the centuries, a broadly diffused infrastructure had been created, which popularized simple Buddhist doctrine and presented understandable visions of heaven and hell. Standardization in belief was promoted by temples throughout the nation—to Tung-yueh (god of the eastern peak), to the kings of hell (especially Yen-lo wang), and to Ti-tsang (the bodhisattva Ksitigarbha who had the power to intervene in hell)—and was supplemented by a well-developed set of visual images of the process of judgment, the torments of hell, and the route to paradise, which were expressed in temple carvings and wall paintings, scrolls hung at funerals, and popular religious book illustrations.[40] The story of Mu-lien's descent into hell to save his mother, transmitted as it was in storytellers' tales and a variety of plays, appears to have been a very important carrier of basic ideas about salvation through Buddhist ritual.[41]

Cheap editions of popular Buddhist sutras (e.g., the *Amitabha Sutra* or the *Diamond Sutra*) were increasingly available in this period so that even the uninitiated could chant something themselves if need be. Doré implies that the general public could even bypass the clergy and go to a specialty shop and purchase the petitions and passports used by Buddhists and Taoists;[42] sectarians also made and sold (very cheaply) passports that could expedite the soul's progress.

Certain rituals relating to the soul were actually managed by the mourners themselves. They burned special paper currency and objects to be used in the spirit world, went to the office of the local earth god to report the death, released the soul from the god's custody by "calling it home," packed the coffin with goods to be used in the next world, and saw off the soul after the encoffining.

Although we do not know their numbers, Buddhist monks and Taoist priests were found throughout the empire (there were fewer nuns and lamas), and funeral rituals were a mainstay of their livelihood. These specialists turned to a large body of written literature and traditional rituals handed down during their professional training. Maintenance of uniformity in ritual depended greatly on these people and these texts. Those monks who lived in large, well-endowed monasteries had libraries and also a community of individuals who were repositories of these traditions. Old editions, rare scriptures, and careful training gave them claims to greater efficacy in their efforts on the soul's behalf. Similarly, Taoists received initiation into esoteric traditions with their own texts and manuals that gave the practitioner access to special deities and to powerful charms and ritual motions unknown to others.[43] Both the Taoist and the Buddhist canons

---

40. Wolfram Eberhard, *Guilt and Sin in Traditional China* (Berkeley and Los Angeles: University of California Press, 1967), pp. 24–55, describes these courts of hell.

41. Eberhard lists a number of these Mu-lien operas; see *Guilt and Sin*, pp. 25, 59.

42. Doré, *Researches*, 1:69–70. He illustrates a variety of special petitions for abnormal deaths (suicides, murder victims, etc.).

43. In "Vernacular and Classical Ritual in Taiwan" (*Journal of Asian Studies* 45, no. 1 [1985]: 21–57), Kristofer Schipper illuminates this murky area with his analysis of the complementary relationship between two kinds of Taoist practitioners: the *tao-shih* 道士 whose rites were based on texts in the classical language, and the less prestigious *fa-shih* 法師 who used orally transmitted ritual texts in the vernacular. Only the former are referred to in my sources.

had been fixed in standard editions and reprinted in the Ch'ing. Among
elite Buddhists and Taoists, standardization of ritual (through common
books and similar training) across time and space was likely to be greatest
and surely accounts for the general similarity in salvational funeral rites
throughout China. Not everyone was well trained (see chapter 5 in this volume), however, and control of quality depended both on education and
on an unwillingness to modify rituals to conform to local practices.

Because the state had long weakened these Buddhist and Taoist establishments, deprived them of the ability to police themselves, and encouraged
decentralization in most religious matters, there was no single church and
few mechanisms for internal control. Competition between monks and
priests of different schools and between professionals and amateurs, combined with this institutional weakness, was in turn reflected in the fact that
the basic stages of the funeral mass were performed differently at different
times and places. Moreover, because the average person did not have access
to the best professionals, the rituals most commonly employed were presumably less orthodox and less standardized.

Regional variation in this track of the ritual reflected this diffused nature
of institutionalized Buddhism and Taoism and the uneven distribution of
monasteries, temples, and clergy in China. Despite the fixed canons and
desultory attempts at licensing by the state, regional and local traditions had
probably developed around certain teachers and particularly around temples. Certainly, some monasteries concentrated on the lucrative business
of performing elaborate rites for the dead and came to be well known for
these.

Because religious instruction was not systematically standardized, ideas
about the soul were often fuzzy or contradictory: how many hells were
there? how did they differ? what were the landmarks on the road to the
underworld? who could intercede most effectively for the deceased? Aspects
of the funeral ritual relating to uncertain areas of articulated belief showed
much variety, were explained in different ways, and were poorly integrated
into the rituals performed on the seven sevens—for example, the exact role
of the earth god, the process of calling back the soul, or the specifics of what
went into the coffin. This sphere of concern was thus characterized by lati-
tude and tolerance of variety within a context of several loosely institutionalized orthodoxies and competing orders of religious professionals.

A third kind of expert brought in at north China funerals in addition to
the diviners and geomancers, the monks and priests, was of a rather different type: invited, not hired, this man's expertise was his classical education.
Funeral rituals were, after all, about the living as well as the dead. Funerals
were intended to give formal expression not only to the feelings of grief and
loss that a death generated but also to the ensuing rearrangement of rela-

tionships. We can see these concerns reflected in many strands of the rites: the ritualized wailing and stylized behavior expected of mourners; the elaborate system of mourning clothing that paralleled degrees of kinship; the fixed methods for notifying the community of the death; the rituals for presenting and receiving condolences; the offerings to the deceased; and the procedure for creating an ancestral tablet. Each had its fixed form and prescribed actions but was not within the purview of the professionals so far discussed.

It is with these aspects of the funeral that classical Confucianism had, in fact, long been explicitly concerned. Funerals were the quintessential expressions of *hsiao*, "filial piety," "reverence toward parents," a value that by late imperial times was imbedded at the core of the orthodoxy accepted by most Chinese. Many of these rituals had names of considerable longevity, were based on ancient precedents quite complicated in their most sophisticated forms, and had been perpetuated by the classically educated elite for many centuries. These rites reflected a deep concern with the proper handling of familial and social relations, and with establishing and maintaining unbroken but hierarchical connections among generations living and dead in the patriline. Because many strands of the funeral rituals drew on this classical Confucian orthodoxy, it is not surprising that people turned to the texts and experts of this tradition for correct explication and procedure.

The ultimate authority for funeral rituals was the Confucian Classics. Confucius himself had established the importance of ritual in general and funerals in particular. The *Li chi* (Treatises on ceremonial usages), *I li* (Rites and ceremonial usages), and *Hsiao ching* (Classic of filial piety) were somewhat later works that had become repositories of model ritual procedures. For centuries, scholars had studied these texts in order to understand and emulate these classical models. Fine editions of these works were available to the elite in Ch'ing times (and more widely in the twentieth century), but their difficulty as texts restricted their readership to the philologically trained. Ritual compendia were also officially printed by the Ch'ing court as guides to imperial ritual, and as Evelyn Rawski shows in chapter 10, at imperial funerals the president of the Board of Rites served as master of ceremonies, and Hanlin scholars, as consultants. Thus scholar-officials, with their access to the classical past, performed the most authentic and elaborate of these rites.

For the person of more ordinary education there was, fortunately, a more accessible reference work, the *Chia li* (Rituals for family life) attributed to the great Sung philosopher Chu Hsi. Although surviving editions of this work seem rather scholarly, the book appears to have circulated fairly widely. Nineteenth- and twentieth-century local histories refer frequently to it, noting the reliance placed on it by educated people.[44] A great many other ritual manuals, many of them illustrated, borrowed the prestige of Chu Hsi's name and the "Rituals for Family Life" title. This more popular *Chia li* genre included simple drawings of mourning clothing and ritual paraphernalia, diagrams of positions and movements, and the texts of many of the written forms necessary for high-status funerals (testimonial banners, announcements, invocations, epitaphs, etc.).[45] Ch'ing literati made concerted efforts to disseminate these works in order to check "Buddhist" influence and rectify what they perceived as vulgar popular customs. The shorter *Classic of Filial Piety* was sometimes distributed at funerals,[46] and it may have been even more widely available. It provided formulaic descriptions of the "filial son lost in grief," which may have inspired behavior (and were sometimes substituted for observation in gazetteer accounts). Although a detailed study of the texts and illustrations of these ritual books is clearly necessary before we can ascertain how much consistency there was between editions for different kinds of reading audiences, it seems fairly clear that books of this sort were basic reference manuals for the elite and were promoted as such.

Equally significant, it was not just the most highly educated who were called upon to dictate portions of the funeral ritual. It appears to have been widely accepted that for matters relating to these aspects of ritual, even a smattering of a classical education produced a specialist. Justus Doolittle (drawing on experiences in Foochow) said of the educated men who made money serving as "professors of ceremony" for the "common people" during funerals: "They . . . are necessarily literary men, of respectable connections, of polite demeanor, able to assume, when occasion demands, a grave and dignified appearance; self-possessed and authoritative, else they could not discharge to the satisfaction of their patrons the function of their calling."[47] During the Ch'ing, the academy and examination system drew in

44. De Groot had obviously seen several editions of this work, which he consulted for his exhaustive study of funeral ritual (*The Religious System*, 1:238; 2:832). Gazetteers called it the *Wen-kung* (文公 or 溫公, another reference to Chu Hsi) *Chia li*. Leon Wieger says of this work: "It is used by the masters of ceremonies in the great families" (p. 504). In 1889 C. de Harlez published a French translation under the title *Kia-li: Livre des rites domestiques chinois de Tchou-Hi, traduit pour la première fois, avec commentaires* (Paris: Ernest Leroux). Patricia Ebrey is currently translating this text; see her 1984 paper for the Conference on Neo-Confucian Education, "Education Through Ritual: Efforts to Formulate Family Rituals During the Sung Period," where she also discusses the question of Chu Hsi's authorship.

45. See, for example, the *Chia li yi-chieh* 家禮儀節 [The formalities of family life] of the fifteenth-century scholar Ch'iu Chün 邱濬, or the *Chu-tzu chia li* 朱子家禮 [Master Chu's rituals for family life], attributed to Ch'iu.

46. For example, see the Chi-tse (1766), Yung-nien (1877), and Jen (1915) county gazetteers.

47. Doolittle, *Social Life*, 1:251–252.

the wealthy from all over the empire and trained them in a classical education and a refined style of behavior. Though many of these men never had careers beyond their native place, they still felt a part of this national elite. Procedures laid out in texts such as the "Rituals for Family Life" provided these men with a source of consistency and continuity. Reliance on this kind of text assured the elite a near monopoly on what, by their own definition (and apparently shared widely by others) was the most high-status, refined, and elegant funeral. These experts disdained other ritual specialists, prided themselves on their amateur status, and were never hired for money.

The prestige of these "Confucian" aspects of funeral ritual made them attractive even to the uneducated. Ordinary people could, of course, simply rely on the orally transmitted expertise of members of the family and community, for in their simplest form the rituals mentioned here (the kowtow, procedures for making offerings, receiving guests, etc.) were commonly used in daily life, and basic "Confucian" ideas about family and hierarchy had long since become part of popular culture. The partially literate could turn also to the sections on funeral rituals contained in popular almanacs, books that often defined the grades of mourning, described mourning attire and the ritual itself, and provided simple texts for the written parts of the ceremony. Such almanacs were said to be widely available in the twentieth century and may have been so earlier.[48]

Nevertheless, the high status associated with elaborate rites and their written components enhanced the desirability of guidance from a member of the elite. To obtain these services, people were encouraged to establish patronage relations with prominent individuals in their communities. Respected and experienced friends of the family were asked to serve as masters of ceremony during the funeral. Someone else was invited to the ceremony of making offerings to the spirit of the soil at graveside and thanked later with a feast. The prestigious ritual of filling in the ancestral tablet called for, ideally, the brief participation of someone of the scholar class. Conveyed to the funeral in a hired sedan chair and welcomed with obsequious fanfare by the host family, this "inscriber of the tablet" thus established his superior position and enhanced the prestige of the rites.[49]

The imperial educational system had provided a nationwide network of "masters of ceremonies" with ritual experience and expertise and access to classical texts, to maintain consistency. Men trained in the classical style of behavior represented the forces of uniformity for this part of the ritual. Among the elite, the formalities orchestrating social and familial relations at

48. See de Groot, *The Religious System*, 1:99–100. Martin Palmer's English version of a modern almanac gives the general flavor but does not contain specific instructions for funerals; see *T'ung-shu: The Ancient Chinese Almanac* (Boston: Shambala, 1986).

49. Wieger's description (pp. 561–563) of the "filling in the tablet" ceremony illustrates clearly the unequal relationship.

funerals were thus relatively standardized nationwide during the imperial period, but became progressively variant as one moved down the social scale.

The three kinds of professionals on whom this discussion has concentrated had specific and different visions of and methods for communicating with the spirit world. Over the centuries, Confucians had tried to stress social relations in this world and discourage both "Buddhist ceremonies" and "vulgar superstitions." (At some point in the past, the orthodox elite appears to have appropriated the rites connected with the transfer of the spirit to the ancestral tablet, making them standardized, more respectable, and in a sense neutralized; the ambiguous position of the geomancer in south China may be part of a similar shift.) These scholars, monks, priests, mullahs, sectarians, geomancers, and diviners promoted different visions of the otherworld that, while perhaps grounded in common assumptions, were never reconciled into a single system. (See M. Cohen in chapter 8 in this volume.) Some practitioners had large but unsystematized canons, while others relied on diffuse textual and oral traditions. These groups competed with one another directly and indirectly as each tried to monopolize different sections of the funeral ritual, and over the centuries their relative positions and areas of expertise have surely shifted. They were probably all agreed, however, that the advice of experts was essential to successful ritual performance.

## CONCLUSION

My intention in this essay has been to sort out the significant variations in funeral rituals in north China in recent centuries, locate predictable differentiation, and examine where and how variations were controlled. I have concentrated on the crucial role of the ritual specialists brought in to deal with interwoven concerns about the deceased and those who mourn him, and noted a general correlation between the training of the ritual specialists and the standardization of particular rituals. But many questions remain unanswered.

These specialists were engaged in part because they controlled special modes of communication with the otherworld of gods, ghosts, and ancestors through offerings, prayers, charms, and divination. The descriptions of funeral ritual used for this essay, however, make no mention of what Michel Strickmann has called China's "ecstatic tradition" of possession and mediumship.[50] These practices, which probably were used to communicate

---

50. Michel Strickmann, "India in the Chinese Looking Glass," in D. E. Klimburg-Salter, ed., *The Silk Route and the Diamond Path* (Los Angeles: UCLA Art Council, 1982), pp. 53–63.

with the otherworld in cases of suicides and other unnatural deaths, seem to have been perpetuated by shamans of all sorts, whose training and methods—and relationships with other professionals—we know about largely through recent south China fieldwork. How different was the situation in north China?

Although each of these specialists prescribed rituals according to sets of underlying ideas about the relationship between the living and the dead, their guidance appears to have been sought out of a concern with performance. As chapter 1 of this volume argues, scrupulousness about correct procedure appears to have outweighed interest in the meaning of those procedures. How might a focus on performance rather than belief have affected the resistance of Chinese ritual to change? Although lay participants were concerned about ritual irregularities, the fact that procedure was separated from belief and put in the hands of specialists removed it from the layman's domain and surely encouraged professional conservatism. The preoccupation of the traditional Chinese elite with ritual seems less surprising if one appreciates (as they did) the importance of a fixed canon not only in creating and disseminating important portions of shared Chinese culture but in slowing the forces of diversity and change.

The changes in funeral ritual in the twentieth century seem clearly related to the changed status of ritual specialists as well as to the vigor with which a new orthodoxy was institutionalized. The legitimacy of the classically trained elite was undermined by the spread of education in this century and was increasingly challenged as new ideas circulated about class, women, and family hierarchy. Rationalist criticisms of popular religion, long a part of elite orthodoxy, were reinforced by missionaries and then by Chinese intellectuals exposed to Western ideas. These criticisms provided a rationale for serious damage to the formal structures of the Buddhist and Taoist establishments, and ordinary people may have been more affected by a lack of traditional practitioners than by attacks on their belief system. Since 1949, as Martin Whyte shows in chapter 12 in this volume, a new orthodoxy has been imposed in urban areas (and accepted?). In the countryside, where old traditions survive but few of the old professionals who had been the mainstays of standardization remain, do we find increased variety, reliance on amateurs, or confusion and anxiety about death and its consequences? It would be most interesting to make a comparison of funerals with weddings, another ritual for which issues of standardization are relevant but the sources of ritual expertise quite different. Who were the specialists? Do we find similar patterns of change?

This essay has also raised the question of regional variation in Chinese culture. I have tried to provide a framework for understanding the ways in which funeral ritual in the north was both similar to and different from rites elsewhere in China, a contrast that other essays in this volume will highlight. Although I have had to rely on written sources rather than on fieldwork observations, I believe that local histories can and should be used to expand temporally and geographically our knowledge of popular Chinese practices. Further work is needed in surveying the geographic distribution of those elements that, based on current knowledge, appear to have been both structurally different and diffused on a broad scale (contrasting grave shapes; secondary reburial of bones; the rites of reporting to the temple, buying water, calling back the soul, and sending winter clothes). With such information, we could begin to see patterns and conceptualize better the other factors with which these rituals were associated.

My larger goal has been an examination of variation and standardization of popular culture generally. In this regard, certain key components of Chinese culture seem to merit further study: not only the ritual specialists and their training, and the written literature that was a source for ideas and procedures, but also (the most difficult problem for the historian) the oral traditions on which people also relied. Studying ritual may be a fruitful way for the historian interested in issues of popular culture to probe the interactions between different sources of authority and understand their relationship to one another. It may also be a way to analyze the development of a common culture over the centuries. This endeavor may convince us that, as Freedman proposed, "the religious ideas and practices of the Chinese are not a congeries of haphazardly assembled elements." But, if at some levels "a Chinese religion exists," at others there were significant differences. The unity that existed may have been created in large measure by pressure toward standardization from above, but it may have survived only through its ability to accommodate diversity. Identifying areas of consensus and divergence and seeing how the tensions between them were handled may begin to give us a real understanding of Chinese popular culture.

# APPENDIX

My data base has been drawn from the "funerals" (*sang-li*) and "offerings" (*chi*) sections of seventy local histories from Chihli (Hopei) province. The names of these counties and departments, with the date of the gazetteer edition I used, are listed below. The dates of these accounts range from 1739 to 1950, but nearly 90 percent come from the period 1870–1945. This basic material has been supplemented with one Japanese and eight English accounts (six from Chihli, two from Shantung, and one from Manchuria). Although colorful descriptions in English are sometimes quoted in this essay, it was the much more comprehensive gazetteer accounts that were the foundation of this study.

Chihli/Hopei gazetteers consulted: An-tz'u (1936) 1.18–19; Ch'eng-an (1931) 10.15–17; Chi 薊 (1831) 2.30, (1944) 3.58; Chi-tse (1766) 8.2–3; Chiao-an (1926) 1.62; Ching-hsing (1934) 10.14–19; Ch'ing-ho (1883) 1.41–44; Ch'ing-yuan (1934) 3.38; Ch'ing-yun (1855) 3.9–10; Cho (1936) 1.10; Fang-shan (1928) 5.17–18; Feng-jun (1891) 3.64–65; Han-tan (1939) 6.5; Hsiang-ho (1936) 5.6; Hsin-ch'eng (1935) 20.4–5; Hsin-ho (1939) 549, 556; Hsin-le (1950) 4.23; Hsing-t'ai (1877) 1.56; Hsiung (1905) 5.1, (1929) 7.2–4; I (1747) 10.2, 10.4, 10.5; Jen (1915) 1.46; Kao-ch'eng (1933) 1.20–21, (1943) 1.6–7; Kao-i (1933) 5.3–4; Kao-yang (1931) 1.22; Kuang-ch'ang (1875) 11.6; Kuang-p'ing (1939) 6.2; Kuang-tsung (1933) 4.2; Lai-shui (1895) 1.25–26; Le-t'ing (1877) 2.14, 2.15; Li (1876) 3.15; Liang-hsiang (1924) 1.9; Lu-lung (1931) 10.3–4; Luan (1898) 8.21–24; Man-ch'eng (1931) 8.5; Nan-ho (1749) 5.16; Nan-p'i (1932) 3.3; Nei-ch'iu (1832) 3.56; Ning-chin (1929) 1.46; Pa (1934) 4.13, 4.46–47; Pao-ti (1745) 7.3–4; P'ing-ku (1934) 3.7; Shu-lu (1937) 8.27; Shun-i (1933) 12.5; Ta-ming (1934) 22.1; T'ang (1878) 2.54–55; T'ien-chin (1739) 13.3, (1870) 8.9–12; Ting (1944) 16.4–5; Ting-hsing (1880) 13.2–3; Tsan-huang (1876) 3.1; Ts'ang (1933) 12.7–10; T'ung (1879) 9.3, (1941) 9.2–3; Tung-an (1935) 8.3; Tung-ming (1933) 16.3; Tz'u (1941) 7.4; Wan (1934) 8.3–4; Wang-tu (1934) 10.4–5; Wen-an (1922) 7.2–4; Wu-ch'iang (1831) 1.11; Wu-ch'iao (1875) 1.12–13; Wu-i (1872) 1.17; Yuan-ch'eng (1872) 1.63; Yung-ch'ing (1779) 11.10; Yung-nien (1877) 7.3.

FOREIGN ACCOUNTS

M. L. C. Bogan. *Manchu Customs and Superstitions.* Peking: China Booksellers, 1928. Pp. 42–45, 67–97. [Mostly about Chinese customs]

Jean Dickinson. *Observations of Social Life of a North China Village.* Peking: Yenching University, 1924. Pp. 29–31. [Chihli: Wu-ch'ing county]

Sidney D. Gamble. *North China Villages: Social, Political, and Economic Activities Before 1933.* Berkeley and Los Angeles: University of California Press, 1963. [Peking area, ca. 1930]

Sidney D. Gamble. *Ting Hsien: A North China Rural Community.* Stanford: Stanford University Press, 1954. Pp. 148, 252–262. [Chihli: Ting county, 1926–1933]

H. Y. Lowe. *The Adventures of Wu: The Life Cycle of a Peking Man.* Princeton: Princeton University Press, 1983; original edition, Peking, 1940–41.

Ida Pruitt. *A Daughter of Han: The Autobiography of a Chinese Working Woman.* New Haven: Yale University Press, 1945. Passim. [Shantung: P'eng-lai]

Takeda Masao 武田昌雄. *Man-Han li-su* 滿漢禮俗 [Manchu and Chinese customary rituals]. Dairen, 1935. Pp. 201–302. [Peking and Manchuria]

L. Wieger. *Moral Tenets and Customs in China.* Trans. L. Davrout. Ho-kien-fu: Catholic Mission Press, 1913. Pp. 524–583. [Chihli generally]

Martin C. Yang. *A Chinese Village: Taitou, Shantung Province.* New York: Columbia University Press, 1945. Pp. 86–90. [Shantung, Ch'ing-tao county]

# FOUR

# Death, Food, and Fertility

## Stuart E. Thompson

*Food comes "between" the relations of men in time and, as a third term
between existing dualities, potentially has the power to unite or to
separate.*—N. J. *Girardot,* Myth and Meaning in Early Taoism *(1983)*

*An ancient Chinese practice is, by the way, curious. They used to bury the
dead in the same position as the foetus assumes in the womb.*—N. B.
*Dennys,* The Folk-lore of China, and Its Affinities with That of the Aryan
and Semitic Races *(1876)*

Food is intrinsic to most Chinese ritual activity. In this essay I focus on the
semantics of food in the context of Chinese death ritual, in which the role of
food is importantly integral—and, like the ritual itself, is multifaceted and
polysemic. Food prestations have been a perennial and indispensable feature
of Chinese death ritual for at least seven millennia.[1] Since food, in one guise
or another, is rarely extraneous to the core aspects of funerary ritual, an
examination of the range of food prestations and food symbolism can help
make sense of Chinese death rites. The role of food in these rituals is neither
uncomplicated nor without conundrums; nonetheless, by focusing on the
semantic significance of food it is possible to distill the often labyrinthine
complexity of Chinese death-related ritual into a concentrate that facilitates
interpretation.

My data base for this analysis is derived mainly from funerals that I witnessed in my fieldwork village and in several surrounding villages situated

Fieldwork on which this essay is based was conducted from March 1981 till August 1982. I
gratefully acknowledge my debt to the Department of Education for Northern Ireland and the
University of London Central Research Fund for funding my research and to Professor Wen
Cheng-i and members of the Institute of Ethnology, Academia Sinica, for their help and hospi-
tality while I was in Taiwan. I wish to thank the conference organizers, Evelyn Rawski and
James L. Watson for inviting me, and for their encouragement. Finally it is my pleasant task to
thank the conference participants for their pertinent comments on the initial draft of this chap-
ter, in particular the essay's shrewd discussants: Emily Martin, Jonathan Parry, and David
Keightley. The flaws that remain do so despite their suggestions.
1. See K. C. Chang, "Ancient China," in K. C. Chang, ed., *Food in Chinese Culture:
Anthropological and Historical Perspectives* (New Haven: Yale University Press, 1977),
pp. 23–52; and David Keightley, "Dead But Not Gone: Cultural Implications of Mortuary
Practice in Neolithic and Early Bronze Age China, ca. 8000 to 1000 B.C.," paper presented at
the conference on Ritual and the Social Significance of Death in Chinese Society, Oracle,
Arizona, January 1985.

near the coast of Yun-lin hsien, on Taiwan's western flank. In all I observed part or most of sixteen funerals.[2] Irrespective of village or the particular contingent of Taoist practitioners conducting the ritual, the funerals shared a similar basic structure. The main factor of variation stemmed from the particular circumstances of death. Those who die a "bad death"—for instance, at a comparatively young age, or away from home, or in an accident—will receive much simpler ceremonies, which are in essence shortened and incomplete versions of the ideal-typical mortuary rites. Though several of the funerals I attended were of the truncated variety, for reasons of space I limit the present analysis by assuming and describing the role of food in a full "orthodox" funeral, a composite picture amalgamating data from all the funerals I witnessed.

The communities whose funerals I describe have in common the fact that their inhabitants are Hokkien-speakers whose predecessors crossed from Fukien mostly in the eighteenth century. Land has been of poor quality in the area, and only in the 1960s, with the drilling of underground tube-wells, has rice displaced sweet potatoes and peanuts as the predominant crop. Many villagers work in Taiwan's cities; even those still resident often earn more in off-farm enterprises; aquaculture has become important in the 1980s. There is no evidence of lineages having developed anywhere in the hinterland—no ancestral halls, no genealogies, no land corporately owned by any agnatic group more extensive than sharing by brothers. The absence of lineage groups, though, does not free the individual villager from the felt obligation to ensure the continuation of his own patriline. To maintain the line intra-village, uxorilocal and (till the 1940s) "little daughter-in-law" marriages have not been infrequent.[3]

I have made a deliberate effort to include the food-motif aspects of funerary ritual as described by other anthropologists (particularly of Taiwan),[4] and by earlier writers, such as the Reverend Justus Doolittle and J. J. M. de Groot (both of whom wrote on death ritual in Fukien, the ancestral homeland of my informants).[5] De Groot describes funeral rites for "the well-to-do classes and families of fashionable standing" of Amoy at the tail end of the nineteenth century.[6] My own ethnographic data is derived from rural

2. Fourteen of the funerals were Taoist, the other two Buddhist. The latter are a rarity in the area, with a frequency of under 5 percent.

3. For a very full analysis of marriage patterns in Taiwan, see Arthur P. Wolf and Chiehshan Huang, *Marriage and Adoption in China, 1845–1945* (Stanford: Stanford University Press, 1980).

4. Especially, but not exclusively, the work of Emily Martin Ahern, who has written incisively and broadly on this subject.

5. Justus Doolittle, *Social Life of the Chinese... with Special But Not Exclusive Reference to Fuhchau* (New York: Harper, 1865); J. J. M. de Groot, *The Religious System of China* 6 vols. (Leiden: E. J. Brill, 1892–1910).

6. De Groot, *The Religious System*, 1:2.

communities whose ancestors left Fukien far from well-to-do, and more than two hundred years ago. And yet, despite the distance in time and social space, it is striking just how many constancies or similarities emerge. Perhaps even more remarkable are the numerous similarities between my own data and the information about Chinese funerals that Susan Naquin has, in chapter 3 in this volume, aggregated for north China. In some respects the thanatopraxis of the Cantonese as described by James Watson is more discrepant,[7] though I will indicate later in this chapter key underlying uniformities.

Ritual involves three prevalent facets in each of which food is immanent. First, ritual aims to transform. In the case of mortuary ritual the main problem is transforming the discontinuity of biological death into a social continuity, of transforming the corpse into an ancestor. Food, as will be shown, plays a crucial part in this process. Second, ritual involves exchanges between the living and the dead, on more or less reciprocal bases. The prestation of foodstuffs to the dead is vital in both senses of the word. Third, ritual is concerned with identity. To be Chinese is to perform Chinese ritual and vice versa; to be Chinese is also to eat Chinese-style food with Chinese-style implements. There is an important concomitance between the two notions. When Arthur Smith wrote that "the essential part of the ceremony is the eating, without which nothing in China can make the slightest progress,"[8] one suspects that it was tongue-in-cheek, but, as they say, "many a true word is spoken in jest."

There seem to be several significant, underlying conceptions about the role of food in Chinese death ritual. Thus, there is a prevalent notion that beings in the otherworld require nourishment from those in this world for their well-being. Ancestors depend on food prestations from their descendants, which gives the descendants a leverage over the dead. However, as Emily Martin (Ahern) has noted, "the living hope to inspire a . . . reciprocal response from the ancestors, to obtain through them the good life as they perceive it: wealth, rice harvests, and offspring."[9] In the broad sense of the word, the descendants hope for fertility from their dead. A common aspect of Chinese death ritual is the frequent appearance of symbols of fertility, very often symbolized in the form of foodstuffs.[10] Both living and dead depend on, but can also gain from, each other. There exists a reciprocal

7. James L. Watson, "Of Flesh and Bones: The Management of Death Pollution in Cantonese Society," in Maurice Bloch and Jonathan Parry, eds., *Death and the Regeneration of Life* (Cambridge: Cambridge University Press, 1982), pp. 155–186; and chapter 5 in this volume.

8. Arthur H. Smith, *Village Life in China* (New York: Revell, 1899), p. 143.

9. Emily Martin Ahern, *The Cult of the Dead in a Chinese Village* (Stanford: Stanford University Press, 1973), p. 91.

10. I deal with the issue of food and fertility in more detail below.

relationship with food as the primary mediating factor. Linked to this reciprocity is the ubiquity of abstinence on the part of mourners to mark the death of a senior agnate, with abstaining from various luxury foods often highlighted. On the death of the emperor the whole court abstained from eating flesh or strong-smelling vegetables, and from drinking wine (see Evelyn Rawski in chapter 10 in this volume). The logic seems to be that the more the mourners fast, the more the dead can feast. De Groot considers that "fasting was at the outset abstaining from food with a view to being able to sacrifice so much the more to the dead."[11] I would suggest that submerged there is a notion (*pace* Maurice Bloch and Jonathan Parry) of "fertility" and the vision of life as a "limited food" [*sic*].[12]

Another common element with respect to the place of food in funerary ritual (though not specific to funerary ritual) are the processes of differentiation, identification, and stratification implicit or explicit in the forms of food offering. Juniors always make offerings to seniors, never the inverse. There is a kinship coding in food presentations, with those differentially related to the deceased, whether agnatically or affinally, offering different categories of foodstuff. The circle of those expected to make offerings widens and narrows as the rites are performed; these are circles of inclusion and of exclusion. The elaborateness or simplicity, the frequency or infrequency of food offerings (there are several junctures even in the ritual for someone who has died a good death when prestations are not mandatory) indicate to the wider community the mourners' social ranking or social aspirations. The feast or feasts that are provided for the living, just as at wedding feasts, are occasions for maintaining, constructing, or reconstructing social networks (see Susan Naquin's discussion in chapter 3 in this volume). Minimally, it seems, there must be a male chief mourner (ideal-typically a son) and a daughter (or niece or other substitute) to make offerings to the recently deceased. Elizabeth Johnson in chapter 6 notes that the Hakka in the New Territories still adopt daughters to participate in funerals. It is common for food to be used in some way or other to establish an identity between the deceased and the chief mourner (irrespective of the sex of the deceased). For example, the wine offered by a succession of relatives as a libation immediately prior to the removal of the corpse is often "received by a live substitute for the subject of respect if he or she has continued the line of descent and reproduced a household."[13] Another widespread practice is for the chief mourner (though not necessarily him alone) to eat foodstuff

11. De Groot, *The Religious System*, 2:656.

12. See pp. 7–9 of their "Introduction" to Bloch and Parry, eds., *Death and Regeneration*, on "fertility" and the vision of life as a "limited good."

13. Stephan Feuchtwang, "Religion and Society in Northern Taiwan" (Ph.D. diss., University of London, 1974), p. 372.

metaphorically associated with or cosubstantial with the deceased or some aspect of the deceased—a theme that I will elaborate on below.

Another standard feature of Chinese thanatopraxis is that, whereas spirit-money, paper houses, paper representations of clothes, a set of real new clothes, and other items are all transmitted to the deceased in the other-world by burning, food is never burned for the dead. It may not, I suggest, be coincidental that food offerings, like the corpse, should not be burnt (see Martin King Whyte in chapter 12 in this volume for attitudes to cremation).

The above represent core Chinese notions about the role of food in funeral ritual. It is also possible to discern an elementary set of food prestations prevalent in Chinese death rites, a uniformity underpinning the heterogeneity of ritual expressions also observable. The chronometric and sequential structure of these common elements is, to an extent, flexible. The sequence is subject to variation at local levels, and the duration between these key elements is often longer in conformity with the status of the deceased—the wealthy tend to have longer funeral rituals, and to include more of the non-mandatory rites, such as marking the forty-nine days after death with special offerings and perhaps a feast every seventh day.

The following seem to constitute the core food prestations.

(1) Foods are presented immediately upon death and at the time of en-coffining. The actual foods given vary, though rice seems common. Some foodstuffs, especially those put in the coffin, are thought to protect the deceased on his "journey": rice or cakes to feed to wild dogs is a recurrent theme. Other food-related items can be used to symbolize the separation of the deceased from the living, his or her expulsion—the breaking of rice bowls is one instance. As a prelude to the expulsion, and to ensure that the deceased does not return malcontented, the deceased's "property" may be symbolically apportioned to his or her heirs, a property division again usually represented by the sharing out of food between deceased and descendants.

(2) After encoffining, food offerings are presented twice a day, or at each mealtime, by the daughter-in-law for the deceased. These offerings continue till the day of burial, at least. Interestingly, offerings are made twice a day even for a dead emperor (as reported by Rawski in chapter 10).

(3) On the day before, or the actual day of, burial, a comparatively bounteous farewell feast is laid out for the deceased, thought of as food in preparation for his or her transformation into an ancestor (eschatologically depicted as a journey). Offerings are made by a wide range of agnatic relatives, but the offerings from affines are particularly stressed. Meat dishes, and particularly pigs' heads, are often regarded as the primary offerings.

(4) Directly associated with the bounteous farewell feast, neighbors and friends bring offerings to satiate the hungry ghosts who would otherwise thieve the food offerings earmarked for the deceased. The Taoist or Buddhist ritual specialists mystically increase the food available for the ghosts to ensure sufficiency, so that they will no longer be hungry. This rite seems to be of Buddhist origin but is also performed at funerals where Taoist ritual specialists orchestrate the proceedings. The rite is known as *p'u-tu*[14] or *fang-yen-k'ou* (feeding the flaming mouths), and is modeled on similar community rituals performed in the seventh lunar month when the gates of the underworld are opened to release all the hungry and suffering souls.

(5) As the last rite before the encoffined corpse is carried out of the bounds of the community a series of threefold presentations of wine is poured as a libation for the deceased. This seems to be a very standard feature for all, including the emperor, irrespective of social status or locality.

(6) Offerings are carried out to the grave and presented after interment. On return of the funeral procession further food offerings are presented to accompany the installation of the temporary ancestral tablet in the household altar room or ancestral hall.

(7) The funeral banquet held for the guests is, as I have indicated above, of great social significance; but, for reasons of space, it is beyond the scope of this essay.

(8) Offerings made to the deceased after the funeral are subject to a great degree of differential elaboration, closely correlatable with the importance or unimportance of lineage groupings. At one extreme are the Cantonese villagers that Rubie Watson describes in chapter 9, who have grave rites to commemorate ancestors who died centuries before. At the other (minimal) extreme, food offerings may be presented to mark the installation of the permanent ancestral tablet (often, though not always, a hundred days after demise); food offerings for the first three years after death at the grave on the occasion of the annual Tomb-sweeping Festival (*ch'ing-ming chieh*); and further offerings given in the altar room to mark the death (and often birth) anniversary of the deceased, eventually to be worshipped as one of the undifferentiated collectivity of domestic ancestors to whom foodstuffs are offered en masse on specific calendrical dates without regard to the individual biographies of the ancestors thereby subsumed.

---

14. For a description of the community *p'u-tu* ritual, see Duane Pang, "The P'u-Tu Ritual," in Michael Saso and David W. Chappell, eds., *Buddhist and Taoist Studies I* (Honolulu: University of Hawaii Press, 1977), pp. 95–122.

Together the above eight demarcations of food prestations constitute a minimal core structure underlying ritual performances for those who died deaths classifiable as good. Data available on the actual foodstuffs offered on each occasion are much scantier, and so generalizations are necessarily more speculative. With one or two notable exceptions,[15] anthropologists and raconteurs alike have been content to vaguely sketch the kind of foods presented, failing to detect the semantic significance entailed in the choice of one sort of offering instead of another. Nevertheless, it is my contention that there is a fundamental and prevalent aspect to Chinese death rituals (certainly for the south of China) associated with the prestation of *rice*, on the one hand, and *pork*, on the other. These two key foodstuffs appear to be ubiquitous, almost canonical and fetishized foods in the context of death rites. The major thrust of this chapter will be an attempt to expound upon and justify the assertion that through the unparceling of the semantic implications of rice and pork prestations crucial ritual concerns are exposed. I proceed by endeavoring to decipher the underlying code of food offerings.

## FOOD OFFERINGS AS CODE

The kind of food given to particular categories of the dead is not an arbitrary product of free choice. Constraints apply, marking one kind of food prestation as appropriate, another as inappropriate. If we regard the range of food prestations as symbolic elements in a semantic field, then certain consistencies, certain patterns, can be deciphered. Mary Douglas has written that "if food is treated as a code, the messages it encodes will be found in the pattern of social relations being expressed."[16] In the Chinese context deciphering the code of food prestations serves to divulge the nature of the social relationship between giver and receiver, irrespective of whether the latter is dead or alive. By the type of food offered rank and status can be upheld—or emulated—and the proximity or distance in the social relationship expressed. Not unexpectedly, the kind of offering given varies according to which of the separate categories of the dead—gods, ghosts, or ancestors—is the recipient.

The most prominent and pronounced structural dichotomy in the food exchanges between living and dead is the distinction between food for the gods and food for ancestors. Food offered to the gods is referred to as *sheng-li* and consists of a platter or plate of meat offerings, with a small glass of wine for each meat item. Food fed to ancestors is called *ts'ai-fan* and consists of rice (*fan*) with a minimum five *ts'ai*, which are side-dishes of vegetable or meat or both. As far as can be ascertained from the writings

15. Ahern and J. Watson are two anthropologists who should be excepted.

16. Mary Douglas, "Deciphering a Meal," in Clifford Geertz, ed., *Myth, Symbol and Culture* (New York: Norton, 1971), p. 61.

of other anthropologists, the distinction between *sheng-li* and *ts'ai-fan* is general for Chinese communities in Taiwan at least.[17]

In the *ts'ai-fan* offered to ancestors "all foods must be cooked." A pot of cooked rice with a serving spatula in it is an omnipresent item. The *ts'ai* provided are as if for immediate consumption, and five sets of chopsticks and five rice bowls are stacked or laid out in front of the ancestral tablets. *Sheng-li* (platter of meats) may be offered if the donors are feeling extravagant, but it is an optional extra, not an essential. The pot of cooked rice is a marked and invariable element in this kind of offering. It must be put, not in the midst of the *ts'ai* offerings, but to the side (in the context a more prominent position), because, as one villager told me, "it is the main offering, and the *ts'ai* are just accompaniments *(pien-li)*."[18] Rice, then, is the essential component of the *ts'ai-fan* offerings.

Gods, contrarily, are not offered *ts'ai-fan*, nor are they offered rice. They are always presented with *sheng-li*. *Sheng-li* vary greatly in terms of elaboration, but, like *ts'ai-fan*, they have one invariable, essential component, namely pig meat *(chu-jou)*.[19] Usually *sheng-li* consist of either "three meats" *(san sheng)* or "five meats" *(wu sheng)*. Whatever the scale of elaboration, the pork element (which can range from a whole pig to a lump of fat pork) is the key component. "It is like the head of the household, the most important." "Pork *is* the *sheng-li*, the other things are just side offerings *(pien-li)*." "If there's no pork in the 'three' or 'five meats' offerings then it's not really good enough." On one occasion, when I listed the elements of *sheng-li* as "chicken, pork, fish," one elderly woman interrupted to say that I should have listed pork first "because it is the most important item." Because the pig meat is the most important part, it is put in the position of prominence—in this case the center.[20] The lavishness or otherwise of an offering to the gods can readily be gauged by the nature of the pork offering alone.

At the root of the structural opposition between *ts'ai-fan* and *sheng-li*, then, lies a further structural opposition between rice and pork. But this duality, in its turn, can be seen as an analogue of the *fan* / *ts'ai* distinction so pervasive in Chinese cooking and eating. Pork, as I have argued elsewhere,[21]

17. See, for instance, C. Stevan Harrell, "When a Ghost Becomes a God," and Arthur P. Wolf, "Gods, Ghosts and Ancestors," both in Arthur P. Wolf, ed., *Religion and Ritual in Chinese Society* (Stanford: Stanford University Press, 1974).

18. I discovered the importance of the positioning of the rice when a neighbor whom I was "assisting" corrected my misplacement of the rice pot.

19. Pork is *the* Chinese meat, and the term "meat" *(jou)* implies "pig meat" unless otherwise specified.

20. On a few occasions I have seen the pork item initially placed to the side, but on each occasion someone made a switch so that the pork item was in the center.

21. Stuart E. Thompson, "Eating and Not Eating the Dead: A Taiwanese Case," paper presented at the London Intercollegiate Seminar Series, December 1982.

epitomizes *ts'ai*. The rice/(pork) meat distinction apparently has a pedigree stretching over two millennia, for K. C. Chang has written of ancient China that "(c)learly grain and cooked meat (main ingredient of dishes) were contrasting items in the Chinese regime of eating."[22] I here suggest, and demonstrate later in the chapter, that the significance of the rice/pork duality straddles much more than the sphere of ethnohoptology alone.

Several anthropologists of Taiwanese society have noted that the degree to which the form and content of an offering approximates a meal, fully prepared and ready for the eating, reflects the closeness of the social relationship between the offerer and the supernatural being.[23] Ahern makes the point succinctly when she states that "supernatural beings are offered food that is less transformed, and therefore less like human food, according to their difference from the humans making the offering."[24] As a measure of the social distance between the living and the beneficiaries of their food prestation this formulation of concomitance is applicable also in my fieldwork area. At the one extreme not only are the offerings to T'ien Kung (the Heaven God) raw and uncut, but a tuft of hair is left on the back and tail of both the pig and the goat, and the tail feathers are left on the whole fowl, the untransformed nature of the offerings indicating the immense social gulf between the Heaven God and his devotees—as between the emperor and peasants in imperial China. There is a series of gradations to the other extreme, the offerings in the compound altar room to family ancestors, where chopsticks and rice bowls are provided, and for which offerings are placed on the table before the ancestral tablets, hot and ready for consumption, just as for a (somewhat-better-than-ordinary) family meal. This indicates the familiarity between ancestors and their living descendants.

A full exposition of coding in food prestations is beyond the compass of this essay, but a third dimension along which food offerings differ is of relevance to the analysis of mortuary rituals. Food prestations differ with respect to their elaborateness or cost. Offerings for the Heaven God are, naturally, the most elaborate and costliest. Food prestations for ghosts at first sight seem to overlap with those for ancestors. They are usually given rice and five *ts'ai*. But the rice they are offered is usually (though not invariably) uncooked, whereas for ancestors it is always cooked. No eating implements are provided for ghosts. The five *ts'ai* are typically simple, cheap offerings—an item or two of fruit, a few biscuits, unelaborate cooked

22. K. C. Chang, "Ancient China," p. 42.

23. See Ahern, *Cult of the Dead*, pp. 166–170; J. L. McCreery, "The Symbolism of Popular Taoist Magic," Ph.D. diss., Cornell University, 1973; Feuchtwang, "Religion and Society," pp. 281–282; and Wolf, "Gods, Ghosts," pp. 177–178.

24. Ahern, *Cult of the Dead*, p. 167.

dishes—nothing fancy. Ghosts are rarely offered *sheng-li* (the effect on them of drinking wine was sometimes given as the reason), and even on those few special occasions when they are offered *sheng-li* the meats look distinctly scrawny in comparison with offerings for high-placed gods. Food prestations for ghosts fall somewhat ambiguously between the offerings made for gods and those given to ancestors. But the lack of elaborateness of food given to ghosts (and the manner in which it is presented) mark ghost offerings off as different.[25]

For the purposes of the present analysis of the role of food in mortuary rites, the key variables are the *ts'ai-fan* (rice) / *sheng-li* (pork) duality; the elaborateness of offerings; and the degree to which offerings approximate a meal ready for consumption.

## FOOD IN THE RITUAL SEQUENCE

Chinese ceremonials of death are premised on the assumption that the deceased continues, in some form, to exist. An individual's biological death is merely a chapter-ending in that individual's more extensive biography. This notion, of course, is widespread and by no means specific to the Chinese syndrome of beliefs and thanatopraxis. The deceased has needs during and after the mortuary rituals, which the living endeavor to satiate in important part by offering food; and the need to offer food to the deceased is proof through ritual practice that the deceased does indeed continue to exist. The one postulate implies and reinforces the other in a tautological bind.

The finality of individual biological death is refuted. But more than that, death is represented as resulting in regeneration. On the one hand, the deceased undergoes a symbolic rebirth as ancestor; on the other hand, from his or her biological death fertility may be symbolically recouped. As Robert Hertz recognized as early as 1907,[26] at death there is a liminal phase during which an unwanted, often dangerous, aspect of the deceased is expelled or expunged, and another aspect of the deceased, credited with the power of yielding fertility, is extracted and continues, in some way, to exist. Maurice Bloch, building on this idea, has claimed that "funerals are a matter of recovering a generative power, this being done by canalising away the polluting side of death."[27] As we shall see in the analysis of the Chinese ritual

25. The divisions are by no means watertight, for otherworld inhabitants are not always unambiguously gods, ghosts, or ancestors. See, for instance, Harrell, "When a Ghost Becomes a God."

26. Robert Hertz, "A Contribution to the Study of the Collective Representation of Death," in *Death and the Right Hand*, trans. R. and C. Needham (London: Cohen and West, 1960).

27. Maurice Bloch, "Death, Women and Power," in Bloch and Parry, eds., *Death and Regeneration*, p. 229.

sequence, this bivocality of retention or continuity, on the one hand, and separation or expulsion, on the other, is reiterated in several guises, including the guise of food prestations. To borrow Stephan Feuchtwang's apposite rendering, Taiwanese death rituals "constitute processes simultaneously of cutting threads and of tying threads of continuity."[28] Food, "as a third term between existing dualities, potentially has the power to unite or to separate," as Girardot suggests,[29] or in Feuchtwang's terminology, to tie and to cut.

Ideally a person should die after being laid out in the domestic altar room, in the presence of his or her children.[30] In this way physical death will occur in the presence both of ancestors (in the form of ancestral tablets kept in the altar room) and of descendants. No tears should be shed till a rice bowl has been smashed.[31] I was told (though never witnessed) that the rice bowl should be thumped down upon a dog's head, causing the bowl to shatter, and the dog (understandably) to rush off howling, which acts as a signal that wailing may begin. The breaking of the rice bowl is clearly a rite of separation.

Soon after death certain food items are prepared. A whole chicken, rice, and an egg seem to be standard items, with other elements being less fixed. In my fieldwork area the whole chicken is cooked and brought out either just before or just after encoffining. It is chopped crosswise, the segment with the head being reserved for the deceased, the remainder of the chicken being shared out among the family members for them to eat. I was told that eating the chicken ensures security and prosperity. But there are other reverberations.

In southern Taiwan the Hokkien word for chicken (*ke*) puns with, and is said to stand for, *ke*, the word for family (*chia* in Mandarin). Perhaps more significant, at weddings a long length of bamboo, with roots intact at one end and with branches and leaves still at the other, is attached to the roof of the vehicle taking the bride and groom from the bride's home to the groom's home. The root of the bamboo is referred to as the *t'ou* (the head), and the branches and leaves are the *wei*, literally the "tails," but with the implicit meaning of offspring or descendants. It is as though the groom's descent line

---

28. Feuchtwang, "Religion and Society," p. 375.

29. N. J. Girardot, *Myth and Meaning in Early Taoism* (Berkeley and Los Angeles: University of California Press, 1983), p. 31.

30. The birth of a child or the acquisition of a bride are similarly "endorsed" in the family altar room.

31. For other instances of bowl-breaking, see Yü Kwang-hung 余光弘, "Lu-tao ti sang-tsang yi-shih" 綠島的喪葬儀式 [Funeral rites of Lutau Island, Taiwan], *Min-tsu hsueh yen-chiu so chi-k'an* 民族學研究所集刊 49 (1980): 154; Henry Doré, *Researches into Chinese Superstitions*, trans. M. Kennelly (Shanghai: T'usewei, 1914), 1:54; and Susan Naquin's discussion in chapter 3 in this volume.

is carried on the roof of the nuptial taxi. By contrast, the switch of bamboo that serves as a soul-flag (*ming-ching*) to direct the soul (*san-hun ch'i-p'o*) has its roots deliberately sliced off, for it represents the separation of the deceased from his or her descendants—the "head" is cut off. In addition, at the end-of-year feast (*wei-ya*) which an employer holds for his employees it is said that if the chicken head points in your direction, that is an indication that you are due to be fired. The imagery of the severed chicken head is, therefore, succinct, but clearly represents the separation of the deceased from his or her descendants.[32]

*rice*

The whole symbolism associated with the exchange of rice in funerals is a theme I will scrutinize more fully below. Here I want to mention that just after encoffining, rice is placed on the coffin lid. In the funerals I witnessed a cloth wrap (sometimes red in color) of uncooked rice is placed on top of the coffin.[33] On Lu-tao island Yü Kwang-hung reports that sticky rice mixed with brown sugar is placed on top of the coffin.[34] De Groot mentions that a large bowl of cooked rice is set on the lid of the coffin.[35] It is said, in each case, that the living members of the family will derive benefit from later consuming the rice.

In some communities rice is put into the hand of the deceased. Henry Doré says the reason is that the deceased "may appease therewith the hungry dogs of the village, which he must cross on his way to the nether world," and that the rice is therefore called *ta-kou fan*, literally "hit-dog rice."[36] Several of these elements—rice in the hand; chicken head severed; beating of a dog—are combined, with different emphasis, in Ahern's fascinating ethnographic rendition of encoffining in Ch'i-nan (northern Taiwan), which merits lengthy citation. Just prior to encoffining, the hand of the corpse is placed in a rice measure (*tou*) "filled with...grains, coins, and nails, the symbols of plenty and offspring." Ahern was told that "it is to let the dead willingly give away the property to the heirs."

> Simultaneously...someone prepares a small bowl of cooked rice and cooked chicken parts—the head, the feet, and the wings...the rice and the chicken head [dumped] on the ground...a dog [is directed] to the food. As soon as the dog has taken the chicken head in his mouth, he is beaten with a long, whip-like plant until he dashes away in a frenzy. It was explained...that the dog represents the dead man, the chicken head the property of the family *first* held by the deceased ([*t'ou*] means both head and first), the wings and feet of

32. At one of the Buddhist funerals a "vegetarian" chicken was divided.
33. Feuchtwang also mentions that a sack of rice is placed on the coffin ("Religion and Society," p. 337).
34. Yü Kwang-hung, "Lu-tao," p. 155. In Yun-lin a similar basin of rice is put on the nuptial bed at wedding time.
35. De Groot, *The Religious System*, 1:98.
36. Doré, *Researches*, 1:48.

the chicken the property held later by the descendants, and the bowl of rice one meal out of the usual three consumed in a day. . . . "The dog, which stands for the dead man, is beaten so that he will run away and not return. He has enjoyed his share of the property, so he should not come back and bother the living."[37]

The resemblances are striking. The theme of separation from or expulsion of the deceased is obvious and is similarly depicted by the division of a chicken. The issue of property division as represented by the sharing out of food is dealt with in detail later in this chapter.

Aside from chicken and rice the other standard food item evident at this stage in the ritual proceedings is the boiled egg. In my fieldwork village an egg and a stone are placed in the hands of the encoffined deceased if he or she is survived by a spouse. The explanation behind this custom is neatly summarized in the words of one villager addressing a corpse: "If you want to marry your husband again you must wait until the duck egg is hatched and until the stone is disintegrated." The use of the boiled egg, then, is another ritual instance of keeping the deceased separate from the living.[38]

Correlated with this expression of separation is the belief expressed by several of my informants that the corpse is potentially dangerous, liable to be triggered into a zombie-like reanimation. I was often told that if a cat (or, unlikely as it may seem, a dog) were to jump over the coffin, then the deceased would sit up and seize the nearest person in an unrelenting grip. De Groot mentions a remarkably similar belief.[39] It is this volatile, unpredictable aspect of the deceased which is ritually discarded.

Another ritual act often performed at this juncture is the putting of food in the mouth of the deceased, or using chopsticks to proffer items of food which are touched to the lips of the deceased.[40] There is an ambivalence evident in such action. On the one hand, this type of feeding can be seen as a gesture of continuity; on the other, it is a farewell gesture performed just before the body is lifted to the coffin, and therefore also interpretable as a rite of separation: it simultaneously unites and separates. It may also be seen as a gesture to placate the threatening aspect of the deceased—in the same way that apportioning the chicken head and bowl of rice to the deceased can

37. Ahern, Cult of the Dead, pp. 197–198.

38. Feuchtwang mentions the same sort of custom and reaches the same conclusion, p. 33. The same message is apparent, in more dramatic fashion, in the "cutting" ritual that occurs in some places just before encoffining. See Ahern, Cult of the Dead, p. 171–172.

39. De Groot, The Religious System (1:43), writes that "if Pussy were not secured, it might occur to her to leap or walk over the death-bed, and so cause the corpse to rise up at once . . . a horrible death in a ferocious embrace would be the inevitable consequence."

40. See Doolittle, Social Life, pp. 129–130, for a particularly elaborate example; also Doré, Researches, 1:48; Feuchtwang, "Religion and Society," p. 339; and Yü Kwang-hung, "Lu-tao," p. 155.

be viewed as an effort to conciliate the deceased. I did not hear of such a custom at firsthand, but this ritual act of feeding the deceased is strikingly similar to the procedure I observed just before a bride leaves her natal home to go to her husband's home. Then an elderly woman picks up pieces of spare-rib pork to offer the tearful bride as she stands facing out of the altar room. The bride's next act is to depart.

It is unusual for villagers to be able to offer any precise formulation of what happens to the soul after death.[41] But the overall gist is that the soul is in limbo, homeless, wandering, in need of comforting and sustenance, unable to differentiate night from day. As Doolittle wrote in 1865, "All beyond death is regarded as dark by the Chinese. The dead are believed to be unable to see how or where to walk."[42] In various ways the living endeavor to direct, succor and nourish this aspect of the soul. One method I encountered was to put dog's hair and rooster's feathers into the coffin. One informant explained, "It's like you don't want to think of the person being dead and not knowing anything anymore, so you put in the feathers because in the morning the cock crows and so the soul will know it is time to get up, and dogs bark in the evening, so the person will be reminded that it is night time."

Offerings of food (and other items, including a lit candle for location) placed on a little table at the foot of the coffin also serve to structure, to give form to, the soul's existence in this liminal stage. Every morning and evening the daughter-in-law leaves out a bowl of cooked rice and a bowl of ts'ai. One pair of chopsticks, positioned vertically, is planted in the food. The food may afterwards be consumed by family members when they have their meal. The ambivalence of the deceased is marked by the fact that he or she can share the family food, but eats separately. The offerings laid at the base of the coffin are intended for a solitary individual, not yet part of the ancestral community in the otherworld. Descendants, at this stage, do not seem to pander to the known tastes of the deceased when alive, which they will do when the status of ancestor is attained. Further, the vertical placement of the chopsticks is unique to mortuary ritual and sets the offering apart from meals shared by the living or offered to established ancestors. The ritual offering constitutes an equivocal package implying fuzzied disaggregation pending redefinition. The mourning family's situation vis-à-vis the wider community is, during this period, analogous to the deceased's situation vis-à-vis the family: ambivalently still *part of* but also *apart from* the wider social segment.

41. See Myron Cohen, chapter 8 in this volume, for a discussion of the Chinese concept of soul; also, C. Stevan Harrell, "The Concept of Soul in Chinese Folk Religion," *Journal of Asian Studies* 38 (1979): 519–528.

42. Doolittle, *Social Life*, p. 126.

Whatever the interval between death and burial, daily offerings of (at least) a morning and an evening repast are made till the funeral rites and burial. Gilbert Walshe has described how a table and a chair were made available for the deceased, and that "regular meals are served to the deceased on this day—tea about 5:00 A.M., breakfast at eight or nine, tiffin at noon, and tea at night, and each time a meal is served the server is expected to wail and cry."[43] In the south of Taiwan the daughter-in-law is also responsible for providing a washbasin and towel for the soul to "have a wash" in the mornings. Nowadays, a plastic mug and a tube of toothpaste are often provided too. Since during the liminal phase the soul is ghost-like in that it is of no fixed abode, such provisions are required to make things easier.[44] The offerings all indicate the ritualized expression of concern for the deceased in this transitory, betwixt-and-between phase; the offerings also indicate that the deceased is represented as akin to a ghost, rather than approximating an ancestor.

In the full mortuary ritual a whole complex cluster of ritual activity and performances commence on the day prior to burial of the corpse. I refer to these rites as funerary rites. Funerary rites continue through the night to conclude, usually in the morning of the second day, with the burial of the corpse and a feast for the living on return of the funeral cortege. These elaborate rites mark the culmination, but not the end, of the various stages of ritually expressed redefinition and reattribution. The daily food offerings mentioned above are made without public fanfare by the descendants— usually the daughter-in-law. With the commencement of the important preburial rites the arena is broadened.

By the time the funerary rites are under way a paper shrine for the soul of the deceased will be made and placed in or just outside the altar room. Food offerings for the deceased are placed at the front of this *fan-t'ing* (literally "rice-hall" or "meal-hall"). For the funerary rites in the *fan-t'ing* there will be a paper effigy representing the deceased, together with effigies for those specified ancestors who have been invited back to accompany and guide the newly deceased; the parents of the deceased are usually included. On the eve of burial food offerings are laid out in front of the *fan-t'ing* for them by the descendants. The food prestation is much as it would be on an ancestor's death anniversary: a pot of cooked rice, five bowls of *ts'ai*, a "three-meat"

43. W. Gilbert Walshe, *"Ways That Are Dark": Some Chapters on Chinese Etiquette and Social Procedure* (Shanghai, n.d.), p. 237. Also Doolittle, *Social Life*, p. 135; de Groot, *The Religious System*, 1:115, and Rawski, chapter 10 in this volume, where a similar practice for the emperor is indicated.

44. For northern Taiwan, Arthur Wolf has reported that the provision of a washbasin and towel is a characteristic feature of offerings made to ghosts—which is not the case in my fieldwork area. Wolf's informants say that gods and ancestors "don't need these things because they have homes of their own." See Wolf, "Gods, Ghosts," p. 178.

*sheng-li*, with three cups for rice wine. Bowls and sets of chopsticks are stacked out, there being one bowl and one pair of chopsticks for each effigy, *including* that of the deceased. For the first time the deceased is not fed in isolation. Being fed jointly with the returned ancestors marks a significant step toward the conferment of full ancestral status.

These offerings, however, are overshadowed by the plentiful and ostentatious offerings which, in the course of the afternoon, are laid out on round tables in the compound courtyard. Left out on display overnight, these offerings are removed only when the coffin is brought out from the altar room prior to its final transference to the burial site. Each table laden with food has a *sheng-li* as the key offering. On tables nearest the coffin a severed pig's head (boiled) with a pig's tail tucked under it, is prominently the central item of the *sheng-li*. Whereas at all other times the number of items for a *sheng-li* offering is always either three or five, on this occasion only "*four* meats" are often (not invariably) presented. The word for "four" (*si*) puns with the word for "death" (*si*) in Hokkien as well as Mandarin Chinese. Taro often constitutes one of the "four meats," for dead people are said to like taro. I was told further that "red turtle cakes" (*hung-kuei*) and *tsung-tzu* (dumplings made by wrapping glutinous rice with pork bits in bamboo leaves) ought also to be provided. Other offerings often include a four-plate offering of various fruits; packets of biscuits, unopened; crates of Taiwanese beer or Seven-Up equivalent, unopened; cans of food and drinks (asparagus juice is a common choice); and sometimes even packets of monosodium glutamate.

This farewell feast, with its alteration in the type and nature of food offered to the deceased, marks a crucial stage in the deceased's transition from ghost to ancestor. The change from daily offerings to the elaborate farewell feast has several dimensions. The elaborateness of the latter, together with the fact that the food offerings are whole and not readied for immediate consumption (meats are cooked but uncut; packets of biscuits, cans, bottles of drinks are all unopened) implies greater distance between the deceased and the donors. *Sheng-li*, especially that of a pig's head and tail, is an honorific offering, an offering of respect, such as is made to gods. Instead of ordinary offerings of a type similar to what ghosts receive, the new *ancestral* spirit, which the returned ancestors are about to take into their fold, so to speak, is feted with extraordinary *sheng-li*. The transformation from ghost to ancestor is both marked and accomplished by the switch in food prestations. There is a shift from *ts'ai-fan* to *sheng-li*, which is also a shift from rice to pork.[45] Concomitantly, those said to be chiefly responsible for providing the offerings switch from agnates to affines.

45. See Doolittle's description of a ceremony held to mark the time when the family ceases to offer rice, *Social Life*, p. 35.

In some cases it is the wife-giving affines who are expected to bring the best offerings. Thus, Ahern found in Ch'i-nan that "the wife-givers try to validate their high status by providing generous gifts that show their wealth and resources," while Feuchtwang states that "the offerings of matrilateral kin are always the most lavish."[46] In other instances, as in the funerals I observed, it is the married-out daughters of the deceased (or, in other words, wife-taking affines) who are expected to provide the most substantial offerings.[47] Whichever type of affines provide the more prominent offerings, it does certainly seem to be the case that offerings from the deceased's agnates alone would be insufficient to achieve the desired transformation from ghost to ancestor. The assistance of affines is required. Ahern has invoked Victor Turner's well-known opposition between "structure" and "communitas" to suggest why wife-giving affines play a key part in effecting changes in the family into which their daughter has married. "In Chinese society," she writes, "patrilineal kin are on the side of relations associated with communitas,"[48] with its connotations of ritual power injecting change into the structural arrangements of a patrilineal family. The logic of such an argument has merit, but it would seem, too, that wife-taking affines, similarly "jurally weak" and lying outside the grid of structural relationships, might also be expected to have the ritual power to alter ties among primary kin.

Concurrent with the offering of the farewell feast, late in the afternoon on the day preceding the burial, food offerings are put out for the hungry ghosts. These offerings are the responsibility of the wider community, of neighbors and friends of the mourners. The prestations for the ghosts are provided outside on the street, the intention being to prevent the ghosts from entering and pilfering the offerings designated for the deceased. It is as though the wider community is erecting a protective cordon around the mourning family. The offerings are nothing elaborate and are usually brought in baskets by women or children. A big turnout is status-enhancing for the mourners and indicative of their "pulling power" within the community. The feeding of the ghosts is a ritual expression of the reactivation of

46. Emily Martin Ahern, "Affines and the Rituals of Kinship," in Arthur P. Wolf, ed., *Religion and Ritual in Chinese Society*, p. 290; and Feuchtwang, "Religion and Society," p. 371.

47. De Groot states that pigs' heads are given by sons and by married-out daughters (*The Religious System*, 1:143); Watson, "Of Flesh and Bones," p. 175, reports that married daughters present a raw pig's head and tail at each parent's funeral; Elizabeth Johnson in chapter 6 in this volume mentions that married-out daughters present pigs' heads; relatedly, Norma Diamond, *K'un Shen: A Taiwan Village* (New York: Holt, Rinehart, and Winston, 1969), p. 46, writes that "the burden of funeral costs are borne by the household of the deceased and the married-out daughters."

48. Ahern, "Affines," p. 307.

the family's ties with its wider social network, and a prelude to its eventual reintegration into the community after the burial.

On the morning of the burial the coffin is carried out from the altar room, amidst a cacophony of loud music and wailing, and is positioned in the courtyard. The elaborate farewell offerings are cleared away. Further along the courtyard, nearer the street, a table has been set up on which are various symbols of the deceased. At the base of the table is a metal washbasin in which is a bunch of scallions (*chiu-ts'ai*) tied into a cylinder shape with white string. Kinsmen and kinswomen of the deceased, in full mourning attire, kneel in succession before the washbasin and, with the help of a master of ceremonies, using both hands, circle a glass of rice wine above the basin, and then pour the contents over the bunch of scallions. This each mourner does three times. In my fieldwork village this rite is called *ching-chiu*, "toasting (the deceased) with wine," though I will refer to the rite as "libation." There can be elaborate differentiation expressed either in the order in which libations are made[49] or by the number of libations each category of mourner makes.[50] Affines may or may not perform the libation.[51] In the funerals I witnessed the wife-giving affines did not take part in the libation ceremony. Nor is there any differentiation in terms of the number of cups of wine offered: all kinsmen and kinswomen who pour wine over the scallions do so three times only, though the sequence of pouring demonstrates proximity to the deceased.

The libation's close juxtaposition with the removal of the corpse—which occurs shortly after the libations have been completed—gives weight to interpretations which see the rite as another cutting off of the deceased from the living. My informants say that the meaning of the libation rite is to "pay respects to" (*chi*) the dead. In the context of a rite I saw performed when someone had accidently killed a cat by hitting it with his motorbike, a spirit-medium "spat-sprayed" a mixture of rice, salt, and water (purificatory agents) "to *chi* the cat's soul." To *chi* in this situation was explained as ensuring that the cat's soul would not return to haunt and harm the culprit. In similar vein, when a pig is about to be slaughtered as an offering for T'ien Kung (the Heaven God) a small measure of rice wine is poured into the pig's mouth "to *chi* the pig's soul," explained by villagers as ensuring that the pig's soul will not come back to seek retribution. So the libation, by the same logic, represents an attempt to get rid of the dreaded aspects of the deceased associated with the corpse and ensure their non-return.

49. See de Groot, *The Religious System*, 1:149.

50. See Watson, "Of Flesh and Bones," p. 177. He also mentions (p. 167) that the Cantonese use their left hands only, not both hands, as I witnessed.

51. Ahern, "Affines," p. 298, gives an example where wife-giving affines are particularly prominent.

One of Ahern's informants told her that to pour wine over the scallion bunch ("the sprout") is to "apply the maxim 'when you weed, get out the roots.' One man said 'It means you must get rid of the dead entirely, not let him become a hungry ghost or come back to do bad things to the descendants.'"[52] This use of wine to exorcise is remarkably parallel to the intent of *chi*-ing the cat and pig. Further, though I never heard the maxim "when you weed, get out the roots," in all but two cases the roots had been "got out," for the bunch of scallions had had its roots sliced off—in the two exceptions the roots remained, but the top of the scallions had been cut off. If we now recall that "roots" can be termed *t'ou* ("head"), which in turn can refer to the deceased, as contrasted with the surviving descendants (*wei*, "tails"), then the symbolic logic of what Ahern's informant said becomes patent. The libation rite is another expression of separating the deceased from the living.

The choice of *chiu-ts'ai* (scallions) does not seem merely incidental or fortuitous. *Chiu-ts'ai* is a perennial vegetable which grows spontaneously every year so long as its *roots* have soil to grow in. Given such botanical properties, it is not surprising that in some wedding rituals "a stalk of [*chiu-ts'ai*] given to daughters to plant in their gardens after the wedding means a long lasting marriage."[53] If planting scallions represents a long-lasting relationship, then for a relationship to be curtailed the roots of the plant certainly need to be "got out."[54] There is, then, an appropriateness in the choice of scallions for the libation rite.

The eviction of the corpse from the environs of its former habitat does not terminate the offering of food to the deceased. At the grave a "three-meat" *sheng-li*—a slab of pork, a whole chicken, and either fish, prawns, or taro—with three small cups for rice wine is a typical offering for the small image of T'u-ti-kung (the "earth god") to thank him for allowing the grave to be built in his precinct. After interment and the *tien-chu* (dotting the tablet) rite, grains, nails, and coins are distributed to the descendants from a *tou* (rice-bucket). Then the *sheng-li* is moved over so as to be offered to the deceased, together with a *ts'ai-fan* offering—a bowl of cooked rice, in which are planted two vertical chopsticks, and five bowls of *ts'ai*. With the exception of the inferior quality of the *ts'ai* dishes, and the vertical placing of the chopsticks, the grave offering approximates the standard sort of offering for

---

52. Ibid., p. 298.

53. Ahern, "The Problem of Efficacy: Strong and Weak Illocutionary Acts," *Man* 14 (1979): 13. *Chiu* puns with the "mystical" number nine in both Hokkien and Mandarin, and also with the word meaning "a long time."

54. I am struck by the similarity in the writing of *chiu* and *fei* ("shroud"), a term which Yü Ying-shih discusses in "O Soul, Come Back: A Study of the Changing Conceptions of the Soul and Afterlife in Pre-Buddhist China," *Harvard Journal of Asiatic Studies* 47 (1987): 363–395.

an ancestor. "Red turtle cakes" and *tsung-tzu* dumplings, together with small cakes, are often offered too.

The offerings are rebasketed for transfer back to the family altar room, where the dotted, temporary ancestral tablet of the deceased is installed. While the guests are seated around tables in the courtyard partaking of the funeral banquet, the family mourners eat the same as the guests,[55] but in the comparative seclusion of the altar room. This ambivalence signifies that the mourners are nearing reincorporation into the community, but that that reincorporation is not yet complete. When the temporary ancestral tablet is replaced with a permanent one (*ho-lu*)—usually after one hundred days— then, concomitantly, the mourning family is essentially freed from the polluting effects of death and fully reintegrated into the community.[56] Till that time, in my fieldwork village, a bowl of rice with a pair of chopsticks stuck vertically in it, together with a single bowl of *ts'ai*, is offered for the benefit of the dead person on the first and the fifteenth day of each lunar month. Not till the *ho-lu* rite is performed is the deceased reincorporated into the family as a fully-fledged ancestor no longer in need of such ghost-like offerings.

Maurice Freedman has noted that "dead ancestors rely for their perennity on the ritual memory of their descendants."[57] On the west coast of Yunlin the ritual memory of the living (as expressed in food prestations) for ancestors *as individuals* is relatively short-lived and does not often outlast the time when no living family member actually knew the ancestor when he or she was alive. Offerings associated with the tablet cult are presented in the domestic altar room, and the type of food prestation is much the same, whether the focus is on a recent individual ancestor on his or her birth- or deathday anniversary, or on the collectivity of earlier unnamed ancestors on fixed calendrical occasions. *Ts'ai-fan* is the standard item, and *sheng-li* is often, though not always, provided. As Arthur Wolf has suggested, "offerings to ancestors are meals, in both form and intent."[58] Several villagers told me, "If you know the sort of thing the ancestor liked eating, then you will serve that."

The offering of food at the grave operates on a much shorter time scale and is associated primarily with the *ch'ing-ming chieh* (tombsweeping) ritual. Families present food for the first three years following the death—in the first year on a date before the festival, in the second year on the date of the festival itself, and in the third year on a date a few days after the festival.

---

55. A restriction on descendants' eating pork is lifted at this time.

56. Some minor markers of pollution still remain.

57. Maurice Freedman, *The Study of Chinese Society: Selected Essays* (Stanford: Stanford University Press, 1979), p. 296.

58. Wolf, "Gods, Ghosts," p. 177.

Subsequently, if a son or grandson marries or if a male descendant is born during the year, then food should be presented at the grave on the following *ch'ing-ming chieh*. Otherwise it is sufficient at the tombsweeping time to tidy the grave, burn spirit-money, and leave colored papers on the grave—there is no need to provide food offerings.

For Ch'i-nan, Ahern found a marked contrast between the type of food offered at the grave and the food presented before the ancestral tablet. As opposed to the food offered in meal-ready form for the tablet cult, she found that grave foods "though potentially edible, are not soaked, seasoned or cooked; most of them are dry and unpalatable... consisting basically of twelve small bowls of foodstuffs."[59] Ahern hypothesizes that the starkness of the contrast between the two types of offerings is indicative of a difference in the conception of the deceased as familiar, indeed a member of the family, in tablet guise, but in grave guise an unpredictable stranger, impersonal, dangerous, and distant.

In the area of Taiwan with which I am familiar the sort of food offered at the grave is not so radically different from that offered in the domestic altar room. A pot of cooked rice complete with spatula, together with five *ts'ai*, often ready as if for consumption, are provided; sometimes, despite awkwardness of carriage, even soup dishes are taken out to the grave. *Sheng-li* are also provided—though first offered to T'u-ti-kung. There are some differences though.

First, the advent of the offerings is often the occasion for women in the family to wail for the deceased, whereas offerings presented before the tablets mark an occasion that is more convivial and familiar. Second, no bowls or chopsticks are provided for the deceased to use. Third, in addition to the *ts'ai-fan* and *sheng-li* offerings, some platefuls or bags of shelled foods—eggs, prawns, clams—are provided, all cooked, but with the shells still intact. These the family members eat at the grave itself, scattering the shells over the grave mound.[60] However, even with these differences, if we allow that the type of food offered is a measure of the social distance between giver and receiver, with readiness for consumption the gauge, then the deceased as grave resident is not as distant, unknown, and potentially threatening as in Ahern's village. I would suggest that the difference may be attributable to the importance of lineage structure in Ch'i-nan and its absence in coastal Yun-lin. The more there are groups with clearly demarcated and circumscribed membership, such as a patrilineage, the greater the ambivalence and potential threat felt toward whatever lies on the other side of the boundary.

59. Ahern, *Cult of the Dead*, p. 167.

60. Among others, Yü Kwang-hung, "Lu-tao," p. 156, also describes the scattering of eggshells on the grave mound.

## OF RICE AND MEN

In the death rites the transformation of the deceased from a wandering, unknowing ghost to a ritually manufactured ancestor is echoed and in part achieved by the switch from ordinary, daily ghost-type offerings to the honorific and elaborate, untransformed pork offerings, congruent with the deceased's conversion in status to that of (near-)ancestor. Further, through analysis of food prestations, the recurrent symbolic representations of separation and expulsion, on the one hand, and retention and continuity, on the other, are manifest. It is evident that much of what is considered polluting and in need of expulsion is embodied by the corpse, though in time the bones will be extracted for retention. But what of those aspects of the deceased that are ritually recouped as regenerative rather than degenerative? Is there any evidence for Bloch's "theme of the retention and re-use of life substance"?[61]

The ancestral tablet is a representation of the deceased as moral ancestor. The *tien-chu* (dotting the tablet) rite is a method of mystically channeling the *li-liang* (vigor) of the deceased onto his or her offspring, whether performed by literatus or Taoist priest. There are more concrete transfers. The nails, coins, and "five grains" (*wu ku*) distributed from the rice-bucket just after lowering the coffin into the grave are a further example of *fertility* (in the widest sense) emanating from death. The nails symbolize progeny, since the Hokkien word for nail puns with the word for adult male; the coins symbolize future wealth for the descendants; and the "five grains" symbolize fertility of crops. The fertility of the descent line tends to be most emphasized. In one extraordinarily unconcealed reference at one funeral I saw the son of the deceased pull a nail from the coffin with his teeth and deposit it into the rice-bucket. The nail was explicitly said to represent future male descendants.[62] Pulling a nail (representative of male descendants) out of a coffin with one's teeth is a remarkable ritual expression of death's being transformed into a source of fertility. Less dramatically, I was told that the taro offered to the deceased ensures that there will be sons and grandsons— taro, a symbol for fertility, is often sent with the bride during a wedding.

In this respect the semantics of rice and pork prestation are most intriguing. I deal first with rice. Rice is the core, the marked element of a meal; the *ts'ai* is an extra, a topping, there to make the rice tastier. Rice is also very much the key food substance shared by members of a family. The eating of rice together in a real sense demarcates the family unit and reinforces kinship bonds. As David Jordan has pointed out, "a family is the unit

61. Bloch, "Death, Women, and Power," p. 222.

62. Compare similar practice described by de Groot, *The Religious System*, 1:5; Doré, *Researches*, 1:49 (in which instance hair of the deceased is entwined around the nail); and Feuchtwang, "Religion and Society," p. 344.

attached to a rice pot."[63] The daily reiterated act of sharing rice sustains and nourishes the family both literally and metaphorically. Rice is ideally not exchanged between families, for it is "substance shared."[64] But, as we have seen, it is "substance shared" by dead family members (ancestors) as well as its living representatives.

Like males within the patriline, rice is not a substance for exchange. In the sense that rice is the product of the land worked by and inherited from ancestors, land which, ideally, should be inalienable to non-agnates, rice can be identified as stuff of the ancestors. And, as ancestral stuff, its retention within the family and descent line makes sense. Bones, as agnatic matter, are similarly retained, for they are exhumed and repotted for preservation. They are retained, not because they are durable (teeth are more durable, but are discarded at reburial), but because, unlike teeth, bones are ancestral stuff. One knowledgeable old man told me, "Only bones are regarded as important. Flesh rots away, but bones are part of your ancestors, so you can't throw them away."

Further, bones are explicitly associated by some villagers with semen. "Bones are connected directly to your ancestors through your father's semen," in the words of one informant. It would seem, therefore, that rice, bones, and semen are coassociable as aspects of ancestral substance, all aspects of a single unity. The coassociability of rice and bones is amply illustrated in a photograph taken by Gary Seaman,[65] in which a man is placing a bowl of rice on the ground where his uncle's grave is to be dug. The caption informs us that the bowl of rice symbolizes the uncle's bones. Rice and semen, to complete the interconnections between the three substances, can also be directly coassociated. In many parts of China there is a saying to the effect that seven bowls of rice need to be eaten in order to regenerate one drop of semen.[66] This correlates with the notion that "a man should regard his semen as his 'precious thing' and should guard it carefully against loss through ejaculation in sexual activity."[67] Anthony Yu tells me that the danger of semen release is ingrained [sic] into the popular consciousness, and that "a man is said to die a little" with each ejaculation.

At a funeral the transmission from deceased to heirs is often symbolized

63. David Jordan, *Gods, Ghosts and Ancestors: The Folk Religion of a Taiwanese Village* (Berkeley and Los Angeles: University of California Press, 1977), p. 118.

64. Here I make use of the distinction between food that is "substance shared" and food that is "substance given," which Ronald B. Inden and Ralph W. Nicholas develop in their book *Kinship in Bengali Culture* (Chicago: University of Chicago Press, 1977).

65. Gary Seaman, "Ancestors, Geomancy, and Mediums in Taiwan," in William H. Newell, ed., *Ancestors* (The Hague: Mouton, 1976), photograph facing p. 309.

66. Vincent Shui, personal communication.

67. Philip Rawson and Laszio Legeza, *Tao: The Chinese Philosophy of Time and Change* (London: Thames and Hudson, 1973), p. 27.

in terms of apportioning rice. In coastal Yun-lin, if the deceased dies after the third meal on the day of death, then a special rite called "begging rice" (*t'ao-fan*) is performed. A *tou* (rice-bucket) measure of rice is divided, two parts (expressed as two meals) for the living, and one part (one meal) for the deceased.[68] In my estimation the contents of the *tou* on this and on other occasions represent not just the property but also the agnatic substance (of which property can be seen as a facet) that the deceased is in danger of hoarding to himself, and which, only through the intervention of ritual procedures, can be transmitted down the patriline to the descendants. I substantiate this claim below.

Also in the mortuary rites a *tou* measure of rice, wrapped in a cloth, is set on top of the coffin. This rice is to be eaten by male descendants of the deceased and their wives; eating this rice is said to ensure peace and plenty. The *tou* plays a very central role in funerary ritual.[69] We can learn a good deal about what death rituals express by unpacking the symbolism associated with it. The *tou* refers both to the traditional standard measure for rice (approximately one decaliter) and to a cylindrical wooden tub which can contain that amount. A *tou* containing the temporary ancestral tablet for the deceased is carried by the son or, preferably, the senior grandson of the deceased in the funeral procession to and from the grave. If the deceased dies without heirs, then whoever carries the *tou* thereby becomes post-humous heir.

If we examine what the *tou* contains in the course of the funerary ritual we can list the following: rice, which is put in a (red) cloth wrap on top of the coffin; the temporary ancestral tablet; the "five grains," coins, and nails, symbols of fertility; short sticks of bamboo, said to represent the sons and grandsons of the dead person. When the son pulled the progeny nail from the coffin with his teeth, he deposited it in the *tou* bucket. My reading is that the items contained in the *tou* are interchangeable, all being facets of agnatic stuff. Pushing the symbolic logic further, and given that the bag of rice on the coffin is an aspect of the deceased, then it follows that the descendants by consuming the rice, an agnatic substance, are metaphorically indulging in endonecrophagy. The substance of one generation is represented as the source of life and substance for the next generations.

The resonances reverberate still more strongly if we consider that the

68. This is notably similar to what Ahern describes above. See *Cult of the Dead*, pp. 197–198.

69. *Tou* is a very complex symbol and has many more layers of meanings than I am able to deal with in this chapter. The symbolization of *tou* is a topic worthy of an essay in its own right. Ahern, *Cult of the Dead*, facing p. 131, provides a photograph of a young man carrying the *tou* and paper ancestral tablet of his father in the funeral procession to the grave. The same photograph forms the dust jacket of her book.

word *tou* "is used by some people in the binome [*chin-tou*] (golden *tou*) both for the urn into which the bones of the dead person are put for reburial and for the red bag into which traditionally women gave birth or, in slang, for female genitals themselves."[70] A *tou* in this broadened terminology can then be a container for semen, for rice, for an ancestral tablet, for reburied ancestral bones, and for a newborn baby—each of which can be construed as aspects of agnatic substance.

Semen, rice, bones, offspring, and ancestors are coassociated and are also elements in cycles of agnation spiraling through time. Semen (agnatic stuff) creates offspring (agnates) who are sustained through life by consuming rice (another agnatic substance). At death an agnate becomes an ancestor preserved as bones and ancestral tablet; but for descendants the death of an ascendant releases life-forces (fertility), of which semen is a facet, thereby closing one cycle and generating another. Agnatic substance is retained, at least metaphorically, within the descent line. Reproductive capacity is not squandered, for, by symbolically eating the deceased-as-rice, it is retained within the descent line. Rice epitomizes the pure, regenerative aspects of the deceased which have been ritually winnowed. It seems that in the mortuary ritual the ideal order being created is one of pure descent, of reproduction by descent alone; of agnatic substance retained from one generation to the next, without reference to inputs from outside. In the world of idealized ritual context the messy world of women, sexuality, affinity, flesh, and decomposition is repudiated. In the terms of Bloch and Parry, "The dominant ideological representation is created out of its contrary," for "the final triumph over death is also a triumph over the necessity for affines and over the world of sexual reproduction which they represent."[71]

But such a reading is biased. It stresses the role of rice, bones, and men while ignoring the significant aspects of death rites concerned with the role of pork, flesh, and women; relatedly, it emphasizes contents, the contained, while neglecting the significance of the container. Besides, it is an unwarranted step to assume that because agnatic fertility is retained within the descent line we are therefore necessarily dealing with a cycle of transfer which is self-sufficient and self-sustaining, requiring neither inputs nor activation from "outside." In the next section I redress the balance.

## OF PORK AND WOMEN

Two aspects of the role of pork in death rituals merit particular attention. First, as I have already indicated, the gorging of the deceased on bounteous pork and other offerings seems to be a widespread way of marking the de-

70. Feuchtwang, "Religion and Society," p. 314.
71. Bloch and Parry, "Introduction," p. 21.

ceased's conversion from (near-)ghost to (near-)ancestor.[72] It seems that the crucial transformation of the deceased into benevolent ancestor cannot be achieved by the offering of rice alone, nor solely through prestations presented by agnates; the affinal presentation of pork, and lots of it, is needed to effect the transformation.

In direct juxtaposition to this gorging of the deceased on pork, there is (widespread in the west Yun-lin region, at least) a taboo on the eating of pork by the surviving agnatic descendants of the deceased and their wives. That is, those family members who will eat the *tou* of rice after the funeral are supposed not to eat pork from the time of death till the funeral banquet that follows the burial. Villagers say that it is filial not to eat pork on the death of an ascendant because "it would be like eating the dead person's flesh."[73] There is a direct equivalence made between pig flesh and the flesh of the deceased.

It is incumbent upon married-out daughters of the deceased to furnish a pig's head and tail for the farewell banquet.[74] Married-out nieces and granddaughters may also provide a pig's head and tail, especially in the absence of a married-out daughter, though supplying a pig's trotter would usually be considered acceptable.[75] Though mandatory for married-out daughters, it is said to be optional for sons to offer a pig's head and tail. Several informants even deny that they do give pigs' heads, despite the fact that empirically sons actually do so. "Sons can, but it's not a must." Further, sons should club together to provide a single head and tail between them (even if they have divided into separate households), whereas married-out daughters always provide one each. The prototypical offering of a pig's head and tail is very much that from the married-out daughter, so much so that it is sometimes referred to as "the daughter's head" (*nü-er t'ou*). Interestingly, even at the two Buddhist funerals which I attended each married-out daughter presented a mock pig's head and tail (fashioned from flour)— a measure of the deep-rootedness of the felt obligation.

72. See Doolittle, *Social Life*, pp. 135–141, for similar marking of the transition.

73. It may not be unconnected that Mu-lien, on his mission, in Orpheus-like fashion, to rescue his mother from Hell has his path blocked because he had eaten meat. The Taoist practitioners' enactment of the Mu-lien story comes strategically just before dawn, and the symbolic leading of the deceased across the bridge into the otherworld.

74. The similarities with the Miao-shan legend, in which Kuan-yin repays her filial debt and saves her father by plucking out her eyes and severing her arms to brew him a life-restoring potion, deserve investigation. See Glen Dudbridge, *The Legend of Miao-shan* (London: Ithaca Press, 1978). The daughter, in presenting the pig's head and tail, has returned from the "death" of marriage (see E. Johnson, chapter 6 in this volume) to save her deceased father by offering flesh (in this case, pig's flesh). I'd like to thank the anonymous reviewer for bringing this and other items to my attention.

75. Some villagers say that a pig is reckoned to have five heads for the purposes of offerings—its actual head and the four trotters.

Though identified with the daughter, the pig's head and tail is actually a prestation from the family into which she married—wife-takers in relation to the deceased. The offerings are acknowledged by villagers as actually being from sons-in-law rather than daughters. Unmarried daughters do not give pigs' heads, since "they have no outside family." The head and tail are boiled before offering, and "those who provide the offering take it home to eat"—though if there is soon to be a "happy event" (*hsi-shih*) at the daughter's marital home, it will not be taken back, for the head and tail is considered somewhat "unclean" (*pu ch'ing-chieh*).[76]

How is the prestation of pigs' heads and tails to be interpreted? The head and tail are said to represent a whole pig, though, paradoxically, it would be inappropriate to offer a whole pig—a type of offering reserved for high-ranked deities. A *sheng-li* offering with a pig's head and tail as the centerpiece is an impressive and respectful prestation, and a few villagers explicitly drew a comparison with the honorific head and tail offered to gods on festival occasions. Given that the deceased is attaining, through the ritual process, the status of (near-)ancestor, an honorific offering makes sense.

A further informant-suggested interpretation relates to the prevalent Chinese notion of *pao*, reciprocity, or balanced exchange. "The pig's head is to *pai* (offer to) the deceased, to thank him and repay his kindness (*pao-ta*)." While rice is "substance shared" by members of a family, pork is very much "substance given," for it is prototypically the foodstuff for exchange and reciprocity between families—it is the primary banquet food.[77] In wedding exchanges, the key food is the pig sent by the groom's family to the bride's. A wife is transferred in one direction, a pig in the other. But the bride's family should return the head and tail of the pig "to show respect to the groom's side." Thus, at the funeral, the wife-takers seem to be reciprocating when they present a pig's head and tail. As James Watson has noted, "The pig's head and tail could be construed as the repayment owed to the deceased by affines,"[78] a balancing of exchanges between each wife-taking family and the deceased (as wife-giver).

In both Cantonese and Taiwanese instances the offering of pig's head and tail is correlated with the phrase *yu t'ou yu wei*, meaning literally "There's a head and a tail." In other contexts this phrase has the connotation of well-rounded completion, and so I concur with Watson that the head and tail may symbolize "a good beginning and a good end" for the deceased in the sense of his (or her) being transformed into a benevolent ancestor.[79]

76. In the Cantonese case that Watson describes, the daughters give only a single, raw pig's head and tail between them, every particle of which must be consumed by, and only by, the immediate descendants of the deceased. See Watson, "Of Flesh and Bones," pp. 175–178.

77. See note 64 above.

78. Watson, "Of Flesh and Bones," p. 176.

79. Ibid., p. 177.

However, I find discrepant Watson's further implication that, through the giving of the head and tail, the affines are paying off their final debt to the deceased, so that "affinity ends at death."[80] The thrust of Watson's argument is that the highly androcentric Cantonese are using the mortuary rites to create an ideal order of pure patrilineal descent, of reproduction by descent alone, an ideal order built on the repudiation of affinity and the role of women in reproduction. In west Yun-lin, though, a married daughter and her husband accompany the corpse to the grave, and the married daughter has important ritual tasks to perform at her deceased parents' postfuneral rites—including initial grave visits at *ch'ing-ming chieh*, and the exhumation and reburial of parents' bones. In the Taiwanese case the offering of pig's head and tail cannot be taken as signifying the ritual termination of affinity, for affinal relationships are continued, ritually and otherwise, during and after the funeral. Besides, sons too usually offer a pig's head and tail.

A more satisfactory interpretation is that the head and tail serves to emphasize family unity and continuity. When the deceased was (near-) ghost, the severing of the (chicken's) head and tail emphasized separation; at the farewell feast, now that the deceased has been ritually manufactured as (near-)ancestor, the (pig's) head and tail are together, and the accompanying chicken offered is intact. The expression *yu t'ou yu wei* indicates the togetherness of deceased ("head") and descendants ("tails"), and thereby the continuity of the descent line.

I was told that food presented to the deceased by his or her daughters, especially the pigs' heads, is regarded as *pu* for the dead parent. In Chinese folk dietetics, foods categorized as *pu* are said to have strengthening or restorative qualities. A woman after giving birth is fed *pu* foods to strengthen her *ch'i* ("vital energy"); similarly, a person suffering from "fright" (*shou-ching*) is often given pig's trotters to help restore weakened *ch'i*. Associatedly, it is reckoned that a part of one's body can be strengthened by eating the same part of an animal—thus, eating pig's liver strengthens the liver of the eater. When a person dies, his or her bones endure and, through secondary burial, are deliberately preserved, whereas flesh and blood are ephemeral and decompose on death. The putrescence of flesh is given cultural emphasis. The deceased only realizes that he or she has died when "T'u-ti-kung takes him to wash in a river and he sees that his fingernails have gone black." Death should entail the rotting away of the deceased's flesh; for it not to do so is arguably good for the deceased but bad for descendants.[81]

---

80. Ibid.

81. Tales are told of graves located in such a conjunction that the geomancy is too good, with the result that the flesh of the deceased does not dissolve at all, with bad consequences for the descendants.

The reader will remember the prohibition on descendants' eating pork flesh, and the equivalence villagers make between pig flesh and the flesh of the deceased. It seems that by furnishing the deceased with substantial amounts of pig flesh (I was told of one funeral where some forty pigs' heads and tails were presented) there is a ritualized effort to replace the flesh which the deceased is losing. The deceased is fed pig flesh to compensate for the loss of his or her own flesh. Apocryphal tales of supreme filial behavior in traditional times cite the practice of cutting flesh from one's own body so as to strengthen an aged and ailing parent.[82] The children of the deceased seem, symbolically, to be doing the same for their parent, substituting animal flesh for their own human flesh. Similarly, it is said to be very filial for descendants to refrain from eating pork prior to burial, the presumed logic being that to do so would be tantamount to depriving the deceased of urgently required reconstitutive flesh. The descendants abstain so there will be all the more for the deceased. "Eating pork is like eating the dead person's flesh," as my informants expressed it.

There is ritual endeavor to recloak the deceased's *yang* bones in *yin* flesh, constituting a symbolic reembodiment of the deceased. Benefits, in the form of fertility, should consequently accrue. The conjunction of ideas is reminiscent of the most common Chinese myth of creation, that of "the Chinese Adam," P'an Ku. As a cosmic, first man, P'an Ku was "hatched" from the primordial chaos through the interaction of *yin* and *yang*. He "then settled and exhibited the arrangement of the causes which produced him."[83] "When his task was completed, he died for the benefit of his creation, animating the whole universe."[84] "He gave birth in dying to the details of the existing material universe,"[85] for the parts of his giant body were transformed into the elements of the universe—his head became the mountains and so on. "He died that his works might live."[86] The term P'an means the shell of an egg; perhaps the eggshells which are widely reported as being strewn on top of the grave are not just an image of rebirth from death but an allusion to the P'an Ku myth specifically. Ideologically, myth and funerary ritual share the concept that the source of natural increase and productivity comes from the dead; death is required for the generation of fertility. The problem with male-type, agnatic fertility, as represented by *yang* bones or rice or semen, is that it is so pure as to be virtually sterile without interaction with female fertile stuff, as represented by *yin* flesh or pork or blood. There is a needed complementarity between the two, a balance of *yin* and *yang*

82. See de Groot, *The Religious System*, 4:386–387.
83. C. A. S. Williams, *Outlines of Chinese Symbolism and Art Motives* (Rutland, Vt.: Charles E. Tuttle, 1974) [orig. Kelly and Walsh, Shanghai, 1941)], p. 313.
84. V. R. Burkhardt, *Chinese Creeds and Customs*, vol. 3 (Hong Kong: South China Morning Post, 1958), p. 1.
85. Williams, *Outlines*, p. 314.
86. E. T. C. Werner, *Myths and Legends of China* (New York: Brentano's, 1922), p. 77.

and other dualities, a dialectical harmony—such as that which engendered P'an Ku.

From a one-sided androcentric viewpoint, pigs and women can be seen as having certain shared characteristics. Both are subject to transfer between families, unlike men, who remain in the bounds of the one family. Indeed, as was already mentioned, in weddings they are exchanged at virtually the same time. They both break out of, and break into, family units. Both are also transformers. The pig converts scrap foods into valuable meat and manure; a woman converts raw foods into meals and semen into children. Pigs are reared (women traditionally are responsible for their feeding) as a form of capital investment which, when money is required, can be sold in market or exchanged with others (often by way of a banquet). They are literally "piggy banks." Women are also reared to be given away to others. In one sense they are similarly "cashed in" (for bride-price), the difference being that they are expected to be goods on which one loses money. Pigs, furthermore, are characterized as depraved, gluttonous, dirty, and licentious creatures, representative of unbridled sexuality and uncontrolled fertility, all in marked contrast to pure, moral, agnatic fertility. Women's sexuality and fertility is also viewed with ambivalence, in powerful ways antithetical to agnatic fertility, but nonetheless essential for providing sons. Women's reproductive capacity is shrouded by notions of pollution, so that the "source of a woman's power [her ability to reproduce descendants] is obscured, if not rendered invisible by a layer of negative sentiment."[87] The sexuality and fertility of pigs and women is strikingly correspondent in two further ways: first, a woman who is always pregnant is referred to as a "mother pig";[88] second, a pig's stomach is said, rather churlishly, to be like a woman's womb, and I was told stories of human souls mistakenly entering pigs' wombs, and vice versa. In a rite called *huan-t'ai* ("changing the womb") a woman who has just given birth to a daughter is given pig's stomach to eat "so that she will have a son next time."

The role of pig flesh in wedding exchanges is also suggestive. Just prior to departing her natal home the bride, on the threshold, is offered pork spareribs. It is said, in maxim form, that she "can eat the flesh, but mustn't gnaw the bones." Several informants said, "It's to do with having sons"; others said it indicates that she will get fatter and prosper (which may be a way of saying the same thing as "having sons"). One key informant told me

87. Emily Martin Ahern, "The Power and Pollution of Chinese Women," in Margery Wolf and Roxane Witke, eds., *Women in Chinese Society* (Stanford: Stanford University Press, 1975), p. 214.

88. Wolfram Eberhard, "On Some Chinese Terms of Abuse," in *Moral and Social Values of the Chinese: Collected Essays* (San Francisco: Chinese Materials and Research Aids Center, Occasional Series, no. 6, 1971), p. 325.

that the pork flesh is *pu* (strengthening), and is to ensure that she will have
*ku-ch'i*. "Pluck" or "courage" is the usual idiomatic translation of *ku-ch'i*,
but the term literally is "bones" plus "vital energy." I suggest that the pork
flesh is female fertile stuff, and that it is proffered to the bride to ensure the
vitalization of her husband's bones, his male fertility. The further implication is that the pigs' heads offered to the deceased, and associated closely
with the daughters of the deceased, are female fertile stuff needed to activate
agnatic fertile stuff, thereby generating fertility for the deceased's agnatic
descendants.

But, first, two other pork transfers at weddings. The length of bamboo
over the nuptial taxi, symbolic of the groom's line of descent, has a small
lump of pork (which should be just flesh, no bones) tied on before it leaves
the bride's home, which ought only to be removed on arrival at the groom's
home. There are auspicious connotations upon which my informants elaborated little. However, my interpretation of pork flesh as catalytic female
fertility is sustained by what Ahern heard in north Taiwan. "'In the early
days a woman wore an underskirt next to her skin on the day of her wedding. . . . Inside the fold was carried: the five grains, a piece of pork, and a
pork heart. When she arrived at her husband's house, she allowed the skirt
to drop unimpeded onto the floor. This was in order to insure the fast birth
of sons.'"[89] In both places the bride brings her catalytic fertility with her in
the form of pig flesh, in the one case attached to her underskirt, in the other
attached to the bamboo length, symbol of the groom's line of descent.

At the time of the wedding the bride's natal family (wife-giving affines)
are clearly responsible for the fertility of the marriage. Ahern, in a stimulating article,[90] has documented other ways in which wife-givers confer fertility on the couple—much of her data is duplicable for the Yun-lin area. At
death the roles are reversed. The married-out daughter or, rather, the wife-
taking affines now reciprocate by providing the pork-flesh needed to interact
with and charge the deceased's bones so as to release fertility for the descendants. The deceased, irrespective of gender, combines male *and* female sexuality and fertility. Like P'an Ku, *yin* and *yang* elements complement each
other: bones and flesh together. There is a duality, but not one that is
dichotomized; rather, it is one of merging and interfeeding elements.
Affines, like pigs and like women, stand apart from, outside, the grid of
agnatic structures; and, like pigs and like women, affines have the power to
transform, to effect transformations in ego's descent group. At the time of
the wedding the deceased's family yielded female fertile stuff, in the form of
daughter and of pork; in the mortuary rites the wife-taking affines recipro-

89. Ahern, "Problem of Efficacy," p. 13.
90. Ahern, "Affines and the Rituals of Kinship."

cate in kind, providing the catalytic female fertile stuff for the agnatic fertility of the deceased's line to be activated, for death to be transformed into regenerative potential.

## TOMBS AS WOMBS

The idea that female fertile stuff is needed to activate the rather weak sexual potency of pure, white bones or semen or rice does not come unheralded from other spheres. Earlier I alluded to the Taoist-inspired notion that a man should not squander his semen, his "precious stuff," for his supplies are thought to be limited. However, a woman's reserves of red, creative sexual potency are reckoned to be inexhaustible. The result is that "the sexual act was to strengthen the man's vitality by making him absorb the woman's *yin* essence."[91] Sexual intercourse was identified as an opportunity for the male to recharge (rather than discharge) his *yang* essence by drawing on the woman's inexhaustible *yin* essence, in the words of Rawson and Legeza, "a kind of sexual 'vampirism.'"[92]

In similar fashion, the pure rice seed cannot sui generis regenerate. It must be planted in the earth, which is "the greatest repository of *yin* energies."[93] Patrik E. de Josselin de Jong, in discussing the "rice-cattle-death-rebirth complex" of South and Southeast Asian cultures, helps us pull the discussion back to the theme of death's engendering fertility. "Rice seeds . . . *are* really buried in the ground, as are dead bodies; and seeing that the buried seed-rice gives birth to a new crop the notion of . . . death bringing forth life is not surprising in an agricultural society that buries its dead."[94] In these respects *yin*, or female, energy is far from passive, neutral, and discountable; rather it is powerful, unlimited, encompassing, and transformative.

If we look carefully we can see that female elements play an important active role in mortuary ritual. Take the crucial rite of dotting the ancestral tablet. At first glance it appears an exclusively male activity; but the final act of vitalizing the ancestral tablet (and with it the transfer of "vigor" [*li-liang*] from deceased to descendants) is achieved by dotting with cock's blood—blood as a life-force, a red vitalizing agent, and a *yin*, or female, substance. In the same manner, a (very *yang*) god-image or even a Dragon Boat is vitalized with dabs of blood.

In Taoist literature red ochre and cinnabar can substitute for blood. David Keightley tells us not only that pigs' heads were buried with the dead

91. R. H. Van Gulik, *Sexual Life in Ancient China* (Leiden: Brill, 1974), p. 46.
92. Rawson and Legeza, *Tao*, p. 25.
93. Ibid., p. 26.
94. Patrik E. de Josselin de Jong, "An Interpretation of Agricultural Rites in Southeast Asia," *Journal of Asian Studies* 24 (1965): 283–291.

in China 3,000 years ago, but also that bones were reddened with ochre and cinnabar as far back as Neolithic times.[95] Some of my villagers were of the opinion that when bones are dug up for reburial it augurs best for the fortunes of descendants if they are dry and *with a red tinge*. Before the bone specialist places the exhumed bones in the ceramic pot, he carefully sorts the bones and reconstructs the skeleton. Larger bones are dabbed with red dye (blood substitute) and tied together with red string; smaller bone fragments may be wrapped in red paper to hold them together. The bones are then placed carefully in the *chin-tou* in a distinctly fetus-like position; they are thus enwombed.

When I asked the significance of the red dye I was told that it was linked with the well-known story (now in school textbooks) of the widow who goes in search of her husband who had died when working on the Great Wall. For convenience I use the version of the story that Ahern has recorded.[96] The widow is unable to locate her husband's bones, so she bites off her fingertip and lets the blood flow onto and down into the ground. "Whenever the blood hit one of her husband's bones, that bone came up and joined together with the others until the skeleton was complete." What the bone specialist was doing was imitative of this aspect of the story. But, at another level, the mingling of *yin* blood with *yang* bones has started to bring the corpse back to life. The widow is advised to carry the skeleton in her arms, and as her tears fall so the more the bones return to life. But T'u-ti-kung's spiteful wife advised her to carry the bones over her back instead, with the consequence that they fell apart, so the widow put them in a pot and buried them. Once again it is the female fertile stuff, blood, which has catalytic effects, vitalizing the male fertile stuff, bones. I rather suspect that carrying the skeleton in her arms is tantamount to carriage in the womb, the *yang* bones being encapsulated as a *yang* fetus, developing toward a return to life. With carriage on the back, the process of enwombment and nourishment (from the widow's tears) is ended, and the widow buries the bones in a substitute womb in the ground.

Terminologically, the ceramic pot in which the bones are placed in fetus-like position is a "golden womb." Birth and death are part of the same ongoing process. Entangled here are Taoist notions of palingenesis and *regressus ad uterum*. "(E)arly Taoism is primarily concerned with the initiatory symbolism of death as a necessary prelude to rebirth. . . . The Taoist must reverse the creation and fall of man and return to the condition of the Beginning: the condition of the closed serenity of the fetus in the womb, the condition of the dead ancestors."[97] The environment of the womb is trans-

95. Keightley, "Dead But Not Gone."
96. Ahern, *Cult of the Dead*, pp. 203–204.
97. Girardot, *Myth*, p. 84.

formative; the *tou* is not just a neutral, passive container for the more vital contents. Indeed the term *tou* has the double referent of container and contents. The *tou* can act as a crucible, as a transformative agent. To alter the sex of the child, it is the woman's womb, not the man's sperm, that is ritually changed. The woman is held responsible for the sex of the child; wife-beating occurs on both sides of the Taiwan Straits when a woman gives birth to a second-best girl.[98] The life-style of the mother's womb is held to heavily influence the future well-being and characteristics of the baby.[99] Again we may be dealing with a South and Southeast Asian phenomenon, for Josselin de Jong reckons that "the important element in the ritual treatment of the jar of [life-giving rice-] beer is not the beer, but the jar . . . symbolic of the underworld in South and Southeast Asian cultures."[100] The contents *and* the container are cojointly vital; it is not a matter of the one to the exclusion of the other. One of the aptnesses of the *tou* as a symbol is that it is simultaneously contents and container, it encompasses and subsumes the duality.

In the Yun-lin area the grave for first burial is as elaborate as that for secondary burial, and the geomantic siting of the first grave is an important consideration for the descendants. The grave mound resembles a pregnant womb in appearance, particularly from a side-on view. Looked on from a bird's-eye view, the configuration of the grave approximates a capital omega. The crucial element of architecture of the tomb is the tombstone, located in the vulva-like opening of the omega. The coffin in the mound swollen above the lie of the land has the foot-end at the tombstone. Villagers readily compare tombs with houses—for example, the multicolored papers put on top of the grave at *ch'ing-ming chieh* are said to be like roof-tiles.[101] Red papers are put on top of the tombstone, "the way we put red paper strips on our doors at New Year, or when there's a wedding." One metaphor, then, is of the tomb as house, with the tombstone as doorway.

But there also seems to be another, submerged metaphor, of the tomb as womb—not unexpected in light of the ceramic pot as a womb, too. In this case the tombstone becomes vulva, or doorway to and from the womb. Descendants gather in front of the tombstone ("wombstone"?), and that is where the tablet is dotted and where the *tou* with its contents signifying agnatic fertility is placed. Bamboo sticks, representing the sons and grandsons of the deceased, are stuck vertically in the grave mound close to the

98. See, for instance, Jeffrey Wasserstrom, "Resistance to the One-Child Family," *Modern China* 10 (1984): 345–374.

99. This syndrome of notions is called *t'ai-chiao*.

100. Josselin de Jong, "An Interpretation," p. 288.

101. De Groot mentions that the wealthy design the layout of their graves on the same basis as their houses; *The Religious System*, 3:1083.

tombstone. At the time of burial, the foot-end of the coffin has holes drilled in it, or may even be smashed open, to let out the *ch'i*; everyone is forewarned to stand clear.[102] After this some earth, presumably pervaded by the *ch'i*, is placed in the *tou*, and the symbols of fertility—coins, grains, and nails—are then distributed to the mourners. Once more, *yin* fertility in the form of *ch'i*-pervaded earth seems to be needed to trigger the *yang* fertile elements. Finally, on the metaphor of tomb as womb, one of the severest curses that can be put on a family is to smear blood of a black dog on an ancestor's tombstone. The ancestors will then create havoc for their descendants. Blood of black dogs is synonymous with menstrual blood, and since "a woman who is menstruating is not 'with child'. . . neither pregnant nor intensively lactating,"[103] the flow of fertility that should emanate from the tomb "doorway" is blocked and the tomb rendered barren—hence the effectiveness of the curse. Insofar as tombs are wombs, and wombs are tombs, the two are aspects of an encompassing synthesis which dissolves distinctions between life and death, degeneration and regeneration.

A third metaphor is equally suggestive. Tombs are like tortoises or turtles (the Chinese term *kuei* does not distinguish the two). De Groot tells us that in Fukien the shape of the grave mound "reminds us of the shape of a tortoise, whence it is popularly styled. . . 'grave tortoise'. . . [there are] many graves the tumulus of which. . . [are] entirely besmeared with plaster in light and dark colours imitating the lines of a tortoise shell."[104] The tortoise, like P'an Ku, whom the tortoise attended in the mythic creation of the world, combines the principles of *yin* and *yang*. It "symbolises the universe. Its dome-shaped back represents the vault of heaven, whilst its flat belly is the earth floating on the waters."[105] A supremely composite creature, the tortoise is said to have "a serpent's head, and a dragon's neck, the outside is bony and the inside is fleshy."[106] The status of a tortoise's head (a slang word for "penis") is wonderfully ambiguous. It is said not only, as above, to be *like a snake*, but to be a snake penetrating its body as a male organ. "One of the Chinese explanations of the Creation is that the world came into

102. The *ch'i* is said to be *tu*, or poisoning, which is why people should stand clear. Allergenic foods in folk dietetics are referred to, also, as *tu*. Somewhat paradoxically, perhaps, *pu* (strengthening) foods are often also classifiable as *tu*. For instance, my villagers say that sesame is the most *tu* and *pu* food.

103. Barbara Harrell, "Lactation and Menstruation in Cultural Perspective," *American Anthropologist* 83 (1981): 805.

104. De Groot, *The Religious System*, 3:1083. In north China the base for stone memorial tablets was often tortoise-shaped.

105. V. R. Burkhardt, *Chinese Creeds and Customs* (Hong Kong: The South China Morning Post, Ltd., 1953), 1:126.

106. Bernard E. Read, *Chinese Materia Medica: Turtle and Shellfish Drugs* (Taipei: Southern Materials Center, Inc. [Chinese Medicine Series], 1977 [orig. Peking, 1937]), p. 7, quoting Li Shih-chen.

existence through the union of a tortoise and a snake."[107] It is famous for "its faculty of transformation,"[108] including a capacity to switch sex. "Assuming female form... were-tortoises haunt rivers, and seduce lewd men,"[109] while in male form the tortoise is still very much associated with licentiousness. In addition, the tortoise is reputed to "conceive by thought alone,"[110] and "to lay eggs and hatch them by its thoughts."[111] So, on the one hand, the tortoise is ambivalently synoecious and bisexual, and, on the other, it can reproduce asexually.

There is not the space to unpack in much detail the constituents of the metaphorical identification of tombs with tortoises. Certainly the funeral prestation of "red turtle cakes" takes on a new and enhanced significance. So, too, since the tortoise is the king of shelly creatures in the Chinese categorization,[112] does the widely reported scattering of egg- and other shells over the carapace of the grave. Consider also that the turtle is famous for its longevity which it owes to "its 'embryo-breathing', that is to breathe underground in the same manner as the embryo breathes in its mother's womb,"[113] and the reverberations become even more intense. Once again tomb and womb, birth and death, are coidentified. The tortoise is a potent miscegenation of inextricated dualities and ambiguity, at the same time fertile, catalytic, and transformative. Fertility is engendered through the dissolution of distinctions, through the coalescent harmonization of *yin* and *yang*. In these aspects it seems to be an epiphany of "the obliterating unity of the *tao*."[114]

In this chapter I have sought to show that a crucial aspect of the significance of food in funerary ritual is concerned with the duality of rice and pork, the semantic ramifications of which help us interpret Chinese death rites. Though not always clearly recognizable, the duality is there in the mortuary and funerary rituals. The dualities can either be dichotomized or amalgamated.

Standard interpretations of Chinese death rituals stress the aspect of Confucian ritual hegemony, the superimposition by the state of standard ritual performances and structures. Deviation from the orthopractical forms could result in punishment. As far as the state was concerned, ritual forms had to conform, which is not to say that all ritual forms, let alone the mean-

107. Burkhardt, *Chinese Creeds*, 2:50.
108. Williams, *Outlines*, p. 405, quoting Mayers.
109. Doré, *Researches*, 5:661.
110. Williams, *Outlines*, p. 405, quoting Mayers.
111. Read, *Chinese Materia Medica*, p. 7, quoting Li Shih-chen.
112. See ibid., pp. 1–2; Williams, *Outlines*, p. 403–405.
113. Van Gulik, *Sexual Life*, p. 9.
114. Werner, *Myths and Legends*, p. 91.

ings attributed to the ritual forms, conformed to the state interpretation. The emphasis in the patriarchal Confucian ideology was on social harmony and moral order, exemplified in the concept *li*, translatable variously as "ritual," "ceremony," or "etiquette." As Watson tells us, *li* is very much at issue during death rites, there being a supposition "that a moral order can be created by proper action," though we cannot a priori know the extent to which participants in the rituals share this state-foisted interpretation. In the hegemonic Confucian paradigm the great fear is "the spectre of disorder [*luan*],"[115] a state of affairs which, in the Confucian definition, prevails when social and moral distinctions are not "properly" maintained. In Confucianism dualities are separated out, thereby emphasizing the "proper" distinctions that ought to apply. And in that separation one part of the duality is given primacy over the other: *yang* over *yin*; *li* over *luan*; men over women; agnates over affines; rice over pork; formal behavior over "what conforms with one's nature"; purity over lewdness; structure over communitas; and so on. In convergent fashion James Watson has depicted the manner in which his lineage-dominated Cantonese villagers stressed one side of the duality while repudiating the other. In the highly structured social world of the single-lineage village the death rituals are interpreted as creating "a pure state of maleness—without sex, affinity, or the messy corrupting necessities of biological reproduction."[116]

However, even in the case of the particularly androcentric Cantonese, the other side of the duality seems to be there in the ritual, though denigrated, poorly recognized, or, perhaps, actively repudiated. We are told, for instance, that "in order to be effective...bones...cannot function without activating the flesh of sacrificial animals."[117] I would favor the interpretation that it is the flesh of the animal (the sacrificial pig) which activates the bones; at any rate, my point is that both sides of the duality (bones and flesh) are there, but the lineage-dominated Cantonese favor the hegemonic Confucian one-sided emphasis on bones when, logically, the emphasis could just as well be focused on the flesh or on the interaction between the two elements. In the Taoist ideology, on the other hand, where the importance of social order and hierarchy is absent, distinctions are happily blurred. In the Taoist way of thinking, "power" is more personalized and not associable or derivable from *social* order and the upholding of distinctions.

115. J. L. Watson, "Of Flesh and Bones," p. 180. Here I am using the terms "Confucian" and "Taoist" in a selective, shorthand fashion, as labels to designate two contrasting perspectives on rice/pork and other dualisms. Other labels might also be applied, for instance "male" and "female" ideologies, as discussed by Emily Martin in chapter 7.

116. J. L. Watson, chapter 5 this volume. Cf. Bloch and Parry's quote, at note 71 above.

117. J. L. Watson, "Of Flesh and Bones," p. 181.

Rather, the stress is on conforming with the way of nature, the *natural* order. The "emphasis is on complementary dualism . . . an equilibrium of opposites as the basic mode of creation, both cosmic and human."[118] Emphasis is on the complementary interaction of *both* elements of dualities: male *and* female; yin *and* yang; flesh *and* bones; rice *and* pork; and so on. *Luan* is seen, not as threatening, but as merely the other side of *li*, both facets of the encompassing meta-level order of the Tao. This Taoist interpretation is subversive of the dominant Confucian interpreting of the meaning that should be given to key ritual dualities. The true Taoist, like the tortoise, has forgotten the eight rules of politeness,[119] and is unable to conform to ceremony, that is, the *li* with which the hegemonic Confucian paradigm is so concerned. In the Taoist counter-ideology reference is to an order beyond the social order and moral harmony stressed in the Confucian emphasis on *li*. In the Confucian paradigm food has the power to separate rather than unite dualities; in the Taoist counter-interpretation food unites rather than separates dualities.[120]

118. Girardot, *Myth*, p. 183.
119. For the tortoise's inability to conform to *li*, see Burkhardt, *Chinese Creeds*, 2:50.
120. My final sentence refers back, palingenetically, to the Girardot epigraph.

FIVE

# Funeral Specialists in Cantonese Society: Pollution, Performance, and Social Hierarchy

## James L. Watson

*Ah-bak [honorific uncle], who are those scruffy outsiders?*

*Not so loud! Don't speak to them and don't go near them. They are [voice in a whisper] ng jong lo. They always come with the coffin. Such men are bad luck and their touch is very filthy.—Elder of the Man lineage to J. L. W. during a funeral in the village of San Tin, 1969.*

Such was my introduction to the subject of funeral specialists in Cantonese rural society. From the moment these men entered the village it was obvious that something extraordinary was happening. Doors and windows were clapped shut as they walked through the narrow lanes, mothers scrambled to remove children from their paths, no one spoke with them, and—most noticeably—heads were turned to avoid their glance. Although I had lived in the community for several months, I had as yet seen nothing even approaching this kind of behavior. "Those who come with the coffin" were treated like lepers—or worse. Later, when I began to probe more deeply into Cantonese mortuary ritual, it became apparent why these men were social pariahs: They earn their living by handling corpses, digging graves, and carrying coffins. Villagers believe that such people are permanently contaminated by constant exposure to the corrupting influences of death. Accordingly, any form of social exchange with them (physical, verbal, or visual) is to be avoided lest the pollution of death be transmitted to the unwary.

This chapter is divided into two major parts. The first, and longest, is primarily ethnographic in that it explores the social backgrounds and ritual roles of funeral specialists who were observed at work in two Cantonese villages. The second part attempts to draw some general conclusions about the nature of funerary ritual and its relation to notions of social order in Chinese society.

The ethnographic evidence suggests that, among the Cantonese, there is a hierarchy of specialists ranked according to relative exposure to the pollution of death. This hierarchy also reflects the standards of skill, training, and literacy required to carry out ritual tasks. Geomancers, whose work demands a high level of skill and literacy (combined with a total avoidance of

polluting activities), rank highest. Next are the priests who learn their trade
through years of apprenticeship; they must also be minimally literate to
perform various mortuary rites. Ranking below the priests are a number of
(usually illiterate) specialists whose ritual tasks do not require a great deal of
skill or training: pipers, musicians, nuns, and general helpers. These middle-
ranking personnel regularly perform at funerals and, hence, are deemed to
be polluted by their activities, but they are careful to avoid physical contact
with the corpse. At the bottom of the hierarchy are the corpse handlers
described in the opening passages. Their tasks involve washing, dressing,
and arranging the corpse; they are also expected to carry the coffin, dig the
grave, and dispose of items most directly associated with death (bedding,
clothing, bandages, etc.). This work is considered to be so polluting it sets
the corpse handlers apart from all other ritual specialists. They are, quite
literally, beyond the pale of normal human interchange.

Readers familiar with the Indianist literature will notice some interesting
parallels between the Hindu and the Chinese conceptions of pollution and
social hierarchy. Both societies have devised elaborate systems of funerary
ritual that require the services of paid professionals; both have highly developed notions of death pollution and its effects on human beings. There
are, of course, important differences between Chinese and Hindu ideas regarding the transmission of pollution and the social reproduction of stigma.
These differences will be explored in the second part of the chapter. At this
point, however, it is important to note that China is by no means unique in
the creation of a complex occupational hierarchy based on notions of pollution.

## ETHNOGRAPHY

### Setting and Background

This study draws primarily on field research carried out in Yuen Long district, Hong Kong New Territories. The author lived in two Cantonese villages, San Tin and Ha Tsuen, where he witnessed sixteen funerals and many
other rites associated with death during twenty-nine months of fieldwork
(1969–1970, 1977–1978). These villages are single-lineage settlements inhabited by the Man and Teng lineages respectively; San Tin has been controlled by the Man for approximately four hundred years, and the Teng
have dominated Ha Tsuen for over six hundred years.[1] Residents of both
villages speak a subdialect of Pao-an Cantonese, known locally as *wei-t'ou*

---

1. On the Man, see James L. Watson, *Emigration and the Chinese Lineage: The Mans in
Hong Kong and London* (Berkeley and Los Angeles: University of California Press, 1975); on
the Teng, see Rubie S. Watson, *Inequality Among Brothers: Class and Kinship in South China*
(Cambridge: Cambridge University Press, 1985).

*hua*, and share the same basic cultural system. There are but minor differences between the conduct of funeral rituals in the two villages. Since the 1920s San Tin and Ha Tsuen have been part of the "marketing community"[2] focused on the market town of Yuen Long. Many of the funeral specialists discussed in this chapter reside in Yuen Long and service approximately fifty Cantonese villages in the surrounding hinterland. This concentration of specialists contributes to the homogeneity of ritual in the area under study.

Cantonese villagers draw an unambiguous distinction between professional and nonprofessional ritual specialists. Anyone who receives payment, in cash or in kind, for information or services associated with funerary ritual is deemed to be a professional and is treated accordingly. In the villages I have studied there are many people (mostly widows) who are well versed in the intricacies of mortuary rites. They are regularly consulted by villagers but do not accept payment; were they to do so, their status would change and they could no longer function as ordinary members of the community. The designation of professional does not imply full-time employment. In fact, some categories of specialists (e.g., funeral pipers) are hard pressed to make a living by ritual activities and supplement their income in other ways. It is not, therefore, the amount of time invested or the percentage of income earned that matters when determining who is and who is not a professional funeral specialist—from the villagers' point of view it is the fact of payment alone that matters. Nonprofessionals are not ranked in the hierarchy of specialists, and being ordinary villagers, they are not thought to be permanently affected by death pollution.

The division between paid (professional) and unpaid (nonprofessional) funeral specialists is reflected in the everyday discourse of villagers. In the jargon of social anthropology this can be called an *emic* distinction; *etic* distinctions, by contrast, are devised by outside observers and are not part of the conscious conceptual apparatus of the people involved.[3] For instance, I find it useful to draw an etic distinction between specialists who provide goods, services, and information (e.g., geomancers, coffin makers, producers of ritual paraphernalia, exhumers) and those who perform ritual services at the actual funeral (e.g., priests, nuns, musicians, corpse handlers). This division is implicit in my informants' conversations, but it is not concretized in marked linguistic pairing. As we shall see, however, important features of the Chinese ritual system are revealed by distinguishing between performers of rituals and providers of goods and services.

2. See G. William Skinner, "Marketing and Social Structure in Rural China, Part I," *Journal of Asian Studies* 24 (1964): 3–43.

3. For a summary of these distinctions, see Marvin Harris, "Emics, Etics, and the New Ethnography," chapter 20 in his *The Rise of Anthropological Theory* (New York: Thomas Crowell, 1968), pp. 568–604.

Rites associated with death and mourning are subsumed under the general emic category of "white affairs" (*pai-shih*), and all who earn income, directly or indirectly, from mortuary rites are associated with that ritual domain. This is contrasted with another emic category referred to as "red affairs" (*hung-shih*), relating primarily to the rites of marriage. In the local symbolic repertoire, white is the color of death and mourning; red is the color associated with life and luck. Villagers make much of this contrast in everyday conversations: "Never mix red and white affairs." Although the two ritual domains are conceptualized as a matched pair, and receive more or less equal emphasis in monetary outlay, only white affairs are presided over by paid professionals. As is outlined below, Cantonese funerals cannot even proceed without the services of a trained priest and other specialists. The rites associated with red affairs, on the other hand, are usually conducted without the intervention of a paid ritual specialist.[4] It is also significant that, among rural Cantonese, performers of ritual services are not interchangeable: funeral priests have nothing whatsoever to do with marriage rites, nor do nuns or funeral pipers (a different piper must be found for weddings). The only exception to this implicit rule prohibiting specialists from engaging in red and white activities is the resident geomancer who often doubles as a fortuneteller for marriages and a locator of auspicious tombs. But, as we shall see, the geomancer's role is unique. It is difficult to categorize him as red or white, given that he is not involved in the actual performance of either set of rites and remains aloof from all other ritual specialists.

### Death Pollution

Most Cantonese villagers have a morbid fear of anything associated with death, and accordingly they do not relish the prospects of attending funerals—even those of friends or close kin. As one elder put it to me: "No one likes to be seen at funerals. It is bad luck and can bring illness." Nonetheless, as is outlined below, certain members of the community (mostly women) are obligated to attend, and these people play an important role in the ritual. The fear of funerals is related to notions of death pollution, described by my informants as "killing airs" (*sha-ch'i*, or *saat hei* in Cantonese). This subject has already been explored in an earlier essay;[5] space does not permit a full discussion here. Briefly summarized, "killing airs" are thought to be released at the moment of death, like "an invisible

---

4. Matchmakers and fortunetellers, of course, are usually paid, but they are not involved in the *performance* of marriage rites. Furthermore, unpaid amateurs can take their place; specialists do not play a role in the formal structure of marriage rites.

5. James L. Watson, "Of Flesh and Bones: The Management of Death Pollution in Cantonese Society," in *Death and the Regeneration of Life*, ed. Maurice Bloch and Jonathan Parry (Cambridge: Cambridge University Press, 1982), pp. 155–186.

cloud," to quote one villager. The airs emanating from the corpse contaminate everything and everybody in the immediate vicinity. This pollution is transmitted to humans by physical proximity, secondary contact, and—most dangerously—by touching the corpse. In the present study and in earlier writings I have chosen to translate *saat hei* as "death pollution," although the English term does not capture the full range and subtlety of the Cantonese concept.

Village men are extremely careful to avoid touching the corpse because physical contact is thought to affect adversely their *yang*, or male, essence. As a local priest explained to me: "After a man touches seven corpses, he can no longer be made clean again." This is why professional corpse handlers are treated with such disdain. It is assumed that they have touched so many corpses that their *yang* essence has long since dissipated. When this happens, according to the priest, killing airs can no longer be resisted, and the living body will be consumed with leprosy, syphilis, and other corrupting diseases. At each funeral only one male villager, the chief mourner, is required to touch the corpse. More will be said about this ritual role in the following section. Suffice it to note here that Cantonese males only take on this dangerous role to fulfill their material obligation, as inheritors, to the deceased.[6] Women are not affected in the same way, given that they are—in villagers' eyes—primarily of *yin* (female) essence. Accordingly, women can handle corpses and attend funerals without the constant anxiety that such actions will permanently corrupt the vital element of their being. This does not mean that women are less afraid of death than their male counterparts, but it does help explain why women, rather than men, are more likely to attend funerals as representatives of their families.

Death pollution, it is important to note, emanates from the decaying flesh of humans, not from the bones. The object of Cantonese mortuary rites is to progress smoothly and efficiently to the stage when it is possible to exhume the bones and cleanse them of the last, corrupting remnants of flesh. The secondary burial system of south China and the manipulation of flesh-free bones is well documented in the ethnographic literature.[7] Of relevance here is the Cantonese equation between rotting flesh and the corrupting influences of death pollution. In the local view, flesh is inherited from the mother and is thereby of the *yin* essence. Bones, on the other hand, are passed in the patriline and, when manipulated properly, are primarily *yang*.

6. Ibid., pp. 169–172.

7. See, e.g., Emily Martin Ahern, *The Cult of the Dead in a Chinese Village* (Stanford: Stanford University Press, 1973); Maurice Freedman, *Chinese Lineage and Society: Kwangtung and Fukien* (London: Athlone, 1966), pp. 118–154; Burton Pasternak, "Chinese Tale-Telling Tombs," *Ethnology* 12 (1973): 259–273; Jack M. Potter, "Wind, Water, Bones, and Souls," *Journal of Oriental Studies* (Hong Kong) 8 (1970): 139–153; and Rubie S. Watson in chapter 9, this volume.

The preservation of bones and the disappearance of flesh reflects the Cantonese conception of the patrilineage as a corporate group of males that exists through time, irrespective of death. The realm of the ancestors is thus exclusively male, or *yang*, in the total absence of women, or the female essence. The androcentric ideology of the ancestral cult is such that Cantonese men seek to create in thought what they cannot attain in life, namely a pure state of maleness—without sex, affinity, or the messy, corrupting necessities of biological reproduction.

Killing airs are in part conceived of as the vital biological forces that are released, untamed and dangerous, at death, as is discussed elsewhere.[8] In order for the spirit of the deceased to be properly settled, these vital forces must be absorbed back into the flesh of living people. All who attend funerals perform a series of acts whereby they voluntarily take upon themselves a portion of death pollution, in varying degrees depending upon relationship to the deceased.[9] In marked contrast to other Cantonese rituals, there are no idle bystanders at funerals. Everyone present is expected to be an active participant who performs an important service for the dead.

Thus, in the local view, the living must assist the deceased to overcome the effects of his or her own death. The chief mourner and female members of the immediate family take upon themselves the major burden of pollution; neighbors and others who are obligated to attend absorb a minor portion carefully prescribed in ritual (see note 9). However, kin and neighbors—alone—cannot absorb all of the killing airs released at death. The full dissipation of death pollution requires that someone actually accept money for taking on this burden. My informants could not, or would not, be more explicit, but it is clear that an exchange of cash is essential for the final transfer of pollution from one body to another.[10] Payment, of course, is only made to professionals who earn their living from white affairs.[11]

In the eyes of the villagers, therefore, the money paid to funeral specialists is of a different order than the currency used in everyday transactions. Money reserved for funeral expenses is often drawn from a bank (in new notes) on the day of burial; the chief mourner always carries it in a separate pocket, where it will not be confused with other notes. Cantonese villagers

8. J. Watson, "Of Flesh and Bones," pp. 172–174.

9. The acts of accepting death pollution include receiving coins and/or bits of white yarn that have been exposed to the coffin, and the offering of incense and wine to the spirit of the deceased. See ibid., pp. 162–163.

10. This notion of pollution transmission is similar to the Hindu system described by Jonathan Parry, "Ghosts, Greed and Sin: The Occupational Identity of the Benares Funeral Priests," *Man* n.s. 15 (1980): 88–111.

11. A clarification is necessary here: As was mentioned above (see note 9), one method of distributing pollution is to hand out coins at the funeral. These coins are spent or given away as soon as possible; they are conceived of more as a burden than a payment. In contrast, professionals accept large amounts of cash for their services.

thus manage to transform a generalized medium of exchange into a highly charged symbol of their own preoccupation with death pollution.[12] The funeral specialists, for their part, treat this money with exaggerated nonchalance, ostentatiously counting the notes in full view of all who care to watch (an inversion of normal behavior in Cantonese society). In so doing the specialists signal that they do not accept the villagers' interpretation of the exchange as a payment for taking on the corrupting influences of death. To villagers the money is a powerful embodiment of pollution; to the specialists it represents payment for services rendered.

The acceptance of contaminated cash is one reason why funeral specialists are perceived as a dangerous category of people. Contrary to the normal order of things, specialists make their living from white affairs, and at least in the eyes of villagers, they thrive on the sorrow and misfortune of others. The fact that funeral specialists use tainted money to buy the rice that sustains them was brought up several times by my informants. In constructing a mental equation that begins with death pollution and ends with eating, villagers are making a powerful statement: Those who live from death must eat from death.

### Community Participation: The Role of Nonprofessionals

Although paid professionals are essential for the performance of Cantonese funerals, neighbors and kin also play an important role in the ritual. Members of the deceased's immediate family perform a series of acts and wear special mourning garb that set them apart from other villagers.[13] The oldest surviving son or designated male heir assumes the role of chief mourner (ch'eng-chi, "heir" or "inheritor"). It is this man who is responsible for paying the specialists and for ensuring that the rites are performed to the satisfaction of the community. Important as he may be, however, the chief mourner cannot carry out his many ritual tasks without a continuous stream of orders from the priest ("Turn left, bow three times, stand up." "No, no! You are going the wrong way. Start again"). Male villagers, as a general rule, know very little about the conduct of funerary ritual; and even if they learn by experience, it is not possible to proceed without professional assistance. The structure of Cantonese funeral rites is such that the chief mourner performs only those acts dictated by the presiding priest. It is always the priest who directs the flow of events, not the chief mourner.

12. For a general discussion of the use of money in ritual, see Michael Taussig, *The Devil and Commodity Fetishism in South America* (Chapel Hill: University of North Carolina Press, 1980), pp. 126–132, and Hill Gates, "Money for the Gods: The Commoditization of the Spirit," *Modern China* 13 (1987): 259–277.

13. See, e.g., Arthur P. Wolf, "Chinese Kinship and Mourning Dress," in *Family and Kinship in Chinese Society*, ed. Maurice Freedman (Stanford: Stanford University Press, 1970), pp. 189–207.

Cantonese villagers are reluctant to attend funerals, as was noted earlier, and they participate only to the extent that obligation defines. The two villages under study have different systems to ensure a reasonable level of community participation. In Ha Tsuen, each of the five major hamlets (well-defined neighborhoods) constitutes a ritual community in the sense that, when a death occurs, every household in the relevant hamlet is obligated to send at least one representative to the funeral.[14] It is inconceivable that a member household would refuse to participate; if they are unable to attend, a stand-in must be provided. The people of San Tin, by contrast, are organized into voluntary associations (*lao-jen hui*, "old people societies") that guarantee a respectable level of attendance at funerals.[15]

The obligations of household representatives are clearly prescribed in ritual, and like all other participants, they perform under the direction of a priest. Unlike members of the deceased's family, however, household representatives are not expected to witness the full sequence of rites (which means that their exposure to pollution is limited). They are summoned by the sound of gongs at a particular stage in the ritual when their services are required. Most perform their duties with rapid precision and leave the scene as quickly as possible. As was noted earlier, women usually fulfill their household's obligation, hence they outnumber men by at least three to one at most funerals. Many societies have a pronounced gender distinction in the performance of funeral rites, and it is often women who carry the burden of pollution.[16] Among the Cantonese a sexual division of ritual labor ensures that women predominate during the early, contaminating stages of the mortuary sequence; later, when the flesh has disappeared, men claim the bones and use the dead for their own political or economic purposes.[17] Women are systematically excluded from participation in the central rites of the Cantonese ancestral cult.

Given that women are expected to perform at funerals, it is not surprising

14. There are, in fact, eleven hamlets in Ha Tsuen, but several smaller ones are combined to form "ritual communities"; see R. Watson, *Inequality Among Brothers*, p. 101. Residents usually attend only the funerals held in their own hamlet/ritual community.

15. On funeral societies, see Bernard Gallin, *Hsin Hsing, Taiwan: A Chinese Village in Change* (Berkeley and Los Angeles: University of California Press, 1966), pp. 121–122; Burton Pasternak, *Kinship and Community in Two Chinese Villages* (Stanford: Stanford University Press, 1972), pp. 64–66.

16. See, e.g., Maurice Bloch, "Death, Women and Power," in Bloch and Parry, *Death and Regeneration*, pp. 211–230; Stanley Brandes, "Gender Distinctions in Monteros [Spain] Mortuary Ritual," *Ethnology* 20 (1981): 177–190; Gary Seaman, "The Sexual Politics of Karmic Retribution," in *The Anthropology of Taiwanese Society*, ed. Emily Martin Ahern and Hill Gates (Stanford: Stanford University Press, 1981), pp. 381–396.

17. See, e.g., Jack M. Potter, "Land and Lineage in Traditional China," in *Family and Kinship in Chinese Society*, ed. Maurice Freedman (Stanford: Stanford University Press, 1970), pp. 121–138, and Rubie Watson in chapter 9, this volume.

that they should know more than village men about funerary ritual. Every hamlet has one or two women—usually widows—who are particularly knowledgeable of white affairs. These women are consulted about proper household procedure (mourning garb, precautions, social conduct, etc.) whenever a death occurs in their hamlet. They also serve as unofficial guardians of the community's well-being, watching carefully to make certain the rites are performed according to established custom. When men return from the grave, for instance, these guardians always station themselves outside the gates of their hamlet to ensure that everyone washes before entering (women do not accompany the coffin to the grave—another element in the sexual division of ritual labor).[18] During the funeral itself the hamlet guardians are always present, serving a dual role as household representatives and observers of the ritual. Although the priests perceive them as nuisances, ordinary villagers rely on these older women for advice during the period immediately following a death. Many of the ritual actions that occur inside the home of the deceased must be performed without delay, and it often takes the priest an hour or more to appear on the scene. Indebted as they may be to these knowledgeable women, villagers are careful not to draw attention to their ritual skills. To do so would be to blur the distinction between specialist and ordinary villager.[19]

### Funeral Priests: Institutionalized Marginality

Funeral priests are referred to in colloquial Cantonese as *nahm mouh lo*, an untranslatable term of uncertain origins.[20] *Nahm mouh lo* has a slight pejorative connotation, given that the Cantonese suffix *lo* (usually translated as "fellow") is also used for corpse handlers (*ng jong lo*) and other unsavory

18. Women do not join the procession to the grave, for two (emic) reasons, according to male informants: (1) They might be so distraught that they would do serious harm to themselves, and (2) crying and wailing at the grave would upset the spirit prior to burial, a critical juncture in the ritual sequence when the spirit must be soothed and settled.

19. It proved difficult to interview these women about funeral ritual, and after some months it dawned on me that I was probably doing them a disservice by drawing attention to their special skills. They do not, in other words, openly discuss this aspect of their lives with anyone. This raises the interesting question of how these hamlet guardians pass on their knowledge to younger women. Funeral laments and ritual duties were taught in "maidens' houses" (C *neuih jai nguk*) where many girls lived prior to marriage, but the knowledge required of hamlet guardians goes beyond this basic level of instruction. In the absence of informant testimony, I am left to speculate that these women are self-taught and that they picked up their skills after years of observation and participation.

20. Villagers often argue that *nahm mouh lo* has onomatopoetic origins, deriving from the priests' low, monotonous chants (which sound, to most observers, like meaningless droning: *"nahm mouh, nahm mouh, . . ."*). However, there is also indirect evidence that this colloquial term has textual origins, deriving perhaps from the Buddhist incantation *nan wu* that appears in many ritual contexts. If there is a textual connection, it no longer has any meaning to ordinary Cantonese villagers.

characters (e.g., C *ngok lo*, "tough guy"; C *gwai lo*, "foreigner" [lit. "ghost fellow"]). It is significant in this context that geomancers are called *feng-shui hsien-sheng* ("mister geomancer"), a title reflecting their high status in the community. Understandably, priests are not always comfortable with the colloquial term *nahm mouh lo*, and many try to invent other, more flattering titles for themselves (such as C *nahm mouh sin-sang* [*hsien-sheng*]). Villagers uniformly ignore these innovations and continue using the traditional form, both as a referent and as a term of address. This linguistic confrontation highlights the ambiguous position of the priest in society: Villagers depend upon him during times of crisis, but during happier times his very presence is an unfortunate reminder of death.

The social position of the funeral priest is somewhat akin to that of undertaker in American small towns.[21] They may reside *in* the community but they are not really *of* the community. Like the American mortician, Cantonese funeral priests are set apart by the nature of their work, and their neighbors—essentially a captive clientele—are never completely comfortable in their presence. Most of the priests I encountered during my research were married and had raised families in the communities they served.[22] The priests themselves often affect an aloof demeanor, but their wives are careful to maintain good relations with neighbors and fellow villagers. The wives of priests also assume the primary responsibility of fulfilling their households' ritual and social obligations.

Priests are acutely aware that their ambiguous position in society stems, in part, from their constant exposure to death pollution. Accordingly, they make every effort to avoid direct contact with the corpse or with the coffin—and they do so in a public manner for all to see. Even indirect contact is avoided if at all possible. For instance, the priest does not accept coins or bits of white cord distributed to household representatives and mourners (such objects are thought to carry pollution; see note 9). Furthermore, unlike other members of the community, the priest does not wear white during the ritual. Instead, his funeral wardrobe consists of red and yellow silk robes decorated with auspicious trigrams; these colors and symbols have, in the local view, prophylactic powers that protect the wearer from

21. See, e.g., Robert Habenstein, "Conflicting Organizational Patterns in Funeral Direct-ing," *Human Organization* 22 (1963): 126–132; E. G. Haley, *How to Conduct a Funeral: A Handbook for Ministers* (Cincinnati: Standard Publishing Co., 1918).

22. Not all *nahm mouh lo* are residents of the villages they serve; some are organized into companies and operate out of the major market towns. When Ha Tsuen celebrated its decen-nial *chiao* (rite of purification and expiation) in 1974, the management committee hired six *nahm mouh lo* from another part of the New Territories to conduct the five-day ritual. Ha Tsuen's resident priest played no role in the organization or direction of this ritual, although, as a member of the community, he was involved as an ordinary participant.

the ill effects of death.[23] At two points in the ritual the priest is required to strike the coffin with a pair of scissors, announcing its imminent departure from the village.[24] These ritual acts are the only instances when the priest comes into physical contact with the coffin, and significantly, he is always careful to protect himself by wrapping the scissors in red yarn. In addition, the priest never accompanies the coffin to the grave, even though all other male participants normally join the procession (*sung-pin*). Given that his services are not needed at the grave, there is no reason for the priest to expose himself to further influences of pollution during the burial.

Cantonese funeral priests learn their trade primarily through long years of apprenticeship, and few have had more than five years of formal education, usually in village primary schools.[25] They are, in other words, only slightly better educated than the average village male, which means that they can prepare ritual forms (paper tablets, memorials to be burned at funerals, etc.),[26] but they have difficulty reading books and esoteric texts. Texts are sometimes used as part of the ritual repertoire (see next section), even though none of the priests, of my acquaintance at least, could actually decipher or interpret more than a few lines per page. Public "readings" from the texts consisted primarily of long chants memorized during apprenticeship.

San Tin's priest was trained by a master (*shih-fu*) who operated in the nearby market town of Sham Chun [Shen-chen]. In several years of apprenticeship he learned chanting (see below), ritual dancing, mime, and paper crafts.[27] As a member of the Man lineage, he had a virtual monopoly over funerals in San Tin until his death in the mid-1970s. The resident priest in Ha Tsuen, by contrast, was not a member of the Teng lineage; he belonged to a minor line of villagers who bear a different surname and live on the fringe of the community. By their own accounts, the Wang (a pseudonym) settled in Ha Tsuen eight or nine generations ago. They

23. Cf., Wolf, "Chinese Kinship and Mourning Dress," p. 193.

24. J. Watson, "Of Flesh and Bones," p. 163.

25. In Rawski's terms, the local priests were "semi-literates" who were far from the "threshold of elite education"; see Evelyn Rawski, *Education and Popular Literacy in Ch'ing China* (Ann Arbor: University of Michigan Press, 1979), pp. 2–4.

26. For a discussion of written communications in Chinese ritual, see Emily Martin Ahern, *Chinese Ritual and Politics* (Cambridge: Cambridge University Press, 1981).

27. One of the esoteric skills priests must master is "dancing" (*t'iao-wu*), a series of precise steps tracing out trigrams ("to settle the spirit of the dead," according to San Tin's priest). Priests also learn to mime the supernatural beings encountered by the spirit during its journey through the underworld. Ha Tsuen's priest was particularly adept at miming the Monkey God (which he performed during a special sacrifice to settle the spirit of a suicide victim in 1978). Most village priests also construct the elaborate paper objects (houses, servants, autos, airplanes, etc.) burned during the funeral sequence.

attached themselves to the Teng lineage as subordinate clients, providing
ritual services that local people were hesitant to undertake. Every generation
since their arrival in Ha Tsuen, one or more Wang males have served as Ha
Tsuen's *nahm mouh lo*. In addition, Wang daughters have monopolized the
role of community shaman, (C) *mahn maih poh* (lit. "ask rice woman")—
mediums who specialize in interviewing the spirits of the dead.[28] Ha
Tsuen's current priest learned his skills directly from his grandfather; his
immediate predecessor was a paternal uncle (it is not clear at this writing
whether a new generation of priests and shamans is being trained among the
five households of Wang who live in Ha Tsuen). The Teng believe that the
Wang are endowed with occult powers, including the ability to extract, (C)
*ning*, small sums of money from the pockets of unsuspecting villagers who
may be miles away. Such stories reinforce the marginality of the Wang and
draw attention to the fact that they earn their living from the misfortune of
others.

### The Priest as Choreographer and Cantor

> In funeral matters there should be regular progress, no retrogressive
> movement.—From the *Li chi*.

In response to my question regarding the most important aspect of his
calling, Ha Tsuen's resident priest responded with something very close to
the ancient maxim from the *Li chi*:

> During a funeral it is my job to make sure everything keeps going forward and
> that nothing stops. Everyone has to be told what to do, quickly, or there will
> be trouble. The worst thing that can happen is for a funeral to start but not be
> finished properly.

This, in a nutshell, is the priest's own vision of his role. He must instruct
his clients on proper procedure and direct the action in such a manner that
the ritual is not interrupted. At nearly every funeral I attended villagers
expressed deep concern that the rites be performed efficiently and that the
burial be accomplished before sundown.[29] Put in our own cultural terms,
the priest resembles a choreographer. He is responsible for directing a com-

---

28. These shamans sometimes communicate with the deceased by spreading husked, uncooked rice in a flat basket and "reading" the designs traced during trance. On women as ritual
specialists, see Jack M. Potter, "Cantonese Shamanism," in *Religion and Ritual in Chinese
Society*, ed. Arthur P. Wolf (Stanford: Stanford University Press, 1974), pp. 207–231.

29. When I asked villagers what might happen if the funeral rites were interrupted or if the
burial were delayed (after the rites had started), my informants said that this would cause
extreme misfortune for the entire community. The spirit, they explained, would surely be lost
and would return someday to haunt the village. One villager also said that, under these circumstances, the corpse might become a horrible monster (cf. Ahern, *Cult of the Dead*, pp. 164,
172).

plicated series of movements and countermovements, all of which must be performed in a regularized sequence. It is by no means an easy task to control the flow of events when many of the key participants are complete novices (i.e., male mourners and teenagers who have little or no experience of funerals).

In reading the anthropological literature on China, it is easy to gain the impression that ritual performances always proceed with stereotypic efficiency and that the people involved know exactly what to do. The illusion of perfection is created by abstracting a generalized series of movements from a number of actual performances. This method of analysis is essential if one's aim is to comprehend the structure of rituals, but it also imparts the false impression that participants behave more like automatons than like people.

The reality of a Cantonese funeral is quite different—some might say shockingly different—from the standard ethnographic accounts: The overriding impression is one of confusion, indecision, and subdued panic. The mourners are often transfixed with fear, incapable in some cases of rational thought or coordinated movement. Fear of the corpse, rather than grief, is the dominant emotion displayed at Cantonese funerals.[30] In order to maintain control over what can easily deteriorate into a chaotic situation, the priest must be very assertive; he may shout at the participants and push them if they lag behind (on one occasion the priest slapped a dazed mourner who was slow to follow his instructions). Women are generally less problematic, given that they often appear as household representatives and know more or less what is expected of them. Men and children, on the other hand, must be nudged, pushed, and cajoled into performing the intricate maneuvers that constitute an essential feature of funerary ritual. To further complicate matters for the priest, one or two older women (the hamlet guardians mentioned earlier) usually stand on the sidelines shouting advice and dissent. Not surprisingly, when the funeral is over the priest is often so thoroughly exhausted that he returns home to sleep for a few hours.

Besides choreography, priests must also learn the esoteric art of chanting. San Tin's priest spent (according to his own testimony) many years memorizing various chants based on long passages from Taoist texts. When asked to identify their religious affiliation, all of the priests I encountered during my research responded that they were Taoist (tao-chiao). However,

---

30. I do not mean to underplay the grief that is evident at many funerals, but most people—including the mourners—display an obvious fear of the corpse and the disembodied spirit. The same seems to be true for Cantonese boatpeople; see Eugene N. Anderson, Jr., *The Floating World of Castle Peak Bay*, Anthropological Studies 4 (Washington, D.C.: American Anthropological Association), p. 181; for a similar reaction to the corpse among Ch'ao-chou villagers, see Daniel Kulp, *Country Life in South China* (New York: Columbia University Teachers College, 1925), p. 198.

other than declaring a link to Taoism—in opposition to Buddhism and Confucianism—they refused to elaborate, saying only that it is their duty to deal with deities (*shen*) and ghosts (*kuei*). All attempts to relate these local priests to a regional, provincial, or national-level hierarchy of religious organizations (monastic orders, schools, priestly lines) failed; furthermore, none of the priests I spoke with could name the texts that they had studied during apprenticeship.

Chanting, like proper choreography, is an integral part of the funeral ritual, and it can only be performed by a *nahm mouh lo*. The chants are delivered in a low monotone that villagers refer to as *yin* ("humming" or "chanting"). The priests have their own specialized vocabulary and distinguish between *ch'ang* ("singing") and *chi-wen* ("sacrificial litanies"). "Singing" is aimed at placating or soothing the spirit of the deceased. "Sacrificial litanies," on the other hand, are special chants deriving from sacred texts (mentioned above) and performed without direct reference to the deceased. One priest observed that *chi-wen* "frighten away ghosts and awaken the gods," but he could not, or would not, be more specific. Villagers confessed to me on numerous occasions that they could not comprehend a single word of the chanting. The priests, for their part, have a ready explanation: Only the dead are capable of understanding the language of the funeral chants.

Chanting is one of the esoteric skills by which priests maintain a monopoly over funeral ritual, and understandably, they do not openly share the secrets of their trade with clients or inquisitive outsiders. Most villagers accept funeral chanting as a necessary if incomprehensible part of the ritual and do not inquire into its meaning or significance. Not everyone, however, is impressed by the mystique of chanting. One local wit observed during a funeral in the late 1970s: "For all we know, the old crook could be calling out the names of the village dogs, but we would still have to pay him." More will be said about belief, skepticism, and the power of ritual, in the conclusion. Suffice it to note here that even our village cynic, who suspects the local priest of being a fraud, did not hesitate to perform under the direction of that same priest when the occasion called for it.

### Music and Musicians: Keeping Spirit and Corpse Together

Piping, like chanting and proper choreography, is part of the formal structure of Cantonese funerary ritual. Mourners, in other words, have no option but to pay for the services of at least one piper—although it is common to see other musicians performing at funerals as well. The pipe is called a *di da* in colloquial Cantonese, or *la-pa* in Mandarin;[31] made of brass, it has a

---

31. I am grateful to Bell Yung and J. Lawrence Witzleben, of the University of Pittsburgh's Music Department, for help in identifying this instrument. The classical term for the Cantonese funeral pipe, according to Yung, is (Mandarin) *so-no*.

wide bell and a reed mouthpiece. The *di da* produces a high-pitched, lyrical sound closely akin to that of the oboe or shawm. The message conveyed by a funeral pipe is unmistakable, and all who hear it are alerted that the dangers of death pollution are nearby. Nothing clears the village paths quicker than the sound of an approaching *di da*.

According to San Tin's priest, the piping attracts the spirit of the deceased, making certain that it does not wander away or get lost in the confusion following death. At several points during the sequence of rites the corpse must be moved from one ritual arena to another (e.g., from the house to a public plaza and, later, from the village to the grave). Piping is especially critical during these transitional states because, as the priest explained, the spirit is easily disoriented by physical movement and may lose contact with the corpse. If this should happen, it would be necessary to delay the funeral (a very inauspicious development) until the spirit is retrieved. The sounds of the *di da* usher the deceased—spirit and corpse together—through the entire sequence of rites, from the moment of death (if possible) to the burial.

The pipers themselves are usually outsiders (*wai-lai-jen*, i.e., not members of the local lineage) who live alone in isolated shacks on the fringe of the larger villages. Those I encountered during my research were elderly opium addicts; other than piping, they supported themselves by running errands for the local priest and by scavenging. Pipers are so closely associated with death that villagers ostracize them and exclude them from community activities. They are hired on an ad hoc basis by priests who also provide the instrument and the reeds. As might be expected, playing a funeral pipe does not require a great deal of skill; it is the *sound* of the instrument that matters, not the virtuosity of the performance. The appropriate range of notes can be learned in one or two afternoons of practice.

Piping is not the only form of music (or sound?) one hears at Cantonese funerals. The priest accompanies himself with small percussion instruments (cymbals, gongs, drums) during his chanting sessions. Percussion, in fact, is used by the priest to announce the most critical transitions in the ritual sequence (e.g., striking the coffin with scissors or beating a gong to summon household representatives). These acts are all part of the formal structure of rites.[32]

A recent innovation in funeral music, introduced in the 1930s, according to my informants, is the Western-style brass band. Every major coffin shop in the New Territories now has its own marching band for hire, at reduced prices for clients who buy coffins. Band members (all male) dress in white uniforms and wear white, military-style caps; they play tubas, trumpets,

---

32. On percussion as a means of marking ritual time, see Rodney Needham, "Percussion and Transition," *Man* 2 (1967): 606–614.

trombones, clarinets, saxophones, cymbals, and bass drums. The band I am most familiar with appeared at several San Tin funerals (1969–1970) and always played the same two tunes ("Onward Christian Soldiers" and "Rock of Ages").[33] The band escorts the chief mourner on his ritual rounds and performs during transitions in the ritual, always at the priest's direction. The piper and the bandsmen often play at the same time, thereby creating a great cacophony of clashing tunes. However, the piping always takes precedence because, at certain critical points in the ritual, the piper plays alone. The brass band is not an essential feature of the funerary ritual.

### Corpse Handlers: The Lowest of the Low

Villagers hire corpse handlers (ng jong lo) to perform the most polluting activities at Cantonese funerals, as was outlined earlier. Their duties begin when they deliver the coffin and place it, lid open, on sawhorses in a public plaza nearest the home of the deceased (the village lanes are too narrow to accommodate a funeral). They are then led to the grave site by a member of the village defense corps.[34] After digging the grave, the handlers return to the village and follow the sound of piping to the home of the deceased (no one needs to direct them), where they begin work without speaking to anyone in the household. One of their most important duties is to wash the corpse with water the chief mourner has "purchased" (mai-shui) from the spirit of a stream.[35] The corpse is then dressed in special clothing prepared specifically for this purpose. When preparations are completed and it is time for removal to the coffin, the handlers carry the corpse—with deliberate speed—through the narrow lanes to the plaza where the public phase of the funeral begins. The handlers then arrange the corpse in the coffin, wedging it tight with stacks of funeral paper to ensure that it cannot move. The transfer of the corpse is accompanied by the sounds of the di da, with the piper playing as loudly as possible. Villagers avert their eyes during the movement of the corpse and the packing of the coffin; similarly, only the chief mourner watches when the handlers hoist the coffin to remove it from the village. In

---

33. The Christian origin of these tunes has no significance to villagers. Among older residents, the emic category for brass-band tunes is "Western music," which subsumes everything from Bach to the Beatles.

34. Every powerful lineage has its own "self-defense corps" (tzu wei tui); corpsmen are responsible for patrolling and protecting the territory claimed by their lineage. Their duties include watching for the intrusion of unauthorized graves on lineage land and verifying the burial sites of lineage members.

35. The water-buying rite is a central element in Cantonese funerary ritual. The spirit, my informants explained, must be cleansed of death pollution before it can begin its journey through the underworld. For a discussion of this rite, see J. Watson, "Of Flesh and Bones," pp. 161–162, 170.

fact, most people never see the *ng jong lo* perform their most important tasks—thereby adding to the aura of malevolence and danger that surrounds them.

The local priest is the only resident who dares to speak to the corpse handlers, and he communicates with a series of abrupt commands. "I must be very careful around the *ng jong lo*," Ha Tsuen's priest said, "because they are like living ghosts." No one, including the priest, ever hands anything directly to the corpse handlers. Items that villagers must provide for dressing or arranging the corpse are placed on the floor or ground near the *ng jong lo*. Cups and bowls used by the handlers are broken and later buried outside the village. There are also restrictions on commensality with corpse handlers. As one resident of San Tin put it: "We would not want to eat at the same table with the *ng jong lo* because they are so filthy. If we go to Yuen Long [the nearby market town] to have tea and we recognize them in the tea house, we would not sit near them." Older informants were convinced that they could pick out a corpse handler in a crowd by the heavy smell of garlic on their breath. Villagers claimed that *ng jong lo* keep cloves of garlic in their mouths to disguise the smell of death that clings to them at all times.

The very utterance of *ng jong lo* is thought to be inauspicious, and many villagers avoid it altogether ("those who come with the coffin" is the preferred alternative). *Nahm mouh lo* and *ng jong lo* are both deeply imbedded in colloquial Cantonese, hence the characters used to represent these terms are rather arbitrary. Nonetheless, my efforts to collect the "correct" characters for *ng jong lo* produced some interesting insights into the villagers' perceptions of corpse handlers. All of the men I asked (women over forty were almost uniformly illiterate) agreed on the last two characters (*jong lo* "burial fellows"), but there was considerable debate regarding *ng*. The majority opted for a character that means "obstinate" or "perverse," whereas the most educated informant insisted that the correct character was another *ng*, a classical euphemism for death (used in a compound to represent "coroner"). The fact that most of my literate informants chose the character for "obstinate/perverse" is no doubt a reflection of the villagers' commonly held view that corpse handlers take perverse pleasure in their work. The *ng jong lo* do comport themselves in a manner that suggests (to me) extreme callousness and nonchalance. At several funerals, for instance, the corpse handlers completely ignored the proceedings and crouched on the sidelines, gambling among themselves. They are always quick to respond to the priest's orders (their livelihood depends on his continued patronage), but the *ng jong lo* never exhibit any interest in the mourners or in the circumstances surrounding the death.

Who are these stigmatized men? My information on the social origins and life-styles of *ng jong lo* is, of necessity, rather limited.[36] Their services are provided by coffin shops as part of the cost of purchasing a coffin. Two handlers accompany the coffin without extra cost, but additional helpers may be employed by wealthy households, particularly if an expensive (i.e., heavy) coffin has been purchased. Corpse handlers are paid by the day and are not under formal contract or binding obligation to the owners of coffin shops. Many are opium addicts who have no other means of support; others are aged drifters with no families or kin in the surrounding region. They live and eat together in the back rooms of coffin shops. There can be no doubt that, in the eyes of villagers and townspeople, these men represent the ultimate form of human degradation.

### Auxiliary Performers: Nuns, Acrobats, and Actors

The priest, piper, and corpse handlers together constitute what might be called the minimal ritual set because without their paid services a Cantonese funeral cannot be performed. More will be said about the implications of this in the conclusion. It is important to note, however, that there are many other kinds of specialists operating in the villages under study. These might be called auxiliary performers in the sense that their services are not deemed to be essential for the proper conduct of the rites, but they do add to the general atmosphere of activity and concern. Villagers gauge the wealth and status of a bereaved family by the number of specialists performing at the funerals of their senior members.

The auxiliaries most commonly seen at funerals are Buddhist nuns (*shih-ku*) who live in small convents scattered throughout the New Territories. Their primary role is to chant Buddhist sutras (*fo-ching*) that are said to have a calming effect on the spirit of the deceased. Nuns are particularly useful when circumstances require that a funeral be postponed until the following day.[37] In such cases, the corpse must be kept overnight in the home, and there is great concern that the spirit might become frightened or disoriented. The nuns chant to the spirit through the night and continue the following day, right up to the moment when the coffin is covered with earth. Like all other funeral specialists, nuns work under the direction of the local priest; they usually perform in sets of two, with as many as eight appearing at the rites of wealthy people.

36. I could not, of course, speak directly to the corpse handlers without alienating my village hosts, and it was too risky to attempt interviews in the Yuen Long coffin shops (news of this would have gotten back to the village). The following information was provided by priests and coffin-shop owners. It will be obvious, therefore, that there is a glaring gap in my analysis of funeral specialists, namely the corpse handlers' own views of their role in funeral ritual.

37. For example, when a villager dies in the afternoon it is generally too late to complete the rites before sundown (see note 29). Similarly, some days are designated by the Chinese lunar almanac as "bad funeral days," which means that the rites must be postponed.

Nuns only visit San Tin or Ha Tsuen during funerals, hence they are closely identified with death. Villagers do not like to interact with them, although they are spoken to on occasion and given direct orders. Buddhist nuns are powerful symbols of role inversion: They represent the antithesis of respectable Cantonese womanhood. Nuns live in the company of other women, which puts them beyond the everyday control of men; they have renounced marriage and are no longer considered members of their natal families. Their bald heads are presumed (by villagers) to reflect a condition of sterility, given that long, healthy hair is associated with fertility and women's sexuality in Cantonese society. At funerals, for instance, one of the most striking aspects of the ritual is the sight of young women (daughters-in-law of the deceased) rubbing their unbound hair on the coffin— thereby absorbing some of the vital life-forces which are released at death and considered essential for biological reproduction.[38] The fact that nuns expose themselves to death pollution but do not transform it into new life is the ultimate inversion, and perversion, of the feminine role.

At funerals, nuns are clearly distinguished from village women. Women wail (*han*) and sing funeral laments;[39] nuns chant sutras. Women avert their eyes during critical transitions in the ritual;[40] nuns do not. Women take whatever precautions they can to protect themselves against the debilitating effects of death pollution; nuns do not. And finally, women do not accompany the coffin to the grave; nuns do. Villagers often commented to me that nuns were "not real women." They are classed, along with monks (*ho-shang*),[41] as a separate gender—a special category of neutered outcastes who live on the margins of society.

Nuns are not the only auxiliaries to specialize in evening performances. Older villagers nostalgically recalled the antics of acrobats and actors (always male) who entertained the community during wakes held for wealthy people. This aspect of funerary ritual ceased during the 1950s and early 1960s, a period corresponding to the introduction of cinemas in the New Territories. According to my informants, the actors were usually apprentice *nahm mouh lo* from nearby market towns. The acrobats were itinerants

---

38. See J. Watson, "Of Flesh and Bones," pp. 172–180.

39. See C. Fred Blake, "Death and Abuse in Marriage Laments: The Curse of Chinese Brides," *Asian Folklore Studies* 37 (1978): 13–33; Chang Cheng-p'ing 張正平, *K'u-ko tzu-t'zu* 哭歌子詞 [Weeping songs] (Hong Kong: Yu Hua Publishing Society, 1969); and Elizabeth L. Johnson in chapter 6, this volume.

40. Among rural Cantonese, there are seven critical junctures in the funeral rites when villagers avert their eyes. They do this, informants maintain, because "we do not want to offend the spirit," which is thought to be angered or disoriented every time it goes through an important transition.

41. Buddhist monks also live in the New Territories, but they do not perform funeral rites for ordinary villagers.

who also performed at temple fairs and periodic markets. The repertoire of wake entertainment consisted of slapstick comedies, coarse jokes, juggling, pantomime, and acrobatic skits depicting the spirit's hazardous journey through the underworld (where it encounters devils and monsters portrayed by members of the troupe). Not surprisingly, these performances drew much larger audiences than the actual funerals. According to San Tin's priest, the primary purpose of the wake was to amuse the spirit and hold its attention, lest it disappear into the night. Ordinary villagers interpreted the wake as a form of entertainment to give the mourners temporary respite from their grief.

## Providers of Goods and Services

There are, in addition to those discussed above, many other types of specialists who earn a living from white affairs in Cantonese rural society. As was noted earlier, it is useful to draw a distinction between performers, who take an active part in the funeral rites, and providers of goods or services, who are not present during the ritual. Perhaps the best known of the latter category is the geomancer (*feng-shui hsien-sheng*). The ethnographic literature on China is replete with discussions of the geomancer's trade;[42] there is little need to belabor the topic here. The essential aspect of the geomancer's role in white affairs is that he never attends a funeral *in his capacity as a geomancer* (he may attend funerals of kin, but even this is rare). Furthermore, geomancers—among the rural Cantonese at least—never deal directly with the grave as such. Rather, they concern themselves primarily with the siting of tombs during the final stage of the three-tiered mortuary sequence (see below), long after the polluting flesh has disappeared from the bones. Geomancers may also earn money by choosing auspicious dates for funerals and lucky hours for important transitions in the ritual (e.g., "buying water," encoffinment, burial), but these services are not deemed to be polluting or tainted in any way.

Providers or makers of funeral goods—such as coffins, paper objects, mourning garb, incense and joss—are in a somewhat more ambiguous position, given that they are associated with the earlier, polluting stage of the mortuary sequence. The most important specialist in this category is the coffin-shop owner. Located in the larger market towns, coffin shops are the focus of many funeral activities. The owner not only supplies coffins, he also acts as contractor for those who need to hire priests, nuns, musicians, exhumers, and others.

Closely associated with coffin shops are purveyors of paper products used during funerals and end-of-mourning rites. The list of items sold in "paper

---

42. See Stephan Feuchtwang, *An Anthropological Analysis of Chinese Geomancy* (Vientiane, Laos: Vithagna, 1974), and Maurice Freedman, *Chinese Lineage and Society*, pp. 118–154.

shops" (*chih-p'u*) would fill several pages of this essay; everything from disposable mourning garb to "Hell Bank Notes" (printed in English) can be purchased there. Villagers avoid keeping such paper items in their homes overnight. It is considered bad luck to do so, which means that each funeral necessitates the purchase of a new package of worship materials (consisting of incense sticks, joss sticks, and stacks of gold paper that can be fashioned into tael-sized ingots). Enterprising hawkers sometimes make the rounds of villages on funeral days, selling these items to people who have not had time to visit paper shops. The paper itself is not considered to be contaminating until it has been exposed to death pollution (after which it is burned immediately). Nonetheless, villagers are wary of spending too much time in paper shops. Major transactions involving the purchase of mourning garb and funeral paraphernalia are often handled by intermediaries, notably older women who know which items to buy and where to find the best prices.

There are three other specializations that need to be mentioned, all of which deal with the mechanics of burial, exhumation, and entombment. When the coffin is lowered into the grave, a professional "settler" (my term, not the villagers') is consulted to make certain that the coffin is level and aligned with the directional flow of geomantic influences (*feng-shui*) from the hills nearby. The settler is not, in any sense, a recognized geomancer, but it is his duty to make the spirit feel "comfortable" in the grave. Since the grave is a temporary resting place until the flesh disappears, the settler is thought to be a carrier of pollution and is not granted a high degree of status. He is careful, however, not to actually touch the coffin; the *ng jong lo* move the heavy case while the settler manipulates an elaborate framework of plumb lines (it often takes an hour or more to settle a coffin in its grave). This service is provided by the coffin shop as part of the purchase price, but there are varying grades of settlers just as there are grades of coffins. The shopowner himself sometimes fills this role for wealthy clients. He sends an assistant (who often doubles as truck driver) to settle the coffin for ordinary funerals. It is essential to note that settlers are treated with a certain amount of respect and that they are never confused with *ng jong lo*.

Seven to ten years after burial, the coffin may be exhumed and the bones removed to a ceramic pot (*chin-t'a*), which is sometimes—but not always—reburied in a horseshoe-shaped tomb. A number of specialists are involved in this process. Professional exhumers open the grave, clean the bones, and arrange them in the *chin-t'a*, which is then moved to a new, pollution-free location. Although villagers often witness the exhumation, they rarely do any of the digging or cleansing of bones themselves. The exhumers are, by the nature of their work, considered to be polluted, but they are not ostracized as thoroughly as the *ng jong lo*.

The last stage in the mortuary sequence is the entombment of the bone pot. The final disposition of the bones is thought to affect future generations of descendants; accordingly, skilled masons are usually hired to construct the tomb. These craftsmen, like the geomancers who direct their work, are not affected by death pollution. Contracts for tomb construction are very lucrative, and those who engage in this specialized occupation are considered to be among the elite of rural workers.

## ANALYSIS AND CONCLUSIONS

### Pollution and the Reproduction of Stigma in Chinese Society

Social anthropologists are captives of a particular methodology: We see the world through the eyes of our most articulate, and willing, informants. They, in turn, have a limited perspective on their own society and wear the blinders of class, locality, gender, and personality. By now it should be obvious that the perspective presented in this chapter is largely conditioned by my discussions with ordinary villagers. For them, funerals are to be avoided if it is at all possible, and specialists who deal with death are either despised or feared. This essay, in other words, is not in any sense comparable to earlier studies that focus on the exegetical virtuosity of China's more sophisticated religious specialists.

Among rural Cantonese, the immediate period after death is perceived as a liminal state during which the deceased is transformed from a dangerous corpse into a settled ancestor. It is inevitable, therefore, that those who earn their living from death should be relegated to the margins of society. They have been drawn so thoroughly into the world of the dead that they exist in what amounts to a permanent state of liminality. From the perspective of ordinary villagers, the stigma associated with accepting payment for funeral services can never be erased.

But is this stigma transmitted to the next generation? Is there, in other words, a permanent category or caste of funeral specialists in Chinese society? The essential feature of Cantonese funeral specialists is that they do not reproduce themselves—biologically—to fill a specific set of occupational niches. Those who perform at funerals are all (save the priest) unmarried or

---

43. See, e.g., Louis Dumont, *Homo Hierarchicus: The Caste System and Its Implications* (Chicago: University of Chicago Press, 1970), and Jonathan P. Parry, *Caste and Kinship in Kangra* (London: Routledge & Kegan Paul, 1979).

44. See Ronald B. Inden and Ralph W. Nicholas, *Kinship in Bengali Culture* (Chicago: University of Chicago Press, 1977), pp. 62–66, 102–107, and McKim Marriott, "Hindu Transactions: Diversity Without Dualism," in *Transaction and Meaning: Directions in the Anthropology of Exchange and Symbolic Behavior,* ed. Bruce Kapferer (Philadelphia: Ishi, 1976), pp. 109–142.

45. This is *not* to say, however, that China was devoid of caste-like categories of people, tied to low status and demeaning occupations. In the Canton delta, for instance, there were (and still are to a limited extent) occupational niches that resemble lower subcastes in the local hierarchies of India. These occupations include tanning, oyster tending, lime smelting, reed gathering, and offshore fishing. Those who engage in such work are thought to be indelibly stigmatized, and the nearby farmers are careful to keep them at arm's length. From a compara-

inherently unmarriageable. The categories of performers I have outlined here are reproduced through purely social, rather than biological, means. One becomes a nun, a piper, or a corpse handler through self-selection or by dint of destitution. The low level of skills and literacy required makes it possible for virtually anyone to perform as a funeral specialist, given the need. The priests represent an interesting variation, given that the occupation of *nahm mouh lo* is sometimes passed in the patriline. But priests do not constitute a category of people who reproduce themselves (and thereby monopolize the priestly trade) through the practice of endogamy. Cantonese priests, like geomancers and coffin-shop owners, marry within their class—not their occupation.

In contrast to the Hindu system of occupational subcastes, therefore, a permanent hierarchy of ritual specialists did not emerge in China.[43] Although the Chinese and the Hindu notions of death pollution are similar in some respects, there are important differences. In China, the stigma of death pollution is ephemeral, and it is not passed to subsequent generations through a transfer of body substance, as is thought to be the case in parts of India.[44] In other words, among Chinese the corruption of death affects only those who deal with it directly, not their offspring (should they produce any). The sons and grandsons of Cantonese funeral priests, for instance, may choose to enter other occupations, and if they do so, they are treated like ordinary villagers. Those who elect to follow their fathers and become priests (a common practice, as was outlined earlier) are motivated primarily by financial considerations; there is nothing inevitable or preordained about their choice. Thus, whereas China and India both have hierarchies of specialists based on relative exposure to the corrupting influences of death, the crucial difference is that the Chinese hierarchy is reconstituted every generation with new recruits drawn from the lower strata of the general population. The reproduction of stigma in the Chinese ritual context is not linked to systems of marriage and inheritance; it is accomplished by informal, self-selective means.[45]

tive sociological perspective, the most interesting aspect of these stigmatized occupational categories is that the people involved tend to be endogamous, and in some regions of the delta they have reproduced themselves as clearly defined groups for at least three centuries (and perhaps longer).

There are, in other words, some interesting parallels between the Hindu system of subcastes and the hierarchy of fringe occupations in the Canton delta. The critical difference, however, is that a ritualized notion of pollution/purity is not the primary ideological component in Cantonese conceptions of stigma. Rather, it is the distinction between proper and improper production that matters most for the Cantonese. This distinction is not tied to any overriding religious or ritual system. A "proper" producer grows crops on land; other forms of production are considered to be marginal and potentially disruptive. This is obviously a different kind of disorder than that associated with death pollution. The chaotic influences released at death are cosmological and ephemeral; they are not rooted in the everyday concerns of work and production.

## Specialists and the Structure of Rites

The list of funeral specialists surveyed above is by no means exhaustive. Limitations of space do not permit a full discussion of all the occupational categories associated with white affairs in Cantonese rural society.[46] If one wished to extend the analysis to other parts of China, particularly major urban centers, the list would grow even longer. De Groot, in his study of Foochow, mentions professional washers of corpses, "hirelings" who dispose of clothing and death bedding, "footworkers" who specialize in carrying coffins, and coroners who earn a living by inspecting the corpses of those who die under unusual circumstances.[47] Twitchett and McDermott note that wealthy lineages sometimes maintained households of hereditary bondservants who served as tomb guardians.[48] Although work in this field is only beginning, it seems likely that a hierarchy of funeral specialists also operated within the confines of the imperial court, and that members of the emperor's household were involved—like all Chinese—in the management of death pollution (see e.g., Evelyn Rawski's discussion in chapter 10 of the conflict between the emperor's mourning obligations and his ritual duties).

Given the vast diversity of Chinese culture—with its class, ethnic, and regional differences—what can one say about the representativeness of the ethnographic data analyzed in this chapter? Does the description represent Chinese society? Cantonese subculture? Canton delta landed peasantry? Hsin-an county? Yuen Long marketing district? Or are we restricted to generalizations about the ritual life of two villages in the New Territories? Fieldworking anthropologists can seldom answer such questions to the satisfaction of historians, sociologists, and others who work at what they perceive to be the macro level of Chinese culture.

Studying the ritual structure of Chinese society is like peeling an onion. Viewed from a distance, there are certain aspects of funeral ritual that appear to be universal: The ritual bathing of the corpse may be one, and the preoccupation with controlling the spirit of the deceased is probably

46. In addition to the specialists discussed above, in the area under study there are professional "watchers," men who are paid to witness end-of-mourning rites (the spirit is said to be upset if no one outside the immediate family witnesses this part of the ritual). Other specialists include wreath makers, fortunetellers, scribes, condolence messengers (who deliver oral as well as written messages), and marchers (who carry flags or banners in funeral processions).

47. J. J. M. de Groot, *The Religious System of China*, Vol. 1 (Leiden: Brill, 1892), pp. 15, 68–69, 89, 97. On coroners, see also Sung Tz'u, *The Washing Away of Wrongs: Forensic Medicine in Thirteenth-Century China*, trans. Brian McKnight (Ann Arbor: University of Michigan Center for Chinese Studies, 1981).

48. Denis Twitchett, "Documents of Clan Administration: I, The Rules of Administration of the Charitable Estate of the Fan Clan," *Asia Major* 8 (1960–61): 19, and Joseph P. McDermott, "Bondservants in the T'ai-hu Basin During the Late Ming," *Journal of Asian Studies* 40 (1981): 686. See also Wolfram Eberhard, *Social Mobility in China* (Leiden: Brill, 1962), p. 18, on "tomb families" who were bound by hereditary obligation to guard imperial tombs.

another. However, as one cuts more deeply into the onion—descending the hierarchy of local systems, class structures, and subethnic divisions (Hakka vs. Cantonese vs. Hokkien vs. Ch'ao-chou, etc.)—it becomes difficult to determine which elements of ritual are variations on a universal theme and which constitute local, or subcultural, departures not reflected in other parts of the whole. Until we can agree that there is a uniform *structure* of Chinese funerary rites, questions of representativeness are essentially meaningless. (The same is no doubt true for discussions of Chinese marriage and marriage rites.)

I, for one, am convinced that there is an overarching ritual structure that distinguishes Chinese from non-Chinese rites. For instance, a close analysis of the *sequence* of Cantonese funeral rites reveals a remarkable similarity to the sequential structure described for other parts of China (see chapter 1). Naquin's survey of funeral rites in north China (chapter 3) strongly reinforces this impression of ritual uniformity.

Another feature of Chinese mortuary ritual that appears to be uniform, over time and space, is the reliance on specialists. Paid professionals always play a key role in the performance of Chinese funerary ritual; they are, in other words, part of the formal structure of rites. Based on a reading of ethnographic and historical sources, I would contend that it is not possible for people who conceive of themselves as "Chinese" to hold what amounts to a do-it-yourself funeral, with untrained and unpaid personnel performing the rites. Among the rural Cantonese a *minimal ritual set* of four specialists is essential for the proper conduct of a funeral. This set includes a priest, a piper, and two corpse handlers. Anyone, it was explained to me, who attempts to bury a family member without the services of these four specialists would be risking serious consequences, namely, the possibility of creating a dangerous ghost and disrupting the entire community. It is the proper performance of the rites which matters most to ordinary villagers (more on this below), and no one without the requisite training would dare to assume the role of priest.

Wealthy villagers, as was noted earlier, may hire up to a dozen specialists for the burial of parents or grandparents; funeral processions in nearby market towns sometimes include over a hundred paid attendants. It is not, however, the funerals of the wealthy that tell us much about the elemental structure of mortuary rites. We learn much more by observing the funerals of paupers, for it is here that the basic form is displayed, devoid of elaboration. I witnessed two funerals for destitute people who died without heirs during my research. In each case the central ancestral hall paid for the coffin, the ritual paraphernalia, and the services of a priest and a piper (the two corpse handlers are provided by the coffin shop). No one acted as chief mourner at these funerals, but the rites had to be conducted in proper (albeit truncated) form, lest the community be haunted by the angry spirits of the deceased. The goal of all funerals, including those for paupers, is a "peaceful burial" (an-tsang), which implies that the rites have been performed according to custom by paid professionals.

The ethnographic data presented in this chapter, combined with evidence drawn from other anthropological and historical sources, lead me to conclude that *performance* is the most critical aspect of Chinese funerary ritual. Among rural Cantonese, for instance, it is the proper conduct of the rites— in the prescribed sequence of movements and actions—that matters above all else. As was noted in chapter 1, the perceptions, beliefs, and emotions of the participants are largely irrelevant. In the emic view, shared by priests and villagers alike, the ritual is performed to control and transform the spirit of the deceased. Accordingly, Cantonese funeral rites are deemed to have an efficacy dissociated from the internal state or perceptions of those who perform the required acts.[49]

In this context, the role of qualified specialists is absolutely crucial. They must take charge of the performance and thereby create the desired state of ritual order which is thought to have a calming effect on the frightened and potentially dangerous spirit. The actions of the priest are particularly revealing: His performance at funerals is always balanced on the razor's edge of credibility, somewhere between mystery and farce. He knows there are many skeptics among his clients, and yet he strives to maintain a dignified atmosphere, appropriate for the task at hand. Mystification is important, but it is not absolutely essential; nor is it a key element in the structure of funeral rites. It matters not what participants believe so long as they execute the prescribed set of acts in the approved sequence.

49. On efficacy in Chinese ritual, see especially Emily Martin Ahern, "The Problem of Efficacy: Strong and Weak Illocutionary Acts," *Man* n.s. 14 (1979): 1–17.

# SIX

# Grieving for the Dead, Grieving for the Living: Funeral Laments of Hakka Women

*Elizabeth L. Johnson*

*We use the occasions of other people's funerals to release personal sorrows.—Lower Yangtze proverb, from Ying-shih Yü*

There are certain characteristic, unforgettable sounds associated with Chinese funerals: percussion instruments beating a solemn rhythm, the chanting of priests, the melodies of the *so-na*, and the lamenting of women. This lamenting, high pitched and penetrating, conveys an intense expression of grief. It is both weeping and singing, repeating melodic phrases that end with calls to the dead and sobs. At certain points in the funeral process several women may wail together, but there may be times when a single woman will lament, entering the site alone and singing in a solitary outpouring of grief.

The fact that women lament at funerals has been recorded by observers of Chinese society, in historical studies as well as contemporary ethnographies. The frequency of such references suggests that lamenting is a basic feature of funeral ritual and has been so for centuries, serving to announce the death as well as to display proper filial behavior.[1] In some studies it is not clear whether laments are expressed in words or are simply formless wailing. De Groot, for example, refers numerous times to wailing, but in only two instances gives the words that were sung. One lament that he presents is a "funeral dirge" that was written down eight hundred years ago. He also gives the words of the laments sung by both men and women in Amoy at the moment of death, describing them as "a melancholy concert of death dirges, a concatenation of complaints addressed to the dead, in accents of reproach for leaving them."[2]

The difficulties attendant on obtaining such information as the words to funeral laments are well known to ethnographers, but a small body of such

---

1. See James Watson's introductory essay to this volume.
2. J. J. M. de Groot, *The Religious System of China* (1892–1910 ed., reprinted Taipei: Ch'eng-wen, 1972), 1:10, 2:801.

information now exists. Fred Blake was able to obtain the words to bridal laments from a notebook kept by newly literate young Hakka women in the Sai Kung district of Hong Kong, but the notebook apparently did not include the texts of funeral laments. He states that both forms are called "weeping songs" (*k'u-ko*), which mourn the departure of a loved one.[3] Eugene Anderson's article on the songs of the Hong Kong boat people also notes the similarity of bridal and funeral laments, stating that both are "talking" songs expressing the singer's feelings at her impending marriage or upon the death of a relative. He recorded and analyzed a number of "salt water songs" and wedding songs, but was unable to study those sung at funerals. He states: "I heard funeral laments, but recording them at the funeral would hardly have been acceptable, and no one would sing them out of context because of the bad luck that would expectedly follow."[4] Chang Cheng-p'ing, working in the Yuen Long area of Hong Kong in the 1960s, recorded over a hundred Cantonese wedding and funeral laments and fragments over a period of two years. His methodology consisted in locating singers immediately after the occasions and asking them to record the laments he had heard, as well as transcribing some that had been written down.[5] More recently, Patrick Hase has described the place of funeral lamenting in one of the Sha Tin villages in the New Territories, and will publish some of the laments he recorded;[6] Chan Wing-hoi has just completed a thesis on the various forms of folk music, including laments, in the New Territories.[7]

My own earlier field notes, from my research in the Hakka village of Kwan Mun Hau in the New Territories of Hong Kong,[8] have a number of references to women's wailing at funerals, including two situations in which women singing alone were quite clearly singing laments with words. In one instance, a woman whose husband had taken a second wife, with whom

3. C. Fred Blake, "Death and Abuse in Chinese Marriage Laments: The Curse of Chinese Brides," *Asian Folklore Studies* 37, no. 1 (1978): 3–33.
4. Eugene Anderson, "Songs of the Hong Kong Boat People," *Chinoperl News* 5 (1975): 13–14.
5. Chang Cheng-p'ing 張正平, *K'u-ko tzu-tz'u* 苦歌子詞 [Weeping songs] (Hong Kong: Yu Hua Publishing Society, 1969), pp. 16–19.
6. Patrick Hase, "Observations at a Village Funeral," *From Village to City: Studies in the Traditional Roots of Hong Kong Society*, ed. David Faure, James Hayes, and Alan Birch (Hong Kong: University of Hong Kong Press, 1984), pp. 129–163, 254–260.
7. Chan Wing-hoi, "Traditional Folksongs in the Rural Life of Hong Kong," M. A. thesis, The Queen's University of Belfast (1985).
8. My research in Hong Kong in 1968–70 was sponsored by the Population Council; my postdoctoral research in 1975–76 was sponsored by the Joint Centre on Modern East Asia. I owe particular thanks to research assistant Jennifer Wun Chi-yee, and to Graham Johnson for his help with Chinese translations. Richard Yau Yan-wai, Connie Lam, and Helga Jacobson also provided assistance.

he had lived, appeared at his funeral and sang at his house, outside the mat-shed where the funeral was taking place, and by his coffin. At another funeral, while the body of the woman who had died was still laid out on the floor, surrounded by her mourning family, a closely related woman came in, knelt by the body, and suddenly began to sing alone.

Both singers seemed to me to be expressing an extraordinary intensity of grief, but I could not understand their words. In my notes I wondered what meaning the first woman was expressing; in the case of the second woman, whom I knew well, I could not help thinking of the tragic life she had had, and the many reasons she had to grieve. Because of the difficulty of understanding sung Chinese, and because the women were singing in Hakka, I could not understand them and certainly could not, in the context of a funeral, record their words.

During my second period of fieldwork, I was fortunate in having one particularly able informant, Mrs. Yau Chan Shek-ying. She was cooperative and interested in our work and had a remarkable memory. She was then in late middle age and so had participated fully in village life before its contemporary transformation. One of her particular contributions was her singing for me of various types of traditional songs and assisting me in recording and in interpreting them. She sang mountain songs, for which the Hakka are well known, which are melodic, ballad-like songs with themes of love. These were sung by women, sometimes in dialogue with men, when they were out working in groups together. Other types of songs include impromptu "flirting" or "teasing" (C *liu*) songs, musical battles between a man and a woman, and the laments sung by brides before their weddings and by women during funerals.[9] It is the group of funeral laments sung by her, some of her own composition and others she remembered from hearing other women sing, which form the body of material cited in this chapter.

It is difficult to understand why she might do something as seemingly inauspicious as singing funeral laments out of context. Perhaps the dangerous aspects of references to death were somehow outweighed by her desire to express feelings and describe situations that were deeply meaningful to her but are quite unknown to the younger generation, who live in such a different world. Certainly the events to which she referred had strong emotional significance for her, and it was important for her to have them heard and recorded. In addition, she took pleasure in singing other women's laments that were particularly well expressed, and took creative pride in those she had composed herself.

The laments, the mountain songs, and the flirting songs all derive from a

9. Texts of some of these songs are given in my article "Great-aunt Yeung: A Hakka Wage-Laborer," in *Lives: Chinese Working Woman*, ed. Mary Sheridan and Janet Salaff (Bloomington: Indiana University Press, 1984), pp. 76–91.

context which within the last thirty years has changed almost beyond recognition. The village where they were once sung is now in the middle of the industrial city of Tsuen Wan. Although it persists as a discrete village with its constituent lineages, its economic base has changed from agriculture to urban occupations and the renting out of urban property. Women are now educated, choose their own husbands, and work in the modern sector. Medical care is available, and the children they bear survive. The themes of these songs are not meaningful to young women, and they have not learned to sing them. In addition, the Hakka language is now being replaced by Cantonese, the dominant language of Hong Kong. Young people have little opportunity to hear Hakka, either spoken or sung. Finally, the mass media have had a devastating impact upon local folk culture.[10] Television now dominates every home. In the past, the radio sometimes featured mountain songs, but the dominant sounds in Hong Kong are now Western and Chinese popular music. Like other aspects of funeral ritual in increasingly Westernized urban Hong Kong, lamentation is fast disappearing. Chan Shek-ying said that older women may still remember how to lament but no longer have the strength to do so. Young women have never learned, which means, as she said, that when she dies there will be no one to lament her.

## WEEPING FOR A BROKEN FATE

Funeral laments are called "weeping" or "weeping for a broken fate" (C *haam* or C *haam laahn mehng*). The fate lamented is that of the deceased, to whom the laments are addressed, as many lines end with a call to him or her. To all appearances, laments are focused entirely on the life that has ended.

The laments recorded in Kwan Mun Hau, however, have a further focus. In lamenting the broken fate of a relative, the singer also laments her own fate. She does, indeed, "use the occasion of others' funerals to release personal sorrows." She may mourn the effect on her life of the death of her relative; this theme is also found in laments from other cultures. In addition, she may criticize others for their treatment of herself or the deceased and may even criticize the deceased for past slights or injustices. Virtually all the laments state her need for recognition and fair treatment, whether from living relatives, the deceased, or the hand of fate.

In their emphasis on the singer and her feelings of hurt and anger, the Kwan Mun Hau laments are strikingly similar to the Sai Kung Hakka bridal laments analyzed by Fred Blake.[11] The form of these laments, and of the

---

10. Eugene Anderson, "The Folksongs of the Hong Kong Boat People," *Asian Folklore and Social Life Monographs*, ed. Lou Tsu-k'uang, vol. 19 (Taipei: Chinese Association for Folklore, 1972), p. 29.
11. Blake, "Death and Abuse."

bridal lament fragments sung by Chan Shek-ying, is similar to that of the funeral laments. The correspondence is appropriate, for the themes of the bridal laments are the injustices inflicted upon the singer by her parents and the matchmaker, the impending loss of her family and lineage sisters, and the misery she anticipates at the hands of her husband's family. The analogy of the wedding process with death is made explicit: the bride describes herself as being prepared for death, and the wedding process as the crossing of the yellow river that is the boundary between this life and the next.[12] She appeals for justice, citing the valuable, unrecognized contributions she has made to her family. Her language is bitter and unrestrained, and she even curses the matchmaker and her future husband's family. Such lamenting can take place only within her parents' household and must cease halfway on the road to her new home, when the invisible boundary has been crossed.

Blake cites evidence to show that this style is not an isolated or a solely Hakka phenomenon, giving scattered examples of such lamentation from elsewhere. It may be that a range of types of laments exist, from those that express the singer's personal bitterness to those that are phrased in the more expected filial and submissive mode. Those laments collected in Cantonese villages in the New Territories by Chang Cheng-p'ing are thoroughly Confucian in their sentiments and very formal in language and presentation.[13] Similarly, C. K. Yang describes lamentation as being an expression of family solidarity, expressing praise, good wishes, and affection for the dead.[14] Anderson quotes a boat people's bride's "talking song," in which the bride expresses good wishes to her husband's family and sets out the contributions she will make to their household, stating her future worth to them.[15] This song shares with the Kwan Mun Hau and Sai Kung laments the fact that the singer is asserting her own merits, however. Chan Winghoi's data suggest that Cantonese laments are formal, learned (in the context of maidens' houses), and concerned with proper kinship behavior, whereas those of the Hakka and boat people are more improvised and personal.[16]

The scattered evidence that exists makes it clear that anthropologists are just beginning to study a very rich resource. Women's funeral and bridal laments, particularly those that are more individual and spontaneous, pro-

---

12. Blake, "Death and Abuse," esp. p. 22. Chan Shek-ying sang a fragment of a funeral lament for a mother or mother-in-law, which advised her as to how she should respond when questioned by the guardian of the bridge over the yellow river.

13. Chang Cheng-p'ing, *K'u-ko tzu-tz'u*. The formality of these laments, which include no Cantonese characters, may in part be an artifact of the difficulty of writing colloquial Cantonese. It may be that Chang found it necessary to write them in this literary form.

14. C. K. Yang, *Religion in Chinese Society* (Berkeley and Los Angeles: University of California Press, 1961), pp. 34–36.

15. Anderson, "Songs," pp. 58–62.

16. Chan Wing-hoi, "Traditional Folksongs," p. 95.

vide an opportunity to explore their thought systems and values.[17] Songs are peasant women's only form of literary expression, as they are almost universally illiterate. Hakka women, at least, have left us little other evidence of their ideas and sensibilities. They were unable to write their ideas and had no time for other forms of artistic creation beyond the weaving of ornamental bands for their clothes.[18] Like the fishing people of Hong Kong, they had little material outlet for their creative energies and so put them into song.[19]

There may be a further parallel between the fishing people of Hong Kong and Hakka peasant women. As Barbara Ward has stated so convincingly,[20] the boat people have existed in a particular relationship to the dominant Chinese ideological model. They were made aware of it through their interaction with members of the wider society and specifically through such media as the theatre, yet they were generally denied the opportunity to learn this model through the usual means, participation in the education system. They share in it to a considerable extent and acknowledge its validity, but they also know that their own cultural model is in some ways different through force of their life circumstances. Likewise, peasant women were denied access to education and formed impressions of the dominant ideology only through observation and through stories and the theater.

An important question raised by Emily Martin in chapter 7 in this volume is whether Chinese women may not have developed a perspective that is somewhat different from the dominant male ideology. Margery Wolf suggests that those social groups most significant to women are different from those important to men.[21] We now need, as Martin states, to begin to study this question, and to learn whether women see other aspects of life, including such fundamental processes as birth and death, differently than men see them. Women's laments provide us with an opportunity to see how women formulate their thoughts in times of personal crisis. Through their laments, women have given us their own statements about their lives in relation to the lives and deaths of others.

Another important question raised by the laments is why, within the con-

---

17. This can and must continue to be done through interviews, but in laments we can expect to find more fundamental statements of values, statements that are difficult to make in ordinary conversation. As Anderson states, "When words fail, song does not" ("Songs," p. 22).

18. Elizabeth Johnson, "Patterned Bands in the New Territories of Hong Kong," *Journal of the Royal Asiatic Society, Hong Kong Branch* 17 (1977): 81–91.

19. Eugene Anderson, "Songs," p. 10.

20. Barbara Ward, "Varieties of the Conscious Model: The Fishing People of South China," in *The Relevance of Models for Social Anthropology*, ed. Michael Banton (London: Tavistock Publications, 1965), pp. 113–137.

21. Margery Wolf, *Women and the Family in Rural Taiwan* (Stanford: Stanford University Press, 1972).

text of a wedding or a funeral, it is permitted for a woman to express herself publicly. In a village context, women are excluded from speaking in those arenas where formal decision-making takes place: village and lineage meetings. There is no formal public forum where they can speak. Older women are not reticent about expressing themselves informally, loudly, and colorfully; but this does not carry the weight of a formal presentation.

During a funeral in Kwan Mun Hau, priests and lineage leaders speak. Male mourners, however, keep silent. These men, who normally speak in public and control public activities, must be silent and relinquish all control to others. They also do not express themselves through lamentation, although they may weep silently. Women, who are normally expected to be quiet on formal occasions and who follow the orders of men, are permitted to express themselves, giving vent to their personal feelings. Such behavior contradicts Granet's statement about conduct at funerals, a statement deriving from written sources reflecting the dominant ideology: "Les gestes de la douleur ne peuvent être de simples réflexes physiologiques ou psychologiques, désordonés, individuels, spontanés; ils sont tout à la fois les rites de cérémonies réglées, les mots et les formules d'une langue systématisée."[22] Such a statement describes very well the behavior of male mourners in Kwan Mun Hau but is inappropriate to the behavior of women, who follow the prescribed form of lamentation but whose words are idiosyncratic and original. This discrepancy requires explanation.

## WOMEN'S LIVES

What one wants, I thought, . . . is a mass of information; at what age did she marry; how many children had she as a rule; what was her house like; had she a room to herself; did she do the cooking; would she be likely to have a servant?—Virginia Woolf, *A Room of One's Own*

We cannot begin analysis of the laments without at least briefly considering the social and material circumstances of the women's lives from which they derive. In talking with older women one receives the overwhelming impression that their primary concern, and that of others in relation to them, was work. Work for young Hakka women meant carrying heavy loads with a pole. They carried water for the household and manure for agriculture, cut grass on the mountains and carried it down in two large bundles for fuel, and carried food for pigs. Women cultivated rice and vegetables, and some were able to plow. From the late 1920s, Kwan Mun Hau women also worked for wages, carrying cement for dam construction and kerosene and steel for an oil company. They worked together in large,

22. Marcel Granet, *Études sociologiques sur la Chine* (Paris: Presses Universitaires de France, 1953), p. 236.

solidary groups, which gave them an important source of social support and companionship.[23]

In some households, women were solely responsible for subsistence agriculture and wage work if the men had migrated overseas or were opium addicts. Tsuen Wan was not only an impoverished area; it was traditionally also known as an area where the women often supported the men and where the women were hardened by work. This is reflected in one local saying:

> If your foot does not have claws
> You are not a Tsuen Wan daughter-in-law.
> If your foot does not have calluses
> You are not a Tsuen Wan grandmother.

During the 1930s, local work became available to men as well, however. Men not only farmed, fished, and cut firewood but also engaged in business and worked as laborers on the same sites as did the women.

Younger women worked outside the home from dawn to dusk, coming in only for meals. Despite their economic responsibilities, they were treated as inferiors, and meals left for them were the picked-over remains of the rest of the family's dinner. Because of the younger women's absence from home, older women performed the essential tasks of caring for the children and running the household. Children without a grandmother suffered from neglect.

Some older women had considerable economic power, which they gained in acting as managers of the household budget (C *dong ga*). This position was normally held by a senior and particularly able women, who received contributions from all the working members of the household and then decided how the money should be allocated. Kwan Mun Hau women were thus not only producers but also transactors of wealth.[24] By skimping on household expenditures and not reporting them accurately, household managers were able to build up their own individual resources. Women also had nest eggs of money and jewelry, which originated with their dowries and the gifts of money they received during their weddings.[25] This could be supplemented with money kept back from their earnings and used as the woman saw fit, perhaps to buy snacks or clothing for herself or to meet individual or household needs.

Although women had a considerable degree of control over money, the management and inheritance of property were almost solely the domain of

23. For further details, see my article, "Great-aunt Yeung" (n. 9 above).

24. Annette Weiner, *Women of Value, Men of Renown* (Austin: University of Texas Press, 1976), p. 117.

25. See also Myron Cohen, "A Case Study of Chinese Family Economy and Development," *Journal of Asian and African Studies* 3, no. 3–4 (July–October 1972): 167, 172.

men. Lineage trusts and family property were managed by men, who had the right to buy and sell land. This could be done by a woman for her minor sons, and widows sometimes retained the right to give their legal consent before their sons could sell land. In addition, there are occasional cases of women who bought land or houses with their earnings, but these were registered in their sons' names and eventually were transferred to them. In the absence of male heirs, women could inherit property, although such cases were rare. Inheritance of property entailed the obligation to worship the benefactor's soul and to be the principal mourner at his funeral.

Women are not entirely excluded from the worship of lineage ancestors, even though they are not permitted to make decisions concerning lineage property. Kwan Mun Hau has two lineages, each of which has two to three hundred people, including wives and daughters; a hall; and trusts of property. Offerings at the halls on the first and fifteenth of the month and at festivals are more likely to be made by women than men, except at New Year. Married women may participate in tomb worship only at the household level, however, and they rarely if ever do so. Lineage tomb worship is conducted entirely by men, although women may accompany them and assist in carrying offerings and clearing vegetation from the tombs.

At the time of her death, however, a women becomes a lineage ancestor. At the appropriate time,[26] her soul is incorporated into the single hall tablet through the ceremony of C *seuhng toi*, there to be worshipped when offerings are made to the founding ancestor and his descendants. Most commonly, she shares a tomb with her husband, but there are cases of women having separate tombs and geomantic prospects, including the wife of the founder of one of the lineages.

Until the 1940s no woman had any degree of choice in her primary marriage, which was arranged by both sets of parents through a matchmaker. Upon her wedding day she was transferred to her husband's family, and under no circumstances was she able to return to her natal family for anything more than brief visits. Although women left their natal families upon marriage, their relationship with their "outside family" (C *ngoih ga*) remained an important one. Young women went back for brief visits, with the permission of their mothers-in-law. They expected to be able to do this for a few days at New Year and on the occasions of weddings and funerals. When visiting, they carried gifts of food from their husbands' households and brought back reciprocal gifts upon their return. Women were welcomed by their mothers on these visits, fed well, and offered a shoulder to cry on. The members of her *ngoih ga* were seen as the allies of a young woman who had been recently married. They did not offer substantial help if she were mis-

---

26. This ceremony may not be held for junior household members while senior members are still living.

treated, but at least offered moral support. To be without a *ngoih ga* was seen as a serious liability.

The maintenance of affinal relations was seen very much as women's business, and there was a minimum of contact between affinally related families. A woman's husband rarely accompanied her on visits to her natal family. Relations between affines were characterized by distance.[27]

## FORMS OF THE LAMENTS

Indeed, I would venture to guess that Anon, who wrote so many poems without signing them, was often a woman.—Virginia Woolf, *A Room of One's Own*

The musical forms of the Kwan Mun Hau bridal and funeral laments are all similar and consist of a single melodic line, which is repeated with variations, the variations being determined by the demands of the text. Extra notes or melodic motifs are added to the basic line of four to six syllables in order to accommodate additional words. The maximum length of line is about twelve syllables. The melody is not developed beyond the single line but is simply repeated. Each lament has a basic motif tied to certain structural notes. The pitches of some notes are flexible, and musical ornament may be added, giving variety to the otherwise repetitious melodies. According to ethnomusicologist Alan Thrasher,[28] the melodies are narrative rather than lyric in form, and the intervals are not characteristic of Han Chinese music, but instead resemble Southeast Asian or Taiwan aboriginal melodies. A somewhat simplified sample line, omitting sliding pitches and musical ornamentation, is the following.

The laments are like boat people's songs in that they are sung by solo or antiphonal voices,[29] without harmony or the accompaniment of musical instruments. Kwan Mun Hau mountain songs and "flirting" songs were also sung in this form whether by women alone or by a man and woman in dialogue. Singing was not done to the accompaniment of musical instruments, and percussion instruments were and are played only by men, in the context of lineage and life-crisis ritual.

The funeral laments recorded in Kwan Mun Hau are expressed in free

---

27. Rubié Watson describes a similar pattern in the marriages of peasant women into Ha Tsuen village, in "Class Differences and Affinal Relations in South China," *Man* n.s., 16 (1981): 592–615.

28. Dr. Alan Thrasher, personal communication.

29. Eugene Anderson, "The Folksongs of the Hong Kong Boat People," p. 24.

verse and consist of lines that are flexible in length and expressed in language more refined than ordinary speech, although, unlike the laments recorded by Chang, it is not highly formal or classical. Most lines end with a call to the deceased, who is addressed by a kinship term. Mothers are addressed as "beloved" (C *oi*);[30] mothers-in-law as *oi* or "grandmother" (C *poh*), following the singer's children's form of address. Other relatives, according to the examples available, appear to be called by their usual kinship terms. The person addressed is rarely called "you," but instead is respectfully addressed by a kin term. The laments do not include elegiac passages, however, and their purpose does not appear to have been to praise the deceased. At best the deceased is warmly remembered for his or her kindness to the singer.

With reference to herself, in contrast, the singer uses the personal pronoun or highly derogatory, belittling terms, such as "dead-fated person" (C *sei mehng*) or "stinking fate person" (C *chau mehng*). She is, in effect, cursing herself.[31] This self-deprecation is done as a form of reversal, in contradiction to the fact that a basic theme of the laments is the assertion of the singer's rights and merits.

The Sai Kung bridal laments are enriched with striking images, as are the "salt water songs" recorded by Anderson and the Kwan Mun Hau mountain songs. The funeral laments recorded do not share this characteristic. Some images and analogies are used, but they are not as rich or evocative as those in other forms of song.

An important literary device used is that of contrast. Comparisons are made between situations, the singer and another person, or the past and present, before and after the bereavement. For example, Chan Shek-ying lamented for her older brother:

> When other people's aunts and daughters went to visit my older brother
> They were treated well.
> When I went to my brother's door
> I was treated like a distant relative.
> I thought that I would die first
> And my brother would attend my funeral.
> Who could have known that he would die first
> And that I would lament him?

A woman might lament her husband's sister:

> Today I have come to cry for my husband's sister.
> When I came for festivals my husband's sister laughed "ha ha."
> Tonight a white paper has told me that my husband's sister has passed away.
> I came to my husband's sister's door and she was not here.

30. The marriage laments analyzed by Blake include calls to the singer's mother, addressed with the same term. "Death and Abuse," p. 18.

31. See also ibid., p. 24.

This device is also an important feature of Greek funeral laments,[32] and it is common in the bridal laments recorded in Kwan Mun Hau and Sai Kung.[33] The following is a Kwan Mun Hau example:

> From the time I was small I never wore a set of new clothes.
> Today I am wearing a set of new clothes.
> I am like grass being spread in the sun to dry.

The laments sung by Chan Shek-ying had several different origins. Some are those she had created herself for the occasions of the deaths of relatives. Except for the use of certain stock phrases, these appear to be quite original and particular to her circumstances. Others, also particular to individual singers, are those she had heard sung by other people and had remembered because of the impression they had made on her. The third group are those that were not tied to any particular person or context but instead describe situations common to the experience of many women. I suspect that lines of the last type formed part of the repertoire of other singers and were used in composing their own laments as appropriate.

There was no formal system for teaching funeral laments in Kwan Mun Hau, although bridal laments were taught by older women. As the great majority of women were illiterate, the words were not written down. It appears that learning occurred primarily through hearing laments in the context of funerals. Well-expressed laments made a deep impression on the women who heard them; they remembered them, mulled them over, and reviewed them for a long time afterwards. Chan Shek-ying still remembered a very moving lament that she had heard when she was only fourteen years old.

Women not only remembered laments after they had been sung; they also thought about and planned them in advance. Two of the laments sung by Chan Shek-ying had been prepared by her for the anticipated deaths of her mother-in-law and great-aunt. She expressed regret that she had been hospitalized at the time of her mother-in-law's death and so had been unable to sing her prepared lament. She was also capable of composing laments almost spontaneously. When her older brother, whom she had expected to outlive her, died recently, she sang a long lament for him within a few hours of hearing of his death.

Laments are always sung by a woman alone; several women may sing at the same time, but each will be following her own lament. Some women may not be able to take the initiative in lamenting but will join if another

---

32. Margaret Alexiou, *The Ritual Lament in Greek Tradition* (Cambridge: Cambridge University Press, 1974), pp. 165–178.
33. Blake, "Death and Abuse."

leads (C *daai tauh*). If no woman takes the initiative, and all those present are shy, then lamentation may not take place. When two or more women are lamenting, they may alternate so that the singing takes the form of a dialogue. This is the usual form of mountain songs and a prerequisite of "flirting" songs. Greek laments also may take this form, consisting of antiphonal singing between individuals or groups of women, sometimes representing dialogues between the living and the deceased.[34] When lamenting must be sustained over long periods, this device eases the burden on individual singers. Antiphonal singing on the Greek island of Mani is seen as a contest between the singers, and the better singers may be congratulated by the family of the deceased.[35]

Likewise, in Kwan Mun Hau, dialogue singing sometimes took competitive form.[36] The competitive element derived, however, not from the quality of the music but rather from the singers' verbal skill. Such lamenting was done spontaneously, and not every woman had the necessary talent. These laments were not friendly competitions. Women used them as opportunities to express resentments and grievances against other relatives, either other singers or their families, who would be defended by the singers. Sharp musical arguments could result, as one woman rebutted (C *bok*) the other. A woman without the ability to lament in this way lost the advantage. Like the "flirting" dialogues, they convey messages that could not be expressed in ordinary speech, although they did sometimes degenerate into purely verbal arguments. The following general example of a dialogue lament upon the death of an older woman was sung by Chan Shek-ying:

| | |
|---|---|
| Daughter: | You ate well, you spent well. |
| | You treated my mother as a beggar. |
| | She had no good clothing to wear. |
| | She had no good meals to eat. |
| Daughter-in-law: | Every meal I bought fish and meat for your mother to eat. |
| | My mother-in-law didn't eat them. |
| Daughter: | You were so kind, bringing fish and meat for my mother to eat. |
| | Whenever I came to visit her you didn't look at her. |
| | You never appeared pleased to see me. |
| | You didn't pour tea for me. |

If older women neighbors had a good relationship with the daughter-in-law, they might answer the daughter thus:

34. Alexiou, *Ritual Lament*, pp. 40–41, 146–150.
35. Ibid., p. 40.
36. Anderson describes song contests among Hong Kong boat people in "The Folksongs of the Hong Kong Boat People," p. 25.

You shouldn't speak like that to your brother's wife.
She treated your mother well.
Every meal she bought fish and meat for your mother to
    eat.
Your mother didn't eat it.

Daughter:          How do you know this?
                   You only live next door; how could you know this?[37]

Although a lamenting woman may have provoked rebuttal from other women, a response from those who heard her does not necessarily seem to have been expected. Lamentation is a solitary act, and gratification seems to come less from the response of listeners than from the simple act of expressing grief. In the situations I observed, women lamented alone, entering the scene alone and leaving afterwards. Those people who were in close attendance around the body, women and the principal mourners, heard them, but others did not stop their conversation or activities to listen. The laments are explicitly addressed only to the deceased. According to Chan Shek-ying, those male relatives who are close to the woman and know her suffering may weep when they hear her; sympathetic *ngoih ga* women may speak to express their support and reassurance. Most men appear to pay little attention.

What is the effect of the laments on the person for whom the funeral is being conducted? Are they believed to be efficacious for the well-being of the soul? If so, this would help to explain their important place in funeral ritual.[38] Hase states that lamenting is one of the basic features of even a minimal funeral,[39] and de Groot's numerous references to wailing suggest that lamenting (apparently without words) formed an essential part of both ancient and contemporary (nineteenth-century) funerals.[40] On the other hand, Blake, in analyzing bridal laments, says that "these laments were never obligatory to begin with; they are not part of the formal rites. They are, on the contrary, the licensed expression of the bride—in some sense they constitute her personal commentary on the formal rites."[41]

37. Croker quotes an Irish lament with a similar theme, in which a woman brags that her father was able to provide her daily with fresh fish, large potatoes, honey, butter, and whey. Her sister-in-law rebuts her, saying that the potatoes were only those fed to pigs, and the fish were limpets. T. Crofton Croker, "The Keen of the South of Ireland," *Early English Poetry, Ballads, and Popular Literature of the Middle Ages*, vol. 13, The Percy Society (London: T. Richards, 1844), p. 97.

38. Alexiou (*Ritual Lament*, pp. 44, 165) states that the purposes of Greek lamentation are to pay public tribute to the dead and to assuage the potential anger of the soul.

39. Hase, "Observations," p. 161.

40. De Groot, *The Religious System*.

41. Blake, "Death and Abuse," pp. 16–17. Anderson, on the other hand, states that the bridal laments he recorded, with their filial and auspicious tone, were believed to have actual power to bring benefits. "Folksongs of the Hong Kong Boat People," p. 20.

My own information is not clear on this point. Chan Shek-ying stated that lamenting is not essential, and that if no one knows how to lament, it is not done. She expressed no apparent concern for the fate of an unlamented soul. This may be a recent development, however, a pragmatic recognition of the fact that young women no longer know how to lament. Other information she gave me suggests that belief in the importance of lamentation for the fate of the soul may only now be changing, and that some people may still consider it necessary. One of her neighbors, a nearly blind elderly woman who had recently died, had asked that a daughter be adopted to lament her "so that her eyes might be opened in the underworld." Chan also said that her mother-in-law's generation believed that it was essential that souls had daughters to lament them, because the funeral rites would not be efficacious without these laments.[42] Even now daughters are adopted to participate in funerals, although they would not likely be able to lament. She remembered being taken as a child to a funeral in which a woman had been adopted after the death of her "mother." From then on the woman was affiliated to two families, as men are who continue two lines. She was compensated with three *mou* of fields and a cow. Chan Shek-ying heard the first stanzas of her lament:

> When she was alive I did not lament her.
> Mother did not see me lament as a daughter.
> Now my mother has died.
> I was carrying grass down the mountain.
> At the side of the road my brother asked me to be her daughter and lament.
> So I came to lament.

Some laments are tied to specific points in the funeral ritual, and Chang's analysis suggests that while some Cantonese laments are merely descriptive of the particular rite, others function for the benefit of the soul, facilitating its passage into the underworld. One lament he cites is sung at the bridge-crossing rite, for example, and functions to assist the soul of the deceased in crossing the bridge into the underworld. Other laments offer comfort to the deceased, urging him, for example, not to be afraid as he is put into his coffin.[43] Only one of the recorded Kwan Mun Hau laments is related to a particular rite. This lament, to be sung by a daughter-in-law at the water-buying ceremony, offers reassurance and advice to the deceased:

> Every day my mother-in-law washed her face in the middle of the room.
> Today I buy water at the river(?) to wash her face.
> When your face is washed clean you will see the King of Hell.
> Tell him the truth of your origins and why you died.

---

42. Chan Wing-hoi states that his Hakka informants asserted that a daughter's lament is efficacious in helping the deceased through the underworld ("Traditional Folksongs," p. 87).

43. Chang Cheng-p'ing, *K'u-ko tzu-tz'u*, pp. 28–30.

After you have died, do not be afraid.
After you tell your history you will have nothing to regret.
You have a lot of descendants, so you should be satisfied.
At night during supper, your grandchildren don't see your bowl.
When your grandchildren wake up, they don't see grandmother in her
    room washing her face.
Wish your grandchildren peace and good fortune.
Wish peace to the village people who are paying their respects.

## THEMES OF THE LAMENTS

According to Chan Shek-ying, even a woman who was barely able to lament
might sing a few lines on the death of her mother-in-law:

You are now at peace.
In the underworld you have your husband and son.
You are now in the underworld.
You need not bother about any affairs.
You can give up the affairs of this world.
You need not worry about them.
Please don't touch your grandchildren with your hands,
Just look at them.
When you come at night, please come silently;
When you go at night, please go silently.

In these lines, the daughter-in-law is stating that her mother-in-law is now in
a different life. The separateness of this new life is emphasized, as is the fact
that the deceased is urged to maintain this separation and to take care when
she crosses the boundary, returning to see her still-living family, so that she
should not do harm to them.

The laments often begin in this way, stating the fact that the mourned
one is dead, and communicating the impact of this fact upon the singer.

| | |
|---|---|
| Daughter: | During festivals when I came, my mother was here. |
| | During festivals when I came, my mother was here to receive me. |
| | During festivals if I come I will only see my mother's tablet. |
| Daughter-in-law: | Every morning when I open the door |
| | My son cannot call his grandmother. |
| | The grandson and baby now do not have a grandmother, |
| | And cannot call her. |
| | At dinner I put away her bowl. |
| | At dinner I put out one less pair of chopsticks. |

These lines may include statements or wishes that the deceased should now
be at peace, and descriptions of his or her good fortune and prosperity. They
sometimes go on to state that if he had lived longer, his situation could have

been even better, and his descendants could have heaped even more wealth upon him. Chan Shek-ying said that in beginning a lament for her mother-in-law she should wish her well first (C *giu keuih hou sin*).

> Tonight you are very much at peace.
> Now you have a lot of sons and grandsons,
> And gold and silver up to your eyes.
> Now you are in the underworld and can see nothing.
> Now I have raised your grandchildren, but you have passed away.
> If you could have lived two or three more years
> Your grandchildren would have earned money and given it to you to spend.
> A few years ago I was still very poor.
> Now your oldest grandchild can earn money but you have passed away.
> If you could have lived eight or ten more years
> You could have rested at ease.
> If I had money, I could get a wife for your grandson.
> Then you would have great-grandchildren and you would laugh "ha ha."

One of the persistent themes of the laments is the change in social relationships that follows from a death. After a death has occurred, the survivors may interact differently, for an important tie which had linked them is gone. When a married-out woman's mother dies, she must remind her brothers of their new responsibility:

> Today we have lost our parents.
> Do not let others look down on you.
> You two brothers must strive to be restrained.
> If you do not, the uncles and nephews will look down on you.
> Your wives should not be talked about by others.
> You brothers should not be ridiculed by the uncles and nephews.

The death of her *ngoih ga* relatives presents a crisis for a married-out woman because each loss means she has less emotional support available to her. The worst is the loss of her mother. While her mother is still living she can expect a warm reception at her natal home. Her brothers and their wives may not pay special attention to her after her mother's death.

> When I came at festivals and special occasions
> My mother greeted and caressed me.
> Today I have lost my mother.
> Who came to greet and caress this dead-fated person.

When she sang thus, her great-aunts and other relatives might weep, and say that her brothers' wives would receive her just as her mother had, but she would reject this reassurance.

> My sister-in-law acting on behalf of my mother
> Is not like my real mother.
> Whenever I had any problem
> My mother would ask about me.

As the older *ngoih ga* relatives die communication with her natal family becomes less and less warm and frequent. The laments she sings for herself as a bride are only the first in a series marking the progressive stages of separation of the woman from her natal home. Chan Shek-ying's relationships with these relatives were particularly meaningful, as she had lost contact with them when she was a "little daughter-in-law",[44] and had only found them again after some years. She was angry when she was not invited to the funeral of her father's sister, who lived in Sha Tin, and when invited to the ceremony of *seuhng toi*, which may conclude the funeral and in which the soul of the deceased is installed in the single tablet in the ancestral hall, she sang as follows:

> My aunt had only this one niece
> Who went to visit her.
> Now my aunt has died,
> So there is no more relationship with her family.

(The aunt's daughters-in-law cried: "Come back, come back!")

> I had no parents when I was small.
> I could not imagine that I could find my aunt.
> We communicated for eight or ten years.
> Now the connection of the road to Sha Tin has been broken.

(The aunt's daughters said: "Please come!")

As this lament implies, the reorganization of relationships following a death can also be expressed in criticism of the survivors. In this context, family conflicts can be brought out in the open, long-standing resentments and grievances can be expressed, and criticisms voiced.[45] Women may respond to the singer if they are able, defending themselves against criticism. The result of such a dialogue might be that the relationship is no longer maintained.

A married-out daughter might accuse her parents' daughter-in-law of bringing bad fortune into the household and causing their deaths.

---

44. A little daughter-in-law was transferred to her future husband's family when she was still a child. She was raised by that family as their adopted daughter and was married to the son who had been designated as her husband when she was mature. This form of marriage was more economical and may have facilitated the daughter-in-law's assimilation into her husband's household. Arthur and Margery Wolf have written extensively on this subject.

45. An Irish lament by a woman for her brother, quoted by Croker ("The Keen," pp. 87–90), criticizes his wife for neglecting him and causing his death and then sitting dry-eyed at his funeral:

> My darling one—my hope that's gone—you had the cruel mark
> Of a bad wife—who lived in strife—she left you in the dark;
> In summer dry, in winter cold, without a Sunday dress,
> And fasting long—with patient song—your sorrow to express.

Daughter:           My sister-in-law does not have good fortune.
                    My sister-in-law has been here for less than a year.
                    My sister-in-law, I don't know whether you don't have
                        fortune
                    Or whether my father didn't have fortune.
                    My parents took this daughter-in-law
                    To enjoy the fortune of the family.

Daughter-in-law:    I didn't come to cheat your father.
                    The matchmaker came and talked and saw me before tak-
                        ing me.
                    Your father naturally had a short life.
                    How can you complain about me?

Daughter:           As long as my father had not taken a daughter-in-law
                    He had no troubles at all.
                    He had no headaches or any other problems.
                    He experienced none of these problems.

The survivors might also be criticized for their poor care of the deceased. Chan Shek-ying accused her brother-in-law's family of neglecting her mother-in-law:

> Other people are wealthy, but regarded you as a beggar.
> Although this dead-fated person was poor, I still tried to support you.
> I looked after you when you were sick.
> Others are wealthy but regarded you as a leper.

Furthermore, the occasion of a death might be used to criticize relatives for their treatment of the singer. Two of the lengthy laments sung by Chan Shek-ying include this theme. In the lament she had prepared for the anticipated death of her great-aunt, she accused her brother, who had not spoken to her for twelve years, of neglecting her. She said: "I will curse my brother. When my great-aunt dies, I will use the occasion to curse my brother."

> My younger brother is intelligent and is in a good situation.
> Although I am a relative, I am treated like a stranger.
> Even if I were a stepchild, there would be a relationship.
> I am blood relative.
> But there seems to be no relationship.

In the lament she had planned for her mother-in-law she criticized her husband's family for their unfair division of the family property. She said that had she been able to sing this lament they couldn't have responded to her; they wouldn't have dared to respond to her. If they had responded, she would have answered them thus:

> I had a lot of property,
> But it was taken by that thief.
> Those thieves swallowed my property.

The thief swallowed it,
And now can enjoy using it.
Now I have only very little property.

Even grievances the singer had with respect to the deceased could be stated in a lament.[46] One frequently occurring theme is that of a mother-in-law favoring her older daughter-in-law, who is stronger and able to do more work. Chan Shek-ying had planned to sing for her mother-in-law:

In the past you loved only your older daughter-in-law.
You just regarded me as a blade of grass.
My parents died when I was very small.
I was brought up by you.
You cared for me and raised me.
Now your other daughter-in-law is bad.
But you didn't treat me well.
In the past you raised me as your daughter.
Today you know I am not a blade of grass
But that I am a good daughter-in-law.

These general lines might be sung by a woman in such a situation:

My mother-in-law cared about her older daughter-in-law.
I was smaller; I couldn't work as much.
My mother-in-law mistreated this struggling person.
My mother-in-law had only two cups; she refused to recognize a person.
My mother-in-law cared only for her older daughter-in-law.
It is only now she realizes that I am also good.

Sometimes the singer recalls hurtful remarks or actions by the deceased which have continued to fester. One woman's lament recalled her father-in-law's accusation that she was lazy, quoting his words: "My father-in-law scolded me: 'In three days she does not gather one inch of fuel!'" Another woman described in her lament an incident in which her mother-in-law had spurned a bun she had bought for her. Chan Shek-ying recalled that her brother had not inquired about her health when she was ill. A theme lacking in the Kwan Mun Hau laments, however, is that of reproach to the dead for dying and leaving the singer alone or without means of support. Such laments are found in Russian and Greek cultures.[47] In Chinese culture, it is inappropriate to mourn a junior; thus a woman could not publicly lament

46. In only one of the laments does the singer criticize a living household member, however, and he was her husband, who lived with another wife. It appears that criticism of relatives with whom the singer lives is avoided.

47. Alexiou, *Ritual Lament*, pp. 43, 163–164. H. Munro Chadwick and N. Kershaw Chadwick, *The Growth of Literature*, vol. 2 (Cambridge: Cambridge University Press, 1936), p. 230.

the death of a son or daughter. It happens that the laments recorded do not include any for the singer's husband, except for one which Chan Shek-ying said they had heard sung by a Cantonese woman, and greatly admired:

> My husband, you have died.
> Our son is small, my husband.
> Ai ya! husband, you are at peace.
> I am miserable.
> Our son is small, my husband;
> Our daughter is small.
> What do you think will become of me, my husband?

Finally, in some of the laments the singer is not blaming others as much as lamenting her own hard fate. Conditions and events such as poverty and the death of children may be beyond anyone's control. A woman married into a poor household might sing thus upon the death of her mother:

> My mother listened to others
> And married out this dead-fate, struggling girl.
> I am so poor that I carry loads
> Until my shoulders look like rough granite.
> If I had been married better
> I would not be so wretched now.
> My feet are full of holes
> Like a rice-drying basket.

In the following lament, which Chan Shek-ying heard when she was fourteen years old, a woman lamented the death of her father's sister's husband (C *daaih gu jeuhng*) by comparing her fate with his. Five of her six children had died, and her husband had taken another wife, neglecting her and giving her only forty dollars a month.

> My *daaih gu jeuhng*
> You are at peace.
> I have come today.
> I am calling *daaih gu jeuhng*.
> I have come to call *daaih gu jeuhng*.
> My *daaih gu jeuhng*, you are at peace today, *daaih gu jeuhng*.
> You have a son and everything is fine.
> My *daaih gu jeuhng* could never eat all his food,
> Could never spend all his money.
> I met *daaih gu jeuhng* at the head of the street.
> He asked me whether I was well.
> How could I be well? I have only forty dollars a month.
> If I were like other people I would have a good fate.
> I should have children pulling at my blouse,
> Children clinging to my legs.

If my children were still alive,
I would have three pulling at my clothes on the right,
Three pulling at my clothes on the left.
My *daaih gu jeuhng* also had a second wife.
He as a husband treated them both equally.
Towards the second he showed no special favor.

Chan Shek-ying explained: "If she had had a good fate, she would have had lots of children, very cute, clinging to her clothes and her legs. Her own fate was bad. How would you feel, seeing others with lots of children? And so she lamented, crying from the pent-up bitterness (C *gik hei haam*)."

## DEATH, GRIEF, AND CONFLICT

Women's laments in Kwan Mun Hau reveal the sources of their bitterness and in so doing suggest a view of life which in some respects differs from that held by men. Many of the experiences and social relationships that are significant to women are unimportant to men. As a result, certain differences in their perspectives become evident.

The bridal laments suggest a fundamental difference. A man's life is characterized by continuity in his social relations. Marriage for him means the addition of a woman to his family and his bed. To a woman, marriage, until recently, meant a profound break with all that she knew, a break comparable to death as an entrance into the unknown. It is no wonder that a young woman undergoing this transition was said to have (C) *saat hei*, "violent breaths," as does an unsettled corpse.[48] Only when she was safely within the door of her new home did this power, which can do harm to children and pregnant women, disappear. There, although she still represented the power of her potential fertility, she could be forced into the mold of her new family. The bridal laments express dread at having to make such a formidable transition and to make it alone. A Kwan Mun Hau man need never have been alone, unless he was forced by circumstances to emigrate or subjected to the ultimate punishment, ostracism from the lineage. Throughout life he was and is surrounded by his fellow lineage members and the men of the other lineage, with whom he enjoys brotherly relations. A share of the family property is his to use, although he has less individual property than does a woman.[49] A Kwan Mun Hau bride arrived with nothing but her dowry, her fertility, and her physical and emotional strength, with which to build a new life. Her fertility was particularly important. It was through her

48. See J. L. Watson, chapter 5 in this volume.
49. Men serve only as trustees for property owned by the household, and are entitled only to the use of their shares, being able to buy and sell property only by mutual agreement. See also Cohen, "A Case Study," pp. 170, 173.

children that she was able to build a strong personal base for herself.[50] The lament for *daaih gu jeuhng* expresses the tragic feelings of a woman who has been unable to bear surviving sons. This tragedy had for her no satisfactory resolution, whereas her husband was able to take another wife, who he hoped would produce the sons he also needed.

The funeral laments demonstrate repeatedly that, besides her children, those family relationships a woman most deeply values are those with her natal family. The loss of her mother and the aunts who loved her are serious blows, and if members of her natal family treat her with anything less than the consideration she feels she deserves, she is deeply hurt. Being asked after and visited when sick are very important to her.

Finally, the laments reflect a belief in equality and in fair treatment which is not strong in the dominant ideology, although it is a common theme in popular literature. One would expect that a woman's experiences as a bride, having been at the bottom of the family hierarchy, would make her particularly sensitive to any injustice. The favoring of one daughter-in-law or one wife over herself is criticized in the laments, as is an unfair division of family property. In another culture, such laments might have incited revenge.[51] In Kwan Mun Hau, a woman's lament must be her own revenge.

Why should women be permitted this liberty in the context of funerals, when most behavior is so carefully controlled by the ritual process? The preoccupations expressed by the laments suggest one possible answer: that most of the concerns expressed are not shared by men. They deal almost entirely with people and situations in which men have little interest. None of the laments recorded threatens male-dominated structures, such as the household or the lineage. It appears that here, at least, women are not doing that of which they are sometimes accused, working to divide male-dominated groups. Even in the bridal laments, when the bride curses her future husband and his family, she does so only when she is still within her natal home.[52]

Women play a rather prominent role in both wedding and funeral ritual, and thus one might argue that these are appropriate spheres for them to express themselves. On these occasions, one is always aware of the presence of a group of older women, who in weddings superintend the bride and carry the dowry. In funerals they (with men, if the deceased is male) care for and dress the body and lay it out with the proper ritual materials. Hired

50. See also Wolf, *Women and the Family*, pp. 32–41. Discussion of the laments has also given us the tantalizing suggestion that women may have believed that it was important that they have daughters as well as sons, as their lamentation was apparently believed necessary for the soul's transition into the next life.

51. Alexiou, *Ritual Lament*, p. 22.

52. Blake, "Death and Abuse," p. 27.

specialists were not, until recently, used for this work.[53] They also assist and direct the mourners when the priests are not doing so, particularly during the ceremony to end mourning. They draw on their extensive knowledge of ritual at this time.[54]

That women who are mourners should be permitted to lament aloud, and to do so in such a personal vein, may reflect a common characteristic of rituals: that within the ritual frame, reversals of normal behavior may occur.[55] Funerals, in China as elsewhere, are characterized by very different standards of dress and grooming than normally prevail, for example. Weddings also are distinguished by behavior very different from that of daily life, such as the sexual teasing of the bride. Thus, it is consistent that brides and female mourners should be permitted to act in ways that are otherwise forbidden.

There are also structural reasons for believing that funerals are appropriate settings for women to be prominent. Women are *yin* beings and thus should be associated with death and loss, especially with recent death when the body is still present. In Kwan Mun Hau, it is women, and only women, who communicate with the dead through a professional spirit medium, who is invariably female.[56] It is their role to consult with the deceased to determine whether he is settled and in need of anything, and whether he has any advice or comments for the family.

A further social structural explanation for women's lamentation is suggested, indirectly, by Humphreys and King, who say: "One would expect *a priori* . . . that societies in which power is personal and labile will show a more intense interaction between the living on the occasion of death, whereas those in which it is solidly anchored in corporate groups may focus their attention more on the care of the dead."[57] In societies in which power is

53. Hase, in "Observations" (n. 6 above), describes the active participation of village members in all stages of funerals, in a multilineage village in Sha Tin. This contrasts with Watson's description in this volume of most villagers' deep-seated fear of contact with the polluting influences of death in the village of San Tin. The hypothesis should be explored that pollution beliefs may be stronger in large, single-lineage villages, whose relations with neighboring lineages and villages are characterized by hostility. In contrast, small multilineage villages must of necessity maintain relations of cooperation with neighbors. Thus, the principle of opposition, which is fundamental to pollution beliefs, is relatively unimportant in their world view.

54. Hase describes a similar role played by women in Sha Tin, in "Observations," pp. 132–133.

55. See Victor Turner, *The Ritual Process* (Chicago: Aldine Publishing Company, 1969), esp. p. 102.

56. See also Hase, "Observations," pp. 156–157, and Jack Potter, "Cantonese Shamanism," in *Religion and Ritual in Chinese Society*, ed. Arthur Wolf (Stanford: Stanford University Press, 1974), pp. 207–231.

57. S. C. Humphreys, "Death and Time," in *Mortality and Immortality: The Anthropology and Archaeology of Death*, ed. S. C. Humphreys and Helen King (London: Academic Press, 1981), pp. 266–267.

lodged in corporate groups, adjustments in power relationships may not immediately follow the death of an individual. This distinction might fruitfully be applied within Chinese society to women as compared with men. Hakka women's power derives primarily from their personal attributes, and it is power relationships which constitute much of the subject matter of funeral lament; it is they who interact intensely with other women through their laments and dialogues. Male mourners, in contrast, are "solidly anchored in corporate groups," and during funerals they appear deeply preoccupied with the dead. They have little interaction with each other and communicate only minimally with those who come to pay their respects. Funerals, from the male point of view, are occasions to present a public front of family, lineage, and village solidarity.[58] The fact that property division does not normally occur at the time of death facilitates this.

Competition and claims for recognition among men may take place in another arena, that of the annual tomb ritual.[59] This sphere is dominated by men; it is they who direct and participate in the ritual. Rubie Watson, in chapter 9 in this volume, demonstrates that men from large Cantonese lineages use these occasions to press their claims for lineage recognition, pushing for demonstrations of acceptance of their claims through changes in the distribution of pork. I have no evidence that men of the Kwan Mun Hau lineages do this; these lineages, and the village, are pervaded by an egalitarian ambience very different from that characteristic of large lineages. The fact remains, however, that tomb rituals, which are occasions for the assembly of entire lineages, provide a situation where such statements can occur. An important difference between the men's tomb-side quests for recognition and the laments of Hakka women is that the men contend with each other as groups, whereas a woman laments alone. As she has entered her husband's family and built her position through her own resources, so she states her claim for justice alone.

The laments of women are one of their principal contributions to Chinese funeral ritual, together, in some regions, with their preparation of the body and ritual materials, and their advising mourners on the details of proper conduct. Until very recently, laments constituted a basic component of funeral ritual. The form of the laments was learned, and their timing and the nature of their performance was dictated by the structure of the ritual. The performance of lamentation was important in the eyes of the community.

Within this unifying framework, diversity existed. In some regions and dialect groups, the content of the laments appears to have been formal and learned, hence concerned with general social values rather than individual

58. Hase, "Observations," pp. 132–135.
59. This relationship was suggested by Jonathan Parry, in his role as discussant of this essay.

sentiments. In Kwan Mun Hau, certain themes and phrases were learned and standardized, but considerable improvisation was possible. During funerals women's mourning for the dead was intensified by their personal mourning. In this context normal rules of behavior did not prevail, and individual grievances could be publicly and poetically expressed. The ritual context demanded the expression of grief for the dead, but it also permitted the expression of grief for the suffering of the singer.

# TEXTS OF TWO COMPLETE LAMENTS

LAMENT PLANNED BY CHAN SHEK-YING FOR HER GREAT AUNT:

My great-aunt, I, your grandchild, have come today to call you.
My great-aunt acted as my mother, but now she has died.
When I was small, I lost my mother and my older sister.
At festivals and special occasions I would come to visit my great-aunt.
She would be hospitable to me, like a mother.
When my children were three days old and one month old
My great aunt acted as my mother.
Today she is old; her eyes are blind.
She thought of coming, but could not come.
I thought of going, but was also unable to visit her.
I, dead-fate person, was married into a poor household by my mother.
Now my younger brother is rich.
Today I have no great-aunt; I have no place to talk if mistreated.
Your eyes were blind for eight or ten years, but your health was good.
You could have come to visit me.
How could I know your eyes had become blind?
When this dead-fate person has pain and sickness
No one will come to visit me.
My great-aunt was thoughtful, but did not have enough strength.
My great-aunt was thoughtful, but was unable to walk.
I am poor; who would look after me?
If my father were still alive, I would not be in such a miserable situation.
My father has good descendants.
My father has good geomancy.
He produced one intelligent white flower [a son].
He produced me, a stupid person.
In the past my great-aunt treated me like a daughter.
But now, people treat me like a stepchild.
I am your genuine descendant
But why am I treated as though I were not a relative?
My younger brother is intelligent and is in a good situation.

Although I am a relative, I am treated like a stranger.
Even if I were a stepchild, there would be a relationship.
I am a blood relative,
But there seems to be no relationship.

### LAMENT PLANNED BY CHAN SHEK-YING FOR HER MOTHER-IN-LAW:

Tonight you will be at peace.
Now you have a lot of sons and grandsons
And gold and silver up to your eyes.
Now you are in the underworld and can see nothing.
Now I have raised your grandchildren,
But you have passed away.
If you could have lived eight or ten more years
Your grandchildren could have earned money and given it to you to spend.
A few years ago I was still very poor.
Now your oldest grandson can earn money,
But you have passed away.
If you could have lived eight or ten more years
You could have rested at ease.
If I had money, I could get a wife for your grandson.
Then you would have great-grandchildren and you would laugh "ha ha."
Now only one grandson earns money.
If you could have lived eight or ten more years
Your second grandson could have attained fame in his university studies,
And could have begun to work.
He could have earned money and given it to you.
Your life was so short.
You brought up other people's grandchildren,
But they didn't take good care of you.
You brought up other people's grandchildren,
But they said they grew up by themselves.
You brought up other people's children,
But they said they grew up by themselves.
Ask your conscience.
Other people are wealthy, but they regarded you as a beggar.
Although this dead-fate person was poor,
I still tried to support you.
I had a lot of property,
But it was taken by that thief.
Those thieves swallowed my property.
The thief swallowed it.
Those thieves stole all my property,
And now they can enjoy using it.
Now I have very little property.
I looked after you when you were sick.
Others are wealthy, but regarded you as a leper.
In the past you only loved your older daughter-in-law.
You just regarded me as a blade of grass.
My parents died when I was very small.
I was brought up by you.

You cared for me and raised me.
Now your other daughter-in-law is bad,
But you didn't treat me well.
In the past you raised me as your daughter.
Now you know I am not just a blade of grass,
But that I am a good daughter-in-law.

(In this lament, "other people" and "those thieves" refer to her husband's brother and his family.)

# SEVEN

# Gender and Ideological Differences in Representations of Life and Death

*Emily Martin*

Are the ideology and practice of death in Chinese society different, depending on one's gender? This question guides the following essay through a discussion of how men and women might relate differently to death, on the one hand, and birth and marriage, on the other. I argue that male and female genders in China may have developed quite distinct views of how these events are related and what they mean. Throughout I try to see women, not as bit actors in a play written and directed by men, but as persons capable of (and by their different life experience probably inclined toward) producing an altogether different drama.

In this effort I am following the path begun by many other recent ethnographers who have shown beyond reasonable doubt, for a great many kinds of societies including China, that women do not always adopt and act on the same ideology of family, lineage, life, and death as do men.[1] In addition, it has been shown that alternative ways of looking at the world often entail much more room for women's maneuver and resistance to domination than we have been accustomed to expect.[2]

---

1. Margery Wolf, *Women and the Family in Rural Taiwan* (Stanford: Stanford University Press, 1972); Annette B. Weiner, *Women of Value, Men of Renown: New Perspectives in Trobriand Exchange* (Austin: University of Texas Press, 1976); Judith Shapiro, "Anthropology and the Study of Gender," *Soundings* 64 (1981): 446–465; Shirley Ardener, ed., *Defining Females: The Nature of Women in Society* (New York: John Wiley, 1978); James L. Watson, "Standardizing the Gods: The Promotion of T'ien Hou ('Empress of Heaven') Along the South China Coast, 960–1960," in D. Johnson, A. Nathan, and E. Rawski, eds., *Popular Culture in Late Imperial China* (Berkeley and Los Angeles: University of California Press, 1985). Watson is moved to remark that "village women and men inhabit separate conceptual worlds—at least in respect to religion" (p. 321).

2. Daisy Hilse Dwyer, "Ideologies of Sexual Inequality and Strategies for Change in Male-Female Relations," *American Ethnologist* 5 (1978): 227–240; Loring M. Danforth, *The*

I begin with the recent provocative and stimulating essays, by Bloch and Parry, Bloch, and Watson,[3] concerning how life and death are ideologically constructed in relation to gender. Bloch and Parry begin by looking at the contrast between "fertility" and "sexuality." In many funeral rites the untamed, natural sexuality of women plays a crucial role: women may act out lewd behavior, for example. Bloch and Parry argue that this occurs in order for a sharp contrast to be set up: between the wild, natural sexuality of women, on the one hand, and the tamed, social fertility ("a sacred ancestral fertility controlled by men"), on the other. The idea is that the biological birthing that is the preserve of women must be contrasted to, and subordinated to, the social birthing that men do when they bring ancestors of various kinds to a new life after death: "Sexuality is set in opposition to fertility as women are opposed to men."[4] "Sexuality is, we suggest, opposed to fertility. It is associated with flesh, decomposition and women, while true ancestral fertility is a mystical process symbolized by the tomb and the (male) bones."[5]

The same contrast is made in another context: female birth (natural and wild) is regarded as polluting, whereas "social birth" into the (male) descent group through ceremonies such as capping or circumcision makes the child clean, whole, and pure. Women's involvement in unclean birth accounts for their close association with the highly polluting corpse at funerals, and the role they sometimes have of absorbing the corpse's pollution. It is as if at death "the women reabsorb the flesh that is their contribution to the child at birth."[6] In summary:

> The negative aspects of death are commonly seen as inseparable from other biological phenomena (like copulation and parturition); . . . in common with other biological processes, decomposition and decay are often (though not always) pre-eminently associated with women; and . . . this world of biology is elaborately constructed as something to be got rid of so as to make way for the regeneration of the ideal order.[7]

---

*Death Rituals of Modern Greece* (Princeton: Princeton University Press, 1982); Anna Caraveli, "The Bitter Wounding: The Lament as Social Protest in Rural Greece," in Jill Dubisch, ed., *Gender and Power in Rural Greece* (Princeton: Princeton University Press, 1986).

3. Maurice Bloch and Jonathan Parry, "Introduction: Death and the Regeneration of Life," in Maurice Bloch and Jonathan Parry, eds., *Death and the Regeneration of Life* (Cambridge: Cambridge University Press, 1982); Maurice Bloch, "Death, Women and Power," in Bloch and Parry, *Death and the Regeneration of Life*; James L. Watson, "Of Flesh and Bones: The Management of Death Pollution in Cantonese Society," in Bloch and Parry, *Death and the Regeneration of Life*.

4. Bloch and Parry, "Introduction," p. 19.

5. Ibid., p. 21.

6. Ibid., p. 23.

7. Ibid., p. 27.

Bloch and Parry are setting up the following series of oppositions:

| | |
|---|---|
| biological birth | social birth |
| biological death | social death (which is really rebirth as an ancestor) |
| pollution | purity |
| women | men |

Part of what happens at funerals is that the inferior, transient female world of pollution and death is vanquished to make way for the superior, eternal male world of the social order. In this scenario the women themselves play a necessary role: it falls to them, by their weeping and dealing with the corpse, to "take on and take away the sorrow and pollution of death."[8]

Let us begin by seeing whether a prima facie case can be made for an analysis of Chinese material that runs along the lines Bloch and Parry suggest.[9] First of all, birth is clearly seen as dangerous and defiling. In many parts of China, the very fact that a woman had borne children meant that her soul must suffer the fate of the "bloody pond" in the underworld, unless special rites were performed for her by her sons. Into this "immense expanse filled with blood and mire" were "plunged a countless number of women, their hair disheveled and their hands bound with shackles" because

> in giving birth to children they have discharged polluted blood, which offends the Spirits of the Earth. Moreover, they have washed their blood-stained clothes in rivers and streams, whence men and women draw this contaminated water, and make therewith tea, which they afterwards offer to the gods. Offended by such irreverence, these latter despatch a celestial warrior, who writes the names of the guilty in the book of good and evil, then after death, they have to undergo this punishment.[10]

Besides the fate of the bloody pond, which all women who have given birth must suffer, numerous other proscriptions hedge around a woman who is within a month of giving birth, or who is menstruating.[11] The baby and anyone who comes into the room of a postpartum woman is affected by

8. Maurice Bloch, "Death, Women and Power," p. 226.

9. The ethnographic base for this chapter is my own fieldwork in northern Taiwan (in the village of Ch'i-nan near the town of San-hsia) in the years 1969–75. Otherwise uncited material is from my field notes.

10. Henry Doré, *Researches into Chinese Superstitions*, trans. M. Kennelly (1914 ed. reprinted Taipei: Ch'eng-wen, 1966), 1:85. See also Emily M. Ahern, "The Power and Pollution of Chinese Women," in Margery Wolf and Roxane Witke, eds., *Women in Chinese Society* (Stanford: Stanford University Press, 1975), and Gary Seaman, "The Sexual Politics of Karmic Retribution," in Emily Martin Ahern and Hill Gates, eds., *The Anthropology of Taiwanese Society* (Stanford: Stanford University Press, 1981), on the pollution of birth.

11. Ahern, "Power and Pollution."

the same pollution and must wait out the month, or undergo special purifications. Elsewhere I argue that these restrictions are not directed against women per se (sexual intercourse is also polluting for both men and women), but they certainly amount in sum to an impression that there is something profoundly troublesome and disturbing about the whole process of procreation, from menstruation through sex to birth. And of course women are far more heavily involved than men in these events. What is troubling must be avoided, shaved off (as in the head of a newborn), waited out, or finally, as in the ceremony of the bloody pond, expunged at death.

In contrast, the social event that legitimates a birth, namely marriage, is seen, by the male descent group that acquires a woman, as a celebration of new life. Here Bloch and Parry's distinction between sexuality and fertility seems relevant: birth brings one head on against the messy sexuality of female bodies; marriage, the incorporation of a descendant-bearing woman into the group, emphasizes pure, social male fertility. In wedding cere- monies, the symbols of this kind of fertility are many, obvious, and public, tokens of pleasure and hope, not fear and loathing. The ritual impregnation of the bride (opening her private dresser-drawer with a key to "look at" her flowers), the use of plants with prolific blossoms, the repetition of good-luck phrases about fertility,[12] and even the ribald teasing that bride and groom are subjected to, are only a few examples.

Death, much like birth, is hedged round with separations and proscrip- tions. As with birth fluids, the corpse is highly polluting and offensive to the gods. Contact with it is carefully monitored according to one's kinship obligations, and must be waited out or purified in due course by washing, passing over fire, and so on. The pollution of death is not the same as the pollution of birth, to be sure,[13] but they share something: they both involve rapid and threatening change, the one in the process of creating flesh, the other in the process of its dissolution.[14] The brunt of most of the major funeral rituals is, of course, to remove the dangerous and polluting corpse from contact with the living and reduce it to clean, everlasting bones. The goal is to reduce the fleshly *yin* elements of the deceased and cordon them off from the living while enhancing the vital *yang* elements in the bones. Often other *yang* elements are used to aid in this endeavor: a cock riding on the coffin attracts the *yang* part of the soul back to the house; its blood and the power of a mandarin invest life in the ancestral tablet.[15] In the terms

---

12. Emily M. Ahern, "Affines and the Rituals of Kinship," in Arthur P. Wolf, ed., *Religion and Ritual in Chinese Society* (Stanford: Stanford University Press, 1974), pp. 286–288.

13. Watson, "Of Flesh and Bones," p. 183.

14. In Ahern, "Power and Pollution," I argued, in ignorance at the time I wrote of the issues I take up here, that what pollution of birth, death, and other events have in common is change that entails crossing boundaries of the body or social groups.

15. De Groot, *The Religious System of China* (Leiden: Brill, 1892–1910), 1:213.

used by Bloch and Parry, this is part of the effort to create new life, rebirth, in the form of ancestors residing in tablets and tombs, enhancing the "sacred ancestral fertility controlled by men."

In this complex of ideas and practices, it is possible, following Bloch and Parry, to see women's role as one of support to the main tenets: they submit to the restrictions that giving birth makes necessary and take unto themselves the pollution of death, as in James Watson's vivid example of women sweeping their unbound hair along the coffin in order to absorb the corpse's pollution.[16]

The question I wish to raise is whether another view is possible. Could it be that buried within these practices and symbols of birth, marriage, and death is another view of how these experiences interrelate, one that is derived from women's own quite different experience of life and that is stamped with a quite different message? The difficulty in making such an interpretation is that I did not have this possibility in mind when I was in the field, and never made observations or asked questions designed to elicit such a pattern. In fact it is only in the very recent past that *any* anthropologists have asked whether this might be so.[17] Consequently, what I have to work with are shreds at best, fragments of what might be (but have yet to be proven to be) whole cloth.

One caveat: in what follows I will refer to "male" or "female" views of life and death. These terms refer to socially defined male and female genders, not to individual men or women. Although an individual man or woman would probably at times feel more comfortable talking and living the view that is dominant for his or her gender, this is not always so. In certain times, places, and contexts men or women can incline toward or act in terms of the ideology of the other gender. For example, old women, who are after all closest to the kinds of power and prestige men have in Chinese society, are often enthusiastic spokeswomen for what I define as "male" views. They also have the most to gain from the male system of power. An excellent example of this is James Watson's finding that old women, invariably widows, can become community experts on funeral ritual. They gain status, respect, and even awe thereby.[18] The point I am arguing is that because of the different relationship men and women have to their bodies, the different involvement they have in the biological events of birth and death, and the different kinds of work they do, each gender has evolved a separate view of what life and death mean and how they interrelate. These two sets

---

16. Watson, "Of Flesh and Bones," p. 173.

17. See unpublished papers prepared for the session "Rethinking Patriarchy and Matriarchy" organized by Peggy Sanday for the conference "Beyond the Second Sex," Philadelphia, 1984.

18. Watson, "Of Flesh and Bones," p. 183.

of views and practices are available to both individual women and individual men.

Let me begin with birth, for which I have the least evidence—partly because I never witnessed an actual birth in Taiwan and so have only the somewhat abstract, considered commentary on what it means that comes at a distance from the actual event. The ideology described above stresses the pollution created after the event of birth and the need to keep others separate from it, or to clean up or protect the infant from it. Very little attention is focused on the woman's pregnant state or on the process of birth itself. Yet the women I knew in the field who were pregnant, as well as many I have known and interviewed in this country, were scared about impending birth, for first and later births, out of fear of their own or the baby's possible death, or out of fear of pain or damage in labor. I do not know whether there might be special rituals performed by women during pregnancy or labor reflecting those concerns, but Doré has some evidence that there are in some parts of China. He describes numerous goddesses women worship to request expeditious childbirth, including one, "K'o-ku Niang-niang," who was formerly a midwife and "subsequently deified, on account of the services she rendered during her earthly career." She is "worshipped by all the women of the place [An-hui], who organize an annual procession in her honour. Shrines are erected to venerate her, and her tablet occupies a prominent position in the temples dedicated to the other local deities. This tablet is taken from house to house, so that she may extend her protection to all cases of childbirth."[19]

Here the focus is on the process of birth, fraught with both danger to life and the creation of new life. A woman who was renowned for protecting the lives of birthing women is raised to the status of a goddess and brought as a kind of patron saint of birth to the "defiled" birthing room. Further evidence comes from the sectarian literature known as *pao-chüan*. The content of some of these tracts—which were often funded by women, recited by women, and listened to by women—related to the specific pains and anxieties of pregnancy, the sufferings and dangers of childbirth, and the arduous labor of caring for and breast-feeding an infant. They deal with these matters in such a realistic and empathic way that the historian wonders whether they might even have been written by women.[20] If there is a particularly female ideology of birth in China, perhaps it would stress, as against Bloch and Parry, *conjunction* of the antitheses life and death in the same events.

Now we come to marriage. How might women see this event, which

19. Doré, *Researches*, 1:2, 5.

20. Daniel L. Overmyer, "Values in Chinese Sectarian Literature," in Johnson, Nathan, and Rawski, *Popular Culture in Late Imperial China*.

from the male side is a glorious addition to the social strength of the descent group? Here the case for a specifically female ideology is very strong. We have in the accounts of Blake and others evidence of marriage laments, which were learned by women from other women and sung both in their father's house and in their husband's house in the days before and after marriage.[21] How do these laments depict marriage?—often explicitly as death. In the examples Blake compiles, mostly from southern China, the bride calls her groom's family the "dead people";[22] she laments that she is dying, that she needs grave clothes.[23] She images "dying in a land of shadows,/About to see the King of Hell!"[24] She cries that she is changed into a dead person, that her father's daughter is dead, and that moving to her husband's family will be like crossing the yellow river (a symbol of the boundary between life and death).[25]

She despairs over the separation she must undergo:

> The chicken egg is broken,
> The yellow spreads;
> Tonight I am separated,
> The four walls of sister's bathroom are open.
> The white spreads;
> Tonight I am separated,
> The four corners of sister's bathstone are cracked.[26]

Here we see a vision of what marriage means from a woman's point of view that is diametrically opposed to the Bloch and Parry version. If the male descent group sees marriage as associated with life, purity, light, order, heat, prosperity, plentitude, and fertility, the bride sees it as associated with "death, dirt, darkness, confusion, cold, poverty, meanness and sterility."[27]

Even laments that do not explicitly use imagery of death choose the closely related metaphor of war. In an example cited by Liu Wei-min, the bride compares her husband's family to barbarians and her own to the central state. She compares the powerful strategies used by military heroes of

---

21. Fred Blake, "Death and Abuse in Marriage Laments: The Curse of Chinese Brides," *Asian Folklore Studies* 37 (1978): 13–33; Johannes Frick, "Hochzeitssitten von Hei-tsuei-tzu in der Provinz Ch'ing-hai (China)," *Ethnographische Beitrage aus der Ch'ing-hai Provinz* (Peking: Catholic University of Peking, 1952); Liu Wei-min 劉偉民, "Tung-kuan hun-su ti hsu-shu chi yen-chiu" 東莞婚俗的叙述及研究, *Min-su* 民俗 1 (1936): 81–99; Yang Ti-wang, "Ancient Bridal Laments," *China Reconstructs* 12 (1963): 42–44; Elizabeth Johnson, chapter 6 in this volume.
22. Blake, "Death and Abuse," p. 14.
23. Ibid., p. 15.
24. Ibid., p. 19.
25. Ibid., p. 20–22.
26. Ibid., p. 21.
27. Ibid., p. 27.

the past to meet disaster, which are impossibly out of reach for her, to the "small strategies" available to a woman in her bedroom. To her female friends she stresses the images of life, growth, and continuity she associates with being in her natal home:

I thought the Green Emperor would let us be beautiful and stay together
    forever,
And like the plum, bamboo, and pine happily enter the new year together.
I thought the Red Emperor would let us play happily together,
Smiling and showing our peach lips and white skin.

She starkly contrasts these images to others of destruction and suffering, which she associates with married life:

How could I know that the foreign White Emperor
    would cast me into this gloomy mood?
If I told of all the hard times I will suffer, it
    would be like fire melting iron.
I hate the fact that this matchmaker's wrong
Has brought me to the Black Emperor, where I return
.   home late, tired from gathering thorny plants.

Throughout the lament, separation is decried: "This mother-daughter separation is what my heart hates most." And her imminent absence from everyday events, such as comforting her parents or doing needlework with her friends, is mourned very much as if she were about to die.[28]

There is not only a *view* of marriage that sees it as like death, sometimes there is also action predicated on that view. Rubie Watson observed that in the New Territories a groom's party's entrance to the bride's village was blocked by a group of unmarried girls. Only after a substantial sum of money was paid would the girls permit the groom and his party to enter.[29]

A piece of ethnography that may be related to this conjunction between marriage and death is that when women die they wear the dress they wore on their wedding day. De Groot reports that it is a robe of finery that mimics imperial dress.[30] In Taiwan it is a white dress worn under the wedding dress and saved for the funeral. In the past I always thought this was simply a matter of status: that women wanted to appear in the underworld in their finest grandeur to impress the officials of the underworld. This may still be so. Yet now I wonder whether, at another level, women are reiterating the equation they make between marriage and death on their wedding day.

Finally, let us take a look at how death might be seen in this alternative

28. Liu Wei-min, "Tung-kuan," pp. 85–86.
29. Rubie S. Watson, "Class Differences and Affinal Relations in South China," *Man* n.s. 16 (1981): 600.
30. De Groot, *The Religious System*, 1:53.

female ideology. Here we need to consider first the kind of work women do in general and in funerals in particular. Hilary Rose has suggested that what sets off the work women do in almost all societies—child raising and house-work—is that it involves caring labor, that is, labor done for the sake of particular other people with whom one has a caring relationship.[31] As in ordinary life, so in funerals. Many accounts agree that it is the women who predominately wail for the dead,[32] wash the corpse,[33] prepare and offer it food,[34] express terms of endearment toward it,[35] and cry on the day it learns it is dead, so that it will not be the first to know. Here the emphasis is not so much on women's taking upon themselves the pollution of the dead as on their tending to the concrete, material, and emotional needs of the person who died. It is not that men never wail for or sit with the deceased, but it is women's preeminent responsibility.

If women as a gender are deeply involved in the nitty-gritty of the actuali-ties of death, they seem in other ways to bring into funerals concerns that at first glance have no place there. For example, certain artifacts that are used in funerals are associated with children and birth. James Watson's evidence here is by far the most striking. He records that women of childbearing age, daughters and daughters-in-law, wear a piece of green cloth on their person throughout the funeral rites, in which they deal closely with the corpse and take its pollution on themselves. Later this cloth is passed over a fire in purification, and then *made into the centerpiece of the back-strap harnesses they use for carrying infants.*[36]

I never asked about any analogous custom in Taiwan, but in rereading my field notes I discovered something I repeatedly observed but never asked about: At the merit ceremonies on the eve of a funeral the soul tablet of the deceased is made to cross the bridge from the *yang* world to the *yin* world with the help of the earth god. This bridge is invariably represented by one of the long strips of cloth women use to wrap a child to their backs.

What this conjunction of birth artifacts with death suggests to me is that women may be making a statement about their own role in the process of

31. Hilary Rose, "Hand, Brain, and Heart: A Feminist Epistemology for the Natural Sci-ences," *Signs* 9, no. 1 (1983): 73–90. See also Sara Ruddick, "Maternal Thinking," in Joyce Trebilcot, ed., *Mothering* (Totowa, N.J.: Rowman and Allanheld, 1983).

32. De Groot, *The Religious System*, 1:10; Justus Doolittle, *Social Life of the Chinese* (New York: Harper, 1865), 2:200; S. W. Williams, *The Middle Kingdom* (1833 ed. reprinted Taipei: Ch'eng-wen, 1965), 2:243; Sidney Gamble, *North China Villages* (Berkeley and Los Angeles: University of California Press, 1963), p. 261.

33. De Groot, *The Religious System*, 1:14–15; W. Gilbert Walshe, *Ways That Are Dark: Some Chapters on Chinese Etiquette and Social Procedure* (Shanghai: Kelly and Walsh, 1906), p. 230.

34. De Groot, *The Religious System*, 1:29; Gamble, *North China Villages*, p. 257.

35. De Groot, *The Religious System*, 1:95.

36. Watson, "Of Flesh and Bones," pp. 173–174.

existence. Bloch and Parry stress that women in a sense give birth to the corpse, because they are responsible for having created polluting biological matter in the first place. I would suggest that this is very probably a view with which the male gender would feel most comfortable; women themselves may be saying something else—such as that the flesh of the corpse (which in Watson's case contacts the green cloth) is like the flesh of the baby it is later wrapped in. Both emerged from the body of a woman, and it is this that is woman's contribution to the cycle and flow of existence.[37]

Further evidence for this interpretation comes from Stuart Thompson's rich Taiwan ethnography on second burial rites.[38] On a reading that presupposes the Bloch-Parry model, male officiants are attempting to attain a form of pure male fertility represented by rice and the pure, hard, white, male bones. To achieve this, the rotten, corrupt female flesh must be encouraged to rot away. Along the way, the aid of the things explicitly seen as phallic—milky rice washing-water and nails—is enlisted. Yet, inextricable from these elements are the literal *containers* of these male symbols: the rice measure, a cylindrical wooden tub called a *tou*, a term that can also be used for female genitals; the round ceramic pot the male bones are enclosed in, arranged deliberately in a fetal position; and finally the horseshoe-shaped, mounded tomb in which the bone pot is housed. Beyond this, the ancestral bones in their final resting place are dotted with red—often red blood—tied with red string, and wrapped in red paper. One could argue that these red emblems of blood and flesh are somehow transformed so that they are no longer corrupt and female but pure and male, but one could hardly argue that for the vast quantities of pork flesh that are ritually fed to the ancestor, because pork is strongly associated with female links through marriage.

In sum, it is possible to glimpse the outlines of two strikingly different ideologies of life and death. In the preeminently female ideology, women see life *and* death in birth, *death* in marriage, and a cycle of change from death to birth to death in funerals. On the female side we see emphasis on the unity of opposites, denigration of separation (recall the bride's lament over her separation from her family), and celebration of cyclic change. On the male side we see constant efforts to separate opposites, to maintain and make oppositions steadfast, and desire for attainment of eternally unchanging social status.

If we were to put Bloch and Parry's series of oppositions (which I suspect may be largely male-gender oppositions) themselves in the context of a larger comparison to female categories, the two might look something like this:

37. Annette B. Weiner gives a powerful account of how, among the Trobriand Islanders, women's role at funerals is to regenerate the bodily substance out of which the matrilineal kinship group is made (*Women of Value, Men and Renown*, p. 119).

38. Chapter 4 in this volume.

*Male ideology*
the social celebrated; the biological despised
oppositions and separations celebrated, i.e., life/death; men/women;
    polluted/pure
eternal, unchanging status sought
*Female ideology*
the social and biological incorporated, i.e., focus at a funeral on the end
    of one (biological) body but, through the bodies of women, continua-
    tion of the life of the social body
opposites unified and brought together
cyclic change celebrated

Sangren's recent analysis of female deities in China points out what many of us have overlooked: that the cults of Kuan-yin and other important female goddesses stress activities that match many of the important components of women's social roles: mediation and unity of disparate groups.[39] This fits in a dramatic way with the conclusions of feminist theorists, who are suggesting that it is not just women's social roles, but also the kinds of selves they construct and the kind of work they engage in that lead "toward opposition to dualisms of any sort, valuation of concrete, everyday life, sense of a variety of connectednesses and continuities both with other persons and with the natural world."[40]

I have been influenced in my efforts to perceive an alternative view by recent efforts to describe the relationship among gender, birth, and death as represented in Western civilization, stretching back to classical Greece. For example, Nancy Hartsock's work suggests that men, because of their very different life experiences—in the family and in the division of labor—develop much more rigid boundaries around the self than women do. Based on object-relations theory (whose details are too complex to go into here), this theory sees men as constructing selves with a hostile and combative dualism (self-other) at their hearts.

> Masculinity must be attained by means of opposition to the concrete world of daily life, by escaping from contact with the female world of the household into the masculine world of public life. This experience of two worlds, one valuable, if abstract and deeply unattainable, the other useless and demeaning, if concrete and necessary, lies at the heart of a series of dualisms—abstract/concrete, mind/body, culture/nature, ideal/real, stasis/change. And these

39. P. Steven Sangren, "Female Gender in Chinese Religious Symbols: Kuan Yin, Ma Tsu, and the 'Eternal Mother,'" *Signs* 9, no. 1 (1983): 4–25.

40. Nancy Hartsock, "The Feminist Standpoint: Developing the Ground for a Specifically Feminist Historical Materialism," in Sandra Harding and Merrill B. Hintikka, eds., *Discovering Reality* (Boston: D. Reidel, 1983), p. 297.

dualisms are overlaid by gender: only the first of each pair is associated with the male.[41]

In these contrasts, Hartsock argues, men's experience inverts that of women, who, because of their deep involvement in the concrete processes of birth, child rearing, and housework, experience life as concrete, bodily, natural, real, and changing. For our purposes, the most relevant inversion men make of women's experience is the inversion of life and death. This occurs through the substitution of death for life. First birth (from the body of a woman) is seen as a death sentence (that is, it leads finally to death). Second birth, however, only attainable through *heroic* death, is seen as leading to immortality.[42] Examples in Western thought of how life can be seen as death, and death as life, are easily come by. On seeing death as life, Hartsock's favored examples are from contemporary works such as Ernst Becker's *The Denial of Death* or Georges Bataille's *Death and Sensuality*.[43] Becker, for example, sees "activity designed largely to avoid the fatality of death, to overcome it by denying in some way that it is the final destiny for man" as the "mainspring of human activity."[44] Other examples can be found in the Homeric literature,[45] and of course in what has been written and said to encourage young men to go to war.[46] On seeing life (and particularly *birth*) as death, my favorite example comes from a nineteenth-century gynecologist, who

compared a woman's life-bearing function to a death-dealing one, her womb a gun, her baby a projectile entirely dependent on her for propulsion. . . . The

41. Hartsock, "The Feminist Standpoint," p. 298. See also Mary O'Brien, *The Politics of Reproduction* (Boston: Routledge and Kegan Paul, 1981), p. 59. Hartsock's use of psychoanalytic object-relations theory cannot provide a complete analysis of institutionalized male domination, as Iris Young points out. See Iris Marion Young, "Is Male Gender Identity the Cause of Male Domination?" in Joyce Trebilcot, ed., *Mothering* (Totowa, N.J.: Rowman and Allanheld, 1983).

42. Nancy Hartsock, "Men, Women, War, and Politics," unpublished paper presented to the Mid-Atlantic Seminar for Research on Women, The University of Pennsylvania, 1983, p. 15. Bloch, "Death, Women and Power," pp. 229–30, suggests that Western societies do not need to transform death into fertility, because the source of creativity is extra-human (in the form of God or capital). The corpse may not be seen as a source of fertility, but death can be, nonetheless, through heroism.

43. Ernst Becker, *The Denial of Death* (New York: Free Press, 1973); George Bataille, *Death and Sensuality* (New York: Arno Press, 1977).

44. Becker, *The Denial of Death*, p. ix.

45. Christiane Sourvinou-Inwood, "To Die and Enter the House of Hades: Homer, Before and After," in Joachim Whaley, ed., *Mirrors of Mortality: Studies in the Social History of Death* (New York: St. Martin's Press, 1981), p. 24.

46. David Cannadine, "War and Death, Grief and Mourning in Modern Britain," in Whaley, *Mirrors of Mortality*, p. 195; Judith Stiehm, *Bring Me Men and Women: Mandated Change at the U.S. Air Force Academy* (Berkeley and Los Angeles: University of California Press, 1981).

mother expelled her baby in an act of aggression against the world. It became a hard, death-dealing missile because of its mother's explosive effects upon it.[47]

The substitution of death for life and life for death in these examples comprises, Hartsock argues, a specifically male ideology. In great contrast,

female experience not only inverts that of the male, but forms a basis on which to expose abstract masculinity as both partial and fundamentally perverse, as not only occupying only one side of the dualities it has constructed, but reversing the proper valuation of human activity.[48]

It is ironic that Bloch and Parry refer to their anthropological conclusions that sexuality is depicted ritually as something to be overcome by fertility as a "perverse" suggestion.[49] Hartsock would see their suggestion as not at all perverse, but fitting exactly the way the male gender constructs the world. What *is* perverse is the male contention that life is really death, and death, life.

I have pushed hard for the notion that there may be a view different from Bloch and Parry's which the Chinese data will uphold just as well. The truth of how these ideologies relate to social life is of course immensely complex and involves all sorts of intended and unintended action, from mindless habit to determined strategy. In real life, ideological systems of thought and action do not exist as seamless wholes—they are full of gaps, lapses, and contradictions. My final point will be that one thing can be seen from the Chinese data: Women as a subordinated gender frequently use contradictions in the total ideological field against the system and for themselves. I will illustrate this process with two examples.

First, in the normal course of events it is generally far less likely for a woman than for a man to receive those ancestral rites that can only be performed some time after death. Despite the variety of ways in which the dead can become ensconced in geomantically beneficial tombs or socially symbolic ancestral tablets and halls, it is clear that men, because of their far more central place in the social system of status and property endowment, are much more likely to be granted (or demand) this form of continued existence.[50] (The one exception to this may be social strata in which polyg-

47. G. J. Barker-Benfield, *The Horrors of the Half-Known Life* (New York: Harper and Row 1976), p. 288.

48. Bloch and Parry, "Introduction," p. 19.

49. Hartsock, "The Feminist Standpoint," p. 299.

50. See, among many others, Maurice Freedman, *Chinese Lineage and Society: Fukien and Kwangtung* (New York: Humanities Press, 1966); Arthur P. Wolf, "Gods, Ghosts and Ancestors," in *Religion and Ritual in Chinese Society*; Emily M. Ahern, *The Cult of the Dead in a Chinese Village* (Stanford: Stanford University Press, 1973); Yü Kwang-hung 余光弘, "Lu-tao ti sang-tsang yi-shih" 綠島的喪葬儀式 (Funeral rites of Lutau Island), *Min-tsu hsueh yen-chiu so chi-k'an* 民族學研究所集刊 49 (1980).

Male mourners at funeral (Taiwan).
Photo by Stuart E. Thompson.

Paper altar in the form of a house, for use by the deceased
in the afterlife (Taiwan). Photo by Stuart E. Thompson.

A paper house being burned, transferring it to the
otherworld (Taiwan). Photo by Stuart E. Thompson.

Closeup of funeral scroll, Buddhist monk
Mu-lien saving his mother from hell (Taiwan).
Photo by Stuart E. Thompson.

Entertainers performing at funeral (Taiwan).
Photo by Stuart E. Thompson.

Bones being assembled for deposit
in *chin-t'a* pot (Taiwan). Photo by
Emily Martin.

Cantonese *nahm mouh lo* priest with paper
goods of his own construction to be burned
for the benefit of the deceased seven days
after burial; mourners, led by chief mourner,
in background (Hong Kong New Territories).
Photo by James L. Watson.

Recently exhumed grave with new
*chin-t'a* bone pot packed and ready
for secondary burial (Taiwan).
Photo by Emily Martin.

*Chin-t'a* bone pots being worshipped
during Ching-ming (grave sweeping) festival; pots not yet
placed in permanent tombs (Hong Kong New Territories).
Photo by Graham E. Johnson.

Permanent tomb, southern Chinese style; bone pot is buried underneath inscription plate at center-back of tomb (Hong Kong New Territories). Photo by James L. Watson.

Northern Chinese style graves; a family set in Chihli. Illustration taken from J. J. M. de Groot, *The Religious System of China,* vol. 2 (Leiden: Brill, 1894), p. 375.

Lineage elders worshipping at tomb of founding ancestor;
roast pigs are later divided and eaten by worshippers
(Hong Kong New Territories). Photo by James L. Watson.

Food offerings at tomb of lineage founder, Chung-yang
(Double nine) festival (Hong Kong New Territories).
Photo by James L. Watson.

yny was practiced, so that the graves of women could be geomantically manipulated to differentiate the fortunes of men descended from different mothers.)[51]

Also, in the normal course of events, a person who committed suicide would remain in an unsettled state after death and so neither receive the regular rites nor have hope of becoming socially immortalized through a tomb or a hall tablet. In fact, because the soul is not in its proper place in the underworld, and can harass the living, making them sick, troubled, and unsuccessful, suicide can be used as an act of aggression against one's kin. It is not infrequently used this way by women in the desperate years after marriage while they are still under the thumb of mother-in-law.[52]

In the last dynasty, these two elements of the system could be put together, paradoxically resulting in a fuller, more powerful status for a woman after death than her husband could ever hope for. If a woman killed herself—by drowning, strangling, poisoning, or best of all, public hanging—upon the death of her husband, this ultimate fidelity to her husband's service could be marked by the highest acclaim: attendance at the hanging by eminent local authorities, followed in some cases by imperial honor, such as an honorary inscription over her family's dwelling, an honorary gate, or a place in a temple for the especially chaste and filial. Women chosen for residence in these temples received regular sacrifices from officials "on a par with the divinities of the state."[53] The paradox, and the trade-off, cut both ways: Society transforms the potentially avenging ghost of a suicide into a chaste widow; for her part, the chaste widow, subordinate to her husband even to the point of dying when he dies, becomes not a forgotten ancestor but a goddess in the public realm. The cost for the woman is of course that she must act on the "perverse" dominant male ideology: that immortal life can only be obtained at the cost of forfeiting life through a heroine's death.

My second example forms a kind of counterpoint to the first. At some times and places, Chinese women seem to have taken dominant male ideology at face value and acted on its implicit message. The pao-chüan I mentioned earlier go on at length about the polluting nature of women's bodies in menstruation and birth. This is put together with the real physical and psychic pain women experience in marriage and birth:

> In giving birth to children she befouls heaven and earth, and offends the river god by washing bloody skirts.
> If she is on good terms with her mother-in-law she can visit her mother every year or so.

51. Maurice Freedman, Chinese Lineage, p. 131.
52. Margery Wolf, "Women and Suicide in China," in Wolf and Witke, Women in Chinese Society.
53. De Groot, The Religious System, 2:750.

But if she is not in accord with her mother-in-law's wishes, she is never able to
return to her mother's home.
She thinks of the pain in the hearts of her parents, and of when she will be able
to repay their kindness.
No matter how many plans you might have, women have always submitted to
others and served them.
This is because of serious sins in their former existences.

When a woman is married to a husband for her whole life she is controlled by
him. All her joys and sorrows derive from him. After they are married she
necessarily suffers the pains of childbirth, and cannot avoid the sin of offending the sun, moon and stars with a flow of blood. Now I will speak with you in
more detail about the sufferings women endure in childbirth.[54]

Directly influenced by texts such as these, some women took them to
their logical conclusion and acted accordingly: They resisted marriage and
lived with members of sworn sisterhoods. Material support came from their
wages in the silk filatures in parts of Kwangtung, and the sanction against
being forced to marry was the threat of group suicide.[55] These women
accepted many elements of the male-oriented ideology about birth and
women, added to them their own perceptions of pregnancy and child rearing, only to draw conclusions that completely undercut the desired end of
ideology from a male point of view: They refused to marry, refused to bear
children, refused to be the wives and mothers necessary for male descent
groups to perpetuate themselves.

To return to Thompson's Taiwan case, if men choose to speak only about
rice, nails, tablets, bones, and semen and ignore blood, containers for rice,
tombs, wombs, and flesh, they do so at the peril of ignoring some of their
own ritual, which depicts what is needed to continue actual, not fantastical
descent groups, that is, men and women, semen and blood. It may be that
some sectors of ritual practice and ideology are complexly interrelated male
and female versions of reality, leaving groups of males free—dominant as
they are in the public arena—to construct a version of what is happening
based on a fantasy of reproduction without women.

It is still an open question whether women in certain contexts would
respond to quite other features of the system, as we have seen that they do in
the form of *pao-chüan*. But even here, just as in the dominant male ideology,
we must expect the kind of paradox, contradiction, and conflict inherent in
the following section of the *Liu Hsiang pao-chüan*; although the necessity of
filling the roles of wife and mother and contributing to male descent groups
is rejected, the ideology of female pollution and the desirability of escaping
female status through rebirth as a male is accepted.

54. Overmyer, "Values," p. 251.
55. Marjorie Topley, "Marriage Resistance in Rural Kwangtung," in Wolf and Witke,
*Women in Chinese Society*.

For ten months, while a girl is in her mother's womb, she turns her back to her mother, facing outward, staying aloof. If the mother moves about, the unborn child begins to stir. When the child is born everyone is disgusted. While the child is in the womb, the mother suffers as if in prison; once the child is out of the womb, the mother meets only disgust. Everyone in the family, young and old, is displeased, objecting to us women for being born to our mothers. Our parents have no choice but to raise us, and when we grow up we are married to someone else. . . . When our husband's parents are angry we must hasten to please them with smiles. When our husband furiously curses us we must not answer back. If we slit or tear fine fabrics, it is a sinful crime, and it's a serious offence if we drop the basket in the water when washing rice. We taint heaven and earth when we give birth to children, and in washing filth from our blood-stained skirts we offend the river gods. If we put on make-up we attract attention and are punished for flouting the law as loose women. If our parents-in-law are kind, we may see our own families once or twice in a year. But if we don't meet with their approval we will never return to our homes again. . . . Once you are married to a husband you are under his control for your whole life: all your pleasures and miseries are at his discretion. When you are a man's wife you are bound to know the sufferings of childbirth, you cannot avoid the bloodstained water, and the sin of offending the sun, moon and stars. . . . If you are a wise and clever woman you will eat vegetarian food, recite the Buddha's name and start religious cultivation at once. How favoured and honoured you will be when you migrate from a woman's to a man's body! In your next existence you can once again follow the way to the Pure Land.[56]

56. Glen Dudbridge, *The Legend of Miao-shan* (London: Ithaca Press, 1978), p. 86.

# EIGHT

# Souls and Salvation: Conflicting Themes in Chinese Popular Religion

*Myron L. Cohen*

Chinese popular religion during late traditional times provided several concurrent or alternative versions of the afterlife,[1] including the possibility of personal or individual salvation through rebirth into the Western Heaven of paradise. As far as the religious practices and beliefs most prevalent among the masses were concerned, the salvation thus depicted received its greatest emphasis during the funeral and postfuneral rituals, when the deceased's passage through the underworld and then reincarnation or hoped-for rebirth in the Western Heaven were facilitated and expedited by his or her kin and by the religious specialists they had employed. For certain Chinese, such as lay adherents of orthodox Pure Land Buddhism, and even more so for members of some of the imperially proscribed "heretical" sects falling within the White Lotus and other traditions, the Western Heaven or a similarly envisioned blissful paradise formed a core element within the total arrangement of religious beliefs. For the majority of the population, however, it would appear that this idea of salvation, albeit incorporated into rituals and beliefs concerning the afterlife, was in fact given little room for expression. A religious orientation toward salvation in Western Paradise both functionally and logically yielded pride of place among the masses to ancestor worship, the belief in three souls, the ideal and role of reincarnation, and more generally to a conceptualization of the structure and organization of the cosmos which tightly and interactively linked the living to the dead and to the gods. While internal consistency as such is not necessarily to be expected with respect to the totality of any popularly held body of

---

1. In addition to nineteenth-century sources, I use materials which describe continuities in traditional practices as observed on the China mainland during the first half of the twentieth century, and even more recently in Taiwan and Hong Kong.

religious beliefs and practices, the fact remains that because in the Chinese case belief in the Western Paradise was potentially subversive of other major elements in popular religion, there was an important tension and contradiction built into popular religious ideas concerning the afterlife. It was for the living, obviously, that the afterlife could assume different forms varying in their desirability, and in this chapter I focus on the social interpretation of death with particular reference to the emphasis or de-emphasis of salvation in different popular religious contexts.

It is well established that the beliefs and rituals surrounding death have as three of their major foci the supernatural domains of the gods and ghosts, the grave, and the ancestral tablet.[2] The dead are held to be present as supernatural entities in their graves and tablets; at the same time, they are undergoing judgment—if not worse—at the hands of the magistrates of hell and their demon assistants, and there can be alternative (not concurrent) outcomes to these underworld procedures: return to the earth as a "hungry ghost," ongoing punishment in hell, release from punishment but continued confinement in the underworld, reincarnation (in one of many possible forms and in one of several domains of existence), or entrance into the Western Paradise.[3]

Linked to these multiple and rather different coexisting contexts of the afterlife was the belief, reported by numerous Western observers with respect to widely separated areas of China, that a dead person had three "souls."[4] At the same time, literary and ethnographic materials indicate several alternative systems of classification, but it is noteworthy that all have

2. See, i.e., Maurice Freedman, *Lineage Organization in Southeastern China* (London: Athlone, 1958), pp. 86–87; Arthur P. Wolf, "Gods, Ghosts, and Ancestors," in Arthur P. Wolf, ed., *Religion and Ritual in Chinese Society* (Stanford: Stanford University Press, 1974); Emily Ahern, *The Cult of the Dead in a Chinese Village* (Stanford: Stanford University Press, 1973).

3. Freedman, *Lineage Organization.*

4. M. [Evariste-Regis] Huc, *The Chinese Empire: Forming a Sequel to the Work Entitled "Recollections of a Journey through Tartary and Thibet"* (London: Longman, Brown, Green, and Longmans, 1855), 2:343, quoting from another missionary's description of Honan, is the earliest mention I have found; Justus Doolittle, *Social Life of the Chinese*, 2 vols. (New York: Harper, 1865), 2:401–402, similarly reports on Foochow in the south; John L. Nevius, *China and the Chinese* (New York: Harper and Brothers, 1869), p. 132, has remarks along the same lines which appear to be based upon what he saw in the city of Hangchow; for an observation with respect to Szechuan in western China there is James Hutson, "Chinese Life on the Tibetan Foothills," *New China Review* 1 (1919): 425; for Peking, see Anne Swann Goodrich, *The Peking Temple of the Eastern Peak* (Nagoya: Monumenta Serica, 1964), p. 208, and H. Y. Lowe, *The Adventures of Wu: The Life Cycle of a Peking Man* (Princeton: Princeton University Press, 1983, combined reprint of vol. 1, Peking, 1940, and vol. 2, Peking, 1941), 2:126; and for modern Hong Kong, Cornelius Osgood, *The Chinese: A Study of a Hong Kong Community*, 3 vols. (Tucson: University of Arizona Press, 1975), 3:1145; also see Osgood, *The Chinese*, p. 1186, n. 100, for additional references.

in common the absence of an individuated soul. The fundamental *yin-yang* dualism gave rise to the distinction between the *p'o*—the earthly *yin* soul which went into the grave with the body of the dead, and the *hun*—the *yang* soul of the ancestral tablet. But both the texts and the ethnographies reveal a situation far more complex than that allowed for by a simple dichotomization. Although it is commonly reported that there are three *hun* and seven *p'o*,[5] other Chinese expositions of the subject describe different and various numbers of "souls." Again, although it is asserted that the *p'o* and the *hun* are represented as manifested in or equivalent to the *kuei*, or ghost, and the *shen*, or spirit/god, the Chinese terminology is less than fully consistent; for example, an *o-kuei*, or "hungry ghost"—surely as *yin* as can be—can alternatively be known as *ku-hun* (an "orphaned," "lonely," or "solitary" *hun*, one whose *yang* forces presumably have not been properly dissipated).[6] Nevertheless, the major ethnographic variations seem to be terminological; while in some areas it is said that the three souls with which the living continue to interact are all known as *hun*,[7] in other parts of China terms such as *p'o*, *kuei*, or *shen* can refer to the souls in the grave, the underworld, and the tablet.[8] Also, it is clear that some of these terms were used interchangeably or in different social contexts.[9]

Stevan Harrell has suggested that the apparent contradictions in the Chinese view of the afterlife can be resolved if what he calls the "analytic" perspective of Chinese literary commentary is replaced by the ethnographers' "action" perspective; the Chinese concept of the "soul," he notes, is fundamentally contextual—grave, tablet, and underworld are but three different areas of religious or ritual concern of the living for their ancestors. It therefore can be assumed that there is one "soul," for even if "there is more than one, . . . they are alike and can be treated in the same way at the same time, which makes them fundamentally one."[10] While I do agree with

5. J. J. M. de Groot, *The Religious System of China: Its Ancient Forms, Evolution, History and Present Aspect*, vols. 1 and 4 (Taipei: Ch'eng-wen, 1964 reprint of Leiden, 1898, 1901), 1:70; Stevan Harrell, "The Concept of Soul in Chinese Folk Religion," *Journal of Asian Studies* 38 (1979): 519–528; Jack Potter, "Wind, Water, Bones and Souls," in Laurence G. Thompson, ed., *The Chinese Way in Religion* (Belmont, Calif.: Wadsworth, 1973), p. 227. [Originally published in *Journal of Oriental Studies* (Hong Kong) 8 (1970): 139–153.]

6. My discussion of the various conceptions of the soul draws upon de Groot, *The Religious System*, vol. 4, which is entirely concerned with Chinese ideas on this subject; on p. 22 he remarks on the merging of *o-kuei* and *ku-hun*; see also Harrell, "The Concept of Soul," for a summary of the various Chinese interpretations.

7. See the Huc, Lowe, and Harrell works cited in notes 4 and 5 above.

8. Osgood, *The Chinese*, p. 1145; David K. Jordan, *Gods, Ghosts, and Ancestors: The Folk Religion of a Taiwanese Village* (Berkeley and Los Angeles: University of California Press, 1972), pp. 31–32.

9. See Wolf, "Gods, Ghosts, and Ancestors," pp. 172–173, on the variable usage of *shen* and *kuei*.

10. Harrell, "The Concept of Soul," p. 523.

Harrell's emphasis on the importance of context for an understanding of how the living define and interact with the dead, the weight of the ethnographic evidence does favor the Chinese belief in three souls, a possibility he too does not deny. In any event, his argument in fact serves to underscore the fundamental incompatibility of the differentiation of the soul with the salvationist ideal.

The Chinese view of salvation also needs to be considered in the context of traditional popular religious beliefs concerning the larger cosmos shared by the living, the dead, and the gods, and while for purposes of this essay it is not necessary for me to deal with this subject in any detail, I must provide enough of an outline so as to relate this cosmic arrangement to Chinese concepts of the afterlife. There was then, the underworld (*yin-chien*), the world of living human beings (*shih-chien* or *yang-chien*), and a higher world of the gods (*t'ien, t'ien-fu,* or *t'ien-chieh*).[11] While the Jade Emperor held court over the other (lower-ranking) gods in the highest of the supernatural domains, he also was held to be the ruler of the cosmos as a whole. If among the gods in the Jade Emperor's court there were those who at the same time were the tutelary deities of communities and groups among the living, other, lower deities—such as the various gods of localities (*t'u-ti*), administrative cities (*ch'eng-huang*), and kitchen hearths (*tsao-chün*)—resided on the earth among human beings. This supernatural government extended into the underworld, which included hell (*ti-yü*) and its ten famous yamens, presided over by Yen-lo wang. Here the dead would be judged—and sometimes horribly punished—as they would be transferred from one yamen to the next, each with its magistrate, secretary-attendants, and demoniacal-monstrous underlings.[12]

Although it has been shown how the gods in each of these domains resembled, with respect to appearance, behavior, and hierarchy, the officials of the imperial bureaucracy,[13] it is important for my present purposes to note that hitherto there has not been given due emphasis in the literature on how the projection of the traditional Chinese polity onto the supernatural involved important modifications with respect to organization. Within the supernatural bureaucracy there was an important distinction, as between

11. See, i.e., Tung Fang-yuan 董芳苑, *T'ai-wan min-chien tsung-chiao hsin-yang* 台灣民間宗教信仰 [Taiwanese folk religious beliefs] (Taipei: Ch'ang-ch'un wen-hua kung-ssu 長春文化公司, 1980), p. 130.

12. For descriptions of the ten yamens of hell, see, i.e., Henry Doré, *Researches into Chinese Superstitions*, trans. M. Kennelly, vols. 1, 6–7 (Taipei: Ch'eng-wen, 1966 reprint of Shanghai, 1913, 1920, 1922), 7: 250–302; Wolfram Eberhard, *Guilt and Sin in Traditional China* (Berkeley and Los Angeles: University of California Press, 1967), pp. 24–59.

13. See Hampden C. DuBose, *Dragon, Image, and Demon* (New York: Armstrong, 1887), p. 358; C. K. Yang, *Religion in Chinese Society: A Study of Contemporary Social Functions of Religion and Some of Their Historical Factors* (Berkeley and Los Angeles: University of California Press, 1961), pp. 150–165; Wolf, "Gods, Ghosts, and Ancestors."

"field administration," whereby god-officials in both the earthly domain (i.e., *ch'eng-huang* or *t'u-ti*) and the underworld each had a specific area of jurisdiction, and the "court" comprising the Jade Emperor and the other higher gods.[14] These gods could serve as the patron deities of many communities precisely because their areas of jurisdiction were not defined in terms of a hierarchy of field administration. Rather, as Feuchtwang has pointed out, popular religion (in contrast to the state cult) took as a community god one which at a particular place had demonstrated *ling*, or "supernatural power and its manifestations," on which basis there could be a "division of power" involving the establishment over a wider area of branch temples all dedicated to the same deity.[15] Thus the supernatural arrangements paralleled those among the living, insofar as court and bureaucracy were two major and separately organized components of the traditional imperial government. Yet an obvious and major difference was that popular religion provided both individuals and communities with far greater access to the gods of all ranks in both court and field administration than did the Chinese imperial state provide direct contact with living government officials.[16]

The supernatural court loomed far larger within the overall organization of the gods than did its earthly counterpart. At the same time, the organization of the gods along lines of formal field administration was most complete in the underworld realm, with its ten yamens and numerous clearly designated hells; in the earthly domain, the place and city gods were organized into hierarchies of territorial administration, but communities could also select their patron protectors from among a large variety of gods in the Jade Emperor's court. A court, with its complex interweaving of bureaucratic, personal, and indeed domestic relationships, served as a most appropriate locale for gods to whom appeal was made by individuals and communities on the basis of their personal efficacy. Thus it comes as no surprise how in one area of Taiwan

> the only figure whose position is universally agreed on is the Jade Emperor . . . , who is at the top. Below him is a group of gods who are higher than other gods, but whom one tries in vain to rank. Some Taiwanese place [Kuan-kung] just below the Jade Emperor himself. . . . In Hsikang the Twelve Plague Gods

14. On the Jade Emperor's court, see e.g., Henri Maspero, *Taoism and Chinese Religion*, trans. Frank A. Kierman, Jr. (Amherst: University of Massachusetts, 1981), pp. 88–92; on *ch'eng-huang* , see Yang, *Religion in Chinese Society*, pp. 156–158.

15. Stephan Feuchtwang, "School Temple and City God," in G. William Skinner, ed., *The City in Late Imperial China* (Stanford: Stanford University Press, 1977), p. 590; also see Philip C. Baity, "The Ranking of the Gods in Chinese Folk Religion," *Asian Folklore Studies* 35 (1977): 75–84, on the subdivision of god images.

16. On this point, see Emily Martin Ahern, *Chinese Ritual and Politics* (Cambridge: Cambridge University Press, 1981), pp. 100–102.

are immediately below the Jade Emperor. Some informants insert most of the Buddhist pantheon at this point, including and especially [Kuan-yin]. Others include the gods who preside over the dead.[17]

The reference to Kuan-yin in the preceding quotation underscores the point that while a strict extension of the administrative model onto the supernatural world would leave no room within cosmic organization for female deities, the situation is rather different with respect to the higher domain of the gods. Thus there is also the case of T'ien Hou (Ma-tsu), a most important goddess especially in southeastern China, who in many popular religious contexts plays the same role of community protector as do numerous gods: her case presents no anomaly, given her powerful position in the heavenly court.[18]

Popular religion recognized yet another supernatural domain, one not following the bureaucratic model, although linked to it. Thus Kuan-yin was believed to escort at least a few select and most fortunate souls from the underworld to the "Western Heaven" (hsi-t'ien), presided over by A-mi-t'o-fo (the Amitabha Buddha). This was indeed paradise (chi-le-kuo); here, under circumstances of total bliss, there would appear to have been none of the material and social involvements, concerns, and requirements that loomed so large not only for the living but also—most interestingly—for the dead. Representations of paradise were popularized by woodcuts such as those which "often pictured the sparkling waters of the sacred lake of the Pure Land, the surface of which is starred with lotus-flowers, each bearing in its calyx the spiritual body of those fortunate beings who by the grace of Amitabha or the guidance of [Kuan-yin] have attained the felicity of a rebirth in the Western Paradise."[19] A summary of the textual description of the paradise reads:

> Those who reach it will henceforth escape all subsequent births. There is no fear of becoming a hungry ghost . . . , or an animal by transmigration, for such modes of life are unknown there. It is composed of gold, silver, lapis-lazuli, beryl, ruby and cornelia. There are all kinds of beautiful flowers, which the inhabitants pluck, and offer to the thousands of Buddhas who visit them from other worlds. . . . Fountains bubble up from all sides. In the middle of the lake are lotus flowers, large as a chariot wheel, blue, yellow, red and white, each

17. Jordan, Gods, Ghosts, and Ancestors, pp. 40–41.
18. On T'ien Hou, see James L. Watson, "Standardizing the Gods: The Promotion of T'ien Hou (Empress of Heaven) Along the South China Coast, 960–1960," in David Johnson, Andrew Nathan, and Evelyn Rawski, eds., Popular Culture in Late Imperial China (Berkeley and Los Angeles: University of California Press, 1985); female deities as a class are discussed in P. Steven Sangren, "Female Gender in Chinese Religious Symbols: Kuan Yin, Ma Tsu, and the 'Eternal Mother,'" Signs 9 (1983): 4–25; on the distinction between court deities and posted official gods, cf. Wolf, "Gods, Ghosts, and Ancestors," pp. 138–143.
19. Reginald Fleming Johnston, Buddhist China (London: John Murray, 1913), p. 103.

reflecting brilliant hues of its own colour and possessed of the most perfect and delightful fragrance.[20]

While it is to be expected that lay devotees of Pure Land Buddhism would have in their minds a relatively full picture of the Western Heaven, I have no evidence to show the extent to which in different areas of the country the textually derived descriptions of paradise, or even their pictographic representations, had entered into the imagery of popular religion in general. However, on the basis of funeral practices alone, there can be no doubt that the idea of the Western Heaven of paradise was expressed in popular Chinese religious practice. For example, the phrase *chieh-yin hsi-fang* ("to be guided to the West," usually by Kuan-yin) is very much in view during funerary rituals, often being inscribed on condolence messages, banners carried during the funeral procession, or on flags placed by the grave.[21] Again, incorporated into the image of hell was the possibility that at least a select few might be accorded entrance to the land of bliss shortly after death when, upon entering hell's first court, they are judged to merit immediate release and salvation; and it is also possible that yet other souls may be granted admittance to heaven after a period of time in the underworld.

But the fact remains that much of the content of Chinese popular religion as a whole would be unintelligible if it were based on the assumption that the "Western Paradise" was the immediate or final destination of a substantial proportion of the departed "souls." Indeed, it is significant that there was little if anything in the context of popular ritual and belief which would give those who knew the deceased even an indication that he or she had attained paradise; rather, what was important was that the departed had three souls, as separately manifested in the three different contexts of underworld, grave, and ancestral tablet. These framed much of the cult of the dead, and I deal with each in turn in order to further consider the role played either by salvation/paradise or by its denial.

Salvation as a concern certainly loomed largest with respect to ideas concerning the underworld. As was noted above, there is the possibility that the dead will "pass over" from the courts of hell to the Western Paradise. Yet the popular view held that such an outcome was quite unlikely. Hsu, for example, describes the relevant situation as follows: "Most West Towners are not very explicit about what will happen to their dead, but all banners of condolence from relatives and friends convey the sentiment that the dead is on his or her way to Western Heaven. In fact, however, most informants

20. Doré, *Researches*, 6:112.

21. See J. J. M. de Groot, "Buddhist Masses for the Dead at Amoy," in *Actes du Sixième Congrès International des Orientalistes, tenu en 1883 à Leide, Quatrième Partie, Section 4, de L'extrême-orient* (Leiden: E. J. Brill , 1885), p. 101; Doré, *Researches*, 1: fig. 59.

agree that the majority of the spirits of the dead will have to go through some unpleasant things in the lower world of the spirits."[22]

While the underworld, as was noted above, was the most highly bureaucratized of the supernatural domains, it should be added that it also was most similar to the world of the living. For beyond the courts of hell there was a larger underworld region where resided those souls who either deserved no punishment or had been ransomed by the offerings of their kin. Maspero, basing his remarks on observations of funeral rituals in Kiangsu, notes how, among other paper items, a house is burnt for the benefit of the deceased, who "must live in the infernal plains where, with other souls, it makes up cities and towns around the palaces of the Yama Kings," such that "each one continues his earthly life: some are field workers, others merchants, others receive more or less important positions as infernal officials."[23] A fuller picture of this underworld is provided by Ahern, with respect to modern Taiwan. Her account confirms how the detailed construction of this realm as an image of society on earth provided a religious basis, not only for the living to continue to remember their dead kin, but also for ongoing interaction with them.[24]

Thus, rather than focusing on the salvation of the dead, Chinese funeral and postfuneral ritual was concerned first with aiding the deceased's passage through the underworld's ten courts and then with providing him or her in that very same underworld with as comfortable a material life as possible, until such time as the "soul" would be reincarnated. Because these two goals accounted for much of the death ritual concerning the underworld, this ritual reflected the basic assumption of salvation's nonoccurrence. There were other rituals, carried out by Buddhist clergy, which were aimed at helping the deceased to "pass over" to the Western Paradise; while some were linked to the funeral itself, others were performed periodically (i.e., on a person's death anniversary), thus reinforcing the belief that the dead remained in the underworld. Another reflection of this belief was the custom whereby paper money and paper clothes for those who had died

---

22. Francis L. K. Hsu, *Under the Ancestors' Shadow: Kinship, Personality, and Social Mobility in Village China*, revised and expanded edition (New York: Doubleday, 1967), p. 158. A nineteenth-century Western observer remarked that "the four hundred millions of China believe practically that the departed roam at large in a realm where devils and demons rule, and where they are as entirely dependent on the gifts of their friends as are the captives in a Chinese prison"; see C. F. Gordon Cumming, *Wanderings in China* (Edinburgh and London: William Blackwood, 1888), p. 217; also Maurice Freedman, "Ancestor Worship: Two Facets of the Chinese Case," in G. William Skinner, ed., *The Study of Chinese Society: Essays by Maurice Freedman* (Stanford: Stanford University Press, 1979), p. 296.

23. Maspero, *Taoism and Chinese Religion*, p. 186.

24. Ahern, *The Cult of the Dead*, pp. 220–224; see also DuBose, *Dragon, Image, and Demon*, p. 358, where the underworld is characterized as "China ploughed under."

earlier were included in the offerings made during the funerals of recently deceased kin.[25]

The dead in the underworld were not completely cut off from the living. They could be visited directly through trance or spirit mediums, and it is commonly reported that such communications were prompted by the belief that illness or other troubles among the living were due to the improper treatment of the dead, especially by their closer surviving kin.[26] The unhappy souls may have been wronged while still alive, or may not have been receiving the sustenance that they continued to desire or need after death. In any event, it is clear that popular belief had it that the relationship between the living and the dead was one of interaction. Because the rituals and beliefs concerning the underworld could in some contexts express fear, but in others the solicitude, warmth, and loss felt with respect to the dead by their living relatives, there was highlighted the incompatibility of this ritual complex with the idea of attained salvation.

Ancestors, in the underworld, are ghosts; in the tablets, however, they are "spirits," or *shen*, worshipped on the basis of a reciprocal relationship which both projects and continues ties that among the living are between senior and junior family members and agnates. While there has been disagreement among anthropologists as to whether the ancestors in the tablet, like the souls in the underworld, are essentially benign or can under certain circumstances cause harm to their descendants,[27] there certainly is no doubt that these ancestors need, expect, and demand worship. As *shen*, the ancestors are close by, and because they are seen to have needs and desires similar to those of the living, they certainly are not thought to be enjoying a blissful existence in the Western Heaven. Indeed, if they were held to be in paradise, the cult of the ancestors as popularly practiced would be seriously undermined.

As with those in the underworld and the ancestral tablet, the soul in the coffin and then in the grave provided a focus for interaction between the living and the dead. The siting of the grave importantly involved geomancy (*feng-shui*), such that proper placement was held to be beneficial to the descendants of the deceased, whereas a bad location could bring harm, and there have been differences among anthropological observers regarding the extent to which the dead in their graves were merely the passive objects of sometimes competitive manipulation by the living for the latter's own gain, or in fact were able to actively express pleasure or dissatisfaction regarding

25. De Groot, "Buddhist Masses," p. 34; see also Ahern, The Cult of the Dead, p. 227, and Doolittle, Social Life, 1:193.

26. Ahern, The Cult of the Dead, pp. 201–202; Jack Potter, "Cantonese Shamanism," in Wolf, ed., Religion and Ritual in Chinese Society, pp. 207–232.

27. See the summary of this argument in Wolf, "Gods, Ghosts, and Ancestors," pp. 163–168.

the conditions of their interment.[28] For my present purposes, however, it is more important to note how there is general agreement that the dead had to be properly encoffined; because of practices such as reinterment in southeastern China and delayed burial in the north, there would be variations with respect to the point at which the soul would be settled. In any event, the effort by the living was to control this soul; its salvation was hardly a major concern. That the coffin/grave soul had to be fixed is demonstrated by the reported belief that prior to this the dead were most dangerous to the living.[29] Another interesting confirmation is provided by a description of how in Shantung the soul is placed in the grave even in the absence of the body. According to Johnston, "calling the soul back" involves the burial of an effigy of the deceased; also, as in standard ritual, the spirit of the dead person is entered into the ancestral tablet: "The soul, or rather the combination of souls, has been saved from homelessness, and will in future assume its proper position as an ancestral ghost both in the family graveyard and in the ancestral temple."[30]

Although Johnston does not refer in this context to the soul in the underworld, it is clear from the evidence which confirms the Chinese belief in three souls that through burial and subsequent rituals the Chinese both defined these souls and attended to them by carrying out the proper funeral and postfuneral rites regarding burial, the "dotting" of the ancestral tablet, and the escort of the third soul to the underworld; the Chinese belief, I suggest, was that not all the dead had three souls—only those who were properly buried. As for the rest, they were precisely the ghosts whose presence loomed so importantly, and sometimes so dangerously, in the world of the living.

My hypothesis that ghosts had only one soul might seem to conflict with Wolf's observation that because ghosts were in many ways equivalent to strangers, the spirit which for one person was a ghost could for another be an ancestor. However, Wolf notes that such ghosts are not dangerous,[31] and the same point is made by Harrell: "Most spirits who are ghosts to one person are ancestors to someone else, and as such are relatively neutral and unimportant in the lives of anyone but their own descendants."[32] Although one of the spirits taken to be a ghost by someone who was not a relative is

28. See Ahern, *The Cult of the Dead*, pp. 175–190, and Rubie Watson, chapter 9 in this volume.

29. See James L. Watson, "Of Flesh and Bones: The Management of Death Pollution in Cantonese Society," in Maurice Bloch and Jonathan Parry, eds., *Death and the Regeneration of Life* (Cambridge: Cambridge University Press, 1982).

30. R. F. Johnston, *Lion and Dragon in Northern China* (London: John Murray, 1910), p. 282.

31. Wolf, "Gods, Ghosts, and Ancestors," p. 172.

32. Ibid, p. 193.

described by Wolf as that of "a woman on her way to her son's house to receive deathday offerings made in her honor,"[33] it might be stretching the internal and regional consistency of Chinese popular religious beliefs a bit too far to suggest that such relatively harmless ghosts were generally the "third souls" of cared-for dead which for one reason or another had temporarily returned from the underworld. Nevertheless, I do think that Chinese belief did make a basic distinction between the malevolent ghosts, who had "trapped, uncontrolled souls,"[34] and those spirits—comforted by the support of their descendants—who had three.

Rather than attempt to summarize the large literature on the connection between ghosts and bad death or bad burial I will here merely note some of the more commonly reported contexts whereby the lack of proper attention to the dead is linked both to the appearance of ghosts and to the absence of a full definition of the three souls. Those who in life had married virilocally, produced male offspring, bequeathed to them property of some economic significance, and died at a reasonably advanced age certainly were in the best position to receive proper ritual attention after death;[35] but even the dead thus situated could make their displeasure known if their descendants did not provide the expected worship. There were also persons whose deaths occurred under less than favorable circumstances but who nevertheless left kin behind; those who had died away from home, violently, prior to marriage, or without male descendants could return to torment or even cause harm to their living relatives. Thus the assignment of a male agnate to serve as the "adopted" heir of someone who died childless was common enough, while "ghost marriages" might comfort those male and female spirits who had died as children. Such procedures, it should be noted, often led, finally, to the proper placement of the souls of the unhappy dead in ancestral tablets or in the grave.[36]

Prominent among the ghosts without living kin to attend to their graves or tablets were the mass of the anonymous dead in the underworld. These were the beggar-ghosts; because they had long been forgotten by the living, they too were incomplete and required sustenance, and each year they were released from hell to roam about on the earth during the seventh lunar month, when there would be rituals of propitiation.[37] Spirits who remained

---

33. Ibid, p. 172.

34. Stephan Feuchtwang, "Domestic and Communal Worship in Taiwan," in Arthur P. Wolf, ed., *Religion and Ritual in Chinese Society*, p. 125.

35. Martin, in chapter 7 in this volume, notes that even under such circumstances women did not fare as well as men.

36. See, i.e., Johnston, *Lion and Dragon*, pp. 204–205.

37. Gordon Cumming, *Wanderings*, pp. 218–220; John Henry Grey, *China: A History of the Laws, Manners, and Customs of the People* (London: Macmillan, 1878), 1:261–263, are among the many accounts.

among the living for longer periods included those who at the time of their deaths had been socially isolated; they became the "hungry ghosts" without descendants to worship them, and without ancestral tablets for their souls. Also threatening the living were the fearsome and malicious *li-kuei*, who had died by drowning or through suicide, circumstances under which death not only was violent but often resulted in the loss of the body itself; for such demons, even access to hell was denied. Perhaps the most extreme contrast with the properly dead and their three souls is represented by terrifying creatures such as the zombie-like *chiang-shih*[38] or the *han-pa* drought-demon.[39] What caused these creatures to be among the most dangerous of monsters was the absence of any differentiation whatsoever between the corpse and its souls.

Those monsters who were denied entry to hell somehow had to be destroyed or at least avoided at all costs. The more approachable of these incomplete spirits received ritual attention through the *p'u-tu* or rites for universal salvation and other ceremonies, during which both the "feeding of the ghosts" and their hoped-for salvation in Western Paradise were given prominent emphasis. Yet the ghosts were hungry precisely because they did not have three souls; their need for both food and salvation highlighted the fundamental incompatibility of salvationist religion with one largely based on the continuing interaction of the living with the dead. Yet this incompatibility was itself given emphasis by popular religion, precisely because this religion recognized the idea of salvation—and perhaps even highlighted it as an ideal if not as a hope—at the same time that it was organized on the basis of its nonoccurrence.

In describing the hierarchy of gods in West Town, Hsu notes that his informants distinguish between the "'Higher World of Spirits,'" and the 'Western World of Happiness,' also referred to as 'Supreme Heaven' and 'Western Heaven' respectively."[40] While the "Higher World of the Spirits," ruled by the Jade Emperor, "shows more signs of being an administrative machinery, the [Western Heaven] is more like paradise pure and simple."[41] Yet, of course, both in West Town and elsewhere in China it was from the "Higher World of the Spirits" that most gods of popular religion were drawn; these gods were objects of worship in their own right, and as was noted above, they were linked to the deities of earth and the underworld in a unitary bureaucratized framework.

The essentially human qualities of the gods have been remarked on often

---

38. On the *chiang-shih*, see J. J. M. de Groot, *The Religion of the Chinese* (New York: Macmillan, 1910), p. 76; Nevius, *China and the Chinese*, p. 166.

39. For *han-pa*, see Johnston, *Lion and Dragon*, pp. 295–297.

40. Hsu, *Under the Ancestors' Shadow*, p. 139.

41. Ibid., p. 141.

enough. In their behavior they are said to resemble and reflect the character-istics of government officials among the living and are therefore to be distin-guished from ancestors, who are as living kinsmen.[42] Most of the gods of Chinese popular religion had originally been human beings, either reincar-nated from the underworld to godhood or more directly transformed on the earth from *kuei* to *shen*. Although a god commonly was referred to as a *p'u-sa* (from *p'u-t'i-sa-t'o*), this appellation cannot be taken too literally. The gods of the popular pantheon were not bodhisattvas—their mission was not to lead mortals to salvation, but rather to protect and regulate society, of which they the gods were in fact a part.[43] On the other hand, although paradise provided the salvationist ideal, it contributed relatively little to the total content of popular religious practices.

Ideas concerning reincarnation generally tend to be mentioned en pas-sant, at least in the anthropological analyses of Chinese popular religion. Nevertheless, reincarnation was important,[44] such that in the beliefs of late traditional popular religion there was either continuity with or at least resemblance to the attitudes of those early Chinese Buddhists who "felt obviously less fervent about *ending* the cycle of rebirths than they did about the idea of *rebirth itself*."[45] The procedure was the responsibility of the tenth (and last) yamen-court of hell, and an important goal of much reli-gious ritual was to provide the dead with as favorable a rebirth as possible, a concern obviously reflecting a de-emphasis of Western Paradise.

Popular ideas concerning reincarnation differed in at least two important ways from those otherwise relating to gods, ghosts, and ancestors. First, reincarnation did not directly project onto the dead the current social rela-tionships among the living; and because its outcome was uncertain, neither did it represent the continuation of those social relationships that had existed prior to a person's death; rather, as Freedman has pointed out, the dead underwent rebirth when they had ceased to be remembered by those who were still alive.[46] There was thus little or no tension between beliefs in reincarnation and the religiously important links between the living and the dead.

From the point of view of the individual, transmigration could have dif-ferent results, which as far as popular religion is concerned seem largely to have involved bad rebirth as a demon in the underworld or as an animal; or

---

42. See Ahern, *Chinese Ritual and Politics*; Wolf, "Gods, Ghosts, and Ancestors."

43. See, i.e., Baity, "The Ranking of the Gods," p. 75; Stevan Harrell, "When a Ghost Becomes a God," in Arthur P. Wolf, ed., *Religion and Ritual in Chinese Society*; Maspero, *Taoism and Chinese Religion*, p. 85.

44. Johnston, *Lion and Dragon*, pp. 403–404; DuBose, *Dragon, Image, and Demon*, p. 314; and others; the sources abound with at least references to the subject.

45. Wolfgang Bauer, *China and the Search for Happiness*, trans. Michael Shaw (New York: Seabury, 1976), p. 439, n.50, emphasis in original.

46. Freedman, "Ancestor Worship," p. 278.

rebirth as a human being, an eventuality which could be of varying desirability, depending on the social position assumed in the next life; finally, and most desirable, there could be rebirth as a god.[47] Because an important focus of funeral ritual was to secure for the deceased a good rebirth, there was provided within popular religious belief a positive alternative to the salvationistic ideal. That good rebirth might indeed take pride of place is noted by one observer:

> The Buddhists have a western heaven presided over by Amitabha. . . . There many become Buddhas and are free from sin, sorrow, and suffering. They may also escape transmigration. This appeals to some very devout Buddhists, but not to the Chinese people in general. They want to enjoy the present life or to accumulate merit so as to enjoy a happy and fortunate existence after rebirth. The Chinese . . . prefer life in this world.[48]

Like so much else in popular religion, it is to be expected that beliefs concerning reincarnation would show much variation, by region, class, and gender, or even between individuals.[49] Nevertheless, if these beliefs expressed uncertainty regarding the afterlife, they also had an important affirmative aspect: reincarnation was required for conception, which is the reunion of reincarnated *hun* with the physical *p'o*.[50] Because all living creatures, as well as many of the gods, were believed to have been reincarnated, rebirth was required for the maintenance of the cosmos itself.

Thus it is not surprising that various rites connected with "cosmic renewal" should in fact emphasize the incompatibility of this process with total salvation. For example, this can be seen in the ritual for "universal salvation" (*p'u-tu*), which can be performed independently by either Buddhist or Taoist priests, or by the latter as part of the larger *chiao* ritual, which achieves "cosmic renewal" by maintaining or restoring the proper balance between the forces of *yang* and *yin*.[51] It is true that at the conclusion of the *p'u-tu* some of the "souls" released from hell will be sent to heaven; however, the demon-controller "Ta-shih Yeh" "will first accompany those souls who must go back to the torments of hell," and while he "is leaving, the high priest pulls the silk curtain tightly closed in front of him so that the evil yin influences from those vengeful souls sent back

47. Maspero, *Taoism and Chinese Religion*, pp. 86–87; Jordan, *Gods, Ghosts, and Ancestors*, pp. 35–36.

48. David Crockett Graham, *Folk Religion in Southwest China* (Washington, D.C: Smithsonian Press, 1961), p. 184.

49. Jordan, *Gods, Ghosts, and Ancestors*, pp. 35–36.

50. Doré, *Researches*, 1:137; Lowe, *The Adventures of Wu*, 1:59–60; Marjorie Topley, "Cosmic Antagonisms: A Mother-Child Syndrome," in Arthur P. Wolf, ed., *Religion and Ritual in Chinese Society*.

51. Feuchtwang, "Domestic and Communal Worship"; Kristofer M. Schipper, "The Written Memorial in Taoist Ceremonies," in Arthur P. Wolf, ed., *Religion and Ritual in Chinese Society*.

to the torments of hell will not cause damage."[52] It is important to add that the dead continue to play a role in "cosmic renewal," not only in the context of community-sponsored ritual, but also during their own funeral ceremonies. This, in fact, is the point of James Watson's article dealing with Cantonese death rites. He notes how his informants believe that a spirit newly released by death is powerful, unpredictable, and disrupts "the natural order of the cosmos . . . and then gradually settles. There is thus a shift . . . to total dependence on the part of the spirit by the time final entombment takes place, years after death."[53] More generally, the funeral rites aim at restoring a proper relation between *yin* and *yang* forces through the absorption by the appropriate persons (as defined by social relationships) of death pollution. Although the deceased do finally enter "the realm of the ancestors,"[54] their true fate is best revealed by Watson's remark that "the world order and the social structure of the living have meaning only through the manipulation and preservation of the dead."[55]

Indeed, a major focus of anthropological scholarship has been to show that within the larger supernatural cosmos there also was the projection or representation of critical relationships among the living: gods, ghosts, and ancestors tell us about government, community, kinsmen, friends, and strangers. Popular religion was able to provide a "national" context, as it were, within which some of the most intimate local social concerns might find expression.[56] However, the cosmos of popular religion clearly comprised more than beliefs involving projections from the living to the dead, and included the operation of impersonal forces connected with geomancy or horoscopic prognostications. In the final analysis, there was in popular religion an orientation toward a total cosmic construction within which the positions of both the living and the dead were highlighted precisely because the social circumstances of the former were paralleled by those of the latter, and also, more important, because the arrangements for both were conceived as involved in a yet larger integrated system of relationships, one whose various parts were mutually interdependent.[57]

If salvation was not a major concern of popular religion, it was hardly

---

52. Duane Pang, "The *P'u-Tu* Ritual," in Michael Saso and David W. Chappell, eds., *Buddhist and Taoist Studies* (Honolulu: University of Hawaii Press, 1977), 1:116–117.

53. James L. Watson, "Of Flesh and Bones," p. 180.

54. Ibid., p. 179.

55. Ibid., p. 157.

56. Yang, *Religion in Chinese Society*, pp. 136–137.

57. See ibid.; the linking within one supernatural domain of such impersonal forces together with the representation of imperial administration and local community, kinship, family, and even individual concerns is one basis for arguing that there is what may be called a Chinese religious system. See Maurice Freedman, "On the Sociological Study of Chinese Religion," in Wolf, ed., *Religion and Ritual in Chinese Society*.

given greater emphasis in the religious institutions and rituals sponsored by the state.[58] This suggests that consideration of the relationship between the state and popular religon may shed further light on those ideas regarding death and the afterlife which were dominant in the general population. The state itself defined as "heretical" the beliefs of certain sects that were salvation-oriented (see below); but the religious attitudes of the majority of the people were sufficiently conditioned by the state and its ideology to warrant my use of the term "popular orthodoxy."

In the first place, there are sociological grounds for linking the state's degree-holding elite and the majority of commoners within one orthodox sphere: insofar as degree-holders and others with elite status were members of local communities, they in fact were intimately involved in the religious life and temple affairs of towns and villages, and at the same time they at least symbolized the presence and operation of the imperial system.[59] Also, the state cult and the dominant form of popular religion can be placed together within the realm of orthodoxy on the basis of institutional links: for example, if a major component of the state cult was religion (or ritual) by the elite for the elite as centered especially in the Confucian temples (*wen-miao*), another important element was based in the temples of the city god, who saw to the passage of the dead to the underworld and was of major significance for the religious beliefs of the masses; again, community-based temples might have their chief deities honored or incorporated into the imperial pantheon. In addition, the state gave at least indirect support to belief in good rebirth as preferable to salvation; rebirth as a god could be facilitated for those winning the state's approval, such that a "remarkable personage, whether he be eminent for bravery, virtue, public charity, or any other notable characteristic, may be honoured after death by deification at the hands of the Imperial Court; whereby the State rewards a distinguished public servant or private benefactor."[60] Although such activities by the state and its bureaucratic and degree-holding elites were but aspects of their much larger direct manipulation and involvement with popular religion,[61] the projection of imperial government organization onto the supernatural world is of itself telling evidence of the state's direct and indirect impact on

58. For a discussion of the state cult, see Feuchtwang, "School Temple and City God" (n. 15 above).

59. On "gentry" control of local temples, see Kung-chuan Hsiao, *Rural China, Imperial Control in the Nineteenth Century* (Seattle: University of Washington Press, 1960), pp. 234, 280; it is to be expected that lower degree-holders would be more directly and consistently involved in matters pertaining to popular religion than would literati of the highest ranks.

60. See Alfred C. Lyall, *Asiatic Studies: Religious and Social*, second series (London: John Murray, 1899), pp. 121ff; Feuchtwang, "School Temple and City God," pp. 606–607.

61. See, i.e., Ahern, *Chinese Ritual and Politics*; James L. Watson, "Standardizing the Gods" (n. 18 above), deals with the incorporation of T'ien Hou into the state pantheon.

common religious beliefs. As Wolf has suggested, if the gods were officials, the soul in the underworld was a "citizen of the empire."[62]

However, a consideration of ideas concerning salvation and the afterlife indicates some possibly even more fundamental elite-commoner linkages in late traditional China. If the "high Confucian" attitude toward the dead can be described as focusing on their impact on the living, both as their being exemplars and through rituals which stress that filiality cannot be interrupted by death, the dominant religion of the masses also insisted that the living continued to interact with the dead in the grave, the tablet, and also in the underworld, where they, the dead, affirmed the stability of society on earth by inhabiting a similarly structured supernatural realm. Furthermore, the idea of cosmic stability and continuity loomed large both in state Confucianism and in orthodox popular religion, and for the latter this was achieved by projecting state and society onto the supernatural, by seeing the masses of anonymous dead as essentially chaotic (*luan*) but nevertheless under the firm control of priests or supernatural officials, by believing that the familiar dead continued to reside in a more orderly and earth-like portion of the underworld, and finally by equating release from this underworld more with reincarnation or the assumption of godhood than with salvation. Obviously, there probably were vast differences of religious belief between an elite and high-ranking Confucian degree-holder at one extreme and an illiterate peasant at the other; however, between these two extremes, and within the orthodox religious sphere, it may not be easy to draw a sharp line between elite and commoner beliefs.[63]

That we can take as "popular orthodoxy" this religion of the masses—which incorporated ideas of paradise into its supernatural scheme of things but nevertheless was grounded on the nonoccurrence of salvation—receives further confirmation when it is briefly contrasted with some of the different or alternative popular religious traditions of the "sectarian" cults, where salvation indeed was the major focus.[64] The goal of many practices, such as

62. Wolf, "Gods, Ghosts, and Ancestors," p. 175; also see Yang, *Religion in Chinese Society*, pp. 50–51.

63. For example, de Groot's massive compendium of Chinese religious beliefs and practices was based, he says, on his observations of "well-to-do classes and families of fashionable standing"; see de Groot, *The Religious System*, 1:1–2; also see Yang, *Religion in Chinese Society*, pp. 276–277.

64. See Daniel L. Overmyer, *Folk Buddhist Religion: Dissenting Sects in Late Traditional China* (Cambridge: Harvard University Press, 1976), pp. 156–157; Stevan Harrell and Elizabeth J. Perry, "Syncretic Sects in Chinese Society: An Introduction," *Modern China* 8 (1982): 288–289; Susan Naquin, *Millenarian Rebellion in China: The Eight Trigrams Uprising of 1813* (New Haven: Yale University Press, 1976). Insofar as themes from orthodox Buddhism influenced the sectarian groups, a distinction can be drawn between the Pure Land tradition with its emphasis on the Amitabha Buddha and salvation in Western Paradise, and that which

recitation of the name of the Amitabha Buddha or vegetarianism, was to insure immediate passage at death from earth to paradise: belief was in direct salvation unencumbered by the obligations or threats posed by continuing interaction with the living, by the underworld's bureaucracy, or by reincarnation. An example of such beliefs can be seen from the reaction of one member of a Peking vegetarian sect to his wife's death as a result of a fire in their home; although according to the ideas of the dominant popular religion she might very well be expected to reappear as a ghost, he described her death as follows: "She died gloriously! She's already in attendance by the side of the Eternal Mother (*lao-mu*)."[65] The linking of immediate salvation to an explicit rejection of popular orthodoxy's underworld seems evident in the case of the Lung-hua sect in Amoy, for whose members death is "a most joyful event"; unlike the funeral customs of believers in the dominant religion, among sect members there is no wailing, inscriptions on red paper are not covered with white, nor is paper money burnt.[66] In modern Taiwan, ritual differentiation from the practices of orthodox popular religion characterizes the "Seek the Way Association," a group viewed as peculiar if not fearful by nonmembers; likewise distinguishing the Association is its salvationistic aim: "The ultimate goal is to [*ch'iu tao*] (receive the way), at which point the soul attains direct permanent admittance to heaven; there is no further rebirth."[67]

While the description of popular beliefs and practices must be ethnographic, a concern of much of the literature on Chinese religion has been to relate the ordinary person's religious behavior to the textual traditions and to the ideas and rituals of those who were able to write such texts or at least to read them. Although obviously necessary for understanding the interconnections and contrasts between the elite and popular domains of religious orthodoxy in traditional China, consideration of the relationship between texts and beliefs is also important with respect to the "heterodox" sects; the trend—out of necessity—has been to rely largely on the sectarian literature,

---

focused on the Maitreya, or Future Buddha, who will descend to the human realm; during late imperial times, the orientation of certain sects was toward individual salvation in the Pure Land after death, while others held that the arrival on this earth of the Maitreya Buddha signaled both the imminent destruction of the universe and the salvation in a restructured world of all believers.

65. Li Shih-yü 李世瑜, *Hsien-tsai Hua-pei mi-mi tsung-chiao* 現在華北秘密宗教 [Secret religions in contemporary north China] (Chengtu, 1948), p. 136; the Eternal Mother, or Unbegotten Eternal Mother, is an important divinity in some sectarian traditions; see Naquin, *Millenarian Rebellion*, pp. 9–10.

66. J. J. M. de Groot, *Sectarianism and Religious Persecution in China: A Page in the History of Religions* (Leiden: E. J. Brill, 1903), 1:233.

67. Ahern, *Chinese Ritual and Politics*, p. 70.

from which important syntheses have been made concerning "heterodox" beliefs.[68]

The contents of some of the sectarian documents do reveal striking contrasts with orthodoxy, and on the basis of their simpler literary style and the emphasis on congregationalism and sutra recitation, it seems clear that for many sects within the "heterodox" domain there was indeed a close connection between text and practice, while for others that were more loosely organized the focus was on meditational activities based upon strong teacher-disciple ties.[69] Maintaining themselves through a variety of special organizational means, these sects had rituals and beliefs which in comparison with those of the dominant popular religion were not nearly as "diffuse" nor as "institutionalized" within culture and society as a whole.[70] Thus the preservation of the sects could not be assured by the social and cultural representation and reproduction which maintained the dominant religious beliefs and practices; and neither was "heterodoxy"—at least with respect to its most "heterodox" elements[71]—directly reflective or projectionistic of society at large. Overmyer in fact suggests that a strong desire for permanent institutionalization in territory under their own control was one of the factors which could encourage sectarians to rebel, a factor which

68. See Naquin, *Millenarian Rebellion*; Overmyer, *Folk Buddhist Religion*; Marjorie Topley, "The Great Way of Former Heaven: A Group of Chinese Secret Religious Sects," *Bulletin of the School of Oriental and African Studies* 26 (1963): 362–392; an additional textual source has been the official transcripts of the interrogation of captured sectarians, as in Naquin, *Millenarian Rebellion*.

69. See Naquin, *Millenarian Rebellion*. More recently, Naquin has underscored the important difference within the White Lotus tradition between "sutra-recitation sects," which were dependent upon texts and relatively formal organization, and the "meditational sects," which were more diffusely organized and had as their organizational focus the teacher-pupil tie; see her "The Transmission of White Lotus Sectarianism in Late Imperial China," in Johnson et al., *Popular Culture in Late Imperial China*.

70. See Yang, *Religion in Chinese Society*, p. 20, on "diffuse" and "institutionalized" religion.

71. For example, among elements in the White Lotus religion were beliefs such as in Maitreya messianism, which substituted the legitimacy of a divine Buddha-savior for the orthodox doctrine of a human emperor who was the Son of Heaven by dint of having received its Mandate; the Unbegotten Eternal Mother grieved for her children (humanity) who needed salvation, a pessimistic judgment as to the condition of the world, which rejected the state Confucian perspective that humans through proper behavior would be in accord with the natural order of the cosmos, which was moral and basically good; the end of a kalpa (era), which would bring universal destruction, likewise denied the state's emphasis on cosmic continuity and orthodox popular religion's focus on cosmic renewal; the view that acceptance of sectarian doctrine would lead to a person's salvation, either in Western Paradise or on earth as a survivor of a forthcoming universal destruction, resulted in a differentiation of believers from nonbelievers or of the saved from the doomed which could cut across the ties and social relationships of kinship and community emphasized by both popular and elite orthodoxy. For description and analysis of these and other White Lotus beliefs, see Naquin, *Millenarian Rebellion*, pp. 7–54.

sometimes operated independently of the more obvious provocation presented by government efforts at suppression, or by severe economic pressures and dislocations.[72]

Nevertheless, Overmyer also points out that the sectarian tradition as such cannot be understood merely with reference to the uprisings that did involve some sects at certain times; although beliefs regarding the arrival of the Maitreya Buddha-messiah and the onset of a new "era" (kalpa) might set the stage for an uprising, sectarians were not necessarily rebellious; and when there was rebellion, the original group of sectarian believers might be joined by others for a variety of reasons not linked to religious concerns. Rebellion aside, sects were attractive because to some they offered a generally more satisfying religious life, including the hope for salvation.[73] But if concern with the sectarian salvationistic tradition as an enduring feature of Chinese life is an important complement to an earlier focus on sects as fomenters of rebellion, there is then the question of the social and religious relationships between sectarians and the rest of the population.

Having beliefs and practices which differentiated them from the population at large, the sects commonly recruited members "on an individual, rather than a community basis," and were especially attractive to "less rooted segments of the population,"[74] who for one reason or another were not fully involved in the "natural" network of social relationships based on family, kinship, and community and who therefore had to construct their own social arrangements. Precisely because orthodox popular religion reinforced the "naturalness" or, indeed, the inevitability of customary social patterns among the living by projecting them onto the supernatural as well, such popular religion might have diminished appeal to socially marginal groups such as Grand Canal boatmen[75] or the residents of all-female vegetarian homes.[76] Likewise, because orthodox popular religion stressed the fact that both the living and the dead continued, albeit in somewhat different ways, to be rooted in society, groups who had to create their own alternative social relationships need not have been constrained in their desire for salvation by the limits placed on such a goal by orthodoxy. The

72. See Daniel L. Overmyer, "Alternatives: Popular Religious Sects in Chinese Society," *Modern China* 7 (1981): 187; but for major sectarian rebellions, see Susan Naquin, *Millenarian Rebellion,* and her *Shantung Rebellion: The Wang Lun Uprising of 1774* (New Haven: Yale University Press, 1981).

73. See Overmyer, "Alternatives," pp. 155–169, where additional attractions offered by sectarianism are discussed.

74. Harrell and Perry, "Syncretic Sects," p. 299; Naquin, "Transmission of White Lotus Sectarianism," p. 257.

75. See David E. Kelley, "Temples and Tribute Fleets: The Luo Sect and Boatmen's Associations in the Eighteenth Century," *Modern China* 8 (1982): 337–360.

76. See Topley, "The Great Way of Former Heaven."

sectarian message of salvation was quite attractive in comparison with what
orthodox popular religion had to offer, according to Overmyer: "At best,
general popular religion provided ethical and religious means for a relatively
easy passage through purgatory, followed by a good rebirth on earth, or, for
a few, as a deity."[77] This observation, in a sense written from a sectarian
point of view, echoes de Groot's earlier and very forceful expressions of
sympathy, admiration, and favoritism toward these sects, and his view of
their subordinate position in society largely as being the result of centuries
of persecution by the imperial government and the Confucian elite.[78]

Many observers and analysts of orthodox popular religion would react, I
suspect, with considerable skepticism to the suggestion that belief in the
supernatural system in which the gods and the dead figured so importantly
was purely a negative consequence resulting from government oppression of
far more attractive salvation-oriented groups. There was, rather, an impressive interpenetration of elite and popular religious orthodoxy, and it is
in this context that the ambiguous attitudes and beliefs regarding the afterlife can be considered. There can be no doubt that the belief in multiple
souls was linked to the priority given social role over individual salvation;
both Confucianism and orthodox popular religion firmly linked society to
the cosmos, and both would appear to have stressed that full personal fulfillment was to be found through culturally defined proper living as a social
being. However, a contrast between state Confucianism and popular orthodoxy would of course reveal the richly emotional and expressive quality of
the latter, as well as the strong emphasis it placed on supernatural beings
and forces. A most important contrast was with respect to the idea of salvation, which was indeed represented in the religion of the masses and yet had
to be denied as a universal possibility precisely because it would otherwise
undermine the larger structure of religious beliefs. At the same time, the very
presence of the salvationistic ideal, even if in rudimentary form, serves as a
reminder that even in the beliefs of the majority there was at least the germ
of a critique of the state and the social-religious order that gave it support.
This idea of salvation was a potential link between orthodox popular religion and sectarianism; although it hardly is to be expected that many or
even most Chinese had any contact whatsoever with sectarians or their beliefs, the presence in the dominant popular religion of salvationistic elements presumably could facilitate acceptance of "heterodoxy" when circumstances introduced it.[79]

77. Overmyer, "Alternatives," p. 157.
78. See J. J. M. de Groot, Sectarianism; also his The Religion of the Chinese.
79. I am not suggesting that at the popular level these salvationistic beliefs provided the
only framework for expressing rejection of the status quo. Popularly held ideas concerning
imperial legitimacy—represented in the "secret society" tradition in terms such as Ming res-
torationism, for example—could be obviously subversive as far as the state was concerned.

In most contexts, however, the preservation of the idea of salvation pure and simple within the larger and indeed contradictory framework of mass religion most likely represented a continuing differentiation between personal considerations of one's own fate and the satisfactions provided by one's role in society, which might range from elementary and relatively predictable security to a degree of material comfort, power, and a heightened sense of self-esteem.[80] While I think it is safe to say that for many in China concerns regarding the afterlife loomed larger with advancing age, these had to remain intensely personal feelings and be given highly individualized religious expression, including efforts to accumulate merit for the next life.[81] Individuals could have recourse to temples in the community, to others that were nearby, or to more distant ones through participation in pilgrimages. The Buddhist church as such was largely kept outside of society; its clergy had no important connections with the great majority of temples and played only a relatively small role within popular religion as a whole, even though it in fact helped to maintain the idea and possibility of salvation. Yet, precisely because Western Paradise and a good rebirth on earth (or as a god) could be alternative desirable outcomes in terms of an individual's hopes concerning the afterlife, the potentially powerful social and political criticism or rejectionism implied by a focus on Western Paradise becomes all the more apparent. Thus official support of deification is in stark contrast to the heretical focus on paradise in the West or on the earth itself.

If, by and large, the Chinese state was hostile to salvationistic heterodoxy, it is perhaps a tribute to state power and influence that such beliefs also were subversive of the dominant form of popular religion. In this popular orthodoxy those who when alive were rooted members of families and communities continued after death to be remembered and to interact with and receive sustenance from the kin they had left behind; they each had three souls only because they were worshipped by their living kin as ancestors in the tablet and in the grave and supported by them in the underworld. It is ironic, therefore, that those considered in death to have three souls were those who when alive had attained social fulfillment according to the dominant cultural standards. And by these standards many of those attracted to

---

80. Although not dealt with in this essay, it is clear that such satisfactions in late traditional China would vary not only with respect to a person's social and economic standing but also by gender; women, even if they might have bound feet, were often observed to outnumber men in temples and in other religious contexts that involved seeking a better afterlife, and it is to be expected that this was tied to their markedly subordinate status in Chinese society. For the participation of women in religious activities, see e.g., Nevius, *China and the Chinese*, p. 103ff.; DuBose, *Dragon, Image, and Demon*, pp. 283ff.

81. This might include, for those able to afford them, various charitable acts; also vegetarianism and a variety of ritual procedures could be resorted to in an effort to accumulate merit for a better rebirth; see, for example, Doolittle, *Social Life*, 2:398–399.

sectarianism were not socially complete persons; for sectarians lacking community and kinship ties there might upon death be only one soul, and its involvement in the cosmos of the gods, ancestors, and ghosts was a prospect far less attractive than that offered by paradise. The rejectionistic attitude implied by this focus on salvation meant, for the state, that a sign of heterodoxy was when the three souls became one. And it is additional testimony to the triumph of state ideology and its deep penetration into the dominant popular religion that for believers in this popular orthodoxy the dead with only one soul were ghosts, some the most dangerous of all.

# NINE

# Remembering the Dead: Graves and Politics in Southeastern China

*Rubie S. Watson*

In his essay "A Contribution to the Study of the Collective Representation of Death" Robert Hertz refers to death as a "sacrilege against the social order."[1] It is hardly surprising that, in the face of this "sacrilege," death rituals and grave rites become occasions for reaffirming ideas of regeneration and continuity. Death reminds us not only of our own mortality but also of the fragility of our social institutions and groups.

In this chapter I see mortuary rites as a series of actions that offer, as Bloch and Parry put it in their introduction to *Death and the Regeneration of Life*, not so much occasions for the assertion of already existing groups as opportunities for creating new groups.[2] In worshipping one's ancestors, in building tombs, and in participating in funerals individuals create, change, reaffirm, and deny social relations. The anthropologist Gilbert Lewis has argued that rituals are not simply intellectual puzzles. Rituals, he maintains, are also performed in order "to resolve, alter, or demonstrate a situation."[3]

Maurice Freedman expresses a commonly held view of Chinese ancestor worship: The worship of ancestors, he writes, "was essentially a means of group action in which the power and status structure of the community was given a ritual expression."[4] Ancestral ritual, according to this view, does

1. Robert Hertz, "A Contribution to the Study of the Collective Representation of Death," in *Death and the Right Hand*, Robert Hertz (Glencoe, Ill.: Free Press, 1960 [1907]), p. 77.

2. Maurice Bloch and Jonathan Parry, "Introduction," in *Death and the Regeneration of Life*, ed. Maurice Bloch and Jonathan Parry (Cambridge: Cambridge University Press, 1982), p. 6.

3. Gilbert Lewis, *Day of Shining Red: An Essay on Understanding Ritual* (Cambridge: Cambridge University Press, 1980), p. 35.

4. Maurice Freedman, *Lineage Organization in Southeastern China* (London: Athlone, 1958), p. 91.

little more than reflect or mirror the status quo. It is passive, not active, and becomes a mere reflection of present arrangements. In the above quotation Freedman is specifically writing of the cult as practiced in the ancestral hall. Hall rites are perhaps the most formal and stylized ancestral rituals, and Freedman is probably correct in stressing their conservative qualities. However, those aspects of the cult that focus on the ancestral grave are concerned more with political competition than with glorifying rigid status hierarchies or group unity.

This chapter is limited to a discussion of grave rites. I argue that, at least in some parts of China, the ancestral cult as practiced at the grave does not simply express the present order but is part of the process in which new orders, new status and power arrangements, are created. Grave rites are active; they are part of the process of change itself. The placement of graves and the grave rites themselves are involved in the give and take of local politics. During the rites groups and individuals make claims and counter-claims that alter the status quo. Rituals, we are often reminded, do not speak with only one voice; it is possible to interpret them on many levels.[5] In China the political arena enfolds the grave. Hall rites emphasize power arrangements as they currently stand, whereas grave rites constitute one of the battlegrounds for disputing those arrangements.[6]

## FUNERAL AND GRAVE RITES

In Chinese society funerals and grave rites are at two ends of a ritual continuum that is concerned with the dead. Funeral rites concentrate on settling the spirit immediately after death; grave rites commemorate ancestors who may have been dead for hundreds of years. During the funeral there is a preoccupation with complex ritual forms, with performing the rites properly so that the spirit of the recently dead will not become a threat to the living. Everyone dies and every death produces a potentially dangerous spirit. Funeral rites are concerned with converting this volatile spirit into a tamed, domesticated ancestor.

In China there is a universal aspect to funerals, which, unlike grave rites,

5. For discussion of this point, see, e.g., Edmund Leach, *Culture and Communication* (Cambridge: Cambridge University Press, 1976); Gilbert Lewis, *Day of Shining Red*, pp. 1–38; S. J. Tambiah, "The Magical Power of Words," *Man* 3 (1968): 175–208.

6. Freedman makes a distinction between ancestor worship and what he calls "the geomancy of burial." In the latter, he writes, "the accent it put upon the paramountcy of self interest," whereas in ancestor worship the emphasis is placed on "the supremacy of the common good." This distinction is very useful, but I believe it requires some alteration. The dichotomy, I argue in this essay, is not between ancestor worship and geomancy but between ancestor worship in the hall and ancestor worship at the grave. As I show below, both geomantic practices *and* grave rites exhibit a preoccupation with self-interest and competition. See Maurice Freedman, *Chinese Lineage and Society* (London: Athlone, 1966), p. 143.

do not depend on economic or political requirements for their performance. One might argue that funerals are compulsory, or nearly so, for one of their primary roles is to provide protection for the living. In contrast, grave rites are not primarily prophylactic and are not performed as a matter of course. Many Chinese are not remembered after death, and many graves are lost after a few generations. Only rarely does a grave become the focus for elaborate group rites.

In the funeral rites the dead continue to be individuals; they retain their kinship, gender, and marital status. The longer the ancestor remains in the grave, however, the more depersonalized he becomes.[7] His flesh rots; eventually his bones may be cleaned and reburied; in the end he becomes a symbol not a person. Eventually the ancestor in his grave becomes passive, incapable of volition or of real harm, but he does not pass out of human concern altogether. His grave may become a rallying point for powerful agnatic groups, and as we will see, his bones are thought to become conductors of powerful natural forces. The ancestor in his grave is perhaps best seen as a pawn to be manipulated by descendants for their own political benefit.[8]

Whereas funeral rites are observed with great care and characterized by fear of the unsettled spirit, grave rites are relatively simple in structure and easy to perform. They are dignified but relaxed. Grave rites are focused on the living rather than the dead. Funeral rites, in contrast, are preoccupied with the deceased. At the risk of overstating the case we might say that ritual form dominates individual expression in the funeral rites, whereas the individual and his concerns dominate grave ritual.

## BODY, SOUL, AND GEOMANCY

In China as in many other societies body and soul are thought to be intimately linked even in death.[9] In the mid-nineteenth century, J. J. M. de Groot devoted six volumes to the study of Chinese burial customs. De Groot explained to his Western audience that in China "both the body and the soul require a grave for their preservation. Hence the grave, being the chief shelter of the soul, virtually becomes the principal altar dedicated to it and to its worship."[10] The soul, he argued, can suffer from an improper burial,[11] and if the soul is not settled, the living may also suffer. According

7. I use the pronoun "he" because in the following discussion the ancestors I discuss are all male.

8. Freedman, *Chinese Lineage and Society*, pp. 140–143.

9. J. J. M. de Groot, *The Religious System of China*, vol. 3 (Leiden: Brill, 1892); Hertz, "A Contribution"; James Watson, "Of Flesh and Bones: The Management of Death Pollution in Cantonese Society," in Bloch and Parry, *Death and the Regeneration of Life*.

10. De Groot, *The Religious System*, 3: 855.

11. Ibid., 3: 857–858.

to de Groot the root of the concern with the condition of the body and grave is actually a concern for the soul, "the corpse being merely regarded as the means by which the soul is to be enticed back to the ancestral home,"[12] where it can be cared for and, one might add, manipulated for the benefit of the living. The soul must be tamed or settled in the grave so that it is no longer dangerous.[13]

In many societies graves and the physical remains they contain are believed to be a source of creative power. The Greeks held that the body should be cremated before it showed signs of disfigurement or decay. The perfect body and its transformation in the funeral ritual, it was believed, released a regenerative power that was necessary for the continuation of life and society.[14] In early Christian times the tombs of saints and martyrs were thought to provide shelter and protection to those buried nearby. Ariès quotes a fifth-century author who describes this practice: "The martyrs will keep guard over us, who live with our bodies, and they will take us into their care when we have forsaken our bodies. Here they prevent us from falling into sinful ways, there they will protect us from the horrors of hell. That is why our ancestors were careful to unite our bodies with the bones of the martyrs."[15] In the Arab world saintly men have a power or charisma called *baraka*. While they are alive such saints might wield considerable political power.[16] After death *baraka* may cling to the saint and embue his grave with special powers; such graves often become pilgrimage centers.

For the Chinese,[17] the remains of the dead are not the source of power or renewal; instead they serve as conductors of a power that originates in nature itself.[18] In English the term "geomancy" is used to describe a sophisticated and complex set of ideas that the Chinese refer to as *feng-shui* (lit. "wind and water"). According to Stephan Feuchtwang, *feng-shui* "stands

12. Ibid., 3: 847.
13. James Watson, "Of Flesh and Bones."
14. For discussion of this point, see Maurice Bloch, "Death, Women and Power," in Bloch and Parry, *Death and the Regeneration of Life*, p. 228.
15. Quoted in Philippe Ariès, *Western Attitudes toward Death*, trans. Patricia Ranum (Baltimore: Johns Hopkins University Press, 1974), p. 16.
16. See, e.g., Fredrik Barth, *Political Leadership among Swat Pathans* (London: Athlone, 1965), pp. 92–104; Ernest Gellner, *Saints of the Atlas* (London: Weidenfeld & Nicolson, 1969).
17. The following discussion is restricted to southeastern China, although many of the patterns I describe are no doubt also found in China as a whole. Nevertheless, the southern Chinese and the southeasterners in particular have certain features that are unique or more elaborated than in other parts of China (e.g., secondary burial, complex geomantic beliefs), and it is best to make clear the regional bias of the following discussion.
18. There is disagreement on this point. Freedman argues (and my Ha Tsuen data support this) that ancestors in the grave (the recently dead excepted) are passive agents. They do not make things happen—they simply conduct the forces of nature to their descendants. See Freedman, *Chinese Lineage and Society*, p. 126. Ahern, however, arguing from data collected in northern Taiwan, maintains that "the ancestor himself, not the [geomancy] of the gravesite,

for the power of the natural environment, the wind and the airs of the mountains and hills; the streams and the rain; and much more than that: the composite influence of the natural processes. . . . By placing oneself well in the environment *feng-shui* will bring good fortune."[19] The grave and the bones it contains are thought to act as conductors of the forces of wind and water.

The links between the ancestor in his grave and his descendants is a strong and consequential one. The proper placement of one's ancestor's bones in the landscape has a direct effect on the worldly success or failure of the living. In fact, the care of the ancestor in his grave is unambiguously linked to the well-being of his descendants, whereas the ancestor in his hall tablet, which like the grave also houses an aspect of the soul, is concerned with the general welfare of the descent group as a whole.[20]

The benefits that derive from the proper placement of an ancestor's bones are not freely available to all. In China placing the dead is a complex and expensive procedure. This delicate task is usually left to specialists (*feng-shui hsien-sheng*) who have studied the constellation of wind and water and know how to place the dead to achieve maximum benefit for the living. In general outline the placement or siting of graves seems fairly straightforward, the expertise of the *feng-shui* specialists being the main determinant of success or failure. Based on a cursory understanding of Chinese geomancy, one might expect that people automatically bury all of their ancestors according to strict geomantic principles in order to maximize their own advantage. In fact, this is not the case. Although some ancestral graves are placed with great care and remembered for hundreds of years, many more are forgotten.[21]

To understand why some ancestors are cherished and others abandoned,

---

will bring good fortune." See Emily Ahern, *The Cult of the Dead in a Chinese Village* (Stanford: Stanford University Press, 1973), p. 185. Whether the differences in these views are due to regional or to cultural variations requires further research.

19. Stephan Feuchtwang, *An Anthropological Analysis of Chinese Geomancy* (Vientiane: Vithagna, 1974), p. 2.

20. Freedman, *Lineage Organization in Southeastern China*, p. 84; Rubie Watson, *Inequality among Brothers: Class and Kinship in South China* (Cambridge: Cambridge University Press, 1985), p. 40–41.

21. Ahern argues that in the northern Taiwanese village of Ch'i-nan "graves . . . ordinarily never cease to be worshiped." She notes that lineage members could cite "the location of each of their direct ascendants' graves up to the founding ancestor." It is difficult to know exactly why graves are remembered in Ch'i-nan and lost in the New Territories. One reason may be the different time frames involved. Ch'i-nan was founded less than 200 years ago, whereas many villages in the New Territories are 600 or 700 years old (one or two are nearly 1,000 years old). People are not likely to continue to worship thirty-five or forty generations of ancestors' graves. Furthermore, Ahern's statement suggests that people tend to remember direct ascendants; presumably the graves of men and women who died without offspring would be forgotten. See Ahern, *The Cult of the Dead in a Chinese Village*, p. 166.

it is necessary to know something about burial practices in southeastern China. This chapter is based largely on research carried out in the single-lineage village of Ha Tsuen (1978 population approximately 2,500) located in the Hong Kong New Territories. Ha Tsuen is inhabited by one of a number of localized Teng lineages in Kwangtung's Hsin-an county. All these Teng are descended from Teng Fu-hsieh, who first settled in this part of Kwangtung during the twelfth century. By local standards the Ha Tsuen Teng are a wealthy and politically powerful community.

According to Chinese eschatology the dead have not one soul (or aspect) but many. In the New Territories the treatment of the dead implies a threefold division of the soul; one is found in the grave, one in the ancestral tablet, and the third in the underworld. Immediately after death the spirit of the deceased remains close to the living. As I have already noted, the dead are very dangerous during this period, and many of the mortuary rites are concerned with the safe separation of the soul from the realm of the living.

In Ha Tsuen the deceased is first buried in an unmarked, hastily chosen grave in the hills behind the village. Usually the dead are buried within twenty-four hours of death. At this stage little attention is given to the choice of burial site because it is assumed that this is not the permanent resting place. On the one-hundredth day after death one aspect of the deceased's soul is incorporated into the collective ancestral tablet of the household, the so-called domestic tablet. In Ha Tsuen, households do not keep individual tablets for each ancestor as in the hall; rather the names of immediate ancestors are written on a large sheet of red paper which is displayed on the household's "spirit altar" (shen-t'ai). After each death the paper is changed and the names of the household's most distant ancestors are gradually deleted as new ones are inserted. Most households list only five generations of ancestors on their domestic altars. Although the majority of ancestors cease to be part of the domestic ancestral cult after five generations, they can escape extinction by having a tablet placed in an ancestral hall or by becoming the focus of a corporate estate within the lineage.

Many southern Chinese, including of course the Cantonese, practice a system of secondary burial. After the deceased has been buried for a period of time (usually seven to ten years) the remains of the deceased are exhumed and the bones cleaned by a mortuary specialist. These bones are then put in a large pottery urn, referred to as a "golden pagoda" (chin-t'a). This urn is placed in the hills behind the village, where it is partially surrounded with earth but not reburied. Later, sometimes years or even decades later, the bones may be buried in a permanent tomb constructed of brick. The tomb is marked by a stone inscription giving the name of the deceased and the date of his death. Often a tomb will contain the bone urns of a man and his wife or wives. It is important to emphasize that not all people go through the three stages of interment. In fact, very few achieve the final stage of a marked tomb. The earthen graves or bone urns of the majority are visited only as long as kinsmen remember their locations. Over the years and generations these places of interment which have no permanent markers may be forgotten. As Maurice Freedman points out: "The humble dead . . . never reach a final grave, their bones being left to lie in the urns which, in great numbers, can be seen to dot the New Territories landscape, at the end of their career being toppled, split and desolate."[22] Few attain the kind of immortality they seek. Eventually most ancestors are lost; their names are taken off the domestic tablets, and their graves are forgotten. What saves an ancestor from such an ignominious end?

The deceased's chances of "survival" are greatly increased if he has left enough property to form an estate (*tsu*) in his name. With an estate the ancestor's continued "existence" no longer depends so completely on the vagaries of human memory or emotion. There is little doubt that the wealthy have a better chance of attaining immortality than do the poor. It is, of course, possible that descendants may form an estate in honor of an ancestor who is long dead (see below); however, such events are rare and require both resources and organizational skill.

In 1905 there were, according to Hong Kong's colonial land records, eighty-two ancestral estates in Ha Tsuen. These estates account for about 50 percent of the land owned by the Teng in Ha Tsuen district. The largest estates incorporate up to forty acres of choice rice land. It may be asked why people allow precious land to be tied up in this way. What do the living gain by forming ancestral estates? There is, of course, great prestige attached to creating estates. The descendants are acting in a highly praiseworthy and filial manner, for they are making their ancestor immortal. By honoring their ancestor in this way, they are also separating themselves from their fellow agnates and reserving to themselves alone the often considerable supernatural, economic, and political advantages that membership in an ancestral estate entails. Furthermore, the proceeds from an estate formed by incorporating the ancestor's personal property, excluding of course the cost of ritual observances, are not really lost to the ancestor's immediate descendants. In the first generation, each son's personal share may not differ appreciably from what it would have been had no estate been established.

Wealth brings the reassurance that one will not be forgotten even in death; but is this reassurance merely a comforting fiction or does it really increase one's chance of "survival" after death? Land can be sold, ancestral estates can be disbanded, and the ancestors can be left to their own devices—uncared for and unattended.

Who then are the remembered dead? And who among the dead are relocated to geomantically efficacious tombs? Wealth is obviously a factor, but

22. Freedman, *Chinese Lineage and Society*, p. 121.

this alone does not explain the attainment of "immortality." Forming an ancestral estate has as its primary aim the provision of sacrificial offerings to the ancestors, but the estate is also the basis for a corporation of living worshippers. In uniting the living to the dead, the estate also unites the living to each other. Generally speaking, without an estate there is no group worship at the grave beyond four or five generations. Individual families may provide offerings for their immediate ancestors, but without an estate there may be no joint worship, and after the passing of time even individual worship may stop. Once an estate has been established, however, descendants are united into a corporation of shareholders with ritual, economic, and political interests.

It is this last aspect of the ancestral cult (when politics and ancestral grave worship are joined) that concerns me here. In another study I have shown how ancestral estates are linked to local political organization in the village of Ha Tsuen.[23] Here I will focus on the role of graves in the creation, destruction, and re-creation of political alignments.

## GRAVES AND GROUPS

Many Teng are remembered (their bones are buried in elaborate tombs, and an estate is set aside for worship expenses) because of their personal wealth and reputation. However, some ancestral graves become the center of ritual activity for other, less obvious reasons, and these graves are of special interest in this essay. Not all estates originate from the ancestor's own private wealth; some estates are formed by a process of fusion. In such cases men come together and choose the ancestor they wish to commemorate; money is collected to build a tomb and endow an estate with property; in doing so they form a corporation. A case study may help us understand the way in which graves, estates, and politics become intertwined.

In Ha Tsuen in the 1930s a group of about a hundred men came together and formed an estate around their fourteenth-generation ancestor, Teng Fei-wu (who lived in the late seventeenth century). The men who formed this estate were representatives of the twenty-second and twenty-third generations. Each descendant was asked to contribute a specific amount of rice, which was then converted to cash and used to purchase land for the estate. The rental income from this property underwrites the expenses of worshipping Fei-wu. Members of the estate pointed out that one line of Fei-wu's descendants refused to contribute, hence they have no share in this particular estate; nor do they participate in the group rites dedicated to Fei-wu.

In considering this example it is important to understand why an estate was formed at the fourteenth-generation level and why Fei-wu became the

23. See Rubie Watson, *Inequality among Brothers*, pp. 70–72, 88–90.

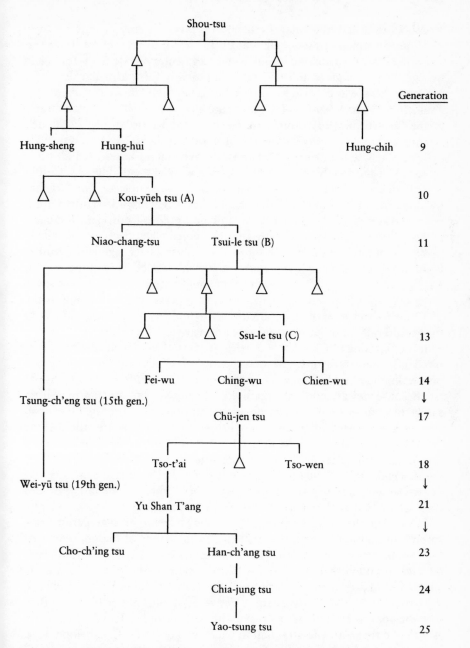

Figure 1. Outline of Major Segments in the Teng Lineage, ca. 1400–1900.

focus. When asked, the villagers themselves give religious reasons for their decision to form an estate: "We wanted to show our respect for Teng Fei-wu," they say. An examination of the segmentary system of the Teng lineage, however, gives an important clue to why this particular ancestor, and not others, was chosen. Kou-yüeh tsu (generation 10; see A on figure 1), Tsui-le tsu (B), and Ssu-le tsu (C) are among the wealthiest ancestral estates in the lineage (in 1905, according to the Land Records, their combined holdings were over sixty-two acres of good rice land). These estates are closely linked, and in recent years a single accountant has served all three estates. The ancestor Ssu-le had three sons, and from the middle son, Ching-wu, are descended the wealthiest families in the entire lineage. The fact that the descendants of Ching-wu are rich and themselves organized into a number of estates gives them great economic and political power in the community. They tend to speak with a unified voice when decisions are made about the running of the three estates. Their control over segment resources is informal, but that does not make it any the less effective. One way in which Ssu-le's unorganized descendants could redress this imbalance was for them to form an estate. In this case, it appears that men living in the 1930s went back over three hundred years to find an ancestor around whom they could rally in order to compete with their wealthier kinsmen.

It is interesting to note that those descendants of Ssu-le who are not organized into an estate (i.e., the descendants of Chien-wu) are among the poorest families in Ha Tsuen. They have no effective voice in running Ssu-le tsu. Because they are poor, unorganized, and largely illiterate they have little say in the management of the larger estates to which they belong. Of course, even after the formation of an estate Fei-wu's descendants are still at some disadvantage vis-à-vis the wealthier Ching-wu branch. Nevertheless, their unification into an estate does give them more cohesion and visibility than the descendants of Chien-wu. During my stay in the village a member of Fei-wu's estate was serving as accountant for all three of the larger estates (that is, for Kou-yüeh tsu, Ssu-le tsu, and Tsui-le tsu).

Obviously, the process of forming estates by fusion or aggregation constitutes an important organizational tool in the hands of the unorganized. The pooling of resources and the creation of an ancestral estate is one method of counterbalancing the political power of the privileged few. It allows a group of men to speak with one voice and makes it possible for them to unify for cooperative action. However, it must not be imagined that only the poor formed estates by fusion. In fact, one of Ha Tsuen's wealthiest estates and the main ancestral hall to which all Ha Tsuen Teng belong were both established in this way.[24] The existence of a corporate estate is impor-

24. See Rubie Watson, "The Creation of a Chinese Lineage: The Teng of Ha Tsuen, 1669–1751," *Modern Asian Studies* 16 (1982): 69–100.

tant, but it is not in itself enough to make the members of that estate power-ful. To be effective an estate must have substantial lands to rent out, for these lands provide both a supplement to estate members' income and a loyal following in the form of tenants.

It took three hundred years for Fei-wu's grave to become a focus for regular group worship, and I think there is little doubt that politics played a role in Fei-wu's "resurrection." Fei-wu and his grave provided an opportu-nity for differentiation from a larger group and the unification of Fei-wu's direct descendants.

Graves and estates may be rallying points for bringing together indi-vidual families; they may also provide a battleground for debate and even violence. One of the Teng's most illustrious ancestors is Teng Tzu-ming, a sixth-generation ancestor of the Ha Tsuen Teng. Tzu-ming's fame seems to be due to a good marriage rather than to any of Tzu-ming's own qualities. According to local genealogies, Tzu-ming's wife was a Sung princess (re-ports vary as to whether she was the emperor's sister or daughter) who married Tzu-ming while she and other members of the court were seeking refuge in what is now the New Territories. Tzu-ming is buried near the present-day village of Sha Tao Kok in the eastern New Territories. Those who are descended from Tzu-ming are very proud of their association with the imperial line and stress this attachment whenever they have the oppor-tunity. During my research among the Teng, the story of Tzu-ming and the princess was told over and over by local residents. In fact, there is an entire genre of folklore focusing on the Teng's imperial connections. Tzu-ming would probably have become a noted ancestor on the strength of his illus-trious affines alone, but there was another factor that contributed to his prestige. Tzu-ming's grave, I was told by many Teng, enjoys excellent *feng-shui*.

It should be noted that Tzu-ming and his grave do not belong to all the New Territories Teng. The Teng have a common ancestor in the first, second, and third generations. The third-generation ancestor, however, had five sons, and from these sons spring the different founders of Teng settle-ments throughout the New Territories (and ultimately the Teng of Hsin-an and Tung-kuan counties). These are referred to as the five *fang*, or branches. The Teng who now live in Ha Tsuen did not establish themselves in an independent settlement until the ninth generation; prior to that they were considered part of the Kam Tin community (five miles east of Ha Tsuen). Both the Ha Tsuen and Kam Tin Teng are descended from the fourth *fang* and therefore claim descent from Tzu-ming. However, the Ping Shan Teng (whose settlement is only a mile from Ha Tsuen) are descended from the second *fang* and therefore cannot claim to be the direct descendants of Tzu-ming.

According to Ha Tsuen villagers, the Ping Shan Teng desperately wanted to associate themselves with Tzu-ming and thus to the Sung imperial line, but the written genealogy does not allow them to make this claim. The Ping Shan Teng, I was told by Ha Tsuen people, therefore tried to "steal Tzu-ming's grave." They did this by burying one of their own ancestors near Tzu-ming. Whether this was originally done because they wished to share the good *feng-shui* of Tzu-ming's grave or because they wanted to usurp the site for themselves is unclear. However, over the years the two graves became confused, and the descendants of Tzu-ming became convinced not only that the Ping Shan Teng were trying to steal the site's good *feng-shui* but that they were attempting to steal Tzu-ming himself (or at the very least intrude themselves into the worship of Tzu-ming). Early in this century a geomancer was brought in to determine which grave belonged to Tzu-ming. I was told that a portion of Tzu-ming's tomb inscription was still legible and it was possible to clearly delineate the two graves. A new marker was erected, and the usurper's grave was, according to my informants, relegated to obscurity.

The rites surrounding Fei-wu and Tzu-ming demonstrate that ancestral graves and grave rituals offer opportunities for both reaffirming and altering existing relationships. In an attempt to participate in Ha Tsuen's political dialogue the descendants of Fei-wu formed themselves into a unified group that was part ritual, part political, and part economic. Ping Shan was also using the framework of ancestors and graves to say something about themselves and their relation to others. They were claiming rights to a *feng-shui* site that did not belong to them and a status to which they were not entitled. In this last case Ping Shan's claims were completely rebuffed, but as we shall see, such demands for restructuring do not always meet with failure.

GEOMANCY, GRAVES, AND POLITICAL PROTEST

Thus far geomancy has been discussed only in broad outline. In order to understand how it was possible, for example, for the Ping Shan Teng "to steal" the *feng-shui* of Tzu-ming's grave we need to know more about geomantic beliefs and how these beliefs translate into practice.

Geomancy is concerned with this world and with individual benefits. Geomancy does not embrace a moral code.[25] "It assumes," Feuchtwang argues, "the right of the individual to benefit without placing emphasis on the social organization within which he is to benefit." These benefits, Feuchtwang goes on to conclude, depend, not on any supernatural aid, but on knowing, through divination, "the laws of natural processes [and] where to place oneself in relation to them; 'riding the *ch'i*' as the manuals say."[26]

25. See Feuchtwang, *An Anthropological Analysis of Chinese Geomancy*, pp. 222–223.
26. Ibid., p. 223.

Among the Teng, geomancy provides a language for competition,[27] for dispute, and for conflict; yet in an important sense geomancy is based on principles of equality.[28] Geomancy implies that if people take proper care in the way they place themselves and their ancestors in the environment, they will be able to advance their own interests. In this system success is not earned through proper behavior or hard work; rather, it is attained by technical manipulation. In Ha Tsuen geomancy was often used as a way of talking about and explaining economic differences.[29] For example, family A is said to be rich because their ancestor's grave was auspicious for making money, or family B has fallen on hard times because rivals have intentionally ruined the good *feng-shui* of their ancestor's grave. In the local view there is no innate or moral difference between rich and poor; one of the major reasons for economic success is simply that the rich have succeeded in locating their ancestors in a more auspicious setting than have the poor.

In the New Territories geomancy is a language for political protest. Today, as in the past, farmers and wage laborers have little direct political involvement in central government and few direct contacts with officials. Their participation is not sought and their views are usually ignored. In such an environment local leaders and decision makers focus their attention on overtly nonpolitical institutions such as temple associations or festival organizing committees. Political discussion (that is, discussion about power and the distribution of resources) is usually couched in seemingly nonpolitical language. Religious festivals may become occasions for showing opposition to the state[30] or for expressing the hierarchical relationships in which one community dominates another.[31] Martial-arts clubs and self-defense corps enforce the claims of ruling elites, while ancestral halls may serve as the framework for organizing local political action and administration.[32]

When direct political action and protest is not possible and is perhaps

27. Ahern argues that in the northern Taiwanese village of Ch'i-nan the geomancy of graves was not competitive. See Ahern, *The Cult of the Dead in a Chinese Village*, pp. 185–188.

28. On this point, see also Freedman, *Chinese Lineage and Society*, p. 123.

29. Rubie Watson, *Inequality among Brothers*, p. 99. It should be noted that geomancy may also be important in explaining illness. On this point, see James Hayes, *The Rural Communities of Hong Kong: Studies and Themes* (Hong Kong: Oxford University Press, 1983), pp. 145–146.

30. See e.g., Emily Martin Ahern, "The Thai Ti Kong Festival," in *The Anthropology of Taiwanese Society*, ed. Emily Martin Ahern and Hill Gates (Stanford: Stanford University Press, 1981).

31. See, e.g., James Watson, "Standardizing the Gods: The Promotion of T'ien Hou (Empress of Heaven) Along the South China Coast, 960–1960," in *Popular Culture in Late Imperial China*, ed. David Johnson, Andrew Nathan, and Evelyn Rawski (Berkeley and Los Angeles: University of California Press, 1985).

32. See Rubie Watson, "The Creation of a Chinese Lineage."

even dangerous, arguments about graves and discussions of *feng-shui* offer a means for saying that which is unsayable. We have already seen that graves and estates may be the focus of political as well as ritual groups. Considering that *feng-shui* is intrinsically amoral and competitively individualistic in orientation, it is not surprising that *feng-shui* should offer opportunities for competing with one's neighbors and for making statements about political alignments.

The man who founded the first Teng settlement in Hsin-an and Tung-kuan counties, Fu-hsieh, is buried very near the modern-day industrial center of Tsuen Wan in the New Territories. The grave is famous for its *feng-shui*. I was told by a number of Teng that it was noted for producing an official every thirty years. To prove the excellence of the site the Teng say that when this spot was dug for the tomb of Fu-hsieh, a stone was found on which a poem was inscribed. The poem had been written by a geomancer and commemorated the beauty and elegance of the site. The fact that two geomancers had chosen this site showed, the Teng believed, that this was truly an auspicious setting for Fu-hsieh's tomb.

In the 1920s the colonial authorities tried to have Fu-hsieh's tomb moved to another location because of the construction of a new road linking the western New Territories to Kowloon. The Teng immediately mounted a protest citing the treaty establishing the New Territories, which, they argued, insured their right to practice local customs. Fu-hsieh's grave, they maintained, is sacred to all Teng in the New Territories. They would not give up the grave's wonderful *feng-shui* for an uncertain, untried locale even if the government would bear the expense of relocation.

The Teng, the wealthiest, most populous, and most prestigious group of *pen-ti* (or native residents) in the New Territories, were no doubt loath to allow or, perhaps more important, to be seen to allow colonial officials to interfere with their most important grave. The relationship between the colonial administration and the *pen-ti* elite has never been easy; each side continues to be deeply suspicious of the other. However, the *pen-ti*, and especially the landed elite among them, have been granted special privileges by the colonial administration.[33] Until 1982,[34] they had advantages in housing and easier access to government authorities than did the post-1945 émigrés, who, incidentally, greatly outnumber the *pen-ti*. The Teng, as the undisputed leaders of *pen-ti* society, have always been jealous of their status. To the Teng their founder's grave is a symbol of unity; it also represents concrete evidence of their long and illustrious history. The colonial government could not have chosen a grave that was more likely to stir up protest.

33. See Chau Lam-yan and Lau Siu-kai, "Development, Colonial Rule, and Intergroup Conflict in a Chinese Village in Hong Kong," *Human Organization* 41 (1982): 139–146.

34. In 1982 a system of District Boards was established to represent everyone in the New Territories (*pen-ti* and émigrés).

Fu-hsieh's grave became a cause célèbre among the Teng all over Hong Kong. Eventually New Territories villagers were joined by protestors from as far away as Canton. A Kuomintang general surnamed Teng (but not a descendant of Fu-hsieh) lent powerful political support when he joined the protest. Finally the Teng and the government reached an accommodation and the grave was not moved. However, because of its location near the industrial city of Tsuen Wan, the grave has faced constant threats of encroachment. Thus far the Teng have prevailed. During the first battles over Fu-hsieh's grave the Teng formed a Grave Protection Society, which eventually purchased the grave and the land around it. The British, it should be noted, had always claimed that the grave was on crown land. In recent years the society leased part of the site to a non-Teng who operates a potted-flower business. The Teng feel that this operation will not disturb the grave, and I was told that "it shows the government that the land around the grave is cared for and put to good use."

In 1977 Teng elders from all over the New Territories gathered at Fu-hsieh's grave to celebrate *ch'ung-yang* (ancestral rites held during the ninth lunar month). Before and after the rites there was much anger and talk about the way the government had allowed a number of tall buildings to block "Fu-hsieh's view" of the sea. The elders, dressed in their grey silk gowns, making their obeisances to Fu-hsieh with high-rise apartment buildings and factories in the background provide one of those anachronistic sights for which Hong Kong is justly famous. That an obscure grave on what was once an isolated hillside should now be the cause of so much protest and high-level government discussion is just one more reminder that the dead may always be pressed into support for the political struggles of the living.

Obviously the *feng-shui* of Fu-hsieh's grave has been affected by enormous changes in the surrounding landscape. Neighboring buildings block the flow of wind and water around and through the tomb; however, now that the grave is both a political and a religious symbol, it cannot be easily abandoned. Of course, if the Teng should suffer any serious reverses, a collective decision could be made to move Fu-hsieh's bones. For now, however, Fu-hsieh's tomb continues to stand as a tribute to Teng unity and Teng power. In thwarting governmental and industrial interests, they created a new institution (the Grave Protection Society) and perhaps a new or at least an enhanced sense of themselves as a special group.

Whether the Teng consciously see their long argument with the colonial authorities over Fu-hsieh's grave as a political battle against government development policies and their own inability to influence those policies is impossible to know with certainty. However, what is clear is that the New Territories *pen-ti* lineages are engaged in a losing battle with a powerful coalition of governmental and industrialist interests. Some Teng have benefited tremendously from the industrialization of the New Territories, and nearly all Teng have a higher standard of living than they had twenty years ago. Yet they have entered a world they do not fully understand, and even more important, a world over which they have precious little control. Many of Ha Tsuen's elders see their culture, their rituals, their way of life threatened. Perhaps their founder's tomb, standing as it does at the very edge of one of Hong Kong's great industrial centers, makes the Teng feel that they can live in two worlds.

It does not take too great an imagination to argue that graves and *feng-shui* offer opportunities for people to defy governmental authority and to express sentiments that would not be tolerated if they were expressed more directly. In a recent publication James Hayes, a Hong Kong administrator and historian, provides a number of examples in which *feng-shui* has become intertwined with local disputes and political tensions.[35] This does not mean that the Teng do not believe in *feng-shui* or revere their founder. But, it does mean that they are not so silly as to decline making a political point when the opportunity is presented to them.

In 1978 the Teng were forced to add the grave of Fu-hsieh's son, located near the market town of Yuen Long, to their list of endangered burial sites. The government had plans to develop the area, and it was feared that once again the Teng would have to do battle with the New Territories administration. In the fall and winter of 1977–78 the Teng held meetings in Yuen Long to determine their course of action. Another Grave Protection Society seemed likely. However, recent changes in land values and the eventual reversion of the New Territories to China has had the effect of cooling the ardor of local developers. The Yuen Long grave is probably safe, at least for the time being.

## HIGHER-ORDER LINEAGE: RITES, POLITICS, AND STATUS

Since at least the seventeenth century the localized Teng lineages of Hsin-an and Tung-kuan counties have formed a higher-order lineage.[36] In the late seventeenth century the Teng's five *fang* built an ancestral hall in Tung-kuan that united Teng from a number of separate communities. The guiding force behind this unification was the Teng's only *chin-shih* scholar, Teng Pao-sang from Kam Tin. Tou ch'ing t'ang, as the ancestral hall was named, was endowed with land, and the income from the estate was used for joint rituals and charitable activities.

Operationally, higher-order lineages serve as an institutional focus for

35. James Hayes, *The Rural Communities of Hong Kong*, pp. 143–145, 147–151.

36. For discussion of higher-order lineages, see James Watson, "Chinese Kinship Reconsidered: Anthropological Perspectives on Historical Research," *China Quarterly* 92 (1982): 608–609.

agnates from different villages and regions. Higher-order lineages tend to be run by and for their wealthier members.[37] They may function as political pressure groups; they may also run schools, recreation centers, and hostels. They provide charity for poor members and allies for wealthy ones.

According to the most complete genealogy in Ha Tsuen (owned by Ha Tsuen's geomancer), Tou ch'ing t'ang brought together eleven localized lineages, including of course the New Territories Teng settled in the villages of Ha Tsuen, Kam Tin, Ping Shan, Lung Yuek Tao, and Tai Po Tao. The genealogy notes that while all Teng elders were encouraged to attend *ch'ung-yang* ceremonies at Fu-hsieh's grave (plus the three graves of his father, grandfather, and son near Yuen Long), each *fang* was to take the responsibility for providing the offerings for these rites in yearly rotation. The five *fang* were focused on the Teng settlements at Jok Yuen, Wai Dak, Kam Tin/ Ha Tsuen, Ping Shan, and Fuk Lung. Since the Communist revolution, however, the border between Hong Kong and China has been closed, and the villagers of Jok Yuen, Wai Dak, and Fuk Lung have been unable to take their turn at the yearly rotation. Now only Kam Tin, Ha Tsuen, and Ping Shan are responsible for the offerings. However, Teng from Wai Dak, Jok Yuen, and Fuk Lung do have the right to participate in the grave worship and some émigrés from these villages who now live in Hong Kong do attend. In 1977 a contingent of Wai Dak migrants were in fact very active in the *ch'ung-yang* rites.

The higher-order lineage focused on Tou ch'ing t'ang offered a framework for Teng cooperation especially among the elite, but the existence of a "super-lineage" did not imply smooth social relations among its members. In fact, the neighboring lineages of Ha Tsuen and Ping Shan have often been in direct and sometimes violent conflict over water, land, and marketing rights. I was told by a number of Ha Tsuen elders that in the mid-nineteenth century the Ping Shan Teng went so far as to forge an alliance with Wai Dak Teng in the hope that they might finally break Ha Tsuen's grip on a number of small tenant villages in the area. In the end Ha Tsuen prevailed but not before they were forced to call on the help of a number of settlements east of Ping Shan (communities that shared with the people of Ha Tsuen a deep mistrust of Ping Shan's intentions). This is not the only instance in which the two lineages came into direct conflict, but it is dramatic proof that members of the same higher-order lineage are not always cooperative allies.

Most Teng antagonisms are not quite so violent as those between Ha Tsuen and Ping Shan, but one does not have to dig very deeply or ask too many questions before rivalries and animosities appear. The large, localized

---

37. On this point, see Woon Yuen-fong, "The Non-localized Descent Group in Traditional China," *Ethnology* 18 (1979): 17–29.

lineages of Kam Tin, Ha Tsuen, and Ping Shan each have smaller, branch communities attached to them. These branch settlements were established by former residents of the larger villages. Of course, according to Teng history Ha Tsuen is in fact a branch of Kam Tin, but what seems to separate larger lineages like Ha Tsuen and those that are not yet fully independent is their size, their ritual status, and their political clout. Branch lineages are small in population and have little political power, whereas Ha Tsuen and Ping Shan are large and tend to dominate local politics. In addition, members of the larger settlements (such as Ha Tsuen) do not return to Kam Tin (from which their lineage originally stemmed) for lineage rituals. Among the Teng perhaps the one thing that defines a descent group as a "branch" of another settlement is that residents of a "branch" return to their parent lineages for major ancestral rites.

There is nothing permanent about the relations between major lineages and their dependent branches. Nor has the relationship among the five *fang* of the Teng higher-order lineage remained unchanged. Political and economic circumstances affect who will be allies and who will be rivals. Their relative status and position are also conditioned by circumstances well outside the system of descent. Lineages may cease to have anything to do with other higher-order lineage members, branches may become independent, and large, independent lineages may be eclipsed by their juniors. How do these changes come about? How are they recognized and justified?

Anthropologists who work on African lineages know that genealogies are political documents and that they are altered and revised when the situation requires. As the genealogy is told and retold generation after generation, links through women, branches descended from one-time slaves, losers in political arguments may be overlooked or forgotten, whereas new alignments may be made to seem preordained. African genealogies are not written, and one assumes that they are more amenable to political manipulation and rationalization than their written counterparts in China. Because of China's long tradition of literacy, genealogies do not readily become the vehicles for making and registering political claims.

Chinese genealogies, on those rare occasions when researchers have examined their reliability, have been found to be generally accurate.[38] There are, of course, differences in the construction of Chinese genealogies. They vary from the elaborate printed versions kept by learned men to the handwritten documents one finds in rural villages. For purposes of demographic research Chinese genealogies leave much to be desired (they often fail to include names of sons who died before reaching adulthood, for example);

---

38. See H. G. H. Nelson, "Ancestor Worship and Burial Practices," in *Religion and Ritual in Chinese Society*, ed. Arthur P. Wolf (Stanford: Stanford University Press, 1974); James Watson, "Agnates and Outsiders: Adoption in a Chinese Lineage," *Man* n.s. 10 (1975): 293–306.

nevertheless, one may feel some confidence in the accuracy with which genealogical relationships themselves are rendered. For example, with an orally transmitted genealogy one might have expected the Ping Shan Teng to have eventually made Tzu-ming their ancestor (and the princess their ancestress). Genealogical manipulations of this sort do not seem to have occurred among the Teng, perhaps because there are so many written records available that it would be difficult to sustain such a fraud for very long. I do not mean to suggest that Chinese genealogies constitute a totally accurate record of descent ties or lineage history; this is certainly not the case. But, compared with unwritten genealogies, they are less prone to alteration and less useful in expressing political and economic changes.

In Chinese society as elsewhere it is all very well for individuals or groups to claim status, privileges, and power for themselves, but it is quite another matter for them to be accorded that status and power. Political arrangements change, alliances outlive their usefulness, and new elites emerge. Change is constant; but how are these changes publicly expressed? and how do people go about making their claims for altering the status quo? In China, one way of making and confirming claims is through ritual performance. As was noted above, rituals are not merely a validation of the status quo; they are in fact part of the process of change itself. Rites may be as much a part of the political terrain as are local elections.

Rituals often provide insights into political alignments that cannot be gained through direct observation and questioning. Nuances and changing power arrangements that informants may be unable or unwilling to discuss are sometimes displayed in ritual. As Tambiah has pointed out, rituals provide participants with "creative understanding." The messages, visions, feelings that rituals conjure up are rarely simple or straightforward.[39] In the remainder of this chapter I examine *ch'ung-yang* rites at the graves of Fu-hsieh's grandfather, father, and son near Yuen Long in 1977. These rites take place on the same day, with worship starting in the morning and continuing into the late afternoon as each of the three graves is visited in turn. The rites are well attended, although there are fewer participants than at Fu-hsieh's grave, which has its *ch'ung-yang* celebration two days after the rites at the Yuen Long graves.

In 1977 it was Ha Tsuen's turn to provide the grave offerings. Because the Ha Tsuen Teng were responsible for organizing the rituals, its *tsu-chang* (lineage master) led the proceedings. The sequence of ritual followed the same pattern at all three graves: First, offerings were made at the grave's protective shrine. Then offerings of five roast pigs, incense, candles, rice, wine, cakes, and a steamed chicken were spread out in front of each tomb. The Ha Tsuen *tsu-chang* led the worship, and once he had made his obei-

39. Tambiah, "The Magical Power of Words," p. 200.

sances, a report (*chi-wen*) was read to the ancestor informing him of the well-being and success of his descendants. Following this each generation came forward as a unit (no distinctions among the different Teng communities were made) to bow and to pour out cups of wine for the ancestor. As they left the grave each man was given a slip of paper confirming that he had attended this ritual and was thereby entitled to receive a share of sacrificial pork. The *tsu-chang* then returned to the grave and made a final bow.

The rites themselves are simple and relaxed. Considering the number of people involved and the cumbersome job of packing and repacking the offerings, the grave rites went off with great precision. The division of sacrificial pork was not, however, such a harmonious affair.

Pork divisions are the centerpiece of most lineage/ancestral rituals. Having a right to a share of the ancestor's pig (in a sense the ancestor himself purchases his own offerings, that is, they are paid for out of estate income) amounts to a public acknowledgment of lineage membership. The proper way to ask if someone is a member of an ancestral estate is to ask "Do you have a share?" The division of pork itself is scrupulously equal: portions are divided according to agreed formulas and each share is weighed to see that all have an equal amount. The whole procedure is watched carefully by the participants. Lineage members receive pork shares throughout their lives. They are given their first portion of sacrificial pork when they are less than one year old, and they continue to receive pork from the ancestors until they die. The sharing of ancestral pork links the living to the dead in a direct and highly dramatic way. Grave rites are, in effect, rites of commensality. In fact, the autumn visits to the graves of ancestors lower in the generational scale than Fu-hsieh often end in picnics. There the sacrificial pig is cooked and eaten by the participants (who, by definition, are also descendants of the ancestor in question). Because of the pig's contact with the grave it is believed to be imbued with cosmic forces (the wind and water) that flow through the grave.[40]

Attendance at the grave rites, where people stand, with whom they worship, all give symbolic expression to lineage ideals of cooperation, equality, and sharing. Among the Teng the division of ancestral pork is perhaps the key symbol of lineage unity; however, paradoxically, pork divisions are often fraught with tension, for it is here that statements about status and political alignments are made.

Five roast pigs were offered at the three Yuen Long graves: Kam Tin, Ping Shan, Wai Dak, and Ha Tsuen each provided a pig. As was noted above,

---

40. For a discussion of the complex relation among graves, ancestors, pork, and living descendants, see James Watson, "Pigs from the Ancestors: Communion and Exchange among the Cantonese," paper presented at University of London, Intercollegiate Anthropology Seminar entitled Death, Food, and Exchange: The Symbolism of Eating, 1983.

because Ha Tsuen people had the responsibility for the annual rotation they brought a second pig purchased from the funds of Fu-hsieh's estate, which after the 1920s comprised the land holdings incorporated by the Grave Protection Society. In 1977 the division of this "communal pig" immediately followed the rites at the last of the three graves. The pig was divided into three portions of nine catties each and two portions of three catties (any remaining pork belongs to those who brought the pig). Ha Tsuen, Ping Shan, and Kam Tin each received nine catties. As soon as the Ping Shan and Kam Tin contingents received their nine catties, they picked up the roast pig they themselves had brought and returned to their home villages where, as was noted above, they shared out their portion of the sacrificial pork. One three-catty portion, I was told by a number of elders, is reserved for other Teng from Tung-kuan and Hsin-an counties who attend the rites. In 1977 only Wai Dak people represented this group, and they took all three catties when they left. Finally, three catties were given to Ha Tsuen's *tsu-chang* as leader of the rites. It was at this point that difficulties began to arise.

First, there was some grumbling about Wai Dak's share of three catties. According to a number of Ha Tsuen Teng, 1977 was only the second year in which émigré Teng from Wai Dak had attended *ch'ung-yang* rites at Yuen Long, and it was the first year they had brought a roast pig. The Wai Dak pig was smaller than the others, a Ha Tsuen elder pointed out to me, but it was nevertheless a respectable offering. In 1976 only one man from Wai Dak participated in the Yuen Long rites; in 1977 there were eleven. Apparently the Wai Dak Teng were trying to rekindle their ties to their agnatic kin in the New Territories. It should be noted that ties to New Territories *pen-ti* can be valuable to émigré entrepreneurs or small factory owners. Whether their claims to be treated as lineage brothers will be successful remains to be seen. Their share of Fu-hsieh's pig does, of course, indicate that the New Territories Teng had decided to grant them formal recognition, but in 1977 no one had quite decided whether the Wai Dak Teng would be accepted completely back into the Teng fold.

Compared with the quiet grumbling over the share of the Wai Dak contingent, the disagreements that followed were heated and, in the end, unresolved. The lineage at Ha Tsuen is divided into two *fang*: *hsia* (bottom) *fang* and *shang* (top) *fang*. Because of their peculiar history, the Ha Tsuen Teng have two founders instead of one (these founders are not brothers but have a common great-grandfather, or FFF); there is an uneasy partnership between the two sets of descendants. In some respects Ha Tsuen is two lineages pretending to be one. The Ha Tsuen Teng have two *tsu-chang* (lineage masters), one for *hsia fang* and one for *shang fang*. However, the master of *hsia fang* usually takes precedence. In fact, *hsia fang* dominates nearly all lineage affairs; it does so, not because it is the senior branch, but because this *fang* has the wealthiest estates and the largest number of descendants. At the autumn pork division the *shang fang* master claimed equal treatment to his *hsia fang* counterpart. This is not new; in fact, such arguments are recurring elements in local rituals. In this case the Ha Tsuen elders decided to pacify the *shang fang* master by giving him one and one-half catties of pork. He was not entirely happy with this arrangement; he had loudly and publicly demanded equality, but he was not granted as much pork as his rival. For their part *hsia fang* elders complained that he should have received nothing. Bowing to such demands, they said, was not a good precedent.

Just as this argument was cooling another, far more acrimonious dispute broke out between Ha Tsuen people and villagers from their branch settlement at Mong Tseng. The small villages of Mong Tseng and Ji Tin were both founded by Ha Tsuen Teng. Mong Tseng is about two miles to the north of Ha Tsuen, and Ji Tin is three miles to the west. They each have a small banquet hall, but they keep their ancestral tablets in Ha Tsuen's main ancestral hall where they celebrate the birth of sons (*k'ai-teng*), marriages, and the Spring and Autumn Rites. As far as the residents of Ha Tsuen are concerned, they have no independent standing; they are simply part of the Ha Tsuen Teng lineage.

In the case of Mong Tseng this lack of independent status is keenly felt and no doubt exacerbated by the fact that they are also Ha Tsuen's political and economic clients. Mong Tseng is located in Ha Tsuen's hinterland; Ji Tin, on the other hand, falls outside of it. In the past the Mong Tseng Teng rented much of their land from Ha Tsuen landlords and estates, they were protected by its self-defense corps, and they made their purchases and sold their crops in Ha Tsuen's walled market. They had the misfortune of standing somewhere between being full-fledged Teng and dependent tenants. Falling between such clearly demarcated status groups could never have been easy, and no doubt that is one reason why Mong Tseng villagers, in contrast to people from Ji Tin, are less willing to accept domination by their agnates in Ha Tsuen. Now that most Mong Tseng people work in local factories or have sons who work in Britain, they are no longer economically dependent on Ha Tsuen. It is perhaps inevitable that economic independence would make the Mong Tseng Teng unwilling to accept second-class status in the larger descent group.

During the 1977 rites the group from Mong Tseng insisted on receiving their share of sacrificial pork at the grave instead of returning to Ha Tsuen for the division, as was the usual custom. By asking for their share immediately following the rites, they were claiming the same status as the major lineages of Ping Shan, Kam Tin, and Ha Tsuen—corporate groups that all receive their shares at the grave. In effect, they were refusing to confirm their dependent status by collecting their share in Ha Tsuen. After considerable argument Ha Tsuen's elders acceded to these demands. The argument did not stop there, however.

The most outspoken of Mong Tseng's contingent was a middle-aged villager who had political aspirations in Ha Tsuen district. For generations the Ha Tsuen Teng have taken their Mong Tseng lineage mates for granted. This man was serving notice that he and the people of Mong Tseng were no longer willing to tolerate this state of affairs. Not surprisingly, there was also a subplot to this drama. Mong Tseng's politician was gaining allies among his own villagers for his outspoken stand against the overbearing Teng of Ha Tsuen. Having gained one point, the Mong Tseng people pressed for another, arguing that they should receive more pork than they were being allotted because so many of their number had attended the rites. There was much shouting, and finally it was agreed that Mong Tseng's contingent should receive three more ounces. Mong Tseng people were not happy with this compromise, but they finally accepted it, took their sacrificial pork, and departed.

Clearly, the Mong Tseng Teng were announcing a change in their relations with Ha Tsuen, and just as clearly, the people of Ha Tsuen were refusing to accept this change. In the view of some Ha Tsuen elders the Mong Tseng Teng had lost more than they had gained by causing a public row (much to the amusement of Kam Tin and Ping Shan elders who watched from the sidelines). Nonetheless, the Mong Tseng contingent had forced a pork division at the grave and they did receive an extra portion. The seeming insignificance of this last concession (only three extra ounces) was viewed by Ha Tsuen people as an insult to the Mong Tseng Teng, and I think that some Ha Tsuen people were secretly pleased that their "dependents" had settled for so little. Eventually the Mong Tseng Teng may negotiate a new status for themselves in these rituals. From their point of view a change in the ritual pork division is long overdue. Although this change may not involve complete ritual independence from Ha Tsuen, at least some of the symbolic bonds that called attention to their dependent status will be discarded.

In a slightly different and perhaps more decorous manner similar arguments were taking place between representatives of Lung Yuek Tao and Kam Tin. The Lung Yeuk Tao Teng, who consider themselves to be the equals if not the superiors of the Kam Tin Teng, settled their status dilemma by simply refusing to accept pork from Kam Tin. Rather than admit to being the status inferiors of their rivals, the Lung Yuek Tao Teng remained aloof from the whole affair. I was told by a Lung Teuk Tao elder that "we now take our own pig so that there is no need to argue." According to Teng elders, disputes over pork divisions are nothing new. Participants all agreed that such disruptions were lamentable, but still the fact remained that dis-

putes seemed to be very much a part of these elaborate grave rites. I was told
by a Lung Yuek Tao Teng that for a number of years Ping Shan and Ha
Tsuen bickered and argued over their share of pork. The dispute finally
reached such a point that youths from the two villages attended the *ch'ung-
yang* rites to back up, presumably with force if necessary, the claims of their
elders for a larger pork share. Each pork division is simply a recognition of
that year's particular hierarchy of status. These hierarchies are under constant negotiation and compromise. Chinese grave rites may celebrate,
create, and sustain agnatic groups, but they also provide occasions for radically altering those groups and their relations one to another.

## CONCLUSIONS

Grave rites, or the cult of the grave, as one might be tempted to label it,
cannot be neatly reduced to a precise set of symbols and actions. The messages conveyed by grave rites, the symbols utilized, and the dramas performed are richly elaborate and multifaceted. They cannot be adequately
analyzed by using the language of Durkheim or by using the models of those
who ignore the social implications of ritual. If we lose sight of the political
and status conflicts that these men are staging within the framework of the
grave rites, we miss one of the most essential aspects of these rituals. Ritual
in this context is about change, transformation, action, and the negotiation
of meaning.

　　In analyzing rituals such as the ones outlined above we are constantly
forced to deal with what Roger Keesing has called "Bateson's problem."[41]
How do we make our analysis of ritual reflect the complex interplay of the
social, political, economic, psychological, and intellectual aspects of life? All
of these forces meet in ritual, but we have yet to find the language for describing this interplay. In my interpretation of grave rites I have stressed the
political; others may take a different approach, emphasizing the unifying
aspects of ancestor worship. It is obvious that both tendencies (unification
and division) have an influence on the orchestration of these rites.

　　Why, one might well ask, do hundreds of grown men care so much about
a few ounces of pork? Obviously the division of pork, the grave rites themselves, and the geomancy of graves continue to be of great importance to the
Teng. The rituals performed at the grave are in many ways tailor-made for
political discourse. Ancestors are, after all, members of the descent group;
they are not "outsiders," like gods and ghosts. They do not have great power;
they tend to be passive and lack volition. It is not surprising, therefore,

---

41. Roger M. Keesing, "Introduction," in *Rituals of Manhood: Male Initiation in Papua
New Guinea*, ed. Gilbert H. Herdt (Berkeley and Los Angeles: University of California Press,
1982), p. 17.

that ancestors should be made to serve the political ends of their descendants. Finally, the grave cult is inextricably linked to geomancy, an amoral and competitive cosmological system. As Freedman has concluded: "[In the context of geomancy] the dead were passive agents, pawns in a kind of ritual game played by their descendants with the help of geomancers."[42]

The role that ancestors play in kinship, their passivity, and their links to geomancy make them excellent vehicles for political and status manipulation. Grave rites inevitably become part of the process by which changes in status and power are confirmed or denied. Both Mong Tseng and Ping Shan villagers tried to force other Teng to accept their claims for a new status. They were not completely successful, but, for our purposes, the outcome of these disputes is not at issue. The important point is that such cases demonstrate that grave rites are not a rigid set of acts to be performed in a precise and unchanging manner. Wealth, status, competition, politics, filial piety, and group unity are all intimately intertwined in the performance of the ancestral rites. In China, the ancestors may be passive, but the dramas performed at the grave do not reflect this passivity.

42. Freedman, *Chinese Lineage and Society*, p. 126.

# TEN

# The Imperial Way Of Death: Ming and Ch'ing Emperors and Death Ritual

*Evelyn S. Rawski*

Death ritual for the emperors had to reflect two at times contradictory aspects of this role. As the Son of Heaven, the ruler stood in a unique position at the pinnacle of the Chinese order. Recipient of the Mandate of Heaven, he relied on his special ritual role in integrating the cosmos and on the symbolic and sacred powers inherited from the imperial ancestors, including those of previous dynasties, for legitimation. The act of sacrificing was central to the emperorship. The Son of Heaven monopolized the right to sacrifice at the most important state altars: "In return for bearing this supreme responsibility, he attained dominion for it was upon his performance that the interconnection of the cosmos depended. While these rituals constituted the cosmic cycle, they also became proof of the emperor's fitness to rule as the man who could...show the unity of Heaven and Earth."[1]

The "grand" or first-rank state rituals, the sacrifices performed at the altars of Heaven, Earth, the Temple of the Ancestors (T'ai-miao) and the Altar of Land and the Harvest (She-chi), were imperial duties; the first was so intimately linked with the imperial institution that for anyone else to worship Heaven was an "act of high treason," signifying "an intention to usurp the prerogative and to seize the throne of the sovereign."[2] This grand

---

1. Angela Rose Zito, "Re-Presenting Sacrifice: Cosmology and the Editing of Texts," *Ch'ing-shih wen-t'i* 5, no. 2 (1984): 52.
2. W. A. P. Martin, "The Emperor at the Altar of Heaven," *Hanlin Papers* (Shanghai: Kelly and Walsh, 1894), p. 358. Robert Oxnam, *Ruling from Horseback: Manchu Politics in the Oboi Regency, 1661–1669* (Chicago: University of Chicago Press, 1975), p. 41. Quotation from C. K. Yang, *Religion in Chinese Society* (Berkeley and Los Angeles: University of California Press, 1961), p. 128. For a structural analysis of the first-rank sacrifices, see Zito, "Re-Presenting Sacrifice." Descriptive material is also provided in E. T. Williams, "The State Religion of China during the Manchu Dynasty," *Journal of the North China Branch, Royal Asiatic Society* 44 (1913): 11–45.

sacrifice to Heaven was the first ritual act performed by the Manchus when they entered Peking and the rite performed at the accession of an emperor. Worship at the altars of deities of the second and third ranks had to be supervised by the emperor: it was he who approved the appropriate dates for worship of each deity, submitted in a religious calendar of worship by the Board of Rites a year in advance.

An emperor's schedule was full of ritual performance, most importantly at the first-rank altars cited above. In addition there were the rituals performed on the birthdays and deathdays of the emperor's ancestors. The significance of these ancestral rituals had itself changed considerably over the long span of historical time. In sharp contrast to the pre-T'ang practice that placed ancestral rites at the heart of the state religion, the T'ang and later dynasties had promoted the worship of Heaven and Earth to the first place.[3] By Ch'ing times imperial death rites combined elements of two traditions: the old tradition, evident from Shang times, that viewed the spirits of imperial ancestors as a source of sacred power, to be monopolized (and manipulated) by the ruler; and the attempt of emperors from the Sung on to use these rites as exercises in filiality that reinforced the legitimacy of the new heir. In the Ming-Ch'ing period, the first tradition was embedded in sacrifice at the Temple of the Ancestors; the second dominated the funeral sequence itself.

Imperial death ritual also replicated many elements of commoner practice found in at least some parts of China. Imperial mausolea were simply larger, more elaborate versions of Chinese tombs. The sequence of the death rituals from the moment of death to the interment of the coffin in a grave was a recognizable variant of the commoner ritual sequence outlined in James Watson's introductory essay in this volume.[4] The areas of imperial ritual that diverged from commoner practice reflected the peculiar social organization of the imperial descent group resulting from the fact that only one man could inherit the throne. Ch'ing alterations in succession practices which heightened the quest for legitimacy on the part of the new ruler became an important motivating factor for mourning observance.

Emperors, like all rulers, were unique beings. Only one man could occupy the throne; partible inheritance, the common practice for males in Chinese families, was not practiced by the imperial family. The bitter contest for succession frequently acted to divide brother from brother. A ruler viewed his agnates as a politically dangerous group to be kept out of politi-

3. Howard J. Wechsler, *Offerings of Jade and Silk: Ritual and Symbol in the Legitimation of the T'ang Dynasty* (New Haven: Yale University Press, 1985).
4. Besides the essays in this volume, commoner death ritual is described in J. J. M. de Groot, *The Religious System of China: Its Ancient Forms, Evolution, History and Present Aspect, Manners, Customs and Social Institutions Connected Therewith*, 6 vols. (1892–1910 ed. reprinted Taipei: Ch'eng-wen, 1969), volume 1.

cal power precisely because they shared his blood claim to the throne. In separating himself institutionally from close agnatic relationships an emperor behaved like virtually none of his subjects. Princes (imperial sons who were not designated heir) were in fact sent out from the capital to live on their own estates in the Ming, a device to keep them from forming political cliques in the capital.[5]

The tension surrounding the succession issue was exacerbated by the Ch'ing, who departed from the Ming practice of public installation of an heir apparent, generally the eldest son, while the heir was still a child. In eleven of the fifteen cases of imperial succession in the Ming, a first son inherited the throne from his father. When an emperor died without sons, a younger brother might be designated his heir; if he died without sons and brothers, an agnate might be chosen. Three such cases occurred in the Ming; there was in addition the forcible take-over of the throne in 1403 by an uncle, the famous Yung-lo Emperor.

The Ch'ing initially practiced a quite different system of rule by council, where the successor either was one of a group of nearly equal leaders or chosen by them. Nurgaci (1559–1626), the founder of the dynasty, was succeeded by his eighth son, Huang-t'ai-chi (T'ai-tsung), who won his own way to the top after Nurgaci died. Huang-t'ai-chi's death in 1643 brought several candidates for the leadership, notably his eldest son and his brother, Dorgon: the latter put Huang-t'ai-chi's ninth son, an infant, on the throne, and dominated the government as regent. The next heir, chosen in 1661 as his father lay dying of smallpox, seems to have been selected partly because he had already had the disease.[6] In fact, no Ch'ing emperor who inherited the throne was a first son.

The case of Yin-jeng, the K'ang-hsi Emperor's heir apparent, posed an excellent argument for the disadvantages of naming an heir.[7] In conformity with Ming practice Yin-jeng had been designated heir apparent in 1676 at the age of two. His personality problems and dissolute life-style, coupled with the emergence of a political faction centered on him, raised the tension between Yin-jeng and his father. In 1708 an attempt on K'ang-hsi's life

5. Charles O. Hucker, *The Traditional Chinese State in Ming Times (1368–1644)* (Tucson: University of Arizona Press, 1961), pp. 8–9.

6. For information on these emperors, see the individual biographies in *Eminent Chinese of the Ch'ing Period*, ed. Arthur Hummel (Washington, D.C.: Government Printing Office, 1941). Frederic Wakeman, Jr., *The Great Enterprise: The Manchu Reconstruction of Imperial Order in Seventeenth-Century China* (Berkeley and Los Angeles: University of California Press, 1985), 1:157–160.

7. Silas H. L. Wu, *Passage to Power: K'ang-hsi and His Heir Apparent, 1661–1722* (Cambridge: Harvard University Press, 1979), chap. 10; Harold L. Kahn, *Monarchy in the Emperor's Eyes: Image and Reality in the Ch'ien-lung Reign* (Cambridge: Harvard University Press, 1971), chap. 12.

prompted the emperor to remove him as heir; he was reinstated in 1709 but removed again in 1712. Meanwhile Yin-jeng's dismissal spurred intense competition among the other sons, the formation of rival cliques around individual contenders for the throne, and one of the most bitter succession struggles of the dynasty. K'ang-hsi refused to name another heir and did not do so until his deathbed in 1722. His successor, the Yung-cheng Emperor (r. 1723–1735), substituted in place of the Ming custom a system whereby the name of the heir was sealed in a coffer, to be opened only upon the emperor's death. Throughout the rest of the Ch'ing dynasty emperors chose secret succession over public avowal of an heir.

These two elements—the secret nature of the decision, not disclosed until the emperor lay dying, and the complete lack of any constraints imposed by birth order on the choice—meant that succession struggles were particularly bitter. Many emperors mounted the throne amid rumors that they or their supporters at court had falsified the late emperor's will and manipulated the succession. In contrast to the predictable succession policy of the Ming, the Ch'ing substituted a dangerous guessing game.

With succession a live issue, competition among an emperor's consorts for the advancement of their own sons was intense. The normal rule dictating that sons of concubines ritually and legally regard the wife as mother was noticeably breached by emperors, whose first acts upon succeeding to the throne were frequently to promote their mothers to the status of empress. Mother-son relationships, commonly warm and intimate, were made even more so by the circumstances surrounding the rearing of princes. The struggle between mothers-in-law and brides was exacerbated by the political power struggles behind marital choices in the emperor's case. Frequently these tensions erupted in disputes over funeral ritual and the placement of ancestral tablets. In short, imperial death rituals serve as a fascinating key to personalities and the "inner story" of the family relations of China's rulers.

The uniqueness of the emperor was frequently underlined by his ritual functions. Yet emperors also spent a great deal of time fulfilling familial roles. This was a deliberate policy decision: the ruler was the exemplar of family virtues for the whole nation. As the K'ang-hsi Emperor noted, "We rule the empire with filial piety."[8] Filiality was the condensed "core" of the family system, and the family system the "core" of the society. When an emperor mourned a parent, he was acting as a role model for the entire empire; he had to be Everyman.

Just as emperors were set apart from their brothers and other agnates, so the line of descent from emperor to emperor was distinguished sharply from the patrilineal descent group, a group of males tracing their descent back to

8. Wu, *Passage*, p. 52.

a common ancestor, found among commoners. Emperors were the heads of the imperial line: that is to say, the direct line of descent, emperor to emperor and ordinarily from father to son, which excluded collaterals. This line was ritually institutionalized in two edifices: the T'ai-miao, the Temple of the Ancestors, situated in Peking, the capital for most of the Ming and all of the Ch'ing dynasty, which was the state temple, and the Feng-hsien tien, or Hall for Worship of the Ancestors, located within the palace grounds almost due east of the Ch'ien-ch'ing gate.

The Temple of the Ancestors was one of the most important religious institutions for the state religion, ranking just after the Altars of Heaven and Earth. The *Book of Rites* states that "the sacrifice to Heaven in the suburbs (at the Altar to Heaven) is the highest act of reverence; the sacrifice in the ancestral temple is the highest expression of human relationship."[9] Worship at the Temple of the Ancestors symbolized the primacy of the emperor's role as exemplar of filial piety. The Temple was located outside the Wu-men, to the east of the great north-south axis leading to the major palace halls for state functions. Its main hall faced south and was reserved for the major sacrifices. Ancestral tablets of emperors and their consorts were housed in the rear hall, located to the north.

Only males in the direct line of succession were commemorated in the Temple of the Ancestors and its adjunct halls. Both the Ming and the Ch'ing included ancestors of the founder in this group: the Ming went back four generations, to the great-great-grandfather of Chu Yuan-chang, and the Ch'ing included their progenitor, Aisin Gioro, and the three generations immediately preceding Nurgaci.[10]

The rear hall of the T'ai-miao permitted only a limited number of chambers *(ch'in-shih)* housing emperors' tablets: in the Ming, nine, and in the Ch'ing, eight. As the dynasty wore on the additional tablets were stored in a rear annex. In all halls, the usual Chinese order prevailed: the first position was the center one, the second the eastern (left) position, the third the western (right) position, and then alternately left and right. By the late sixteenth century, T'ai-tsu, the founder of the Ming, held the commanding central

9. Quoted in E. T. Williams, "The State Religion," p. 23.

10. For information about the T'ai-miao, see the *Ta Ming hui-tien* 大明會典 [Collected statutes of the Ming dynasty] (1587, reprinted Taipei, 1963), chüan 86, and the *Ch'in-ting ta Ch'ing hui-tien shih-li* 欽定大清會典事例 [Collected statutes and precedents of the Ch'ing dynasty] (1886), chüan 423. See also Edward T. Williams, "Worshipping Imperial Ancestors in Peking, " *Journal of the North China Branch, Royal Asiatic Society* 70 (1939): 46–65. The deathdays observed in the Ming (up to the Wan-li reign) are listed in *Ta Ming hui-tien*, 89:3a–4a; the Ch'ing deathdays are provided by J. M., "Mourning Days at the Court of Peking," *China Review* 15 (1886–87): 181–182, and G. M. H. Playfair, "Days of Official Mourning in China," *China Review* 17 (1888–89): 47–48.

position in the T'ai-miao; the first position in the Ch'ing T'ai-miao was occupied by Nurgaci's tablet.[11]

Rituals at the Temple of the Ancestors used the same kinds of musical instruments, dancers, choir, and so forth stipulated for the other first-rank altars. The five regularly scheduled rituals were the *meng* rites in the first, fourth, seventh, and tenth lunar months, and the *hsia* sacrifice at the close of the year. On such occasions, the ancestral tablets were brought and placed on the main hall's altar. Different sacrifices called for different displays: each dynasty published elaborate rules specifying the arrangement of tablets for each rite.[12]

Like the Temple of the Ancestors, the Hall for Worship of the Ancestors housed only the spirit tablets of emperors and imperial consorts; both were therefore completely unlike the ancestral halls of commoners, where a collection of collateral agnates would be collectively worshipped. Although the two halls housed the same tablets, we can see a distinction in Ch'ing placement of tablets of ancestors who had died before 1644: these were separately housed in the Temple of the Ancestors, whereas in the Hall, all ancestors in the direct line of descent were housed in one chamber and placed on the altar for sacrifice.

The Ming and Ch'ing also recognized a broader kinship group consisting of all persons descended from an emperor, and set this group apart in terms of ritual obligations and privilege.[13] In fact, the very first institution treated in the *Collected Statutes* of both dynasties was the Imperial Clan Court (*tsung-jen fu*), which was in charge of all matters relating to imperial descendants. The Imperial Clan Court was responsible for keeping the genealogy of the descent group, the *Yü-tieh*, which was divided into the genealogy of the imperial descent line (*tsung-shih*) and the genealogy of collaterals (*chueh-lo*).[14] Rank within the descent group was determined by degree of separation in descent from the imperial progenitor and by seniority within the agnates of each generation. Although every son of an emperor could be invested as a prince of the first rank (*ch'in-wang*), the award of princely ranks was at the discretion of the ruler. The first- and second-rank princely titles were passed from eldest son to eldest son. New *ch'in-wang* were added

11. *Ta Ming hui-tien*, chüan 86; *Ch'in-ting ta Ch'ing hui-tien shih-li*, chüan 423; de Groot, *The Religious System*, 3:1268–1276.

12. *T'ai-ch'ang hsu-k'ao* 太常續考 [Study of the Court of Imperial Sacrifice] (1643), 4:26ab.

13. The Imperial Clan included male descendants of the founding emperor and of subsequent emperors, as well as the daughters of such persons; on the female side inclusion lasted only one generation, since the offspring bore not the mother's but the father's surname.

14. Ch'ü Liu-sheng 屈六生, "Ch'ing-tai yü-tieh" 清代玉牒 [The Ch'ing imperial genealogy], *Li-shih tang-an* 歷史檔案 no. 1 (1984): 83–87.

with each generation, so the number increased in the course of the dynasty. Other sons of princes received lesser ranks; with each generation, younger sons' ranks declined, but all imperial male descendants remained marked off from the rest of the population. Princes were divided into twelve ranks; these ranks were of course linked to privilege.[15]

Although excluded from commemoration in the Temple of the Ancestors and the Hall for Worship of the Ancestors, the imperial descent group had the birthright to worship at these temples, and beyond that they could substitute for the emperor at the grand sacrifices at the first-rank altars. Their ritual eligibility was of course the reason why emperors drew a sharp line between themselves and these potential claimants of the throne.

### SELECTION OF TOMBS

Unlike ordinary citizens, the selection of a burial site was usually made by an emperor during his lifetime, in accordance with the principles of geomancy, or *feng-shui*. The geomantic virtue of the site was assumed to affect dynastic fortunes, so proceedings were generally protracted and occasionally rancorous. Burials were assumed to be permanent; double burial was not practiced.[16]

Imperial tombs were clustered in areas designated as imperial cemeteries. With the exception of the founder of the dynasty and his son, the Ming emperors and their empresses were all buried at a site 45 kilometers northwest of Peking called Ch'ang-p'ing, preserved by the succeeding Ch'ing house, which also buried the last Ming emperor with full rites.[17] The Ch'ing emperors and their empresses were buried in two cemeteries, one to the east and the other to the west of the capital. Both dynasties also designated the burial places of the progenitors of the founder of the dynasty (the same ancestors whose tablets reposed in the Temple of the Ancestors or its adjuncts) as *ling*, or imperial burials. Such a designation automatically ensured that a certain number of households would be assigned to care for the site in

15. Hucker, *The Traditional Chinese State*, pp. 7–10; H. S. Brunnert and V. V. Hagelstrom, *Present Day Political Organization of China*, trans. A. Beltchenko and E. E. Moran (Shanghai: Kelly and Walsh, 1912), pp. 4–8; de Groot, *The Religious System*, 2:453; 3:1172.

16. The movement of graves of the Manchu remote ancestors as the fortunes of the Aisin Gioro clan rose is described by de Groot, *The Religious System*, 3:1354–1358.

17. *Ta Ch'ing Shih-tsu Chang huang-ti shih-lu* 大清世祖章皇帝實錄 [Veritable records of the Shun-chih reign] (all Ch'ing *shih-lu* in 1964 Taipei reprint ed.), 5:3b–4a; Oxnam, *Ruling from Horseback*, p. 41. The imperial burial sites are described in the *Collected Statutes* of each dynasty, under the section on the Board of Rites. The Ming tombs were also described by Ku Yen-wu 顧炎武, *Ch'ang-p'ing shan-shui chi* 昌平山水記 [Record of the Ch'ang-p'ing cemetery], in *Ku T'ing-lin hsien-sheng yi-shu shih chung* 顧亭林先生遺書十種 [Collected writings of Ku Yen-wu] (1885); de Groot, *The Religious System*, 3:1177–1253, 1256–1282; and Ann Paludan, *The Imperial Ming Tombs* (New Haven: Yale University Press, 1981).

perpetuity and that the area would be guarded by a garrison. The tombs were of course closed to ordinary visitors.[18] Each imperial tomb had a sacrificial hall, which housed the spirit tablets of the deceased emperor and empresses buried there. Regular worship took place on the first and fifteenth of each month. At stipulated times of the year, the three most important being ch'ing-ming, the Lantern Festival, and the winter solstice, a high-ranking imperial kinsman or official would be sent to perform sacrifices at the tombs. An official was also sent at the New Year, the end of the year, and on the birthday and deathday of every emperor and empress to perform rites at their mausolea. From time to time, emperors would make pilgrimages to the cemeteries. Grave worship thus occurred with much greater frequency for imperial burials than the once-a-year grave rites of commoners.[19]

The imperial cemeteries were reserved for the emperors and their principal consorts; concubines, like princes, were buried at other sites, although in the early Ming and again in the early Ch'ing, concubines and sometimes servants accompanied their master into death. In the Ming, two emperors failed to receive imperial burial at the behest of their successors: the second emperor, Chu Yun-wen (r. 1398–1402), was overthrown by his uncle, who refused to even acknowledge his reign, and Chu Ch'i-yü (r. 1449–1457) was buried in the cemetery for lesser imperial kinsmen by his brother, the Cheng-t'ung Emperor (r. 1435–49, 1457–64), whose capture by the Mongols in 1449 had led to Ch'i-yü's accession, and whose coup in 1457 ended Ch'i-yü's reign.[20]

If rulers could be denied legitimacy by exclusion from imperial burial by their successors, a non-ruler could of course obtain imperial treatment by edict. Named successor to the childless Cheng-te Emperor in 1521, Chu Hou-ts'ung, cousin of the previous ruler, forced the officials to promote his father, Prince of Hsing, to posthumous imperial status. He installed his

18. For information on these low-status tomb households, see Paludan, *The Imperial Ming Tombs*, pp. 214–215.

19. The Ch'ing tombs are discussed by de Groot, *The Religious System*, 3:1282–1373. On imperial visits to the tombs, see Ray Huang, *1587, A Year of No Significance: The Ming Dynasty in Decline* (New Haven: Yale University Press, 1981), p. 121; Charles Gutzlaff, *The Life of Taou-Kwang, Late Emperor of China: with Memoirs of the Court of Peking, Including a Sketch of the Principal Events in the History of the Chinese Empire during the Last Fifty Years* (1852 ed. reprinted Wilmington, Del.: Scholarly Resources, 1972), pp. 94–97; de Groot, 3:1371. On commoner grave rites see Maurice Freedman, *Chinese Lineage and Society: Fukien and Kwangtung* (New York: Humanities Press, 1966), p. 142.

20. Details on Ming immolation can be found in *T'ai-ch'ang hsu-k'ao*, 4:3b–6b. On the early Ch'ing practice (which was abolished by the K'ang-hsi Emperor), see Oxnam, *Ruling from Horseback*, p. 61. A list of the individuals interred in the Ch'ang-p'ing cemetery is provided by de Groot, *The Religious System*, 3:1188–1191. On Chu Ch'i-yü, see Paludan, *The Imperial Ming Tombs*, chap. 19.

father's ancestral tablet in the T'ai-miao, erected a special hall within the
palace grounds for his father's commemorative rites, and having decided
against moving his father's coffin from An-lu department, Hupei, to the
Ch'ang-p'ing cemetery, made his father's burial site a *ling*.[21]

Interment in a *ling* did not automatically confer entry of the ancestral
tablets of women into the T'ai-miao. A Ming empress or a concubine posthumously raised to the rank of empress because she had given birth to an
emperor was buried in the same underground chamber as her spouse; the
Ch'ing altered this custom in 1717 when they ruled that thenceforth widows
of empress rank would be interred in separate tombs, placed next to the one
in which the emperor was buried. In both dynasties, the practice of elevating
imperial mothers to empress meant that frequently several women were
buried with an emperor. Since the Ming ruled that only the first empress
would have her tablet installed in the T'ai-miao, women subsequently raised
to this status and buried at Ch'ang-p'ing in imperial tombs were denied this
privilege: in five of the seven Ming cases, the women were mothers or grandmothers of emperors, promoted from concubine status for this reason. The
Ch'ing permitted the tablets of several consorts to be placed in the T'ai-
miao; the sole example of exclusion is the case of Hsiao-hsien, concubine of
the Shun-chih Emperor, who promoted her to empress upon her death in
1660. Despite this promotion and her inclusion in the Shun-chih Emperor's
tomb, her tablet was not placed in the T'ai-miao, perhaps because the
emperor's extreme devotion to her was regarded with great bitterness by his
mother, and his arrangement for her death rites was denounced as "excessive" in the will (probably forged) left after his death.[22]

It was always possible (if rare) for a ruler to select a new burial site, as did
the Yung-lo Emperor, who took the throne from his nephew and established
a new imperial burial ground in 1409 near his capital, Peking. In Ch'ing
times, the Yung-cheng Emperor, who displayed extreme filial piety in his
mourning for his father (of which more later), nonetheless built his
mausoleum in a completely different location in the opposite direction from
the cemetery in which his father and grandfather lay, citing bad *feng-shui* as
the reason. His successor, the Ch'ien-lung Emperor, chose to place his tomb
in the earlier eastern cemetery, arguing that if he followed his filial desire to
be buried near his father, successive generations would do likewise and the

21. Charles Hucker, "Confucianism and the Chinese Censorial System," in *Confucianism
in Action*, ed. David S. Nivison and Arthur F. Wright (Stanford: Stanford University Press,
1959), p. 201, describes the official resistance to this action. See Chu Hou-ts'ung's biography in
*Dictionary of Ming Biography*, 1:315–322. The *Ta Ming hui-tien*, 89:12b–19b, describes the
shrines erected by the Chia-ching Emperor to commemorate his father.

22. Details of the death of Hsiao-hsien are in *Eminent Chinese of the Ch'ing Period*,
1:255–259. Oxnam, *Ruling from Horseback*, pp. 60–62.

tombs of the Shun-chih and K'ang-hsi emperors would be isolated. Emperors should henceforth be buried alternately in the eastern and western cemeteries, and this rule was generally followed.[23]

Because an imperial mausoleum was a very large project, involving coordination of large numbers of workers and expenditure of vast sums, imperial favorites were frequently appointed to supervise the work. Appointment to this post was an extremely risky political proposition. There were numerous potential grounds for demotion and punishment. The most horrible possibility was the flooding of the underground chamber in which the emperor's coffin would eventually rest. Since tombs were built in valleys (a reversal of commoner practice, which placed tombs on hills),[24] and the construction of a huge earth tumulus over the underground chamber tended to make drainage difficult, this was a recurrent phenomenon. Such an accusation during construction of the Wan-li Emperor's mausoleum brought dismissal of the memorialist from the civil service when the charges proved false; the Tao-kuang Emperor's discovery that his tomb was flooded led to exile for the minister in charge.[25]

In other ways, imperial mausolea were constructed on principles that were common to other Chinese tombs. The major elements of an imperial burial site—mammoth arches, the stele pavilion, stone figures of animals and humans guarding a spirit road, palace-style buildings centered around a sacrificial hall, arranged in a series of courtyards above ground, an underground funeral chamber beneath a man-made tumulus, surrounded by a fortified wall—were replicated in the tombs not only of imperial kinsmen but of officials. Tomb buildings resembled the secular dwelling quarters of the deceased in their layout. The Ming and Ch'ing enacted sumptuary regulations specifying the dimensions of the burial ground; the height of the tumulus; the number of stone figures; and the dimensions of the stele permitted to princes, their consorts, descendants, hereditary nobles, and officials by rank.

23. Paludan, *The Imperial Ming Tombs*, pp. 7–10; de Groot, *The Religious System*, 3:1292–1297. For an exception to this rule, see Hsu Kuang-yuan 徐廣源, "Tao-kuang ling pan-ch'ien shih-mo" 道光陵搬遷始末 [The details of the move of the Tao-kuang emperor's tomb], *Ku-kung po-wu-yuan yuan-k'an* 故宮博物院院刊 no. 4 (1983): 59–62. My thanks to Sue Naquin for this reference.

24. In actuality, the imperial siting of tombs in valleys probably predates the commoner practice (in south China) of siting tombs on hills; the Bronze Age tradition was to erect man-made tumuli over royal graves. The Ch'ing dynasty were thus following ancient Chinese precedent in siting their tombs on low ground, then building a tumulus to conceal the underground grave chambers. In north China, even commoners' graves followed this pattern; but of course the flat terrain of the north China plain did not permit the elaborate geomantic grave siting followed in south China.

25. Ray Huang, *1587*, p. 81; Gutzlaff, *The Life of Taou-Kwang*, pp. 93–94; Hsu Kuang-yuan, "Tao-kuang ling," p. 60.

The only difference between the emperor's mausoleum and those of his subjects was its scale.[26]

## DEATH RITUAL

The sequence of rites that punctuated the death of an emperor was fundamentally the same as the sequence of commoner death ritual, as we have already noted. The *Collected Statutes* of a dynasty presented the regulations attending imperial death in elaborate detail.[27] The ritual sequence included public notification of death, the donning of mourning dress, the washing of the corpse, encoffining, transfers of food and goods to the dead, the creation of a spirit tablet, the use of music and percussion at key points of the ritual, and the expulsion of the corpse from the community. Professionals (the officials in charge) were employed. These rites echoed the core sequence of commoner funerary ritual. Burial rites (what Watson calls the "rites of disposal") for emperors paralleled the rites for commoners in north China. Imperial death ritual did depart from the commoner mode at certain points, but the major distinction lay in the grander scale of the commemoration attending imperial death. Deaths of commoners affected, in precisely prescribed degrees, the mourning circle of relatives, or *wu-fu*, and friends; in villages the whole community was drawn into some phase of the ritual observance. In the case of imperial death, mourning activities were carried out, in precise gradations, by immediate kin, the larger descent group, by officials, and, since the emperor's whole realm could be deemed his "community," by every person living in the empire, and by tributary states.

Chinese imperial death rituals differ sharply from those found in premodern Europe, where conceptions of kingship sometimes heavily influenced the ritual relationship of a dead king and his successor. There is nothing like the

26. The excavation of Ting-ling, the tomb of the Wan-li Emperor, provides details on the underground construction: see Hsia Nai, "Opening An Imperial Tomb," *China Reconstructs*, no. 3 (1959): 16–19; "Ting-ling fa-chueh chan-lan" 定陵發掘展覽 [Exhibition of excavations from Ting-ling], *Wen-wu ts'an-k'ao tzu-liao* 文物參考資料 no. 10 (1958): 23–25; "Ting-ling fa chueh chien-pao" 定陵發掘簡報 [Condensed report of the Ting-ling excavation], *K'ao-ku t'ung-hsun* 考古通訊 no. 7 (1958): 36–47; *K'ao-ku* 考古 no. 7 (1959): 358–368; Paludan, *The Imperial Ming Tombs*, chap. 5; de Groot, *The Religious System*, 2:451–452, 3:1164–1177.

27. *Ta Ming hui-tien*, chüan 96, can be compared with the Ch'ing regulations in *Ta Ch'ing hui-tien*, chüan 96, and *Ch'in-ting ta Ch'ing t'ung-li* 欽定大清通禮 [Collected rituals of the Ch'ing dynasty], compiled in 1736, chüan 45. Yin Te-wen 尹德文 , "Ch'ing T'ai-tsung Huang-t'ai-chi huo-tsang k'ao-lüeh" 清太宗皇太極火葬考略 [The cremation of Ch'ing T'ai-tsung, or Huang-t'ai-chi], *Ku-kung po-wu-yuan yuan-k'an* 故宮博物院院刊 no. 1 (1985): 63–64, 52, states that until the Yung-cheng reign, the Manchu practice of cremation was observed for the Manchu rulers. The *hui-tien* regulations thus represent the sinicized practice of the post–K'ang-hsi era.

royal funeral ceremony in Renaissance France, where conflict between two traditions of kingship was embodied in the elaborate feeding of an effigy of the dead king, deemed to be sovereign until his burial. For the Chinese, sovereignty was transferred as soon as the emperor died, although the cere- mony of accession did not occur until an auspicious date shortly thereafter. When the Shun-chih Emperor died, his infant son was put on the throne two days later. The Yung-cheng Emperor ascended the throne seven days after his father's death.[28]

Death could occur anywhere: out in the suburbs, where the Ming and Ch'ing emperors had palaces, or in Jehol, where the Ch'ing rulers spent the summer months. It was customary for rulers to dictate their last testament on the deathbed. In the Ch'ing period the heir was frequently not named until this point. After the emperor's death, his "last will and testament" (*i-chao*) would first be read to the officials and then promulgated through- out the empire by his successor. In it, the ruler surveyed his reign; he left hortatory injunctions for his heir; and he concluded with directives about the funeral and mourning observances.

The actions of the principal mourners from this point on were spelled out in the dynasty's code. "At the demise of the emperor, the princes and minis- ters forthwith remove the ornaments from their caps, and all the inmates of the inner apartments of the Palace, from the Empress Dowager, the new Empress and the deceased's concubines of all ranks down to the lowest all do the same with regard to their headgear." The mourners must wail. Upon the death of the K'ang-hsi Emperor in 1722, Father Ripa, while talking with Father Angelo, "heard an unusual murmuring noise, as if arising from a number of voices within the palace. Being acquainted with the manners of the country, I instantly caused the doors to be locked, and remarked to my companion that either the Emperor was dead, or else that a rebellion had broken out at Peking."[29]

The death of the emperor was announced to the officials in Peking; dispatches were sent to inform the government officials in the provinces. Notification of the emperor's death was quickly followed by issuance of the mourning regulations. The Board of Rites was in general charge of the whole process; the agencies in direct charge of death ritual were the Court of Sacrificial Worship (T'ai-ch'ang ssu) and the Court of State Ceremonial (Hung-lu ssu). The latter, and on occasion the Court of Banqueting (Kuang- lu ssu), supplied the sacrificial offerings of fruit and foods, while the rituals

28. Ralph E. Giesey, *The Royal Funeral Ceremony in Renaissance France* (Geneva: Librarie E. Dorz, 1960); *Ta Ch'ing hui-tien*, 96:5a, 97:8b.

29. De Groot, *The Religious System*, 2:632–633, translating from the *Ch'in-ting ta Ch'ing t'ung-li. Memoirs of Father Ripa*, trans. Fortunato Prandi (London: John Murray, 1844), p. 129.

were led by officials from the Court of Sacrificial Worship. Hanlin scholars
were employed to write the ritual texts, and the president of the Board of
Rites frequently acted as a kind of master of ceremonies. The Board of
Works had to build tombs, erect lodgings along the route to the cemetery,
create spirit tablets, and arrange facilities within the T'ai-miao. Imperial
Household officials were also active participants and codirectors in many
ceremonies.[30]

Imperial death was differentiated from all other deaths by virtue of the
requirement that mourning be observed by every citizen. Since the funeral
rites took place in Peking, there was a ban on butchering in that city for
forty-nine days. The signs on the shops were covered over to conceal "all
that is gilded and colored." Anything red disappeared. The onset of imperial mourning was thus immediately evident to anyone living in the
capital: S. Wells Williams reported on what "surprising contrast to their
usual gaiety" the streets presented the morning after the death of the T'ung-
chih Emperor in 1875.[31] During the period of mourning the official red seal
was replaced by one of blue; visiting cards and stationery, normally red,
were yellow instead. The title and columns of the Peking *Gazette* were
printed in blue. Peking residents in the Ming were required to wear "plain
clothes" for twenty-seven days, as opposed to only thirteen days for commoners residing elsewhere. All commoners were forbidden to marry for one
month; there was a ban on music for a month in the Ming (one hundred
days in the Ch'ing). The ban on marriage prompted many to hasten to conclude matches that would fall within the prohibited period. Doolittle noted
in Foochow that "before official news of the emperor's decease arrived,
and after reliable intelligence of this event had reached this port, a large
number of marriages were celebrated among the people."[32]

Imperial death was also marked by definitions of mourning obligation
which went beyond the normal framework set in the *wu-fu*, or five mourning grades.[33] In contrast to the normal mourning system, the degree of
mourning obligation was determined by rank as well as by degree of

30. The three agencies are described in Charles O. Hucker, "Governmental Organization
of the Ming Dynasty," *Harvard Journal of Asiatic Studies* 21 (1958): 34; and in Brunnert and
Hagelstrom, *Present Day*, no. 933, 934, 935.

31. S. Wells Williams, *The Middle Kingdom: A Survey of the Geography, Government,
Literature, Social Life, Arts, and History of The Chinese Empire and Its Inhabitants* (1833 ed.
reprinted Taipei: Ch'eng-wen, 1965), 2:250.

32. Justus Doolittle, *Social Life of the Chinese: with Some Account of Their Religious,
Governmental, Educational, and Business Customs and Opinions* (New York: Harper, 1865),
1:371.

33. On the normal *wu-fu* structure, see Han-yi Feng, *The Chinese Kinship System* (Cambridge: Harvard University Press, 1967), pp. 38–43, summarized in diagram IV, p. 42. The
historical precedents of the system are described in de Groot, *The Religious System*, 2:490–
546; pp. 547–562 present the Ch'ing regulations on the *wu-fu*.

relationship. The Ming regulations originally decreed that first-degree mourning, for "three years" (in actuality, twenty-seven months), would be observed by not only the sons, grandsons, daughters, the empress dowager (wife of the deceased), the deceased's concubines, and empress (daughter-in-law), but by agnates with princely ranks one and two (*wang*, their heirs, and *chün-wang*) and their wives. In the course of the dynasty, many of these princes would have fallen outside the *wu-fu*. The stringent requirements outlined above were soon relaxed, and it was customary from the mid-fifteenth century for emperors to direct that "days be substituted for months"; that is, that the twenty-seven months be reduced to twenty-seven days. In the Ch'ing, the most strict mourning was observed for only a hundred days by the new emperor, the empress dowager, widow of the deceased, and the new empress. All of the others cited above observed full mourning for only twenty-seven days, and secondary mourning for the rest of the twenty-seven-month period. Both dynasties also required first-degree mourning of all officials serving in the capital and their wives. The same observance was required during the Ch'ing dynasty of officials of the Eight Banners.

First-degree mourning entailed not only dress but dietary abstinence; alterations in residence; and a ban on normal grooming,[34] the wearing of ornaments, sexual activity, and festivities. The heir and new emperor served as the chief mourner. He left his normal residence to dwell in a side-apartment, wore deep mourning, neglected to comb his hair, abstained from meat and wine, and led the death rituals. During the period of most intense mourning, his decrees were signed with blue ink. After completion of the initial phase of full mourning, the emperor could "bestow care on His hair again"; full mourning was exchanged for "plain dress" or secondary mourning attire. Full mourning clothes would still be put on when he went to offer sacrifices before the altar set up for the death rituals. This reduced mourning lasted for the remainder of the twenty-seven-month period.[35]

In general, the emperor's body was brought back to the capital for the death rites. This was, of course, an exception to the usual prohibition on entry of corpses into any walled city. In the case of the Hsien-feng Emperor, who died in Jehol on August 22, 1861, the body was encoffined the same day; it was returned to the capital for the death rites, and did not arrive in Peking until October 26. In the more usual circumstance, when death

---

34. This ban included a ban on combing one's hair; note the Manchu modification to express extreme grief, which was (for men) to cut off the queue. On the significance of hair in mourning and its links with the absorption of death pollution and fertility, see James L. Watson, "Of Flesh and Bones: The Management of Death Pollution in Cantonese Society," in *Death and the Regeneration of Life*, ed. Maurice Bloch and Jonathan Parry (Cambridge: Cambridge University Press, 1982), pp. 173–174.

35. De Groot, *The Religious System*, 2:633–634.

occurred within the capital or its suburbs, the body was often brought back to the palace before the ritual of encoffining occurred.[36]

The imperial records do not provide many details on the washing and clothing of the corpse (*hsiao-lien*) and the placement of the corpse in a coffin (*ta-lien*), although excavation of the Wan-li Emperor's tomb provides us with a detailed description of the clothing, textiles, jewels, and other paraphernalia placed with the body in a double coffin.[37] The heir, empress dowager, empress, princes, officials and persons in the Imperial Household donned mourning, and the men cut their queues after the encoffining ceremony. The coffin was placed in a palace, frequently the Ch'ien-ch'ing palace; an altar table was erected before the coffin; and a temporary spirit tablet was installed on the table before which libations and offerings were made twice a day, to continue until the interment of the coffin. The spirit pennon (*ming-ching*), bearing the name and titles of the deceased, and the imperial equipage (*lu-p'u*) were assembled. The offerings presented before burial included the burning of the personal possessions of the deceased, including clothing, furniture, utensils, and so forth—all of the things the deceased person might need in the next life. Additional possessions were taken to the cemetery as part of the funeral cortege and burned there before interment of the coffin. The remainder of the dead emperor's clothing was generally preserved in chests, but we know of at least one instance in 1820 when an emperor directed that these clothes should be distributed among the courtiers.[38]

Officials in the capital were directed to assemble in mourning dress to hear the will being read. During the first three days after the death was

36. De Groot, *The Religious System*, 3:842. The Board of Rites could issue special permits for all cities except Peking, where the emperor's consent was required. The transport of the Hsien-feng Emperor's coffin was unusually prolonged: compare with the earlier 1820 Chia-ch'ing Emperor's case, recorded in *Ch'in-ting Li-pu tse-li* 欽定禮部則例 [Collected regulations of the Board of Rites], 147:1b. Information for the death rituals described in this section were obtained from the *hui-tien*, the *Ch'in-ting Li-pu tse-li*, c. 147–150, the *Ch'in-ting ta Ch'ing t'ung-li*, 3:40a–55b, c. 45, and accounts of the death rites for the Wan-li Emperor's mother, 1614, the death rites for the K'ang-hsi Emperor, 1722, the death rites for the Ch'ien-lung Emperor's mother, 1777, and the death rites for the Ch'ien-lung Emperor, 1799, reported in *Ming Shen-tsung shih-lu* 明神宗實錄 [Veritable records of the Wan-li reign] (1964 Nankang ed.), c. 517–521; *Ta Ch'ing Shih-tsung Hsien huang-ti shih-lu* 大清世宗憲皇帝實錄 [Veritable records of the Yung-cheng reign], c. 1–13, 17, 26, 28; *Ta Ch'ing Kao-tsung Ch'un huang-ti shih-lu* 大清高宗純皇帝實錄 [Veritable records of the Ch'ien-lung reign], c. 1025–1032; *Ta Ch'ing Jen-tsung Jui huang-ti shih-lu* 大清仁宗睿皇帝實錄 [Veritable records of the Chia-ch'ing reign], c. 37–52.

37. See Hsia Nai, "Opening An Imperial Tomb," p. 19; "Ting-ling fa-chueh chien-pao," p. 46.

38. *Eminent Chinese of the Ch'ing Period*, 1:575. For illustrations of the various items in the imperial equipage, see *Huang-ch'ao li-ch'i t'u-shih* 皇朝禮器圖式 [Illustrations of ritual objects for the dynasty] (1759, reprinted Taipei, 1976), chüan 10.

proclaimed, all presented themselves twice a day before the altar to offer incense and prostrate themselves, lodged at their offices, and practiced abstinence. Officials in the provinces were to change into mourning clothes when notified of the death, assemble to hear the will being read, and assemble for three days to wail and carry out mourning rites. After the first three-day interval, provincial officials would wear "plain clothes" for the rest of the twenty-seven-month period.

The interval between the encoffining of the corpse and its eventual placement in the imperial cemetery could be extremely long. Sometimes construction of the tomb was not yet completed. Even in the best of circumstances, when the tomb stood ready to receive its occupant, the process of lacquering the coffin seems to have taken a considerable time. We are told in one instance that forty-five coats of lacquer were applied, and that on average each coat took ten days to dry. The elaborate preparations of the coffin extended the period during which the coffin remained within the capital city, but the practice of keeping the coffin for long periods before burial could also be found among well-to-do commoners.[39] In the Ming the coffin remained in the hall or palace in which the encoffining had taken place during this period; but the Ch'ing erected a special building, the Shou-huang tien, located outside the palace walls on Coal Hill (Mei-shan), to house the coffins in this interval. The Kuang-hsu Emperor's coffin rested in this hall for six months.[40]

The most important imperial ritual in this interval was the conferral of a posthumous name (shih). This was also a practice found among well-to-do commoners.[41] Only the emperor and his major consorts received a posthumous name; concubines of lesser rank did not. The emperor would ask his chief ministers to deliberate and select the name by which his predecessor would be known on his spirit tablet and grave. The ritual conferring the posthumous name was preceded by three days of abstinence, with sacrifice at the first-rank altars of Heaven, Earth, the Temple of the Ancestors, and the Altar of Land and the Harvest. The document with the posthumous name was presented at the mortuary altar before the coffin in an elaborate ceremony led by the emperor and attended by the court. Before conferral of the

---

39. See de Groot, 1:106, on well-to-do commoners varnishing coffins; H. Y. Lowe, *The Adventures of Wu* (Princeton: Princeton University Press, 1983), 2:100; Martin C. Yang, *A Chinese Village: Taitou, Shantung Province* (New York: Columbia University Press, 1945), p. 87, states, "The richer the family, the more elaborate the decoration of the coffin and the length of its retention."

40. E. Martin, "Les Funerailles d'une Imperatrice de Chine," *Revue d'Ethnographie* 1 (1882): 230; Camille Imbault-Huart, "La Mort d'une Imperatrice Régente en Chine," *Journal Asiatique* 7e série 19 (1882): 265. Ch'in-ting ta Ch'ing t'ung-li, chüan 45. 44b–45a, states that 49 coats must be applied; Williams, "Worshipping Imperial Ancestors," pp. 61–62.

41. See de Groot, 1:175.

posthumous name, the deceased emperor was referred to in the records by his full official name and title, prefaced by the characters *ta-hsing*. Thenceforth the deceased was called by his posthumous name. This name was inscribed on a tablet (*shih-ts'e*), made of wood but sometimes of jade, which was buried with the coffin. At the same time, a seal (*pao-yin*) was made, for the same eventual destination. Both objects rested in front of the coffin on the mortuary altar.[42]

Before the funeral procession took place, the coffin bearers were carefully drilled to ensure that the heavy bier would be carried without any mishap. The Board of Public Works repaired the streets that would be used. Imbault-Huart, observing the rites for the Empress Dowager Tz'u-an in 1881, watched the army repairing the bridges between the palace and the Shou-huang tien:

> For several days, one saw a curious spectacle on this spot: whole regiments evening out the high part of the boulevards, ordinarily full of ruts. . . . At the same time the divided walls that circle Mei-shan were repainted red, as were those neighboring houses before which the cortege must pass. It is only surprising that the roads of the capital must be in such a bad state that one waits for the death of an emperor or empress for repairs.[43]

The removal of the coffin from the palace (*fa-yin*) was preceded by three days of abstinence. During this interval it was forbidden to slaughter animals or to play music. An official was sent to announce the date of the removal of the coffin to the first-rank altars. The emperor himself announced the removal date in front of the mortuary altar. On the day before removal of the coffin, sacrifices were made to the major bridges and gates through which the cortege must pass, to be repeated when the funeral procession arrived at these points.

The actual rite preceding the movement of the coffin resembled the parallel ceremony described in de Groot. The emperor led the ritual, attended by those mourning in the first degree. He bowed before the spirit tablet standing on the mortuary altar. Libations were offered. A document announcing the burial (*wang-i*) was read, then burned. The servitors removed the curtains around the coffin, signifying that the "wiping of the coffin" was completed. The spirit tablet, the *shih-ts'e*, or tablet inscribed with the posthumous name, the imperial seal, the spirit pennon, and the coffin were moved out of the hall to form the essential components of the funeral cortege. A last sacrifice was made before the coffin, already mounted on a catafalque.

---

42. *T'ai-ch'ang hsu-k'ao*, 4:3b–6b. The tablet and seal found in the Wan-li Emperor's tomb are reported in "Ting-ling fa-chueh chien-pao," p. 47, and in *Ti-hsia kung-tien* 地下宮殿 [The underground palace] (Peking, 1958), p. 29; also photos on p. 30.

43. Imbault-Huart, "La mort," pp. 264–265.

Funeral processions differed only with respect to their length and degree of "show," as de Groot noted. Imperial funeral processions were of course the most elaborate and showiest of all. Amiot observed the cortege of the Dowager Empress Hsiao-sheng, mother of the Ch'ien-lung Emperor, in 1777:

> The convoy left the palace...towards 7 A.M. Those in the Imperial House-hold went first. After them came pennants, parasols, and canopies, five of each, in five different colors...followed by camels and horses, two by two, loaded with provisions as if for a long trip. . . . Articles of use, jewels, all that the Princess used while she lived, such as mirrors, fans, etc., . . . were carried separately by servants, forming several ranks, after which was carried, with much respect, the little stick which she used during her old age. The grand officers of her household immediately preceded the coffin, along with the sons and grandsons of the Emperor. . . . The wives of the Emperor, those of the Princes, Counts and other Greats, women in service in the palace, all on horse-back, and after them Eunuchs, also on horseback, were immediately after the coffin, guarded by several companies of pikesmen. . . . After the women and the Pikesmen, on foot, came Manchu and Mongol Counts and Greats...each by rank.[44]

Amiot does not describe the spirit tablet, the tablet bearing the post-humous name, and the seal, but these may have been housed in the "two enormous palanquins, covered with yellow silk," and the third palanquin, "decorated with gilded sculpture," preceding the coffin bearing the body of the Empress Dowager Tz'u-an, witnessed by Martin in 1881. The procession was accompanied by drums, cymbals, and "clarinets"; in short, by percus-sive and reed instruments whose playing would fend off malevolent spirits—precisely as in the funeral processions of commoners. The shops along the route were closed, their signs removed, their doors and windows shut so that no one could see the convoy. In marked contrast to the mourning reg-ulations that forbade display of red, the coffin bearers wore red, the color with which the walls and houses along the way were repainted.

The reasons for use of red, an inversion of the usual practice (which was followed in the general mourning regulations, presented earlier in this chap-ter) are not clear. We know that it was common for Cantonese villagers attending funerals to wear a patch of red as a prophylactic against death pollution, and that funeral priests (see James Watson in chapter 5 in this volume) wore red and yellow robes as a prophylactic measure as well. De Groot tells us that at commoner funerals musicians wore red uniform coats, and hats with red tassels; the coffin (when the deceased was male) was con-

44. Amiot, "Mémoires Concernant Les Chinois," *Mémoires Concernant L'Histoire, Les Sciences, Les Arts, Les Moeurs, Les Usages, etc. des Chinois par les Missionaires de Pé-kin,* vol. 6 (Paris: n.p., 1780), pp. 356–358. My thanks to Sue Naquin for this reference.

cealed with a red cover as it was carried in the funeral procession. Was the appearance of red in imperial funerals an amplification of this prophylactic function? Alternatively, might it have symbolized the almost "god-like" status of the emperor and his role as Son of Heaven? But it should be noted that the same red appeared in the funerals of empresses as well.[45]

The imperial procession to the Ming cemetery at Ch'ang-p'ing or to the Ch'ing eastern and western cemeteries took several days and of course required a great deal of advance planning, since the coffin, the chief mourners, and the large retinue had to be properly accommodated along the way. The coffin was placed each night in a "black hall" (lu-tien); libations were poured before the coffin each morning and evening during this journey. If the emperor accompanied the cortege, he was housed in a "traveling palace" (hsing-kung) or imperial camp (yü-ying), erected for this purpose. In 1777 the Ch'ien-lung Emperor accompanied the coffin of his mother to the western imperial cemetery. The distance of over 300 li from the capital to Hsi-ling was covered in five days: nine kung were constructed along the route as resting places for the emperor. Since the emperor saw off the coffin each morning then went by a separate route to receive the coffin at its resting place that evening, a separate road for the coffin was constructed for the occasion. All along the route, the local officials waited, kneeling as the coffin passed. In each locality able-bodied men thirty to forty years of age and of about the same height were recruited to help as coffin bearers. Amiot states that each such band of 128 porters carried the coffin for only 312 steps. The official porters who bore the coffin from the palace carried it to and from its resting place at night and in the morning. The citizen bearers received compensation for their services, just as the localities through which the procession passed were rewarded for their efforts with tax remissions.[46]

Upon arrival at the cemetery, the spirit tablet, posthumous-name tablet, imperial seal, and coffin were deposited in the sacrificial hall of the tomb. The earth deity and mountain deity of the cemetery site received sacrifices at this time. An auspicious day for the interment having been selected, the final burial ceremonies commenced with the chief mourners kneeling before the coffin. The spirit of the deceased (ling) was requested to enter the underground burial chamber. The coffin, the posthumous-name tablet, and the

---

45. Martin, "Les Funerailles," p. 232; Amiot, p. 358; W. Lockhart, "Notes on Peking and Its Neighborhood," *Journal of the Royal Geographical Society* 36 (1866): 156, says that the poles supporting the bier were also "varnished red." On red in death ritual, see Arthur P. Wolf, "Chinese Kinship and Mourning Dress," in *Family and Kinship in Chinese Society*, ed. Maurice Freedman (Stanford: Stanford University Press, 1970), p. 193; James Watson, "Of Flesh and Bones," p. 168; de Groot, *The Religious System*, 1: 157, 175, 181. My thanks to Sue Naquin for the Lockhart reference.

46. *Ta Ch'ing Kao-tsung Ch'un huang-ti shih-lu*, 1030: 19a–1031: 5a. Amiot, "Mémoires," pp. 361–365.

seal were placed on the raised dais in the chamber. Sacrifices were presented outside the door of this chamber; after a final series of prostrations and ritual wailings, the tomb chamber was sealed. Sacrifices were presented before this sealed chamber, and an official was sent to sacrifice to the earth and mountain deities.

The ceremony of dotting the spirit tablet followed the sealing of the burial chamber. For this ceremony, participants (with the exception of the emperor) changed into court dress. A high official performed the actual dotting; in the Ch'ing period, it was customary to have a Manchu and a Chinese official perform the rite. The dotted tablet was placed in a box; the official in charge knelt to request that the spirit of the deceased emperor enter the tablet. Kneelings, prostrations, libations, and prayers as well as ritual wailing were performed. The tablet was moved with appropriate ceremonies from the tomb site into the sacrificial hall, where it was placed on the altar for performance of the *yü* ceremony, the sacrifice of repose offered on the burial day. The Ming required that this sacrifice be repeated nine times, the last one being conducted upon the return to Peking, where the tablet was met by officials outside the city walls, escorted into the city, received by the emperor, and placed in the T'ai-miao. In the Ch'ing, morning and evening libations were poured before the spirit tablet as it journeyed back to the capital, just as morning and evening libations had been poured before the coffin as it traveled to the tombs.

On the day of its return to Peking or on the next day the tablet was installed in the Temple of the Ancestors. Ceremonies installing a second tablet in the Hall for Worship of the Ancestors (attached to the Altar of Heaven) followed. A prince was delegated to carry out rites installing a third tablet in the sacrificial hall attached to the tomb. The tablet in the Temple of the Ancestors was brought out for a special rite (*ta-hsiang*) on the second anniversary of the death; on the third anniversary, marking the end of the full period of first-degree mourning, the *t'an-chi* rite was performed by a prince (*ch'in-wang*, son of the deceased emperor) before the tablet at the sacrificial hall of the tomb. The tablets also received regular sacrifices through the year. The deathdays of emperors and empresses were commemorated through the life of the dynasty: on these days the emperor and officials attending court wore "plain clothes," the main gates of government offices were closed, and no auspicious events were held.[47]

Death provided the ideal opportunity for a new emperor to display filial piety (and affirm his legitimacy) to his officials and subjects. This was especially the case when the new emperor was a mature adult. Yin-chen, the K'ang-hsi Emperor's fourth son, had to counteract a history of bitterness

47. *Ch'in-ting ta Ch'ing hui-tien shih-li*, chüan 415; J. M., "Mourning Days," pp. 181–182; Playfair, "Days," pp. 47–48.

over the succession and challenges to the legitimacy of his accession when he came to the throne in 1723, a man in his forties. The official record testifies to Yin-chen's lavish displays of grief. He told his officials that he had always been an obedient son, but he wished to disobey his father in one matter, the command that he limit his observance of full mourning to twenty-seven days instead of the customary hundred days. Yin-chen visited his father's coffin, deposited in the Shou-huang tien, three times a day; he escorted the coffin to the cemetery in the third month, went back in the ninth month for the interment, and was persuaded against revisiting the site on his father's first deathday by officials who pointed out the added hardship another imperial visit would put on the citizens of the locality.[48]

Ritual constituted a structure in which individual feelings could be expressed in purposeful deviations from the norm. This is the way in which we should interpret the Yung-cheng Emperor's performance of the "three kneelings and nine prostrations" at additional points in the death ritual of his father. Yin-chen's use of this ritual act to report his accession to the throne before his father's coffin, to mark the end of deep mourning after twenty-seven days, and upon inspection of his father's posthumous-name tablet and seal shows how a ruler could heighten his show of respectful grief by artful modifications of the prescribed acts.[49]

The mourning regulations for empress dowagers were only slightly less stringent than those for emperors. Here, even more strongly than in the mortuary rites for emperors, what was being illustrated was the principle of filial piety.

An infant when his parents died, the K'ang-hsi Emperor was very close to his grandmother, the Great Dowager Empress Hsiao-chuang, who directed his upbringing. This woman "became one of the most influential grandmothers in Ch'ing history." K'ang-hsi used his grandmother as the object of his filial devotion, for the edification of his sons and subjects. Her death in January 1688 prompted the K'ang-hsi Emperor to express his grief by breaking several imperial traditions: he cut off his queue (previously done only for the death of one's father or grandfather); he refused to allow his grandmother's body to be moved out of the palace before the New Year; he mourned for twenty-seven months instead of twenty-seven days, and slept

---

48. *Ta Ch'ing hui-tien*, 97:2a–43a; *Ta Ch'ing Shih-tsung Hsien huang-ti shih-lu*, 1:8ab, 1:11ab, 1:22b–24b, 2:5ab, 5:19a–20b, 4:3a, and 7:27b–28a, 8:3a on similar exchanges concerning mourning for his mother, who died in 1723. Silas Wu, *Passage*, chaps. 14, 15, and p. 186; Hsu Tseng-chung 許曾重, "Ch'ing Shih-tsung Yin-chen chi-ch'eng huang-wei wen-t'i hsin t'an" 清世宗胤禛繼承皇位問題新探 [A new approach to the question of the succession of the Yung-cheng Emperor], *Ch'ing-shih lun-ts'ung* 清史論叢 4 (1982): 111–140.

49. *Ta Ch'ing Shih-tsung Hsien huang-ti shih-lu*, 1:18a, 2:14a, 4:22b, 4:23b, 4:24a, 11:3b. The *Ch'in-ting Li-pu tse-li*, *Ch'in-ting ta Ch'ing t'ung-li*, and *Ta Ch'ing hui-tien* present information on the ritual regulations which changed over time.

in a tent outside his normal quarters in the Ch'ien-ch'ing palace, despite the winter temperatures.[50] He also acquiesced with her desires in breaking the tradition of burial with one's spouse. According to the emperor:

When the Grand Empress-Dowager Grandmother was sick and was about to depart this life, she ordered Us: "The coffin of T'ai Tsung, the Emperor Wen (Abahai), having been put to rest already a long time ago, it may not be disturbed in my behalf with levity. Moreover, I feel such an attachment to your Imperial father and yourself, that I cannot bear the idea of going far away. Try therefore to find an auspicious plot close to the Hsiao ling, and bury me there, then my mind will not feel sad." This order being given Us with such impressive emphasis, how can We presume to disobey it.[51]

In actuality, however, the K'ang-hsi Emperor merely stored the coffin of his grandmother in a hall awaiting the construction of her tomb; she was not buried until 1725.[52]

One of the most extensive exercises in filiality was conducted by the Ch'ien-lung Emperor on the death of his mother, the Empress Dowager Hsiao-sheng. Hsiao-sheng was a concubine who was retroactively made empress when her son was selected to succeed. During his long reign, the Ch'ien-lung Emperor became noted for his filial devotion: he took Mother on four of the six southern tours, three of five official visits to the sacred mountain Wu-t'ai shan, three of five pilgrimages to the Confucian temple in Ch'ü-fu, Shantung, and on numerous occasions to the summer retreat in Jehol. Daily visits to Mother with inquiries after her health, personal attention during her illnesses, and elaborate birthday celebrations that "became veritable orgies of filial solicitude" conveyed the appropriate message to officials and citizens: the Son of Heaven was a model son.[53] When Mother eventually died in 1777 at the age of eighty-five, Ch'ien-lung observed the most stringent mourning for her. We have not only the *shih-lu* record of the death rituals for Empress Dowager Hsiao-sheng, but a Western account.

The Empress Dowager Hsiao-sheng died on the twenty-third day of the first month in the forty-second year of the Ch'ien-lung reign, in her palace outside Peking. Her corpse was returned to the capital, and placed in the main hall of the Tz'u-ning palace. Here the emperor, having cut his queue and changed to deep mourning, supervised the washing, clothing, and encoffining ceremonies. Despite the empress dowager's injunction that full mourning be limited to twenty-seven days, the emperor declared that his observance would be extended to one hundred days. In sharp contrast to the Wan-li Emperor, who pleaded illness for failing to carry out his role in the

50. Wu, *Passage*, pp. 51–52.
51. Cited by de Groot, *The Religious System*, 3:1291–1292.
52. De Groot, *The Religious System*, 3:1292.
53. Kahn, *Monarchy in the Emperor's Eyes*, chap. 5, pp. 86–90.

death rituals for his mother (1614),[54] the Ch'ien-lung Emperor led the
twice-daily rituals before the coffin, accompanied the funeral cortege to the
cemetery, and escorted his mother's spirit tablet back to Peking. So assid-
uous was his observance that the officials complained that he did not leave
sufficient time for the lacquering of the coffin. Amiot notes how taxing the
ritual observances were, even for young men; the emperor was already
sixty-six. In the midst of the funeral, the emperor's eldest surviving son,
Yung-ch'eng, Prince Lü, died; fatigue also claimed the life of Shu-ho-te, a
Grand Councillor.[55]

If extreme grief and reverence in mourning for parents was praiseworthy,
imperial excess over the death of wives was criticized. One of the more
bizarre episodes in imperial records concerned the consort of the Shun-chih
Emperor, Hsiao-hsien, who died in September 1660. "Overwhelmed by
grief," the Shun-chih Emperor posthumously made her empress, staged an
elaborate funeral in which several maids and eunuchs committed suicide to
accompany the consort into the next world, and cremated her body. This
emperor was later made to express self-criticism in his will for "extravagance" in burying Hsiao-hsien.[56]

## MOURNING VERSUS RITUAL ROLES

Burial of the corpse and the dotting of the spirit tablet initiated rites designed to incorporate the imperial dead into the state cult. The creation of
the spirit tablet and its installation into the Temple of the Ancestors were in
fact classified under "auspicious rituals" and not death.[57] Imperial *manes*
became important adjuncts to the deities worshipped on the most important
state altars. The spirit tablets of the eight Ch'ing emperors that occupied the
major chambers in the Temple of the Ancestors were also deposited in the
Huang-ch'iung yü, next to the Altar of Heaven, and brought out for the
great sacrifice to Heaven at the winter solstice. Another set were placed in
the Huang-ch'ien tien, a building behind the Ch'i-nien tien, to be used in the

54. This death is mentioned briefly in Huang, *1587*, pp. 94–95. For details on Empress
Dowager Tz'u-sheng, see *Dictionary of Ming Biography*, 1:856–859. A Western account of
the death rites is found in Alvaro Semedo, *The History of That Great and Renowned Monarchy of China*, trans. into English (London, 1665), chap. 17, but this account diverges at various
points from the official record, *Ming Shen-tsung shih-lu*, 517:3a–520:15b.

55. Amiot, "Mémoires," pp. 360–361. The details of the empress dowager's death rituals
are taken from *Ta Ch'ing Kao-tsung Ch'un huang-ti shih-lu*, c. 1025–1031. Yung-ch'eng's
death is reported 1027:21b; Shu-ho-te's death, 1031:9b–10b.

56. Oxnam, *Ruling from Horseback*, p. 61; the Shun-chih Emperor was himself cremated
(Hummel, *Eminent Chinese*, 1:257–258; Yin Te-wen, "Ch'ing T'ai-tsung"), being the last
Manchu ruler to adhere to the traditional practice. K'ang-hsi's corpse was buried in accord
with Han Chinese custom by his successor.

57. Covered in *Ch'in-ting ta Ch'ing-t'ung-li*, 3:40a–56b.

prayer for a fruitful year, performed in the first *hsun* of each new year. Another set was deposited at the Altar of Earth, and used in the great sacrifice performed there.[58] The sacrifices that marked the pinnacle of state religion thus underlined the continuing linkage of ancestor worship with state ritual. Placement of the tablets at these grand sacrifices indicates that they ranked only below the tablets of Heaven and of Earth. The deified ancestors were thus important pillars of the state religious system, to be worshipped exclusively by the emperor or his designated representative.

Nor were the deified ancestors of previous dynasties ignored. The emperors of earlier dynasties were worshipped in the Temple of the Emperors and Kings of Successive Eras (Li-tai ti-wang miao), one of the second-rank altars in the state religion. Earlier imperial mausolea enjoyed the protection of the state, and Ch'ing emperors issued edicts ordering that they be maintained in good order and that sacrifices be offered. Designated numbers of households were assigned to care for them, as for the tombs of the dynasty in power.[59]

Mourning and performance of state ritual were similar in many respects: both required purification and dietary abstinence, prohibited music and entertainment, and specified sacrificial offerings, the most common denominator being incense, wine, and silk. The coffin and then the spirit tablet were presented on major ritual occasions with animal sacrifice, just as were the state altars.[60] But the obligations of mourning also conflicted with the ritual obligations of the emperor in the state religion. As we noted earlier, these rituals could not be performed in mourning dress. Mourning, offensive to man, was even more offensive to the gods. Those who were mourning in the first degree were banned from taking part in "auspicious events," among which were included the sacrifices to state deities. Further, persons wearing mourning dress were prohibited from entering government buildings, including the palace. Officials who had to enter the court on business during the period of full mourning changed into "plain clothes" for the period of their court appearance.[61]

The great sacrifices at first-rank altars normally required the wearing of court dress (*ch'ao-fu*, *li-fu* when applied to imperial dress), the most formal of the three categories of clothing designated for the court. For ordinary

58. E. T. Williams, "The State Religion," pp. 25, 29, 38, 39; Andrew Happer, "A Visit to Peking," *Chinese Recorder* 10, no. 1 (1879): 29, 31, 32–36. The ritual is described in *Ta Ming hui-tien*, c. 82–83.

59. *Ta Ming hui-tien*, c. 91, shows it was a third-rank altar honoring dynastic founders and the mythical first rulers in that era; *Ta Ch'ing hui-tien*, 90:2a–15a; on mausolea, see de Groot, *The Religious System*, 3:925–934.

60. *Ta Ming hui-tien*, c. 96; *Ta Ch'ing hui-tien*, c. 96; *Ta Ch'ing Kao-tsung Ch'un huang-ti shih-lu*, c. 1025–1032; E. T. Williams, "Worshipping Imperial Ancestors," pp. 62–64. Sacrifices performed at the sacrificial hall in the cemetery are described in Paludan, *The Imperial Ming Tombs*, pp. 216–218.

61. De Groot, *The Religious System*, 3:842; *Ta Ming hui-tien*, 96:2b, 96:3b.

court appearances, the emperor and his officials wore *chi-fu* (auspicious clothing); the emperor wore *ch'ang-fu* (ordinary dress) for informal private occasions.[62]

The obligations of mourning produced compromises in dress. "Plain clothes" was in between the "filial dress" (*hsiao-fu*) worn during the period of most intense mourning and *ch'ang-fu*. The requirement that the grand sacrifices must exclude all persons who were mourning could not eliminate the need during death ritual to use the T'ai-miao, where the prohibition against mourning dress caused the mourners to change from "deep mourning" to "plain dress" for the rites. Because the dotting of the spirit tablet was an auspicious rite, participants donned court dress for this ceremony. In fact, full mourning dress was appropriate only when presenting offerings at the mourning altar, erected in front of the coffin.

In short, state ritual requirements enjoyed priority over mourning regulations when the two conflicted. Indeed, a standard feature of imperial wills was the injunction that the ruler should not neglect performance of the first-rank rituals, which was one of his primary duties. One of the arguments used by officials opposing the Yung-cheng Emperor's desire to override his father's will and observe the full mourning period was that the sacrifices could not be conducted by the emperor while he was in mourning. The Wan-li Emperor, whose indolence was infamous, was made to confess in his will that despite initial inclinations "to govern well," "afterwards, being hindered by several infirmities for many years, I left off the care of having the wonted sacrifices celebrated to Heaven and earth: neither did I cause the offices and ceremonies to be performed, which are due to the memory of my Ancestours."[63] The primacy of state ritual over mourning was made explicit in discussion of yet another dilemma: When one of the major state rituals fell within a period of full mourning, who should perform the ritual, and in what manner should the ritual be performed?

In 1777 the period of full mourning for the Ch'ien-lung Emperor's mother, Empress Dowager Hsiao-sheng, encompassed the period when the annual sacrifice was to be performed at one of the first-rank state altars, the Altar of Land and the Harvest. The occasion called for court dress and music, both forbidden during the period of mourning. A search revealed contradictory precedents, and the emperor ordered the Grand Councillors to deliberate on this issue. The emperor could not perform the rituals in person, because of the prohibition against participation by anyone in

62. The three categories of Ch'ing imperial dress are illustrated and described in *Huang-ch'ao li-ch'i t'u-shih*, chüan 4. See Helen Fernald, *Chinese Court Costumes* (Toronto: Royal Ontario Museum, 1946), pp. 13, 15–18, 23–24.

63. *Ta Ch'ing hui-tien*, 97:8b–11b; *Ta Ch'ing Shih-tsung Hsien huang-ti shih-lu*, 1:22b–24a, 1:24b. The Wan-li will is cited from Semedo, *History*, p. 84; for the original, see *Ming Shen-tsung shih-lu*, 596:11b–12a.

mourning—yet should this prohibition be observed for the full three-year period? Was this not an evasion of his responsibilities as Son of Heaven? The Board of Rites returned its recommendations some days later. During the period of full mourning (a hundred days), an official would be delegated to perform the first-rank rituals in place of the emperor, but the emperor himself would perform them thereafter. Performance of the state sacrifices would be marked by a lightening of the mourning dress of the emperor and his officials. Mourning modified but did not prevail over the dress requirements for state ritual.[64]

The principle that state ritual took precedence over imperial mourning was reaffirmed in the Chia-ch'ing reign (1796–1820), when conflicts over observance of deathdays and the dates for sacrifices were resolved by an imperial decision (1814/15) to give priority to the sacrificial calendar for first-rank altars.[65] The second-rank sacrifice became the dividing line between assertion of state ritual obligations and the observance of ancestral deathdays.

Imperial death ritual confirmed the preeminent and unique position of the emperor in the Chinese world view; at the same time it permitted the ruler to serve as a role model reinforcing the basic familial values that underlay the Ming and Ch'ing state. Death ritual reflected the Chinese conception of kingship, which was inextricably tied to performance of ritual roles in the state religion. Death transformed fallible rulers into deified ancestors, who shared in the great sacrifices not only at the Temple of the Ancestors but at the great state altars of Heaven and Earth. Emperors in their post-mortem aspect were integrated into state religion.[66] Through the mourning obligations they bequeathed to their descendants, they remained at the core of tension between the dual obligations of a ruler to sacrifice and to mourn. What made this tension particularly acute in the Ch'ing period was the complex way in which mourning itself enabled a new emperor to affirm simultaneously the cardinality of filial piety and, by taking the role of chief mourner, his right to the throne.

---

64. The Ch'ien-lung decision was reaffirmed during the Tao-kuang and Hsien-feng reigns: these cases are reported in *Ch'in-ting ta Ch'ing hui-tien shih-li*, chüan 415.

65. *Ta Ch'ing Kao-tsung Ch'un huang-ti shih-lu* 1025:31a–34a, 1026:17b–22a, 1030:4b–5b, 1031:27a–28b; *Ta Ch'ing hui-tien*, c. 415, 423; deliberations reported in *Ch'in-ting Li-pu tse-li*, 147:22b–27b.

66. The central role of imperial ancestors in the state religion echoes the pre-T'ang period, when the imperial or royal ancestors were the primary focus of the state religion; for an ambitious theoretical attempt to trace the evolution of Asiatic civilizations using data from ancient Chinese history, see J. Friedman and M. J. Rowlands, "Notes Towards an Epigenetic Model of the Evolution of 'Civilisation,'" in *The Evolution of Social Systems*, ed. J. Friedman and M. J. Rowlands (London: Duckworth, 1977), pp. 201–276.

# ELEVEN

# Mao's Remains

*Frederic Wakeman, Jr.*

## PROLOGUE

While in Peking in 1984, I requested a visit to Mao's Chi-nien t'ang (Memorial Hall). Although the monument was not then open to the public at large, the Chinese Association of Science and Technology arranged for the small delegation I headed to see the hall early on a cold January morning. One of those sharp, bitter winds so common in the dead of a Peking winter was whipping across T'ien-an men, snapping flags and ruddying the cheeks of the Military Police standing guard, when our cars drew up beside the group of huge statuary figures at the northeastern corner of the shrine. In between these titanic representations of socialist heroes past and present, dwarfed by comparison, were silently attentive groups of real men and women, many dressed in uniforms of the People's Liberation Army, waiting for their units to be admitted to the hall. The northerly wind carried down upon us strains of a military band, playing what I later learned was the Sudanese national anthem, as an African general in full battle dress laid a wreath at the foot of the Revolutionary Heroes' Cenotaph in the distance, toward the Forbidden City.

I got out of my car, pulling my overcoat around me, and had time to take just one photograph of the scene across the great square before the atten-

Research for this essay was facilitated by a grant from the Center for Chinese Studies (Institute of East Asian Studies) and the Committee on Research at the University of California, Berkeley. The author wishes to express his appreciation to Blaine Gaustad, Carolyn Wakeman, Jeff Wasserstrom, and Yeh Wen-hsin for their help in gathering materials and revising the text. He is also grateful to members of the California Regional Seminar in Chinese Studies who read and discussed the essay, and especially to Professor Joseph Esherick, Jr., and Professor Rudolf Wagner.

dants behind the ropes that delineated the approach to the mausoleum sharply reproved me. Moments later we were sandwiched in between two of the waiting groups and rushed, nearly at a trot, down the rope-lined avenue, up the steps, and into the outer room where sits Mao Tse-tung's statue, three meters high and carved in white marble. Lights were low, the mood hushed, and I realized that this was not to be a tour of the entire hall but rather a visit to pay respects to the remains of Chairman Mao. I let the group behind me shuffle on through the carved hardwood doors into the refrigerated room at the heart of the shrine where Mao's remains lie. As I lingered in the anteroom (which one Chinese friend has told me was inspired by the Lincoln Memorial), the lights suddenly brightened to camera-ready brilliance and a television crew appeared from the side to film the Sudanese general and his entourage now climbing up the steps of the hall. Attendants quickly spotted me, however, and motioned me on to the much darker and colder room where Mao lay in state under a trapezoidal crystal upon a black catafalque of granite from Mount T'ai, inscribed with gold national, party, and army emblems, as well as his own dates (1893–1976). The catafalque, surrounded by mountain flowers and a low crystal balustrade, was only a meter high, so that—passing by on the right—one looked down upon the sallow, wrinkled face of the late Chairman, bathed in yellow light. There was too little time to feel any emotion, be it awe or impatience, though my eye was caught by the phrase inscribed in the green marble on the southern wall to the memory of "our great leader and teacher Chairman Mao Tse-tung: forever eternal without corrupting" (*yung ch'ui pu hsiu*).[1] Just as the irony of that phrasing (rumors were rife in 1980 that the embalmed corpse was decomposing) sank in, I found myself with my fellow delegation members walking rapidly down the southern steps that face the Ch'ien-men where our cars were waiting to take us on to the day of negotiations ahead.[2]

Before getting into the limousine and out of the wind, I turned to look back at the imposing structure behind me. On either side were groups of statues showing the people of China carrying out Mao's final commands, and around these fluttered thirty red flags representing the peoples of the provinces, municipalities, and autonomous regions of China. Stationed along the steps, as frozen as the statues, were fur-hatted guards standing in silent vigil. I suddenly, impiously, remembered a joke making the rounds among particularly defiant Peking intellectuals in the summer of 1977. A

---

1. For the importance of calligraphic symbols to Hua's succession, see Helmut Martin, *Cult and Canon: The Origins and Development of State Maoism* (Armonk: M. E. Sharpe, 1982), p. 54.

2. For the rumors about embalming difficulties, see Jay and Linda Mathews, *One Billion: A China Chronicle* (New York: Random House, 1983), p. 327.

*t'u-pao-tzu* (bumpkin) from the countryside visits his city cousin, who takes him to see Mao's tomb. "Ai-ya," the bumpkin says. "It's so big! Chairman Mao always wanted to be just like one of us. He never wanted to distance himself from the masses. How could you build him such a big and imposing *ling-mu* (mausoleum)?" "Oh," answers the city cousin, "just to prove that he's really dead."

## REVOLUTIONARY SAINTS

The term *ling-mu* (or, in some cases, even *ling-ch'in*, once used to describe the tomb of a member of the imperial family) suggests some of the problematical awkwardness surrounding the physical remains of a modern secular political leader like Mao Tse-tung. A simple grave (*mu-tsang*) was traditionally the normal resting place of common corpses. Royal remains might merit mausolea that were both monuments and tombs, but revolutionary saints—while deserving of public worship—were usually buried apart from their historical monuments.

The impulse behind this separation was egalitarian: to create a public mausoleum was tantamount to creating a public shrine, and thus a public cult singling out one among many leaders of the revolutionary movement. As Teng Hsiao-p'ing candidly explained:

> In the fifties, Chairman Mao had said that at their death, all the leading comrades in China should be cremated and only their ashes maintained. No grave site for the leaders, no mausoleums. The proposal had been caused by the lesson learned after the death of Stalin and had been materialized in the form of a document. Chairman Mao had been the first to put his name on it, and many other high-ranking officials had their names on it too, including myself. In fact, that Chou En-lai was cremated makes you know that document still exists.[3]

Though the party's cremation policy was ostensibly directed against the formation of a cult of personality like Stalin's, such worship originated with Lenin himself, whose faith "holds that a legendary past will deliver a utopian future."[4] Indeed, it was precisely the embalming and public display of Lenin's corpse in the USSR that inspired the initial practice in Republican China of creating a *ling-mu*—a conjoined tomb and shrine—for the greatest of early revolutionary saints, Sun Yat-sen himself.

---

3. Oriana Fallaci, "Deng: Cleaning up Mao's 'Feudal Mistakes,'" *Washington Post Outlook*, August 31, 1980, p. 4.

4. Nina Tumarkin, "The Remains of Lenin," *New York Times* (April 30, 1983), p. 23. For Stalin's use of the Lenin cult to entrench himself in the leadership, and for the origination of the tradition later adopted in Vietnam and China of interring the leader in a mausoleum, see Martin, *Cult and Canon*, p. 145.

## THE BURIAL OF SUN YAT-SEN

Dr. Sun Yat-sen's funeral rites in 1925 aroused intense conflict between his Christian relatives and the left wing of the Kuomintang. Leaders of the Kuomintang, and especially the head of its political bureau, Eugene Chen, brought great pressure to bear upon Madame Sun (Soong Ch'ing-ling), Sun Fo, and the Soongs to refuse a Christian ceremony altogether.[5] When Sun Yat-sen's family insisted on a Christian service in the privacy of the Peking Union Medical College's chapel, members of the party's left wing announced that they would have no part in it. As the glass coffin ordered by the Kuomintang had not yet arrived, a massive Chinese hardwood casket stood beneath a large framed photograph of Dr. Sun, banked with white flowers, on the chapel's altar. When the service was over, the coffin was brought out, borne by twenty-four pallbearers to the street, and a procession of party members was formed to take Sun's body to Central Park, where it was to lie in state for two weeks. As planes circled overhead the funeral cortege moved with great solemnity through the streets, its progress marked by military salutes fired at five-minute intervals. Eventually, the coffin was placed in the Central Park's great pavilion upon a flaming red bier, the gift of Ambassador Karakhan. Then, to bring an end to the civil ceremony, Sun's will was read aloud to the multitude.[6]

After the Nationalists' Northern Expedition reached the capital and Chiang Kai-shek paid a dramatic visit to Pi-yun ssu (Temple of the Azure Clouds) where Sun Yat-sen's silver casket lay, the physical remains of the late *tsung-li* (director) were moved to Nanking and placed in the imposing memorial built on Purple Mountain east of the Nationalist capital. The mausoleum became "the national shrine of modern China," and—unlike imperial tombs—a place of public pilgrimage.[7] Just as Sun Yat-sen had repeatedly sought to legitimate his own revolutionary movement by conducting ceremonies at the Ming tombs, so did his successors enshroud their government in the aura of Sun's mausoleum. Even before the shrine was built,

5. Edna Lee Booker, *News Is My Job: A Correspondent in War-Torn China* (New York: Macmillan, 1940), pp. 185–186. There was also a putative ideological conflict between Sun's conservative Confucian supporters and the left wing, cited in Mary Clabaugh Wright, *The Last Stand of Chinese Conservatism: The T'ung-Chih Restoration, 1862–1874* (New York: Atheneum, 1966), p. 304.

6. Leon Wieger, ed., *Chine moderne*, vol. 6 (Sienhsien, 1925), pp. 170–171. See also the account preserved in L. Carrington Goodrich's diary and quoted in C. Martin Wilbur, *Sun Yat-sen: Frustrated Patriot* (New York: Columbia University Press, 1976), p. 280. There are many photographs of these scenes in the Sidney Gamble Collection, Princeton University. Booker, *News Is My Job*, pp. 186–187.

7. M. L. Rosholt, "Magnificence, Grandeur of New Nanking Makes Deep Impression on Foreign Traveller Revisiting Nation's Capital," *China Press Double Tenth Supplement* (October 1935), p. 56.

the new Nationalist government sought to use the anniversary celebrations of Sun's death to enhance its own authority by holding "elaborate ceremonies" on March 12, 1928, in Nanking where it was decreed that thenceforth the "planting ceremony" of Chinese arbor day would be held on the anniversary of the death of the "father of the country."[8] The funeral rites on June 1, 1929, when Sun Yat-sen was reinterred on Purple Mountain, provided the occasion for all of the regime's leaders to ritualize their rule by accompanying the *tsung-li*'s coffin as it was solemnly carried up the stone steps for burial in the mausoleum above.[9] Afterwards, the ceremonial climax of any official visit to the Nationalist government at Nanking was a trip to Dr. Sun's memorial, and more than any other single object—including the presidential offices in the capital—the tomb represented the Kuomintang government.[10] The mausoleum constituted a new sacral center for the Republican state: a sign of revolutionary authority that had to be acknowledged by all succeeding rulers. When Wang Ching-wei and Chou Fo-hai inaugurated their puppet government in Nanking in 1940, for example, the first place they visited was the tomb, where Wang read Dr. Sun's will and cried aloud, tears running down his face. Similarly, when the Nationalist government formally reestablished its capital in Nanking on May 5, 1946, Chiang Kai-shek celebrated the occasion by "personally leading his civil and military officials in conducting a great victory ceremony before the tomb of the father of the country (*kuo-fu ling*)." And, less than three years later, when the Generalissimo resigned as president, the very last act he performed was to pay a final call of respect at Sun's tomb.[11]

Even today the Nationalist regime on Taiwan ceremonially addresses the tomb on important state occasions. After a new Kuomintang government was sworn in on January 20, 1984, President Chiang Ching-kuo and Vice-President Li Teng-hui held a special ceremony in the Great Hall of the Pres-

8. "Summary of Events and Conditions in the Nanking Consular District, March, 1928," *Records of the Department of State Relating to the Internal Affairs of China, 1910–1929*, 893.00, volume 68. Left-wing Kuomintang members of the Peiping branch attempted to use the ceremonies commemorating the fourth anniversary of Sun's death and held in the T'ai-ho Palace courtyard in the Forbidden City on March 14, 1929, to protest Chiang Kai-shek's "packing" of the Third Party Congress. "Memorial Services for Kuomintang Founder Held Despite Severe Dust Storm," *North China Standard*, March 14, 1929.

9. For photographs of the reinterment ceremonies, see *A Pictorial History of the Republic of China: Its Founding and Development* (Taipei: Modern China Press, 1981), pp. 252–255.

10. For the use of the tomb as a symbol of the regime, see *Ten Years of Nationalist China. The China Press Weekly Supplement* 3, no. 16 (1937): 1–80.

11. Gerald E. Bunker, *The Peace Conspiracy: Wang Ching-wei and the China War, 1937–1941* (Cambridge: Harvard University Press, 1972), p. 226; *Tsung-t'ung Chiang kung yi-hsun yü hsun-yeh* 總統蔣公遺訓與勛業 [President Mr. Chiang's bequeathed instructions and meritorious honors] (Taipei, 1975), pp. 226, 261 (quote from p. 226).

idential Palace in Taipei. While solemn music was played, Chiang "made offerings at a distance" to the "tomb of the father of the country," burning incense and tendering flowers in the direction of Nanking before leading the participants to bow three times to the portrait of Sun Yat-sen hanging in the Palace's Great Hall.[12]

## CREMATION VERSUS PRESERVATION

There were thus two conflicting impulses within the revolutionary tradition that the Kuomintang and Kungch'antang inherited from Sun's United Front years. One, evinced in the Communists' signed promise to accept cremation, both turns one's physical remains into ashes and enforces a certain egalitarianism among the "older generation" of party leaders. The second, coming from Lenin through Sun, is the tradition of the single dominant leader of the party (the *tsung-li*, *tsung-ts'ai*, or *chu-hsi*) having his remains preserved as an object of civil religious devotion.[13]

The decision to preserve the remains brings many problems, including the persistent trope of physical corruption. It was said in the case of Sun Yat-sen that the famous crystal sarcophagus from Russia was not airtight and that (as rumors later attested about Mao's remains) the dead leader's body was decaying.[14] Even if the person's corpse were perfectly preserved, there remained the risk of later physical defilement—a practice far from uncommon in Chinese imperial history or in the Republican period. Certainly the dismemberment of Ch'ien-lung's and Tz'u-hsi's remains by Sun Tien-ying's soldiers in 1928 represented a malice beyond that of ordinary grave robbers.[15] Leaders who feared posthumous political reversals during the civil war between the Communists and Nationalists were also concerned lest their bodies be disinterred and defiled.[16]

---

12. *Shih-chieh jih-pao* 世界日報 [World journal] (February 22, 1984), p. 1. The ceremony was held on January 21.

13. The remains include, of course, ideological remnants, often embodied in a last testament or in the "living thought" of the dead leader. As Ambassador Karakhan said at the February 1924 commemoration for Lenin in Peking: "The brilliant star that guided us has been extinguished by death. But the thought of Lenin survives. It will continue to shine throughout the world." "Feu Lenine, 93," in Leon Wieger, ed., *Chine moderne*, vol. 5, 2d ed. (Sienhsien, 1934), p. 207.

14. Percy Finch, *Shanghai and Beyond* (New York: Charles Scribner's Sons, 1953), p. 67.

15. Henry McAleavy, *A Dream of Tartary: The Origins and Misfortunes of Henry P'u Yi* (London: George Allen & Unwin, 1963), pp. 185–189.

16. When Tai Li was buried by his followers in 1946, for example, the tomb in Nanking was so heavily encased in concrete that his former Bureau of Investigation and Statistics lieutenants were unable to unearth his body to take it to Taiwan three years later. Shen Tsui 沈醉, "Wo suo chih-tao te Tai Li" 我所知道的戴笠 [The Tai Li I Knew], in Shen Tsui and Wen Ch'iang 文强, *Tai Li ch'i jen* 戴笠其人 [Tai Li the man] (Peking, 1980), p. 172.

Nor did the danger of defilement end with the civil war. During the Cultural Revolution Red Guards smashed open the grave of former Party Chairman Ch'ü Ch'iu-pai—whom Mao had indirectly accused of betraying the revolution while in a Kuomintang prison—and scattered his remains.[17] Remembering this as he lay dying of cancer in January 1976, Premier Chou En-lai insisted that his body be cremated and his ashes scattered.[18] After Chou's death word spread that his corpse was to be sent to the crematorium; only the intervention of Chou's widow prevented popular resistance to the cremation.[19] The agitation then, and later during the tumultuous outpouring of grief in the April 4 demonstration on grave-sweeping day before the Revolutionary Heroes Monument in T'ien-an men Square, reflected complex political concerns.[20] But these public demonstrations over the disposition of Chou's remains and the commemoration of his spirit also represented a kind of psychological displacement. For, especially during the Cultural Revolution, one of the most intense anxieties experienced by survivors of the dead was their inability to attend properly to the traditional rituals of death and dying.[21] Even individualized access to the crematoria— where bodies lay about unattended, awaiting anonymous mass disposal unless it could be proved in writing by one's unit that the person was not a "black gang" member and had not died as a result of being beaten or having committed suicide—was restricted; and elaborate back-door procedures were required to obtain illicit burial grounds in the Fragrant Hills west of the capital.[22] The handling of Chou En-lai's remains, therefore, must have touched many who were unable openly to mourn loved ones who had died while under political attack.[23]

17. Mao had insinuated that Ch'ü had lost his revolutionary integrity when he wrote *Superfluous Words*. Xu Guomin, "The Tragedy within China's Communist Palace: the Wu Hao Incident and Relations between Chairman Mao and Premier Zhou," M.A. thesis, San Jose State University, April 1983, p. 105. For the controversy surrounding *Superfluous Words*, see also Tsi-an Hsia, *The Gate of Darkness: Studies on the Leftist Literary Movement in China* (Seattle: University of Washington Press, 1968), pp. 45–54; and Paul G. Pickowicz, *Marxist Literary Thought in China: The Influence of Ch'ü Ch'iu-pai* (Berkeley and Los Angeles: University of California Press, 1981), pp. 210–221.

18. Xu Guomin, "Tragedy," p. 104; David S. Zweig, "The Peita Debate on Education and the Fall of Teng Hsiao-p'ing," *China Quarterly* 73 (1978): 149–150.

19. *New York Times*, January 8, 1977, p. 1. See also Roger Garside, *Coming Alive: China after Mao* (New York: McGraw-Hill, 1981), pp. 7–9. For photographs of the procession, see *Jen-min te tao-nien* 人民的悼念 [The grief of the people] (Peking, 1979), pp. 14–15.

20. The intense emotionality attending Chou's death, as well as the passionate demonstrations at T'iananmen on April 4 and 5, are well described in two important eyewitness accounts: Garside, *Coming Alive*, pp. 7–11, 128–132; and Zweig, "The Peita Debate on Education," pp. 146–147, 154–157.

21. Anne F. Thurston, "The Cultural Revolution in Retrospect: Voices of the Victims," unpublished paper, pp. 22–24.

22. Personal testimony by a Chinese informant.

23. One is reminded of a Chinese aphorism: "Borrow the mourning hall to cry out one's sorrows."

## THE DEATH OF MAO TSE-TUNG

Mao Tse-tung's death in the early hours of September 9, 1976, at the age of eighty-two was another matter.[24] People felt more "at a loss" (*mang-jan*) than grief stricken. In meetings some people cried openly, and there was public weeping over his corpse, but most people in Peking seemed mainly concerned about who was going to take over the country in the succession struggle certain to break out now that the Chairman was gone.[25] The government—that is, the Central Committee and the Military Commission of the Chinese Communist Party, the Standing Committee of the National People's Congress, and the State Council—issued two announcements on September 9, 1976, in order to coordinate public mourning for the dead leader and to reiterate the policies then being carried out by the coalition later vilified as the "Gang of Four," who were uneasily allied with Mao's successor, Hua Kuo-feng, against a "right deviationist" wing represented by Teng Hsiao-p'ing.[26]

Characteristically, the policy statement came first. After brief remarks extolling Chairman Mao's role as founder of the Communist Party of China, the announcement praised him for his leadership during the various "line" struggles against "opportunists" and against "counter-revolutionary revisionists." As a Marxist, Mao was singled out for having been the first to point out that "there are still classes and class struggle after the socialist transformation of the ownership of the means of production," and for having reached the "scientific conclusion" that the bourgeoisie was "right of the Communist Party."[27] His historical accomplishments had earned him the love and respect of the Chinese people as well as of revolutionaries throughout the entire world, and even though "the radiance of Mao Tse-tung thought will forever illuminate the road of advance of the Chinese people," his death was "bound to evoke immense grief" among them.[28] Nevertheless, the Chinese were enjoined to carry on the cause he had left behind by "taking class struggle as the key link," in order to rally around the party, to

24. Mao died at ten minutes past midnight, probably of advanced Parkinson's disease or cerebral arteriosclerosis. Andres D. Onate, "Hua Kuo-feng and the Arrest of the Gang of Four," *China Quarterly* 75 (1978): 540.
25. Edoarda Masi, *China Winter: Workers, Mandarins and the Purge of the Gang of Four*, trans. Adrienne Foulke (New York: E. P. Dutton, 1982), p. 88. My impressions are based on conversations with Chinese friends—nearly all intellectuals—living in Peking at that time. See also Garside, *Coming Alive*, pp. 139–140, 149.
26. The "Gang of Four" was present at the discussions drafting these messages, but its members were reported to have said nothing. Onate, "Arrest," pp. 542–543.
27. "Message to the Whole Party, the Whole Army and the People of All Nationalities Throughout the Country," NCNA-English (Peking, September 9, 1976), CMP-SPRCP-76-37, pp. 250–251. Mao's statement about the "bourgeoisie" being in the CCP can be found in *Peking Review* 19, no. 1 (March 12, 1976): 4. See also Richard Curt Kraus, *Class Conflict in Chinese Socialism* (New York: Columbia University Press, 1981), pp. 17, 97.
28. "Message," pp. 251–252.

deepen the criticism of Teng Hsiao-p'ing and repulse the "right deviationist attempt at reversing correct verdicts," to strengthen the building of the army and militia, to continue the struggle to liberate Taiwan, to adhere to proletarian internationalism and struggle against imperialism and social-imperialism, and to go on studying Marxism–Leninism–Mao Tse-tung thought.[29]

The second announcement declared that mourning services would be held in the Great Hall of the People during the seven days from September 11 to September 17, culminating in a memorial rally in T'ien-an men Square on September 18 at 3:00 P.M.[30] The government also announced that it had decided not to invite "foreign governments, fraternal parties or friendly personages to send delegations or representatives to take part in the mourning in China."[31]

Party organizations at all levels responded to the radio broadcast of the first announcement by sending messages of condolence that essentially affirmed the statement of policy itself. In the first of many identical rituals held throughout China, a Peking Garrison guard unit gathered before the huge, black-draped portrait of Mao on the red wall of T'ien-an men to take "a solemn vow" to "discharge our duty well, defend the Party Central Committee, defend T'ien-an men and keep the five-star red flag hoisted by Chairman Mao in its place over T'ien-an men Square forever."[32]

## MOURNING MAO

The mourning services that commenced on September 11 placed Mao's corpse on public view and established the roster of the new government. While 50,000 inhabitants of the capital prepared to file through the Great Hall of the People on that single day, party and state leaders in hierarchical order (Hua Kuo-feng, Wang Hung-wen, Yeh Chien-ying, Chang Ch'un-ch'iao, Soong Ch'ing-ling, Chiang Ch'ing, Yao Wen-yuan, and so on down to Chiang Hua, President of the Supreme People's Court) gathered at 10:00 A.M. to pay silent tribute before Mao's bier while a PLA band struck up solemn funeral music. As the "Varshavyanka" march played on, group after

29. Ibid., pp. 252–254.

30. "Announcement," NCNA-English (Peking, September 9, 1976), CMP-SPRCP-76-37, p. 256.

31. Ibid. The only foreigner to participate in the mourning services was Ieng Sary, Deputy Prime Minister of Kampuchea. "Chairman Mao's Magnificent Achievements Will Always Shine, Over 300,000 People in Capital Deeply Mourn Chairman Mao and Pay Last Respects to His Remains," NCNA-English (Peking, September 17, 1976), CMP-SPRCP-76-39, p. 186.

32. "Whole Party, Whole Army and People of Whole Country Mourn Passing Away of Great Leader and Teacher Chairman Mao," NCNA-English (Peking, September 10, 1976), CMP-SPRCP-76-38, p. 26.

group of mourners—selected from key units by the funeral committee in order to symbolically confirm the policies then in effect—filed through the hall. Most stopped for a moment in respectful silence in front of the bier, through some cried out: "Chairman Mao, Chairman Mao, you'll always live in our memory!"[33]

The hall contained the many funeral wreaths presented by the Standing Committee of the National People's Congress, the State Council, and other state and party units, plus a group of "patriotic compatriots from Taiwan province."[34] The order of precedence of the official roster, which completely displaced Mao's family, was in this single respect shifted to accommodate the special status of Mao's private dependants. A wreath from the family was placed just before his coffin and given special attention in the accounts of the ceremony, but there was nothing else, apart from those flowers, to signal the family's position as mourners.[35] The chief mourners remained the carefully listed state and party leaders, and more important than Mao's relatives were the representatives sent to the services from areas where Mao had "undertaken great revolutionary activities": Shao-shan, the An-yuan Colliery, Jui-chin county, and so on.[36] Mao as a person, with family and friends, was displaced by Mao as a transcendent revolutionary leader without a private domain of his own.

Elsewhere in China, at specially designated places, similar public observances were held—the mourning ceremonies continuing in this fashion for seven days.[37] Increasingly stressed, as time went by, was the commitment of carefully chosen units to the cause bequeathed them by the dead leader. Pledges to carry on the cause—the policies initiated during 1976 against Teng Hsiao-p'ing—were repeatedly voiced. Official accounts of the mourning services emphasized again and again the magnitude of the numbers of people who paid their respects to Mao. During the seven days, more than 300,000 cadres, workers, peasants, soldiers, and people in the capital "with

33. "Solemn Mourning Services Begin in Chinese Capital—Party, State Leaders, 50,000 People Mourn Great Leader Chairman Mao with Profound Grief," NCNA-English (Peking, September 11, 1976), CMP-SPRCP-76-38, pp. 86. The mourners included Red Guards from the Chingkang Mountains, Long March survivors, Eighth Route Army veterans, young Red Guards "who fought in the van of the Great Proletarian Cultural Revolution," and so forth.

34. Ibid., p. 87.

35. Ibid., p. 85. Of the forty condolence messages published in People's Daily between September 10 and September 12, only six provinces and five military regions specifically offered their condolences to Chiang Ch'ing, and none of the eleven devoted more than a single sentence to her. Chiang Ch'ing failed to appear in the receiving lines during the memorial services. Onate, "Arrest," p. 545. See also Ross Terrill, The White-Boned Demon: A Biography of Madame Mao Zedong (New York: William Morrow, 1984), p. 368.

36. "Solemn Mourning Services Begin," p. 89.

37. This was in marked contrast to the mourning for Chou En-lai, which was declared at an end once the funeral ceremony had been held. Garside, Coming Alive, p. 12.

grief and esteem and love, came to the mourning hall in the Great Hall of the People to pay last respects to the remains of Chairman Mao."[38] The choreography of each group's visit—the assembling by column in assigned spots on T'ien-an men, the quick responses to the attendants' orders to come forward, the reverential shuffling past the bier with its honor guard, and then the march down the steps of the Great Hall to return to the vast square below—was analogous to a work of art: "an abstract, livid performance of a funeral in which everyone played a prearranged role, a moment that exists outside time and becomes forever fixed in images."[39]

## MOURNING CHIANG

In some ways equally impressive, if only because it appeared to be so spontaneous, was the public mourning for Chairman Mao's archenemy, Generalissimo Chiang Kai-shek, who had died seventeen months earlier, on April 5, 1975, at the age of eighty-seven. Chiang Kai-shek had been in retirement since July 1972.[40] The day that he died, April 5, was the lunar grave-sweeping festival, traditionally considered an especially dangerous time for the ill because the forces of death are then so strong. His demise shortly before midnight coincided with an ominous thunderstorm.

> As midnight approached, the clear starlit night was suddenly darkened with clouds. Rain fell, and many people in Taipei were awakened by the peals of thunder and flashes of lightning. It was as if Heaven itself was pouring out its anguish and grief. Those who had been awakened wondered at the sudden change in weather. None knew that at 11:20 the president was stricken with a heart attack. Emergency treatment was administered to no avail; by 11:50 Chiang Kai-shek, leader of the Republic of China for half a century and the last of World War II's "Big Four," was dead.[41]

The ministers who learned of Chiang Kai-shek's demise in the early hours of April 6 reached his residence at Shih-lin at about 2:00 A.M., to find the dead man "resting serenely" on his bed while his son, Premier Chiang Ching-kuo, knelt beside him.[42] The last written instruction given to his eldest son was a couplet: "Take up the responsibility for the rise and fall of the nation first./ Place your own life and death beyond consideration."[43]

38. "Chairman Mao's Magnificent Achievements Will Always Shine," p. 186.
39. Masi, *China Winter*, p. 99.
40. *Vista*, 1975, no. 3, *A Nation Mourns*, p. 3.
41. *A Nation Mourns*, p. 3.
42. Chiang Wei-kuo was in southern Taiwan at the time of his father's death.
43. Chung-yang jih-pao 中央日報, eds., *Ling-hsiu ching-shen wan-ku ch'ang-hsin: Tsung-t'ung Chiang kung ai-ssu shih-lu* 領袖精神萬古常新：總統蔣公哀思實錄 [The spirit of the leader will be constantly renewed through the ages: Veritable record of the grief over General Chiang Kung] (Taipei, 1975), *Chung-yang jih-pao*, p. 2; *Vista*, pp. 3, 42.

Reports in Taiwanese sources stressed the overwhelming sense of shock when the news of Chiang Kai-shek's death hit the streets of Taipei at 10:30 A.M. on that same morning. While Chiang's corpse was being taken to Veterans General Hospital, crowds began to appear before his residence in Shih-lin, bringing gifts as tribute. And on April 9, when Chiang's bronze casket was moved from the hospital to the Sun Yat-sen Memorial Hall, hundreds of thousands of people lined the sidewalks, even though the streets were swept with rain. When the cortege finally appeared, the sun suddenly came out, like a counter-omen to the thunderstorm four days earlier.[44] The contrast between these individual groups of mourners, some of them businessmen who had closed their shops for the day, holding up white wreaths or joss sticks, as Chiang's cortege paraded by, and the serried ranks on T'ien-an men, could not be sharper.

Yet, once Chiang's body was installed in the Sun Yat-sen Memorial Hall, there were certain points of similarity between the last rites of the two leaders. Chiang Kai-shek's coffin was placed on a stage decked with flowers and evergreen trees, under a giant portrait of the former president.[45] Around the funeral bier, which was flanked by an honor guard of soldiers, were eighty-eight white candles—one for each *sui* of Chiang's life. An arrangement of white flowers from Madame Chiang Kai-shek stood directly in front of the casket itself, which was covered with a transparent glass top. Once the hall was opened the following day, lines of mourners began to file by the casket, wearing black armbands. Attendants in military-style uniforms helped those who were infirm or stricken in the sweltering heat.[46]

The appearance of similarity (the leader's openly displayed corpse, the evergreen plants and white flowers, the family flower arrangement, the honor guard, the many mourners viewing the corpse) was barely superficial; there were telling differences between Mao's and Chiang's mourning services, even in these visible details. The honor guards flanking the Nationalist leader's coffin and cortege were dressed in chrome G. I. helmets and American-style military uniforms.[47] The white flower arrrangement presented by Madame Chiang Kai-shek was in the form of a cross, symbolizing the Christian resurrection. And whereas state and party clearly took precedence over family in the services for Mao, Chiang Kai-shek's dynastic family— Madame Chiang Kai-shek with Chiang Ching-kuo and Chiang Wei-kuo on either side, dressed in traditional Chinese robes—occupied center stage throughout the funeral ceremonies.[48]

44. *Tsung-t'ung Chiang kung*, pp. 44–45, 61; *Vista*, p. 10.
45. *Tsung-t'ung Chiang kung*, p. 49.
46. *Vista*, pp. 8–10.
47. *Tsung-t'ung Chiang kung*, p. 43.
48. Ibid., pp. 66–67; *Vista*, p. 15.

Even the arrangements made by the funeral committee were quite different. Mao's funeral preparations required mobilizing units around the capital, assigning times for their representatives to appear at the Great Hall of the People, and then moving them in an orderly fashion through the hall. The presidential funeral committee formed in Taiwan had to deal with a quite different problem: unanticipated numbers of seemingly spontaneous visitors. Though the committee eventually decided to keep the hall open twenty-four hours a day, a huge crowd remained when the building was finally closed at midnight on April 14 to make preparations for the public funeral service on April 16. By then, two and a half million mourners had passed through the memorial hall: one-sixth of the island's entire population.[49]

Giving due weight to the propaganda bias of the official accounts that lent textual permanency to the occasion, one still cannot mistake the sincerity of the grief among the Taipei mourners—a grief that could find no customary channel in established public ritual. Although the atmosphere inside the hall was described as dignified and serene, befitting an elite funeral dominated by the Generalissimo's aristocratic widow, "sobs, cries and sometimes even uncontrollable wails occasionally echoed through the huge auditorium."[50] The public outpouring of sentiment is illustrated in photograph after photograph, as Chiang's funeral cortege passed through streets lined with altars laden with fruits, candles, and offerings.[51]

In contrast to the detailed reports of individuals and groups in Peking speaking before Mao's bier of the causes for their sorrow, the accounts of Chiang Kai-shek's death seldom gave specific reasons for the public's grief, although anxiety about the future of Taiwan itself must have been an important stimulus.[52] The older generation of native Taiwanese allegedly felt they had lost a father, because Chiang had freed them from Japanese occupation in 1945 and had later liberated them from the ruinous rents on the lands that they tilled. The Generalissimo was mainly extolled for his dynamic economic leadership as well as his historical stature: his closeness to Sun Yat-sen during the exile of the *kuo-fu*, his command of the Northern Expedition, his leadership against the Japanese, and his firm stance against the Communists. His international prominence, including his status as one

49. *Tsung-t'ung Chiang kung*, pp. 62–63, 65; *Vista*, p. 10.

50. *Tsung-t'ung Chiang kung*, pp. 27, 30–33, 37, 52–57; *Vista*, p. 9. "The only incident that occurred was when an unfortunate foreign journalist...asked someone waiting in line outside the memorial hall how much he was being paid by the government to queue up. The newsman was beaten" (*Vista*, p. 10).

51. *Vista*, p. 17.

52. American observers reported that the authorities, who were concerned about hostile Taiwanese reactions at this time (just at the U.S. was withdrawing from South Vietnam), temporarily stationed tanks in culverts about the capital.

of the Big Four, was especially underscored to account for Chiang Kai-shek's importance to his countrymen.[53]

The Nationalist government tried to use the public's grief over Chiang's death to rededicate the regime to its anticommunist crusade, to recovery of the mainland, and to economic development. Almost parodically, the major corporations on Taiwan extended condolences to the family of the late President while simultaneously pledging themselves to ongoing economic growth. Typically, businesses like Clinton Taiwan Corporation or Texas Instruments would take out a half or full page in the special *Vista* edition commemorating Chiang's death, and feature a photograph of the Generalissimo with brief comments below. The Industrial Development and Investment Center simply placed the following reassuring fiscal solicitation in a black-ringed box:

> Based on the policies laid down by our late President Chiang Kai-shek, economic decisions in Taiwan, the Republic of China, are designed to foster price stability, business prosperity, and social welfare. Despite world economic disruptions, Taiwan offers numerous lucrative investment opportunities.[54]

These capitalist appeals for investment were one way of carrying out the injunction of the Kuomintang leadership "to transform grief into strength" (*hua pei-shang wei li-liang*), a motto that was widely proclaimed in Taiwan just after Chiang Kai-shek's death.[55]

## TRANSFORM GRIEF INTO STRENGTH

Curiously enough, exactly the same formulaic language appeared in major propaganda media in the People's Republic of China just after Mao's death; it was quickly adopted as a slogan uttered automatically by mourners at all levels the first few days after the Chairman passed away. By September 16, the next-to-last day of the Peking mourning services, the phrase had become part of the litany of pledge-taking before Mao's remains: "We will turn our grief into strength, live up to your consistent teachings and always advance valiantly along the revolutionary path you blazed."[56]

While the transformation of grief into strength on Taiwan elicited promises of more capital investment and better managed economic development,

53. *Tsung-t'ung Chiang kung*, pp. 7, 74, 105–112; *Vista*, pp. 4, 6, 42; *Free China Weekly*, Supplement B (April 6, 1975).
54. *Vista*, p. 20.
55. *Tsung-t'ung Chiang kung*, pp. 98, 116–117.
56. "Mourning Services," NCNA-English (Peking, September 16, 1976), CMP-SPRCP-76-39, p. 101. It also became closely associated with the left-wing repetition of the phrase "Act according to the principles laid down." One of the most militant articles in support of that adjuration appeared in *People's Daily* on September 30, entitled "Turn Grief into Strength." Onate, "Arrest," p. 552.

on the mainland it inspired spurts of labor productivity reminiscent of Great Leap Forward mobilization efforts. At the Shanghai Number One Steel Plant, the death of Chairman Mao prompted the workers to step up their pace by turning out record heats of steel on each shift.[57] And at the Fu-shun Mining Administration in Liaoning province coal miners went in groups to the areas visited by Chairman Mao in 1958 and topped production quotas by 17 percent in six days.[58]

The most intense expressions of grief over Mao Tse-tung's death appeared to come from older people, for whom Mao was a great emancipator, and from the very young, whom he had metaphorically fathered and nurtured. A group of poor and lower-middle peasants from P'ing-ku county traveled more than 100 kilometers into Peking to see his body, bringing their village customs of unabashed public mourning with them.

> These peasants, who were emancipated by Chairman Mao from the oppression and humiliation imposed on them in the old society, burst into tears when they stepped into the Great Hall of the People and saw the kindly and serene face of Chairman Mao. The mourning hall was filled with the sound of loud weeping and crying. They bowed at every step and said with profound emotion: "Chairman Mao had all the labouring people at heart. Chairman Mao was always one with us poor and lower-middle peasants. But for Chairman Mao, we poor and lower-middle peasants would not have been what we are today."[59]

Similar feelings of bereavement were expressed by the five T'ang-shan coal miners who were rescued at Mao's behest after being trapped underground for fifteen days as a result of the 1976 earthquake; by aged proletarians like the woman textile worker from Shanghai who had had her teeth knocked out and had been stabbed by reactionaries before liberation; and by young Red Guards from Peking and Tsing-hua Universities, who recalled the hectic months of the Cultural Revolution when they were supported by the Great Helmsman, and who cried out tearfully now, "Oh, Chairman Mao, we miss you so much!"[60] Chairman Mao, whose benevolence was "higher than the

57. "Chairman Mao Lives in the Hearts of Chinese People," NCNA-English (Peking, September 13, 1976), CMP-SPRCP-76-38, p. 250.

58. "Whole Party, Whole Army and People of All Nationalities Throughout China Mourn Great Leader and Teacher Chairman Mao with Concrete Action," NCNA-English (Peking, September 17, 1976), CMP-SPRCP-76-39, p. 182.

59. "Mourning of Mao Tsetung," NCNA-English (Peking, September 16, 1976), CMP-SPRCP-76-39, pp. 102–103.

60. "Peking People Continue Solemn Mourning Over Death of Great Leader and Teacher Chairman Mao, Pay Last Respects to His Remains," NCNA-English (Peking, September 15, 1976), CMP-SPRCP-76-40, p. 108; "People in Shanghai Mourn Chairman Mao at Revolutionary Site," NCNA-English (Shanghai, September 16, 1976), CMP-SPRCP-76-40, p. 115–116; quote from "Mourning of Mao Tsetung," September 16, p. 104.

mountains and deeper than the sea" (shan-kao, hai-shen—language once reserved for the Son of Heaven), had become a kind of cosmic savior, no man or god greater than he.[61]

As these waves of public grief washed out from Peking to the provinces, and thence to the minority peoples who proclaimed Mao their liberator, a kind of symbolic national constituency was created. The constituency was repeatedly linked together with locations Mao had visited, worked in, or touched during his revolutionary activities—places like Jui-chin and Yenan where, in effect, his sainthood had been realized.[62] The cult of Mao had been best symbolized at its apogee by the famous mangoes the Chairman sent around in 1968 in an effort to bring unity to the warring factions of the Cultural Revolution. Mourners at Tsing-hua University now recalled the moment on August 5, 1968, when their propaganda team had received the "precious gift" of mangoes from the Chairman, and activists at Peking University, who passed "the most grievous moments of their lives" when news reached them of Mao's death, recalled that same boon and vowed to transform their grief into strength through the study of Mao's writings.[63] Units throughout China consequently decided that after the seven days of mourning services were over they would renew the daily study of the Chairman's Selected Works.[64]

## MAO'S MEMORIAL RALLY

The mourning services came to an end on September 17. The following day a mass memorial rally, involving one million people, was held on T'ien-an men Square. The square was dominated by a high red ochre platform arrayed with decorations that included a new wreath made by Chiang Ch'ing from sunflowers, corn, ears of wheat, rice, and millet—"five grains" (wu ku) like the life-renewing offerings once made to Heaven itself at the Altar of the Soil and Grain (She chi) in the old Ch'ing palace nearby. The rostrum above the platform was accentuated by a huge black memorial

61. See, for example, "Mourning of Mao Tsetung in Peking University," Jen-min jih-pao (Peking, September 18, 1976), CMP-SPRCP-76-39, p. 249.

62. For the minority nationalities, see: "Minority Nationalities in China Deeply Mourn Passing of Great Liberator Chairman Mao," NCNA-English (Peking, September 15, 1976), CMP-SPRCP-76-40, p. 109; "Miao Nationality Centenarian Deeply Mourns Chairman Mao," NCNA-English (Peking, September 16, 1976), pp. 121–122; "Peking Papers Continue to Mourn Death of Chairman Mao," NCNA-English (Peking, September 16, 1976), CMP-SPRCP-76-40, p. 124; "People in Yenan Deeply Mourn Chairman Mao," NCNA-English (Sian, September 16, 1976), CMP-SPRCP-76-39, p. 117.

63. "Mourning of Mao Tsetung in Peking University," Jen-min jih-pao (Peking, September 18, 1976), CMP-SPRCP-76-39, p. 252.

64. See, for example, "Whole Party, Whole Army and People of All Nationalities," p. 183.

streamer that ran below the portrait of Chairman Mao mounted on T'ien-an men Gate, where "27 years ago . . . the great leader Chairman Mao himself hoisted the first five-star red flag,"[65] proclaiming the founding of the People's Republic of China.

At precisely 3:00 P.M. Wang Hung-wen declared the memorial rally open and the mourners observed a three-minute silence. All across the country people stood in respectful attention, at their radios, while sirens sounded in mourning.[66] After the national anthem and the "Internationale" were played, Hua Kuo-feng delivered the memorial speech.[67]

Hua's eulogy described the nation's sorrow and recapitulated Chairman Mao's accomplishments. Calling Mao "the greatest Marxist of the contemporary era," Hua laid the greatest stress upon Mao's point that "there are still classes and class struggle after the socialist transformation of the ownership of the means of production." Yet though he emphasized the Chairman's admonition never to forget class struggle, he did not once mention the phrase favored by Chiang Ch'ing (who stood enshrouded in a large black shawl) and the ultra-left: "Act according to the principles laid down."[68] Rather, before calling for the liberation of Taiwan, he pointedly enjoined his listeners to support the "Three Dos and Three Don'ts" of Chairman Mao: "Practice Marxism, and not revisionism; unite, don't split; be open and aboveboard, and don't intrigue and conspire."[69] These were the same words Mao had used on May 3, 1975, to reprimand the Shanghai "Gang of Four" for factional maneuvering, and when Hua uttered them now—at the culmination of the late Chairman's memorial ceremony—the point was obviously made, especially to those who were watching the rally on television and who saw Wang Hung-wen arch his eyebrows and pointedly peer over Hua's shoulder at the text of the speech itself.[70]

Hua Kuo-feng concluded his speech with an appeal to accept the leadership of the Party Central Committee in order to carry through to the end the proletarian revolution that Chairman Mao had pioneered. The strains of "The East is Red" rose above T'ian-an men Square:

> The east is red,
> The sun rises.

65. "Mass Memorial Rally for Mao Tsetung," NCNA-English (Peking, September 18, 1976), CMP-SPRCP-76-39, pp. 261, 263.

66. Masi, *China Winter*, p. 98 (n. 25 above).

67. Ibid., pp. 263–264.

68. Garside, *Coming Alive*, p. 148 (n. 19 above).

69. "Memorial Speech by Comrade Hua Kuo-feng, First Vice Chairman of Central Committee of Communist Party of China and Premier of State Council, at Mass Memorial Meeting for Great Leader and Teacher Chairman Mao Tsetung," NCNA-English (Peking, September 18, 1976), CMP-SPRCP-76-39, pp. 273–279. Quote from p. 278.

70. Garside, *Coming Alive*, pp. 148–149; Masi, *China Winter*, p. 99; Terrill, *White-Boned Demon*, p. 370 (n. 35 above).

China has brought forth a Mao Tse-tung.
He works for the people's happiness,
He is the people's great savior.

The rally ended at 3:30 P.M.[71]

In spite of the assurances that the thought of Mao Tse-tung was invincible and would live forever, the tone of Hua Kuo-feng's exhortation—the adjuring quality of his appeals to grasp the key link of class struggle—suggested less than total confidence in future outcomes. One senses, both in his speech and in those reported from the mass memorial meetings held throughout China just as soon as the T'ian-an men rally was over, that those factions of the Party momentarily successful in attacking Teng Hsiao-p'ing and his "right deviationist line" were far from certain that they would continue to prevail over their opposition.[72] In each of the subsequent memorial meetings (usually held in front of a portrait of Chairman Mao decorated with evergreen boughs and flanked with wreaths presented by local units) the speakers pledged to "turn grief into strength" by "acting according to the principles laid down" and by deepening the criticism of Teng Hsiao-p'ing. Always there were the raised fists and fervent oaths before Mao's picture, but the vows of determination sounded shrill and belabored.[73]

## CHIANG KAI-SHEK'S FUNERAL SERVICES

The situation more than a year earlier in Taiwan, after Chiang Kai-shek's death, was quite the opposite. There was no succession crisis to speak of at all. Premier Chiang Ching-kuo first tendered his resignation, "in keeping with the ancient Chinese tradition that calls for the withdrawal from government service after the death of a parent."[74] The Central Standing Committee of the Kuomintang, however, refused to accept the premier's resignation. Vowing to carry out Chiang's last instructions, to "persevere in the face of adversity and redouble [their] efforts to fulfill the responsibility of the National Revolution without fail," the Central Standing Committee endorsed the succession of Vice-President Yen. At 10:00 A.M. on April 6, in accordance with Article 49 of the Constitution of the Republic of China, C. K. Yen, facing a portrait of Sun Yat-sen, was sworn in as president in Taipei.[75]

The first major ceremonial duty of the new president was to lead the funeral services for Chiang Kai-shek at the Sun Yat-sen Memorial Hall,

71. "Mass Memorial Rally," pp. 268–269.
72. Masi, *China Winter*, p. 98.
73. "Mass Memorial Rallies Mourning Mao Tsetung," NCNA-English (Peking, September 19, 1976), CMP-SPRCP-76-39, pp. 329–334; Masi, *China Winter*, p. 96.
74. *Vista*, p. 6.
75. *Vista*, pp. 3, 6–7. See also *Ling-hsiu ching-shen*, p. 1; *Free China Weekly*, supplement A, April 6, 1975.

where Premier Chiang Ching-kuo had appeared daily before the bier.[76] The elder son's filial piety represented his personal claims to the Generalissimo's remains, as well as his public commitment to the traditional values of his father's regime.[77] The contrast between his stepmother's Christian devotion and Ching-kuo's Confucian attachment may have created a certain private dissonance, but their joint piousness served to mediate between family rituals and government ceremonies. The funeral rites for Sun Yat-sen had been completely dichotomized between family and state—the remains, so to speak, being split between private and public spheres; but the memorial services for Chiang Kai-shek eclectically combined familial and state interests, appropriate to the man himself.

The services began at 8:00 A.M. on April 16 with a eulogy by President Yen Chia-kan. After he presented a wreath, the immediate members of the late president's family gathered around the open coffin and looked on while three of Chiang's most highly prized medals were placed in the casket along with the four books "which had guided him through life": Sun Yat-sen's *Three Principles*, the Christian Bible, an anthology of T'ang poetry, and *Huang-mo kan-ch'üan* (Streams in the desert), a Christian inspirational work by Mrs. Charles E. Cowman.[78] After the coffin was closed, the audience—which included notable foreign dignitaries—bowed three times and observed a minute of silence. The state ceremonies were concluded after a Kuomintang flag was laid on top of the coffin and then a national flag draped beside that. The Christian service, conducted by the Reverend Chou Lien-hua, ended with the singing of Chiang Kai-shek's favorite hymn, "Lead, Kindly Light," by the Hua Hsing Taipei Children's Choir.[79]

The ceremonial process that followed essentially rendered Chiang's remains private once more. This was possible because as yet there was no final resting place on Taiwan for the Generalissimo, given his perennial mission to return to the mainland as its leader. Whereas Sun Yat-sen's family lost control over his remains, Chiang Kai-shek's family recovered and retained them—until such time as they could be moved on to their final resting place on the Chinese mainland.[80]

The site selected for the temporary resting place was President and Madame Chiang Kai-shek's tile-roofed villa at Tz'u-hu.[81] As the couple's

76. *Vista*, p. 8.

77. For Chiang Ching-kuo's own account of his filial devotion, see "Shou fu ling i yueh chi" 守父靈一月紀 [Record of one month of watching over my father's soul], reprinted in *Tsung-t'ung Chiang kung*, pp. 123–151.

78. *Tsung-t'ung Chiang kung*, pp. 66–67; *Ling-hsiu ching-shen*, pp. 14–17. See Kaoman fu-jen 高曼夫人 (Mrs. Cowman), *Huang-mo kan-ch'üan* 荒漠甘泉 [Streams in the desert], trans. Wang Chia-yü 王家棫. 2 vols. (Taipei, 1970).

79. *Tsung-t'ung Chiang kung*, pp. 70–71; *Vista*, p. 14.

80. *Vista*, p. 19.

81. *Tsung-t'ung Chiang kung*, p. 89.

former country house, Tz'u-hu symbolically represented filiality, inner family life, and retirement to the mainland itself. Now, the president's remains were solemnly carried out of the Sun Yat-sen Memorial Hall by twelve of Chiang's former aides and placed upon a flower-covered hearse decorated with a Christian cross on the top and a Kuomintang star in the front. While family members held on to tassels at the back, the members of the state funeral committee grasped long white streamers that came along both sides of the hearse. Behind them slowly walked the foreign dignitaries past a crowd that was estimated to number a million and a half all along the route from the hall to Tz'u-hu. As the funeral cortege passed, many of the onlookers dressed in mourning knelt or kowtowed in reverence.[82]

The cortege stopped at the intersection of Jen-ai and Kuang-fu roads, where Madame Chiang—still the primary trustee—bowed her thanks to all those who attended the funeral. At Tz'u-hu the casket was carried into the main hall of the house. There, on a white marble floor, stood a black granite catafalque built by the Retired Servicemen's Engineering Agency (Jung-min kung-ch'eng shih-yeh kuan-li ch'u), the construction company formed by Chiang Kai-shek to give jobs to ex-servicemen.[83]

The remains were still at this juncture shared between family and state, but a final ceremony now privatized them, with the ultimate trusteeship being conferred directly upon the elder son. After the casket was sealed inside the catafalque, President C. K. Yen led the members of the funeral committee in three final bows. Then he and his entourage walked slowly around the granite monument. While his stepmother watched, Chiang Ching-kuo bowed deeply to each of the official mourners in turn. The official entourage then walked back out the front of the small building, leaving the presidential corpse behind.[84]

State and party retained the right to recover Chiang's corpse whenever their own mission to resume control of the mainland was realized. Though the fragility of this conceit was obvious if unspoken, reunion with the mainland might eventually occur in unforeseen ways, and in that event, the final disposition of Chiang's remains would have enormous symbolic significance. For the moment, however, they were more safely disposed of in the family's hands, resting in their temporary private grave, with public veneration reserved for less personal monuments in the state's domain.[85]

82. *Ling-hsiu ching-shen*, pp. 19, 28–29; *Vista*, pp. 13–16; *Tsung-t'ung Chiang kung*, pp. 76–77.

83. "The workers had done the job in less than ten days, working on the catafalque night and day in shifts—many with tears running down their faces as they cut, polished and put the granite slabs together" (*Vista*, p. 17).

84. *Tsung-t'ung Chiang kung*, p. 88.

85. Important visitors to Taiwan, who would have been taken out to Tz'u-hu in 1976, were brought instead to Chiang's memorial hall after it was opened in 1980.

## MAO'S PERSON AND THOUGHT

Chiang Kai-shek's personal remains could be entrusted to his family because state and party were in the hands of his natural heir. Mao's corpse could not be so easily disposed of, because his political heir, Hua Kuo-feng, could not afford to let the late Chairman's family claim possession of the body—a body whose very corporeality continued to radiate the charisma of Mao Tse-tung's personal power.[86] As Mao's anointed successor, Hua must have seen it to be in his own interest to keep the remains intact, especially since he was doing all that he could to highlight the physical resemblance between himself and the late Chairman.[87] The problem, therefore, was to preserve the body without losing control of it. In this respect, the disposition of Mao's person was analogous to the treatment of his thought.

Though Mao's voice was stilled, his thought survived both as ideas and as written texts.[88] As ideas, "invincible Mao Tse-tung thought" was said to represent the Chairman's eternal legacy. The constitution of Mao Tse-tung thought, however, could be defined in many different ways.[89] In its most recent guise, it tended to accord with the policies of those who had risen during the Cultural Revolution and who wanted to use it as a weapon against the "right deviationists" represented by Teng Hsiao-p'ing. To the latter, on the other hand, Mao's ideology represented an indispensable form of legitimation. Consequently, a compromise had to be worked out at the highest levels of the party and state in order to try to come to an agreement upon a common exegesis of Mao Tse-tung thought. The result was no compromise at all and the ensuing arrests of the "Gang of Four."

Hua Kuo-feng, because of the way power was handed down to him by Mao, favored the six-character formula that celebrated the moment the Chairman had selected his successor: *Ni pan-shih, wo fang-hsin* (With you in charge, I'm at ease).[90] He also liked to refer to the "Three Dos and Three

---

86. Evidently, Chiang Ch'ing planned to have Mao's ashes placed in a plot at Pa-pao-shan, which would eventually be her grave as well. Yet when the Politburo asked her to take responsibility for disposing of Mao's remains, she refused. Hua Kuo-feng insisted that there had to be an immediate autopsy so as to prevent deterioration. He agreed to assume complete responsibility for the handling of Mao's corpse. Chiang Ch'ing suggested that he make this decision public, but Hua refused to do so on the grounds that the memorial service had not yet been scheduled. Later it was charged that Chiang Ch'ing had been trying to prepare the ground for a future attack upon Hua for having disregarded Chairman Mao's land usage policy. Onate, "Arrest," p. 542; Terrill, *White-Boned Demon*, p. 373.

87. Martin notes that Hua had himself photographed working in a train, in emulation of a famous photo of Mao, and in addition changed his hairstyle and calligraphy to better match Mao's. Martin, *Cult and Canon*, pp. 53–54 (n. 1 above).

88. "Even during Mao's lifetime the texts often functioned almost independently of him" (Martin, *Cult and Canon*, p. 4).

89. Ibid., pp. 46–49.

90. Mao's statement was probably made with reference to Hua Kuo-feng's handling of the campaign against Teng Hsiao-p'ing during April 1976, but Hua and his supporters sought

Don'ts" to remind Chiang Ch'ing and her allies that the former Chairman had been deeply opposed to their factional intrigues. Nevertheless, Hua Kuo-feng initially favored yet another oracular pronouncement by Mao Tse-tung, which simply enjoined: "Act according to past principles." The original Chinese version of this statement was loosely vernacular: *Chao kuo-ch'ü fang-chen pan*. But after the T'ang-shan earthquake, Chiang Ch'ing allegedly had taken the original document out of the Party General Office and altered the sentence to read: *An chi-ting fang-chen pan* (Act according to the principles laid down). The term, *chi-ting*, which means "already decided" or "laid down," made Mao's exhortation sound much more definitive and authoritative, and that was entirely consonant with the wishes of the left wing of the party to continue to follow the policies associated with the Chiang Ch'ing faction and to prevent "revisionist chieftains" from tampering with the late Chairman's radical programs.[91]

In the weeks following Mao's death, the growing struggle between Hua Kuo-feng and the Chiang Ch'ing faction came to center upon which of the available slogans was most readily used in the descriptions and commemorations of the Chairman's funeral rites. Generally speaking, the propagandists in favor of using "act according to the principles laid down" prevailed.[92] Yet Mao's thought was not so easily prescribed. It remained a set of manifold ideas that people carried within themselves and that were susceptible to private interpretations. As unwritten texts, these ideas were much more open to individual exegesis (especially for those who had taken Mao at his word in believing that *tsao-fan yu-li*, "to rebel is justified") than the standard editions of Mao's printed works already being readied for distribution throughout the country.[93] Since only some four volumes of Mao's collected works had appeared and a fifth was due to be published, and since there would soon have to be a newly compiled edition of the Chairman's *Selected Works*, the opportunity to set a much more permanent imprint upon the

---

to extend it to a mandate for their succession. Onate, "Arrest," pp. 549–551. See also Martin, *Cult and Canon*, pp. 52–53.

91. There is a careful and detailed discussion of these textual questions in Onate, "Arrest," pp. 548–549, 553–554. See also Martin, *Cult and Canon*, pp. 52, 169. Bonavia reports, however, that, according to the official charges at the time of the trial of the "Gang of Four," it was Yao Wen-yuan who made the alterations. David Bonavia, *Verdict in Peking: The Trial of the Gang of Four* (New York: G. P. Putnam's Sons, 1984), p. 109.

92. As the competition between Chiang Ch'ing and Hua Kuo-feng accelerated within the Central Committee, the "principles" slogan appeared forty-two times in *People's Daily* and *Kuang-ming Daily*, while the Three Dos and Don'ts were featured only eleven times. One of the acts that appear to have triggered the arrest of the "Gang of Four" was a militant article by the Liang Hsiao group on the importance of making the "principles" notion "known to the broad revolutionary masses" lest a Teng Hsiao-p'ing spread revisionism among the people. The article appeared in *Kuang-ming Daily* on October 4, 1976. Onate, "Arrest," pp. 553–554.

93. "The Imposing Revolutionary Writings Will Be Passed on from Generation to Generation," *Jen-min jih-pao* (Peking, September 22, 1976), CMP-SPRCP-76-40, p. 3.

content of Mao Tse-tung thought than merely arriving at brief, oracular formulas was obviously at hand.[94] Hua Kuo-feng therefore sought to arm himself with the authority to issue those texts under his editorial imprimatur, in this way both bringing Maoist fundamentalism under control and establishing himself as the leading doctrinal disciple of his predecessor, the Chairman.[95]

Hua Kuo-feng's claim to be the editor of the Chairman's works depended on his gaining and maintaining control over Mao's ideological remains: the texts themselves. That was why the issue that actually provoked Hua's arrest of the "Gang of Four" was the question of archival access. It was when Hua learned from Wang Tung-hsing, the head of Mao's "8341" palace guard, that Chiang Ch'ing was taking documents out of Mao's archives and altering them for her own use that he swiftly moved to seize her and her three chief accomplices and to purge their closest henchmen.[96]

Just as the Mao archives were a source of textual authority, so did Mao's physical remains symbolize a source of charismatic authority. Mao's person and his persona were still linked in people's minds. Wanting to tap into that charismatic relationship, Hua Kuo-feng favored enshrining Mao's remains in a public monument in order to immure Mao's person directly under his own aegis. In the long term, routine visits to such a memorial would take the place of spontaneous demonstrations of devotion like the April 1976 T'ien-an men gatherings in Chou En-lai's memory. And in the short term, the erection of a monument to Mao would help close national ranks after the arrest of the "Gang of Four" on October 6, 1976.[97] At that time, though some leading party members argued that the tomb should be kept apart from the monument, Hua Kuo-feng persuaded the Central Committee to support his plan to establish a memorial hall.[98] The plan for a memorial hall, announced on October 8,[99] went hand in hand with the project to issue a new selection of Mao's works. In subsequent reports the building of the memorial hall and the publication of Mao's works were closely identified with Hua Kuo-feng and his victory over the "Gang of Four."[100] The "Gang of Four" was accused of resorting to "underhand manoeuvres to criminally

94. On the editing process before Mao's death, see Martin, *Cult and Canon*, pp. 44, 56.

95. Hua's appropriation of the role of official interpreter of Mao Tse-tung thought occurred abruptly on October 8. Martin, *Cult and Canon*, pp. 55, 62–63.

96. Onate, "Arrest," pp. 547–548.

97. Ibid., p. 540.

98. Personal communication from a Chinese informant. The decision to establish a memorial hall was made on October 7, only hours after the "Gang of Four" was put under arrest. Onate, "Arrest," p. 542.

99. "Decision on Establishment of Memorial Hall for Great Leader and Teacher Chairman Mao Tsetung," NCNA-English (Peking, October 8, 1976), CMP-SPRCP-76-42, p. 64.

100. "Chinese Capital Celebrates Publication of Volume Five of 'Selected Works of Mao Tsetung,'" NCNA-English (Peking, April 16, 1977), CMP-SPRCP-77-17, p. 184. By the end of

interfere with and sabotage the preservation of Chairman Mao's remains" in order to usurp party and state power, and Comrade Hua Kuo-feng was praised for "representing the wishes of hundreds of millions of people throughout the country" by having "smashed the plot of the 'Gang of Four'" and by having properly arranged for Chairman Mao's remains to be preserved.[101] "What Chairman Hua did," the Field Headquarters for Building the Chairman Mao Memorial Hall announced, "was what we desired"; and the hall was later to be described as the crystallization (*chieh-ching*) of the "aspirations of hundreds of millions of people."[102]

## THE CONSTRUCTION OF MAO'S MEMORIAL HALL

During the debate within the party over the memorial hall several different locations were suggested as building sites. Hua Kuo-feng proposed that the single building be placed in T'ien-an men Square itself between the Revolutionary History Museum and the Great Hall of the People, a site of considerable symbolic significance.[103] After his view prevailed, Chairman Hua personally initiated the construction work on Mao's shrine on November 24, 1976, before a huge color portrait of Chairman Mao and with earth movers and cranes standing by.[104] The announced purpose of building the memorial hall was "to perpetuate the memory of Chairman Mao Tsetung" so that "people for generations to come will be able to pay their respects here to Chairman Mao's remains, recall his magnificent contributions, review his teachings, and be personally touched by the education and inspiration that Chairman Mao gave."[105] The monument was not meant to be a

---

that same month, 28 million copies of the volume had been distributed. Martin, *Cult and Canon*, p. 68.

101. "Solemn Ceremony of Laying Cornerstone for Memorial Hall for Great Leader and Teacher Chairman Mao Tsetung Held in Peking," NCNA-English (Peking, Nov. 24, 1976), CMP-SPRCP-76-48. See also "Conference Representatives Take Part in Construction of Memorial Hall for Chairman Mao," NCNA-English (Peking, December 24, 1976), CMP-SPRCP-77-61, p. 164. For having chosen to build the hall in the first place, Hua was said to have "read the minds of the people." "Project for Future Generations," NCNA-English (Peking, November 25, 1976), CMP-SPRCP-76-48, p. 34.

102. "Deeply Cherish the Memory of Chairman Mao, Offer Our Red Hearts in Building the Memorial Hall," *Hung-ch'i*, no. 9, September 4, 1977, CMP-SPRCP-77-31, p. 61; caption under photograph of the Chairman Mao Memorial Hall on the front page of *Jen-min jih-pao*, NCNA-English (Peking, May 25, 1977) CMP-SPRCP-77-23, p. 15.

103. Private communication from a Chinese informant.

104. "Project for Future Generations," p. 34; "Solemn Ceremony of Laying Cornerstone for Memorial Hall for Great Leader and Teacher Chairman Mao Tsetung Held in Peking," NCNA-English (Peking, November 24, 1976), CMP-SPRCP-76-48, pp. 218, 220.

105. "Chairman Hua Kuo-feng's Speech," NCNA-English (Peking, November 24, 1976), CMP-SPRCP-76-48, p. 222.

sealed tomb, or *ling-mu,* which was traditionally reserved for the ruling class and set apart from the people.[106] Rather, it was designed to be a memorial hall, or *chi-nien t'ang,* that would preserve Mao's remains in order to objectify the memory of Mao, until then carried within the hearts and minds of the Chinese people.[107] This reification was also intended to lay the former Chairman to rest "amid pines and fresh flowers," as though his serene repose would somehow ensure social peace and tranquility.[108] The construction site itself, covered with fluttering red flags, became a symbolic arena where the speed and intensity of the work were interpreted as signs of devotion to Mao, Hua, and the people of China.[109] The style of work was that of the Great Leap Forward, charged with images of militant political struggle, devoted to the daily reading and discussion of Chairman Mao's new *Selected Works,* guided by model worker-heroes, and inspired by the revolutionary spirit of the Long March.[110] Devising a number of their own technical innovations "simply by thinking of Chairman Mao," the workers had by March 22, 1977, completed the construction of the 34-meter-high edifice for the Chairman Mao Memorial Hall.[111] The accomplishment in less than six months of this "unprecedented feat in the history of Chinese architecture," involving the labor of more than 700,000 people from all over China, represented "the crystallization of the will power and strength of the 800 million people of various nationalities."[112]

106. The architects at first drew up plans for a tomb with a blockhouse-like structure on the surface and with the remains preserved entirely or partly underground. After they were reminded that they had "to be sure to draw a clear line between [Mao's memorial] and a *ling-mu* of the ruling class" in which the building was intended to demonstrate the distance between the rulers and the people, the architects resolved to design a memorial hall instead of a tomb. "Mao chu-hsi chi-nien t'ang kuei-hua she-chi" 毛主席紀念堂規劃設計 [The planning and design of the Chairman Mao Memorial Hall], *Chien-chu hsueh-pao* 建築學報 [Journal of architecture] 4, no. 13, (1977): 32–33.

107. "Mao chu-hsi chi-nien t'ang," p. 33. The "permanent preservation of Chairman Mao's body" by a medical team drawn together from all over the country took ten months, as did the design and manufacture of a spotless crystal coffin. "Chairman Mao Memorial Hall Completed," NCNA-English (Peking, August 29, 1977), CMP-SPRCP-77-36, p. 179.

108. "Deeply Cherish the Memory of Chairman Mao, Offer Our Red Hearts in Building the Memorial Hall," *Hung-ch'i,* no. 9, September 4, 1977, CMP-SPRCP-77-31, p. 61. "The memorial hall is a place where Chairman Mao rests peacefully forever. This great project is of profound political significance, extremely solemn in nature and broadly meaningful to the masses" (ibid., p. 63).

109. "Conference Representatives," p. 164.

110. "Construction of Edifice for Chairman Mao Memorial Hall Completed Ahead of Schedule," NCNA-English (Peking, March 26, 1977), CMP-SPRCP-77-13, p. 164; "Deeply Cherish the Memory," pp. 62, 63; "Builders of Chairman Mao Memorial Hall," NCNA-English (Peking, March 28, 1977), CMP-SPRCP-77-14, p. 45.

111. "Deeply Cherish the Memory," p. 64; "Construction of Edifice," p. 164. NCNA also gives May 24 as the date of completion of the edifice. "Construction of Chairman Mao Memorial Hall Completed," NCNA-English (Peking, May 26, 1977), CMP-SPRCP-77-25, p. 65.

## CHIANG KAI-SHEK'S MEMORIAL HALL

Three years later surprisingly similar language was used to describe the Chiang Kai-shek Memorial Hall (*Chung-cheng chi-nien t'ang*): "This stately, elegant, huge construction is the crystallization (*chieh-ching*) of the blood and sweat of its building engineers, and it has drawn together in an ever more concentrated way the deepest veneration of the Chinese people, at home and abroad, in commemoration of revered Mr. Chiang."[113] In contrast to the Peking project, however, it was the engineers (*kung-ch'eng jen-yuan*) whose energies were vaunted in building Taipei's monument; and it was an individual designer and foreign technology that enabled the Chiang Kai-shek Memorial Hall to be constructed over three years' time, slowly growing "like a pupa" in its scaffold, by the Retired Servicemen's Engineering Agency.[114] Monetary donations from the public covered most of the U.S. $70,000,000 needed to finish the hall.[115]

Although the planners of the Chiang Kai-shek Memorial Hall wanted to use the most modern engineering and construction methods available throughout the world, they also wanted the building to "express the spirit of Chinese culture."[116] In the end they decided upon a classical Chinese palace

---

112. "Construction of Edifice," p. 164; "Construction of Chairman Mao Memorial Hall Completed," pp. 66, 179. For other references to the "unprecedented" nature of this "landmark" accomplishment, see: "Builders of Chairman Mao Memorial Hall," p. 45; "Worksite of Chairman Mao Memorial Hall on Eve of May Day," NCNA-English (Peking, April 28, 1977), CMP-SPRCP-77-19, p. 91; "Construction of Chairman Mao Memorial Hall Completed," p. 65.

113. Wang Ch'i-jung 王琦榕, "Hao-jan chih ch'i, ta-chung chih cheng: chü-yu to-chung yi-yi ti Chung-cheng chi-nien t'ang lo-ch'eng ch'i-yung"浩然之氣,大中之正:具有多重意義的中正紀念堂落成啓用 [Spirit of magnanimity, great mean and extreme rectitude: the completion and public opening of the profoundly significant Chiang Kai-shek Memorial Hall], *Kuang-hua* 光華 [Sinorama], vol. 5, no. 5 (May 1980), pp. 2–13, quote from p. 3.

114. Wang Ch'i-jung, "Hao-jan chih ch'i," pp. 3, 5, 13. Ground-breaking took place on October 31, 1976, the 90th birthday anniversary of the late President. Yü Kuo-hua 俞國華, "Chung-cheng chi-nien t'ang chih ch'ou-chien"中正紀念堂之籌建 [Planning the construction of the Chiang Kai-shek Memorial Hall], *Chung-yang yueh-k'an* 中央月刊 [Central Monthly], 12, no. 6 (1982): 29–34.

115. Wang Ch'i-jung, "Hao-jan chih ch'i," p. 3; "Chung-cheng chi-nien t'ang lo-ch'eng k'ai-fang"中正紀念堂落成開放 [Completion and opening of the Chiang Kai-shek Memorial Hall], *T'ai-wan hua-k'an tsa-chih* 臺灣畫刊雜誌 [Taiwan Illustrated Magazine], May 1980, p. 3.

116. Yü Kuo-hua, "Chung-cheng chi-nien t'ang," p. 31; Wang Ch'i-jung, "Hao-jan chih ch'i," p. 7. This was in keeping with the spirit of the construction of Sun Yat-sen's tomb, for which "everything was set up according to a scientific method." Lü Yen-chih 呂彥直, "Sun Chung-shan hsien-sheng ling-mu chien-chu t'u-an shuo-ming" 孫中山先生陵墓建築圖案説明 [An explanation of the architectural plans for Mr. Sun Chung-shan's mausoleum], *Liang yu* 良友 [Young companion] 2 (March 1926): 13.

style copied from the T'ien t'an (Altar of Heaven) in Peking.[117] The building, 70 meters high, was to be approached by a 215-meter processional boulevard through high white marble gates inscribed with the characters *Ta-chung chih cheng*, which included Chiang Kai-shek's name, Chung-cheng.[118] In finished form, the building's colors and shapes were intended to syncretize cherished values.

> The square (*cheng*) shape of the building represents the spirit of the mean and of rectitude (*chung-cheng*, which is also Chiang Kai-shek's name); the three-tiered staircase symbolizes the Three Principles of the People; the two-tiered eight-cornered roof eaves, built in the shape of the character *jen* (man) and coming together at the *pao-ting* (summit) converge with the sky (*t'ien*), symbolizing revered Mr. Chiang's belief that "Heaven and Man are One" (*T'ien jen ho i*).[119]

The main colors used in the building—blue and white—were those of the flag of the Nationalist regime, where they symbolized liberty and equality, while the color of the *pao-ting* suggested the Golden Mean.[120] The memorial hall was therefore intended to represent "the pure sincerity of our Leader that will be forever remembered by his fellow countrymen throughout the entire nation."[121]

It was thus the ethical stature and moral eminence of Chiang Kai-shek that were most heavily stressed in the intended design of the memorial hall. Less a monument to a historical giant or a shrine to a revolutionary demiurge, it was to be a tribute to a moral paragon, a glorification of the Generalissimo's lifelong devotion to public duty and his ethical commitment to self-cultivation.

> On entering the main hall, the visitor first sees a bronze statue of the late President... standing 9.8 meters high. The statue is so lifelike that one almost expects a kindly word or a gesture of benediction from the late President. His will is inscribed on the base of the statue, and six big characters, *lun-li* (ethics), *min-chu* (democracy) and *k'o-hsueh* (science) are inscribed on the marble statue. The late President's famous saying "To live is to seek a better life for all mankind; the meaning of life lies in the creation of a life beyond life" is engraved on the two sides of the main hall.[122]

The bronze statue of Chiang, dressed in traditional scholar's gown and seated squarely in a massive chair looking out and down upon the viewer, was meant to be looked up to, to be revered. Distant in death as in life, the

---

117. Wang Ch'i-jung, "Hao-jan chih ch'i," p. 4.
118. The phrase is taken from Wang Yang-ming's *Ch'uan-hsi lu.*
119. Wang Ch'i-jung, "Hao-jan chih ch'i," p. 4.
120. Ibid., p. 7. Yü Kuo-hua wrote that the color of gold represented "ascendant China in splendid brilliance"—*sheng hua kuang-hui.* Yü Kuo-hua, "Chung-cheng chi-nien t'ang," p. 32.
121. Yü Kuo-hua, "Chung-cheng chi-nien t'ang," p. 29.
122. Wang Ch'i-jung, "Hao-ran chih ch'i," pp. 7, 9.

leader's persona was to be approached respectfully in a spirit of remote devotion rather than one of intimate worship.

## MAO'S MONUMENT

The marble statue of Mao Tse-tung, on the other hand, was designed to present the late Chairman in a much more accessible pose. One-third the size of Chiang's likeness, the statue of Mao portrayed the Chairman with book in hand, legs casually crossed, head slightly askew, and a kindly smile upon his face as if he were about to receive a visitor.[123] The effigy was meant to be approached at eye level, directly and forthrightly; and if this was not in fact the way viewers usually drew nigh, it was not because of the statue itself. Rather, it was the very hall in which the statue sat that imposed inhibitions upon the visitors to the monument.

The Mao Tse-tung Memorial Hall was intended to be "a magnificent and imposing structure in national style."[124] It was deliberately designed not for visitors but for "homagers."[125] The building's materials and accoutrements were a synthesis of all things Chinese, beginning with the workers themselves, who were drawn together from many different parts of the country.[126] Visitors from Yenan brought soil from the cave where Chairman Mao had lived, and Hunanese lumbermen cut the best fir they could find to be sent as timber to the capital.[127] Building stone came from all over China: granite, white marble, and terrazzo from Fukien, Shantung, Kiangsu, Szechwan, Chekiang, Liaoning, Sinkiang, Kwangtung, and Hupei.[128] And placed alongside the foundation stone were rocks brought from the summit of Mount Joimo Lungma (Everest), while the mortar for building the base was prepared with water from the Taiwan Straits.[129] In the same fashion, the landscaping of the Memorial Hall was done with as many different regional plants as possible, and paintings within the Memorial Hall depicted scenes from the revolutionary past drawn from places all around China.[130]

123. "Chairman Mao Memorial Hall Completed in Peking," NCNA-English (Peking, September 1, 1977), CMP-SPRCP-77-37, p. 76. The original plan called for him to sit with legs apart and with a red halo painted imposingly on the wall behind him. This was deemed too formal. "Mao chu-hsi chi-nien-t'ang," pp. 36, 45.

124. "Solemn Ceremony of Laying Cornerstone," p. 219.

125. "Worksite of Chairman Mao Memorial Hall," p. 92; "Mao chu-hsi chi-nien-t'ang," p. 36.

126. "Worksite of Chairman Mao Memorial Hall," p. 93.

127. "Conference Representatives Take Part," pp. 307–308.

128. "Wide Support in Building Chairman Mao Memorial Hall," NCNA-English (Peking, June 10, 1977), CMP-SPRCP-77-25, p. 89; "Mao chu-hsi chi-nien t'ang," p. 37.

129. "Chairman Mao Memorial Hall Completed in Peking," p. 76.

130. "Wide Support in Building Chairman Mao Memorial Hall," p. 88. See also "Construction of Chairman Mao Memorial Hall Completed," pp. 65, 76.

The architects who designed the hall were keenly conscious of spatial relationships within T'ien-an men Square, the surface of which was now expanded by several hectares of roadways around the monument.[131] The human capacity of the square—which was now 500 meters wide and 800 meters deep—grew from 400,000 to 600,000 people: no small consideration, since the memorial hall was explicitly intended to overlook mass rallies yet to come.[132] The latter expectation also dictated the precise location of the *chi-nien t'ang*. The designers decided to put the hall directly in between the cenotaph and the gate and consciously broke with "tradition" (*ch'uan-t'ung*) by making the northern side of the hall its entrance.[133] In this way, they hoped to use Mao's Memorial Hall to draw together and complete all of the other structures facing onto the square: the Revolutionary Museum to the east, the Great Hall of the People to the west, and T'ien-an men itself to the north.[134]

For many people the actual effect was otherwise. The vista from T'ien-an men Gate down to the Cheng-yang Gate was now blocked by the shrine. Mao himself sat on the northern side of his monument, facing the Forbidden City. Whereas an emperor in life and death always faced south, overlooking the vast *t'ien-hsia* beyond Ch'ien-men, the Chairman's effigy reversed the direction, looking up at the old imperial palaces, bringing the openness of the square to a close. Visually, the anticipated sweep of space—the accepted scope of charismatic political authority, so to speak—was abutted by this placement. The architects had designed the memorial hall to represent the permanence of Chairman Mao's revolution, but the unintended effect was quite the opposite. The building interrupted the continuities of the square. Symbolically, the unending flow of temporal change—Mao's own vision of permanent revolution—was blocked and then truncated. The mausoleum seemed to seal off history rather than to enlarge it.

## THE CHIANG CULTURAL CENTER

Whereas Mao's Memorial Hall interrupted what had been open space, Chiang Kai-shek's monument enclosed what had been 250,000 square meters of crowded urban residential areas in the southeastern part of Taipei.[135] The buildings there were razed to make room for the memorial hall itself, plus a vast park designed by one of the most experienced horticul-

131. "Deeply Cherish the Memory of Chairman Mao," pp. 65–66.
132. "Mao chu-hsi chi-nien t'ang," p. 4.
133. Precedent for this could be found in Mao's earlier decision to have the Revolutionary Heroes Monument face north, as a way of focusing political rallies between the cenotaph and the rostrum at T'ienanmen. Ibid.
134. Ibid., pp. 4, 13.
135. Wang Ch'i-jung, "Hao-jan chih ch'i," p. 5.

turalists in Taiwan for recreational use by the public.[136] Eventually, a national opera house and a concert hall will be built on either side of the approach to the memorial hall, while—most telling of all—land under the complex will be excavated to make room for a 600-vehicle parking lot.[137] The result will be to reinforce even more the secular qualities of the Chiang Kai-shek Memorial as a civic center, which is already spoken of as only one of many similar architectural structures around the world.[138]

The Chiang Kai-shek Memorial Hall was opened by President Chiang Ching-kuo on grave-sweeping day (April 4), 1980, in a special dedication ceremony to commemorate the fifth anniversary of the Generalissimo's death. The main room of the exhibition hall on the first floor was dominated by an enormous oil painting of Sun Yat-sen and Chiang Kai-shek together on the eve of the Northern Expedition. In the display cases themselves were exhibited over three hundred memorabilia of the late president, uniforms and medals, and more than a hundred historical photographs. In a separate theater within the memorial hall documentary movies were shown depicting important moments in Chiang's career. Throughout, the Generalissimo's piety, studiousness, and benevolence were strongly emphasized.[139] The inauguration of the memorial hall was meant to laud the dead leader's personal virtues and historical accomplishments while setting them firmly in the past.[140] The commemorants who met that day to observe the anniversary of Chiang's death did not celebrate his immortal presence in their midst. Instead, they "reflected back upon (*chui-nien*) the former president's moral accomplishments (*te-yeh*) and gracious benevolence (*en-tse*)."[141]

## THE OPENING OF MAO'S HALL

A quite different tone pervaded the ceremonies during the grand rally in Peking held on September 9, 1977, marking the first anniversary of the death of Chairman Mao and the opening of his memorial hall. In contrast to

136. Ibid., pp. 3, 9.

137. Ibid., p. 13; "Chung-cheng chi-nien t'ang lo-ch'eng k'ai-fang," p. 3.

138. "The monument will undoubtedly take its place beside the Washington, Jefferson, and Lincoln memorials in Washington and even the Taj Mahal in India." Wang Ch'i-jung, "Hao-jan chih ch'i," p. 5.

139. Ibid., pp. 3, 5; "Chung-cheng chi-nien t'ang lo-ch'eng k'ai-fang," pp. 4, 9; Ho Ying-ch'in 何應欽, "P'ei-i yü tao tse min shu shih te li-shih wei jen" 配義於道澤民淑世的歷史偉人 [A great historical figure, dutiful to the Way, bountiful to the people, beneficent to the world], *Chung-yang yueh-k'an* 12, no. 6 (April 16, 1982): 19–22.

140. The historification began the moment official mourning ended. The closing of his casket, which marked Chiang Kai-shek's separation from the Chinese people, was "a historically significant moment" (*li-shih hsing te shih-k'o*). *Tsung-t'ung Chiang kung*, p. 3.

141. "Chiang kung shih-shih wu chou-nien" 蔣公逝世五週年 [Fifth anniversary of revered Mr. Chiang's death], *Mei-tsai Chung-hua* 美哉中華 [Beautiful China!], May 1980, p. 4.

the Kuomintang ceremony, Chairman Mao's rally was meant to celebrate a force still alive in people's hearts and minds. In his speech to the homagers, Hua Kuo-feng said: "Chairman Mao will always be with us; he will always be in the hearts of each comrade and friend among us; he will always live in the hearts of the Chinese people and of revolutionary people the world over."[142]

Yet even though the slogan "Chairman Mao lives in our hearts forever" was heard across China, there was a certain tiredness in its repetition; and the fact that it was most widely spread in the form of an eight-fen postage stamp suggests how phantasmal that living presence was becoming.[143] Hua Kuo-feng might well insist in his rally speech that "all attempts by class enemies at home and abroad to make our party change its Marxist-Leninist line, which was formulated by Chairman Mao, are no more than reactionary daydreaming."[144] But Teng Hsiao-p'ing now sat smiling in the front row of the audience, and time was running out for Chairman Hua.

As Hua Kuo-feng's position in the leadership began to slip and then drastically slide, the memorial hall that he had ordered built began to become something of an embarrassment. After the Third Plenum in December 1978 set China on an entirely new political and economic course, visitors from abroad who asked to visit the mausoleum were politely discouraged.[145] Rumors began to spread that the embalming of Mao's corpse had been a failure, and that his remains were decomposing. In January 1979 there were even demonstrations alongside the Memorial Hall calling for a monument to be built for Chou En-lai in between the Chairman's mausoleum and the Revolutionary Heroes Monument.[146] As other Communist leaders were honored by special posthumous rehabilitation ceremonies, Mao's spiritual hegemony was challenged. By 1980 it was an open secret in Peking that

142. "Hua chu-hsi tsai lung-chung chi-nien wei-ta te ling-hsiu ho tao-shih Mao chu-hsi shih-shih i chou-nien chi Mao chu-hsi chi-nien t'ang lo-ch'eng tien-li ta-hui shang te chiang-hua" 華主席在隆重紀念偉大的領袖和導師毛主席逝世一週年及毛主席紀念堂落成典禮大會上的講話 [Chairman Hua's speech at the ceremonies solemnly marking the first anniversary of our great leader and teacher Chairman Mao's death and the inauguration of the Chairman Mao Memorial Hall], Chien-chu hsueh-pao 建築學報 [Journal of Architecture] 4, no. 2 (1977). See also "Chairman Hua's Speech at Grand Rally Marking First Anniversary of Death of Chairman Mao and Opening of Memorial Hall," NCNA-English (Peking, September 9, 1977), CMP-SPRCP-77-39, p. 105.

143. "Peking Papers Carry Articles and Photos Marking Anniversary of Chairman Mao's Death," NCNA-English (Peking, September 7, 1977), CMP-SPRCP-77-39, p. 49; "Commemorative Stamps on Anniversary of Chairman Mao's Death," NCNA-English (Peking, September 8, 1977), CMP-SPRCP-77-39, pp. 104–105.

144. "Chairman Hua's Speech at Grand Rally," p. 108.

145. Mathews, One Billion, p. 327 (n. 2 above); Fox Butterfield, China: Alive in the Bitter Sea (New York: Times Books, 1982), p. 302; and Martin, Cult and Canon, p. 111 (n. 1 above).

146. Martin, Cult and Canon, pp. 111–112.

some party leaders actually wanted to tear down the Chairman's Memorial Hall. Teng Hsiao-p'ing, now firmly in power, told Oriana Fallaci: "Regarding the mausoleum, I can tell you that I do not agree in changing things. Now it is there, and it is not appropriate to take it away. It was not appropriate to build it, it would not be appropriate to take it off. Should we demolish it many people would be hurt and there would be a lot of rumors. Yes, many people are speculating on the subject, but we don't have such an idea."[147] The result was a compromise: the memorial hall would be kept, but Mao would have to share it with other important party leaders as a historical monument.

## THE HISTORIFICATION OF MAO

During 1979–1980, both at the highest levels of the party and among the populace itself, there was a fundamental reevaluation of Mao Tse-tung's historical role.[148] By 1982—when preparations commenced for the ninetieth anniversary of Mao's birth—leaders' opinions began to move toward a more balanced view of the late Chairman's historical accomplishments.[149] Public opinion quickly followed suit, and as a spate of movies about Mao, including an eighty-minute documentary of his life which played to packed audiences in Peking theaters during December 1983, were released to coincide with the birthday celebrations, the media began to praise Mao once more with enthusiasm—albeit tacitly qualified by the observation that Mao was only one among a number of meritorious Communist Chinese leaders. At the same time the official press denied that there had ever been an intent to denigrate the late Chairman, despite the fact that his economic policies had been utterly changed.[150]

The rehabilitation of Mao Tse-tung was safely accomplished in several different ways. The first was simply historiographical. It was claimed that, in a longer perspective, Mao's positive contributions to the revolution over-

147. Mathews, *One Billion*, p. 326; Fallaci, "Deng: Cleaning up Mao's 'Feudal Mistakes,'" p. D-6 (n. 3 above).

148. Martin, *Cult and Canon*, pp. 116, 129, 138. The phrase *fei-Mao-hua* (de-Maoization) began to appear in the Chinese press in March 1979. My conception of historification owes much to Joseph Levenson's notion of the "(merely) historically significant." Joseph R. Levenson, *Confucian China and Its Modern Fate*, volume 3, "The Problem of Historical Significance" (London: Routledge and Kegan Paul, 1965), p. 114.

149. This is based on the author's conversations with party historians in China. The official document that eventually summed up the compromise accepted by the top party leadership was the resolution adopted by the Sixth Plenum of the Eleventh Central Committee in June 1981: *Kuan-yü chien-kuo yi-lai tang te jo-kan li-shih wen-t'i te chueh-i* 關於建國以來黨的若干歷史問題的決疑 [Resolution of certain questions in the history of our party since the founding of the People's Republic of China] (Hong Kong, 1981).

150. *New York Times*, December 27, 1983, p. A-3.

shadowed his many errors after liberation. Second was the notion that Mao Tse-tung thought was not the creation of Chairman Mao alone; it was the summation of the party's collective experience in applying the principles of Marxism-Leninism to the Chinese revolutionary moment. Naturally, the greatest individual contribution—the "principal element"—was Mao's union of Marxist theory with Chinese practice; but taken altogether, Mao Tse-tung thought "was the crystallization of our party's collective wisdom," the distillation of the recent history of the Chinese people.[151] What had begun as one man's theory of universal class struggle ended by becoming an ideology of national consciousness, a "spiritual mainstay" of the Chinese people, somewhat like Sun Yat-sen's *San-min chu-i.*[152]

Third, Mao was given a particular niche in modern Chinese history—a history that had produced him during turbulent times long passed by. As Chairman Hu Yao-pang put it on the ninetieth anniversary of Mao's birth: "Periods of great struggle necessarily produce outstanding personages. Conversely, outstanding personages at the same time push history forward. Comrade Mao Tse-tung was precisely the greatest and most outstanding figure during those hundred years or more."[153] Party propagandist Lu Ting-yi extended this historicism by positing a two-stage theory of the Chinese revolution. He argued that each of these stages (the revolutionary phase before 1949 and the stage of socialist construction after liberation) had in turn distinct periods of youth and maturity. Many failed to realize that even though the party had reached maturity in its revolutionary phase, it was still in its infancy in the stage of socialist construction. Lu thus implied that while Mao's revolutionary praxis had perfectly met the needs of the revolutionary era, it was not well suited to an age when the greatest priority was to build a "wealthy and strong China" (*fu-ch'iang te Chung-kuo*).[154]

Fourth, Mao was turned into an object of history rather than its subject and master. This transformation accompanied the appearance, at the time of his ninetieth-birthday celebration, of a collection of 372 of Mao's letters, dating from 1920 to 1965. The letters were represented as an entirely new category of Mao's writing which would be of important use to "theoretical,

151. "Mao Tse-tung ssu-hsiang yung fang kuang-mang" 毛澤東思想永放光芒 [Mao Tse-tung thought will shine forever], *Jen-min jih-pao* 人民日報, December 26, 1983, p. 1.

152. As Dr. Weigelin-Schwiedrzik suggests, this "relativization" of Mao's role in the history of the party implies both a less individualistic theoretical contribution and a more collective political role. Susanne Weigelin-Schwiedrzik, "Parteigeschichtsschreibung in der VR China—Typen, Methoden, Themen und Functionen." Inaugural doctoral dissertation, Ruhr-Universität Bochum, 1982, pp. 69–70.

153. Hu Yao-pang 胡耀邦, "Tsui hao te chi-nien" 最好的紀念 [The best memory], *Jen-min jih-pao*, December 26, 1983, p. 1. One instantly thinks of Plekhanov's historiography.

154. Lu Ting-yi 陸定一, "Yung Mao Tse-tung ssu-hsiang tso-hao cheng tang kung-tso" 用毛澤東思想作好整黨工作 [Use Mao Tse-tung thought to carry out the work of rectifying the party], *Jen-min jih-pao*, December 24, 1983, p. 3.

intellectual and cultural workers for the study and research of Mao Tse-tung thought and for the study and research of our Party's history."[155]

The final way of confronting the late Chairman's persona without either destroying or succumbing to it was to place Mao among a pantheon of party elders. As the ninetieth anniversary of his birth drew near, Mao was increasingly identified as one of an "older generation of proletarian revolutionaries" who were founders of the Chinese Communist Party, the People's Liberation Army, and the People's Republic of China.[156] Finally, on December 23, it was formally announced that Mao's mausoleum would be "enriched" with a new exhibit containing mementos honoring Mao, Liu Shao-ch'i, Chou En-lai, and Chu Te.[157] The four "commemorative rooms" were devoted to the historical activities of these revolutionary figures. Upstairs, a movie theater ran fifteen-minute showings of a documentary called "Brilliance Forever Lasting" (Kuang-hui yung ts'un) about these leaders, while a gift shop sold thermometers, chopsticks, and other souvenirs inscribed with the name "Chairman Mao Memorial Hall."[158]

Clearly, Chairman Mao was meant to be receding, like his comrades, into the collective memory of the Chinese people. Their "meritorious service (hsun-yeh) survives forever"—People's Daily said—"illuminating one thousand autumns."[159] Yet the museum had not altogether ceased being a mausoleum, which—after all—had always been its dominant architectural function. China's top leaders did visit the memorial rooms (shih), but they also felt obliged to "pay their respects to the remains of Comrade Mao Tse-tung" in the larger hall (t'ang) where his body still lay in the crystal-covered sarcophagus.[160] One cannot simply go and gaze at the historical exhibits detachedly, like paying a call on the Museum of Revolutionary History on the eastern side of T'ien-an men, just across that great square. One must approach t'ang and shih together, with due reverence and awe for

155. Editorial, Jen-min jih-pao, December 25, 1983, p. 1. It was just such a group of historians who gathered at Ch'ang-sha on the anniversary of Mao's birth and who were told by Wang Chen, director of the Central Party School, that "the formation and development of Mao Tse-tung thought is a glorious chapter in our party's history."Jen-min jih-pao, December 27, 1983, p. 4.

156. Jen-min jih-pao, December 24, 1983, p. 1. Earlier in 1983, Mao's long overshadowed patron, Li Ta-chao, had been celebrated in a special ceremony at his gravestone in Wan-an Cemetery in Peking's western suburbs. China Daily, October 31, 1983, p. 1.

157. Associated Press Release, San Francisco Chronicle, December 23, 1983, p. 18. See also Lowell Dittmer, "Death and Transfiguration: Liu Shaoqi's Rehabilitation and Contemporary Chinese Politics," Journal of Asian Studies 40, no. 3 (May 1981): 479.

158. Jen-min jih-pao, December 24, 1983; New York Times, December 27, 1983, p. A-3; Michael Browning, "Chinese Officially Remember Mao: All His Flowers, Violins and Smiles," Miami Herald, December 20, 1983, p. A-14.

159. Jen-min jih-pao, December 27, 1983, p. 1.

160. Ibid.

the body still housed there.[161] In that sense, the monument remains a *lingmu*. The boundary between person and persona, between thinking and thought, is indistinct. The central tomb and the axial rooms awkwardly contain both parts of Mao, so that the personal shrine and the public memorial are mutually denatured. Like Chiang Kai-shek's corpse, which is said to be only halfway home to its final resting place, Mao's body is preserved in a kind of limbo, uneasily caught midway between individual transcendence and collective immortality. Sun Yet-sen's corpse was more definitively entombed, immured in the side of Purple Mountain. And the ashes of Chou En-lai, after all, were finally returned to the ancestral dust of China. Chairman Mao's remains, in the end, survive, uncomfortably, vulnerable to public view.[162]

161. Mathews, *One Billion*, pp. 327–328.

162. According to rumor, a deranged woman who claimed that Mao Tse-tung had killed her entire family made an attempt to destroy his corpse during the summer of 1984.

# TWELVE

# Death in the People's Republic of China

## Martin K. Whyte

*If this movement [for cremation] really gains headway, it will mark one of the sharpest breaks with tradition since the philosopher Mo Tzu vainly fulminated against the Confucianists for encouraging lavish funerals [in the fifth century B.C.].—Derk Bodde, Peking Diary (1949)*

*If there is any feng-shui at all, the Communist Party and the cooperatives will be enough feng-shui.—Chinese peasant slogan (1958)*

*The struggle between the old and the new does take place not only on the barricades, not only in the economic and political field, but also in the resting places of the dead.—Soviet ritual specialist (1970)*

Communist revolutions are something out of the ordinary because they attempt a thorough transformation, not only of political and economic structures, but of the very way people live—their family lives, rituals and customs, and values. Even the way people deal with death and funerals becomes a political issue, as the final opening quotation indicates.[1] Our fascination with the Communist revolution in China, a country with such ancient traditions and deeply honored rituals, comes in part from curiosity about what happens in this sort of situation where "irresistible force meets an immovable object." Funeral reform efforts have been initiated by the Chinese Communists since before 1949, and in this chapter I attempt to assess those efforts. In particular, I am concerned here with why and how the Chinese Communist Party (hereafter CCP) has attempted to change "the Chinese way of death," how successful these efforts have been, and what the meaning and implications of the current set of funeral practices are.

The evidence for many of the generalizations about changes in funeral customs that I will present is admittedly less solid and systematic than would be ideal. For the most part I will be piecing together information from scattered press reports and observations by visitors to China. One

---

1. Opening quotations are from Derk Bodde, *Peking Diary* (1950; reprint edition New York: Fawcett, 1967), p. 196; Albert Ravenholt, "The Gods Must Go!" *American Universities Field Staff Reports, East Asian Series*, Nov. 22, 1958, p. 5; and G. Gerodnik, cited in Christel Lane, *The Rites of Rulers* (Cambridge: Cambridge University Press, 1981), p. 83.

more systematic type of evidence will be used: detailed reports on forty-one
rural and seventy-nine urban funerals carried out in China during the 1960s
and 1970s, but even these permit only tentative conclusions about what has
happened to funeral rituals in the People's Republic of China.[2]

## THE OBJECTS OF CHANGE

Funeral customs in China in 1949 for the most part still reflected "traditional" practices. As other chapters in this volume describe, and the existing
literature on the topic elaborates in greater detail, these practices involved
a complex and fairly standardized set of ritual activities surrounding
the funeral itself, the procession and burial, and subsequent mourning
obligations.[3] I will not give a detailed description of the various rituals here.
However, several general points should be noted.[4] First, even in urban
areas, most individuals died at home and death rituals were centered around
the home. Hospitals, funeral parlors, and other public facilities had not in-
truded much into funeral activities in mid-twentieth-century China. Second,
there was not much difference between funeral rituals in urban and rural
places. In fact, the distinction is somewhat arbitrary for pre-1949 China,
since many urbanites were transported back to their native villages after
death (if they had not already gone there in their declining years) to be

2. These descriptions of funerals were collected during two large interviewing projects
conducted in Hong Kong jointly with William Parish. The first project, in 1973–74, focused on
village life, and the second, in 1977–78, focused on urban life. The limitations of these cases
should be clear. In addition to the modest numbers involved, the rural interviews all concerned
villages in only one province, Kwangtung, and obviously include no cases for the years after
1974. The urban funerals described include cases in a variety of cities and towns in China, but
since they stop at 1978, they also include virtually no cases of funerals in the post-Mao period.
See the sections on funerals in William L. Parish and Martin King Whyte, Village and Family in
Contemporary China (Chicago: University of Chicago Press, 1978); and Whyte and Parish,
Urban Life in Contemporary China (Chicago: University of Chicago Press, 1984).
3. See, in addition to other chapters in this volume, J. J. M. de Groot, The Religious
System of China, 6 vols. (Leiden: Brill, 1892–1910); Annie Cormack, Everyday Customs in
China, 4th ed. (Edinburgh: Moray Press, 1935); Ku Chieh-kang 顧頡剛 and Liu Wan-chang
劉萬章, Su-Yueh ti hun-sang 蘇粵的婚喪 [Marriage and funerals in Kiangsu and Kwangtung]
(Canton, 1928); Emily Ahern, The Cult of the Dead in a Chinese Village (Stanford: Stanford
University Press, 1973); Laurence Thompson, "Funeral Rites in Taiwan," in his The Chinese
Way in Religion (Encino, Calif.: Dickenson, 1973), pp. 160–69; and James L. Watson, "Of
Flesh and Bones: The Management of Death Pollution in Cantonese Society," in M. Bloch and
J. Parry, eds., Death and the Regeneration of Life (Cambridge: Cambridge University Press,
1982), pp. 155–186.
4. Here and throughout, I will be dealing only with the funerals of Han Chinese, rather
than those of China's many minority groups. I will also ignore the funeral practices of Chinese
Christians.

buried there. And many of our most detailed descriptions of "traditional" funerals come not from rural areas but from China's cities.[5]

That is not to say that funerals were entirely uniform, however. In addition to the modest regional variations in funeral observances that are extensively discussed elsewhere in this volume, there were other important bases of differential behavior in marking death. Perhaps the most important involved wealth and social status. The wealthiest families, whether rural or urban, were obligated and able to observe funerals in a lavish way, with great expenditure, conspicuous displays, and scores of hired priests of various types, musicians, bearers, and others participating.[6] In addition, only the wealthy were likely to maintain extensive mourning obligations over several generations and build expensive tombs and conduct worship at them. The poor, in contrast, usually had to make do with a bare minimum of expense and ceremony at funerals, and they were unlikely to be able to afford the expenses of a tomb, so that after a couple of generations their dead ancestors would be effectively "forgotten."[7] Other important sources of variation in funeral practices were age and marital status. The most elaborate funerals were held for those, male and female, who had lived full lives and had many descendants. For those without offspring or who were unmarried, things were much simplified, and the death of a child produced very little ceremony at all. In all cases those in older generations did not don mourning and observe rituals for deceased relatives younger than themselves. So when the Chinese Communists came to power they confronted a complex set of funeral rituals that differed more by wealth and family status than by rural or urban location.

## CCP POLICY TOWARD FUNERALS

The Communists were not the first Chinese rulers to try to change funeral practices. Down through the centuries Confucianists had criticized what

5. For example, Amoy is the site observed by de Groot in *The Religious System of China*; Peking, by Cormack in *Everyday Customs in China*; and Foochow, by Justus Doolittle in *Social Life of the Chinese* (New York: Harper and Brothers, 1865).

6. Some idea of the pomp involved can be gained from the sketches and photographs included in some of the works already cited, such as those by de Groot and Cormack, or from the funeral procession in Peking in the 1930s shown in Wang Ta-kuan's hand scroll, "The Capital in Late Winter." See Geremie Barmie, "A Vision of Old Beijing," *Chinese Literature*, Summer 1984, pp. 127–134.

7. One source notes an unusual claim by local officials in the 1950s—that before the revolution many peasants were so poor that they could not afford to bury their dead decently and just left them "lying around anywhere." See Adalbert de Segonzac, *Visa for Peking* (London: Heinemann, 1956), p. 194. The implication was that the revolution made it possible for poor peasants to meet a traditional obligation—to provide a decent burial for deceased relatives.

they saw as excessive superstition and heterodox religious elements in funeral rituals. And a fairly successful effort was made from the Sung dynasty onward to prohibit the cremations that Buddhist influence had made increasingly popular earlier and to require burial of the dead.[8] The Republican Revolution in 1911 ushered in efforts to foster simpler and Westernized forms of funerals. The hostility toward Confucianism of the May Fourth period added to this trend, and we have a fascinating account from Hu Shih in 1919 of how he agonized over what "modern" customs should be followed in his mother's funeral. For example, he wanted to do away with all offering of sacrifices for his mother, but when he was implored by his grandmother, he allowed one consolidated sacrifice session, but with bowing rather than the full kowtow expected. And he intended to wear only the black armband being popularized by the Republican government, but on seeing all of his relatives in full hempen mourning garb he consented to wear hemp, but with no hat, no mourning staff, and no straw belt, as were customarily required.[9] Still, as in so many other realms, it seems that the effort to replace traditional funerals with black armbands and simple funerals made little headway before 1949 except among Westernized intellectuals.

When the CCP came to power they more ambitiously set out to change the entire range of funeral behavior. What did China's new leaders find objectionable about complex and arcane death rituals, which might seem irrelevant to questions of political power and economic construction?[10] In fact, just about every element except showing respect for the deceased was repugnant to the CCP. In part the traditional rituals reflect a set of religious

8. See F. Lisowski, "The Practice of Cremation in China," *Eastern Horizon* 19 (1980): 21–24. Cremation was still used for many Buddhist monks and nuns and some lay persons into the twentieth century, but otherwise burial had become universal. On this point I would quibble with James Watson's claim in chapter 1 that the required structure of Chinese rituals concerned funerary rites only, and not rites of disposal, and that cremation was an accepted option. While we do not have systematic data for many different parts of China, I am not aware of regions in the twentieth century in which cremation was commonly practiced by Chinese not affiliated with certain Buddhist sects, and there is plenty of anecdotal evidence that the switch to cremation the CCP tried to enforce, to be discussed below, was experienced by many as a traumatic violation of the required ritual sequence.

9. See Hu Shih 胡適, "Wo tui-yü sang-li ti kai-ke" 我對於喪禮的改革 [My reform of funeral rites], *Hsin ch'ing-nien* 新青年 6 (1919): 568–77, translated in E. T. C. Werner, *Autumn Leaves* (Shanghai: Kelly and Walsh, 1928), pp. 69–95.

10. The pages that follow are based on a variety of sources. Particularly useful are Donald MacInnis, *Religious Policy and Practice in Communist China* (New York: Macmillan, 1972); Holmes Welch, *Buddhism under Mao* (Cambridge: Harvard University Press, 1972); Richard C. Bush, Jr., *Religion in Communist China* (Nashville: Abingdon Press, 1970); and Ho Ta-chang 何大章 et al., *Yu mei-yu keui-shen ho ming-yun?* 有沒有鬼神和命運 [Do ghosts and spirits and fate exist or not?] (Canton: Kwangtung People's Press, 1963).

beliefs that the CCP considers superstitious and harmful.[11] The idea that there are spirits (ancestral or otherwise) and ghosts who have to be worshipped or ritually appeased, and that an individual's fate is affected by the performance of such acts, challenges the CCP's contention that there is no supernatural world or hereafter, and that man is the master of his own fate. Concern about whether one will have male descendants to conduct the proper activities to keep one's soul well cared for is also one source of the preference for sons that poses a major obstacle to the official birth-control program. Also, the idea that the proper siting of graves can have an effect on later generations conflicts with the same philosophy, and *feng-shui* beliefs also may interfere with "rational" plans for constructing roads and buildings.[12](Maurice Freedman would have argued, as does Rubie Watson in chapter 9 in this volume, that belief in *feng-shui* also fosters individualistic or family-based competition for wealth. This competition conflicts with the broader solidarity and asceticism espoused by the new order.) Funeral practices also help to reinforce kinship ties and lineage rivalries, conflicting with the universalistic creed promoted by the CCP. Loyalty should be directed toward the party and the nation, rather than toward one's own family and lineage, and control over choice burial sites should not be used to express dominance over other families and lineages. In addition, the ritual specialists relied on are particularly hated, not only as quacks earning money by false pretenses, but as potential rival authority figures.

Another set of CCP objections is related more to economic and social status. CCP analysts argue that traditional funeral customs involve substantial wasteful expenditure. In part there is waste to the nation. The number of trees that must be cut annually to supply the heavy wooden coffins endangers China's forests and may foster erosion. Similarly, the cloth used

11. In most periods the CCP has attempted to make a distinction between religion and superstition which seems artificial to Western anthropologists. Religion refers to the worship activities of Islam, Christianity, and Buddhism, and is tolerated under various Chinese constitutions, in spite of the official atheism of the government. Other traditional religious practices, such as those associated with Taoism and folk religion and therefore including almost all elements of funeral ritual, are defined as superstition, which is seen as harmful and subject to state coercion. See the discussion in Ya Han-chang, "On the Question of Religious Superstition" and "On the Difference between the Theist Idea, Religion, and Feudal Superstition," in MacInnis, *Religious Policy and Practice in Communist China*; and Pan-yueh-t'an editorial board, "Do Away with Feudal Superstitions," *Pan-yueh-t'an*, no. 24, December 1983, translated in Foreign Broadcast Information Service, *Daily Report: People's Republic of China* (hereafter *FBIS*), Jan. 17, 1983, pp. K-17–22.

12. See Maurice Freedman, "Chinese Geomancy: Some Observations from the Hong Kong Case," in his *The Study of Chinese Society* (Stanford: Stanford University Press, 1979). By the same token, traditional pollution fears associated with death can cause objections to the construction of new hospitals, old-age homes, and funeral parlors.

for both burial and mourning clothes is seen as competing with more essential daily needs for clothing. Perhaps most important, the land taken up with scattered graves is considerable, and in many parts of China barren hillsides are neither available nor preferred. Thus a large amount of arable land is used for graves, aggravating China's problem of shrinking farmland. In addition, graves scattered in the fields make mechanized farming next to impossible. (Some commentators suggest deep burials with no headstones as a compromise solution—in other words, you can bury someone in the fields, so long as you don't mind their being plowed over.) There is also the manufacturing capacity that is given over to spirit incense, paper ritual objects, and other ritual paraphernalia which would be better off put to other uses.[13] In addition, the ritual specialists who make their living partly or wholly from funerals would be more usefully employed in "productive" labor.

Waste also affects individuals and families, it is argued. In general financial terms, funerals constitute a heavy burden, and poor families often feel they must spend beyond their means and go into debt to provide a proper funeral for their parents or other kin. John Buck estimated that the average peasant circa 1930 spent about three months' family income on a funeral. A study in Peking in 1926–27 found that funeral expenses varied from one-eighth of a month's income (for a two-year-old child of a poor family) to almost four years' family income (for a wealthy widow); in the same period a study of Shanghai textile workers found that funeral costs ranged between two days' and more than four months' family income.[14] Furthermore, funerals provide an arena for status competition, as wealthier families use their resources to engage in lavish displays and processions to demonstrate their superiority (and perhaps persuade their poorer neighbors that in doing so they are ensuring the continued prosperity of their descendants). At least until recently, open status competition of this sort, particularly based upon wealth, has been anathema to the CCP. One might, of course, question whether the CCP objection is to the expenditures involved per se, or whether what is at issue is more the fact that these are simply expenditures that the government has no effective control over. In other words, the concern here may be as much political as economic.

13. In 1958 an article appeared in the press that attempted to quantify these various forms of "waste" for Shantung Province: see Chao Chien-min, "Reform Funeral Customs, Encourage Thrifty Burials without Coffins and Graves without Sepulchral Mounds," translated in MacInnis, *Religious Policy and Practice in Communist China*, pp. 312–322. A similar and more recent effort on a national scale is presented in Zhang Weimin, "Chinese Burial Customs Are Undergoing Change," *China Daily*, Nov. 30, 1983.

14. See John L. Buck, *Land Utilization in China* (Nanking: University of Nanking, 1937), p. 468; Sidney Gamble, *How Chinese Families Live in Peiping* (New York: Funk and Wagnalls, 1933), pp. 200–201; and Simon Yang and L. K. Tao, *A Study of the Standard of Living of Working Families in Shanghai* (Peiping: Institute of Social Research, 1931), pp. 33, 77.

## THE CCP ALTERNATIVES

The alternatives developed by the CCP to replace the traditional funerals can be summarized briefly. The dead should be cremated rather than buried. Traditional funerals should be dispensed with completely. Instead, there should be a paying of last respects to the deceased and a memorial meeting. (Sometimes these take place as separate activities, and sometimes they are combined.) Paying last respects involves workmates, friends, and also relatives filing past the body—either in a special room in a hospital or in a funeral parlor—and then expressing their condolences to members of the immediate family. The memorial meeting may be held before or after the cremation and involves an audience assembled in a hall in the funeral parlor, where they listen to eulogies in honor of the deceased, usually delivered by leaders in the deceased's work unit. These should stress the contributions he or she made to society. Generally a large picture of the deceased will be present, plus wreaths sent by various collective units (e.g., workshops in a factory, university departments). After the eulogy or eulogies, those attending stand in silence, then bow in unison several times (but do not kowtow), and then file out—perhaps again with individuals stopping to express condolences to the immediate family. No references to spirits, ghosts, or the hereafter should be made during these activities; there are no food offerings and no burning of ritual items; and expenditures are minimal. There is a charge for renting the hall, for cremation itself, and for the ash box that the ashes of the deceased are placed in, but these are modest compared with those of a traditional burial (e.g., 50–100 yuan as opposed to 200–1,000 yuan), and are often fully or partly paid by the deceased's work unit.[15] (Coffins may be used for the memorial meeting, but they are reused rather than burned, unlike the practice with many cremations in America.) The wreaths sent by mourners also require some expenditure, although these are often rented rather than bought, making the charge quite modest. Mourning clothes are not worn; only a black armband or black or white patch on the pocket for men, and the same or a white cloth flower on the pocket or in the hair for women, will signify mourning. If cremation cannot be arranged, the same activities should be followed, with a ritually barren burial as a conclusion.

15. Regulations for employees of state enterprises provide that for retired staff members 50–100 yuan can be spent as a "funeral supplement," and the members of the immediate family may receive the equivalent of six to nine months of the deceased's pension payments as a one-time "sympathy payment." When active employees die, especially in work-related accidents, the funeral supplement may be larger, and the immediate family is entitled to regular monthly payments until the children are of working age, with the amount depending on such things as the pay level and seniority of the deceased. See Fukien Provincial Revolutionary Committee, *Lao-tung kung-tzu wen-chien hsuan-pien* 勞動工資文件選編 [Labor and wages document collection] (n.p., 1973), pp. 310, 315, 414–415.

The simplicity of the espoused rites is somewhat modified in the case of leading personages of the new political system. When important officials die, the memorial meetings will be held in large public halls, and the expenditures on decorations, wreaths, and other items will clearly surpass the figures quoted above. In Peking their remains will be placed in Pa-pao-shan cemetery, which is specially reserved for "heroes of the revolution." In earlier years individual tombs were constructed there, but more recently the shortage of space has meant that the ashes of such worthies are all placed in a central mausoleum in Pa-pao-shan. Similar, if more modest, elite cemeteries are found in other major cities. In the case of revolutionary China's foremost leader, Mao Tse-tung, of course, the ideals of frugality and simplicity were thrown completely to the winds, with the mass mourning rituals and construction of a special mausoleum described by Frederic Wakeman in chapter 11.

Ashes of ordinary citizens may be left in repositories attached to funeral parlors or cemeteries, although after three to five years they have to be reclaimed or they will be disposed of. Families may visit and request the ash boxes of family members at ch'ing-ming and on other occasions, and the system in these ash repositories apparently works much like a lending library. Although flowers may be placed by the ashes and moments of silence observed, in general burning paper ritual items, placing out food offerings, and praying are frowned upon, unless there are special circumstances (such as with overseas Chinese).[16] Similarly, if individuals have been buried, visits to clean the graves are allowed, but traditional graveside rituals and offerings are discouraged. Also, a new ritual of encouraging visits by schoolchildren to the graves of revolutionary heroes and martyrs at ch'ing-ming has been popularized. The implications of these simplified, secular funeral activities will be taken up after a review of the nature and relative success of the efforts to bring about funeral reform.

## IMPLEMENTING FUNERAL REFORMS

The detailed process by which funeral reforms were fostered by the CCP, particularly in the early years, is not entirely clear, but some significant turn-

16. Overseas Chinese—both those who return from abroad and those who simply have relatives abroad—have generally been entitled to a number of special privileges since 1949, including the ability to buy new private homes in cities and to select burial rather than cremation. For a description of overseas visitors burning ritual paper in a Tientsin crematorium in 1972, see Eileen Hsu-Balzer, Richard Balzer, and Francis L. K. Hsu, China Day by Day (New Haven: Yale University Press, 1974), p. xxxiv. More recently, burial plots with favorable feng-shui have been offered for sale in Shen-chen across the border from Hong Kong for those Chinese abroad who want to be buried in the motherland.

ing points can be described.[17] Mao Tse-tung was already on record in 1944 as favoring memorial meetings instead of traditional funeral rituals. In a eulogy he delivered at such a meeting for Chang Ssu-te, a Long-March veteran who had died when a charcoal kiln collapsed on him, Mao said:

> From now on, when anyone in our ranks who has done some useful work dies, be he soldier or cook, we should have a funeral ceremony and a memorial meeting in his honor. This should become the rule. And it should be introduced among the people as well. When someone dies in a village, let a memorial meeting be held. In this way we express our mourning for the dead and unite all the people.[18]

By 1949 the CCP was also on record as favoring cremation, as the opening quotation from Derk Bodde shows. However, funeral reform was clearly not a high-priority goal for the new government, and little sustained effort to directly change popular behavior in this realm occurred until the Great Leap Forward. Indeed, one Chinese source claims that Peking did not open its first public crematorium until 1957.[19] (But Tientsin and some other large cities clearly had such crematoria earlier, and there were also the crematoria that were attached to most Buddhist monasteries.) Memorial meetings were held for important personages who died, but they still had not been popularized generally.[20]

Even in these initial years changes in funeral behavior began, though, induced by some of the other changes in society. Hostility toward superstitious cults and secret societies created a hazardous atmosphere for funeral specialists to have to work within, and some were pressured to forsake their trades for "productive labor." Given the new hostility against wealth and conspicuous consumption, engaging in lavish funeral processions also seemed a risky step, to say the least. One foreign observer in Peking claimed that already in 1950 colorful funeral processions had become rare.[21] (However, this judgment may have been premature. A foreign observer in

17. See, in addition, the discussion in Deborah Davis-Friedmann, *Long Lives* (Cambridge: Harvard University Press, 1983), chap. 5.

18. See Mao Tse-tung, "Serve the People," in *Selected Readings from the Works of Mao Tse-tung* (Peking: Foreign Languages Press, 1971), p. 311.

19. See Zhang Weimin, "Chinese Funeral Customs Are Undergoing Change." Another source claims that a single crematorium built by the Japanese during their occupation served Peking until two new facilities, using furnaces imported from Czechoslovakia, opened in 1958. See Shen Ji, "Cremation Taking Root," *China Daily*, Oct. 28, 1986, p. 6.

20. Clearly, the memorial meeting format owed something to Soviet influence, but the details on how this influence was transmitted to China are unclear. For descriptions of approved Soviet funeral rituals, see Christopher Binns, "The Changing Face of Power: Revolution and Accommodation in the Development of the Soviet Ceremonial System," Part 2, *Man* 15 (1980): 179–180; Lane, *The Rites of Rulers*, pp. 82–86.

21. Peter Lum, *Peking, 1950–1953* (London: Robert Hale, 1958), p. 23.

the same city six years later, just on the eve of the socialist transformation campaign, observed a traditional burial procession under way, with drums and horns and ranks of mourners in varied-colored mourning garments; residents along the street followed, bringing out tea to serve to the mourners as they paused on their way. The procession proceeded for an hour out into the suburbs, where a dispersed burial was carried out, with wailing at the side of the grave. The inquisitive foreigner was told that the entire affair cost 600 yuan.)[22] In the countryside the land reform campaign, completed by 1952, deprived landlords and lineages of the property and resources that were used to support ritual displays, and the class struggle fostered during the campaign also helped to undermine the solidarity of kin groups. Then in the socialist transformation and collectivization campaigns of the mid-1950s, remaining ownership of land and other property by families was lost. These changes clearly helped to weaken the conception that one's fate was bound up with a line of patrilineal descent and property transmission, a conception that was at the heart of the traditional funeral practices. Nonetheless, for most Chinese, particularly in the countryside, funeral practices during the 1950s continued to be largely traditional in form, although often engaged in on a more modest and simplified scale.

The Great Leap Forward brought the first concerted attempt to change popular funeral customs. It was during the hectic production campaigns of this period that the arguments about funerals wasting scarce resources were most fully elaborated. Crematoria were being opened in large cities, and resort to them was strongly advocated. In the increasingly better organized urban health care system more and more people were dying in hospitals rather than at home, and medical personnel were supposed to encourage the delivery of the bodies of those who died to the new funeral parlor/crematoria. Those who continued to favor burials found new obstructions in their path. In the mass construction projects of the Leap many urban and suburban cemeteries were condemned. Public notices required people to come and claim the remains of their ancestors or else lose them to the bulldozer.[23] And in the land scarcity of the period, bans against new burials within city limits began to be imposed. With the enlarging of city limits to include suburban counties at this time, some efforts were made to include these suburban areas under the new bans as well. Burials were not them-

22. See Peter Schmid, *The New Face of China* (London: George Harrap, 1958), pp. 33–35. The author, a Swiss journalist, includes in his book some pictures of the procession and burial.

23. Actually, this process of condemnation of cemeteries started earlier as a result of the economic and urban expansion initiated in the early fifties. For example, some of the thirty or more institutes and universities built in those years in the suburbs of Peking displaced burial grounds in this manner. See Schmid, *The New Face of China*, p. 52. But the Great Leap Forward accelerated this process.

selves forbidden, but it became increasingly difficult to arrange for the transmission of a corpse to a distant burial place.[24]

Perhaps more significant, the funeral reform effort of the Leap was not
confined to the cities. Some crematoria began to be opened in county towns,
but most of the rural effort focused on simplifying and secularizing the activities surrounding burials. Accounts of the period mention new-style coffins
made of thin planks, reeds covered with mud, or even concrete. Burial in
out-of-the-way places was required, freeing the fields for agriculture, and
ritual specialists were struggled against. Ancestral tablets were taken out of
some peasant homes and replaced by Mao portraits, and then the tablets
and other wood items, such as coffins stored in advance, were hammered
together to make farm carts, while metal god images were melted down in
communal smelters to make ball bearings![25] I have no solid information
about how widespread such changes were, but at least it is significant that a
major effort was being made to change peasant funeral customs.[26] Nor do I
know the long-term impact of another force for funeral simplification produced by the Leap. The mass famine brought on by the campaign caused so
many deaths in certain regions that those who were left were not physically
or financially able to arrange proper burials for all.[27]

After the collapse of the Leap the attention to funeral reform efforts
abated. While memorial meetings continued to be advocated and increasing
numbers of crematoria came "on line," urbanites who wished to arrange for
funerals and burials felt that it was again somewhat easier to do so. Occasionally an elaborate funeral procession could be seen on the street again in
this period.[28] One foreign observer noted in July 1965 that you often saw
coffins piled up in railway stations, awaiting shipment out to rural locales
for burial.[29] But there were already some ominous signs of changes to come.
During the rural "Four Cleanups" campaign of 1964–65 ritual specialists

24. Difficult, but not impossible. We have one account from this period of a wealthy
Shanghai family selecting a grave site in the hills in their native Ningpo—with the assistance of
a *feng-shui* specialist—in anticipation of the death of the parents. See Chow Ching-li, *Journey
in Tears* (New York: McGraw-Hill, 1978), pp. 231–232.

25. See Ravenholt, "The Gods Must Go!" and Yue Daiyun and Carolyn Wakeman, *To the
Storm* (Berkeley and Los Angeles: University of California Press, 1985), p. 98.

26. The accounts I have of such assaults on death ritual items come from widely scattered
parts of rural China—from Fukien, Hopei, Shantung, Chekiang, and Kweichow, for instance.
But I do not know how typical or atypical such assaults on traditional customs were in each
area.

27. See Thomas Bernstein, "Starving to Death in China," *New York Review of Books*,
June 16, 1983, pp. 36–38.

28. See Colin McCullough, *Stranger in China* (New York: William Morrow, 1973), p. 49.

29. See Delia Jenner, *Letters from Peking* (London: Oxford University Press, 1967),
p. 101.

were struggled against once again, some were driven out of business, and local cadres came under fire for spending lavishly on funerals of family members. A Canadian reporter in China in this period noted a newspaper article advocating the removal of tombs in Hangchow of poets, scholars, and courtesans from the imperial era. These tombs had become attractions for Chinese tourists and were blamed with "spreading the foul odor of the reactionary ruling classes among the visitors."[30]

It was the Cultural Revolution, and particularly the "Destroy the Four Olds" stage in the fall of 1966, that ushered in the period of greatest hostility to traditional funeral practices. Coffin shops, astrologers, spirit-incense makers—all of the specialists required for such funerals—were essentially tabooed in the cities and in many rural areas as well. Red Guard groups in the cities and in some villages broke into homes, looking for "four old" items and confiscating or burning ancestral tablets, god images, and in some cases even the lacquered coffins that were stored in anticipation of death. Chinese quickly adapted by pasting portraits of Chairman Mao in their homes, often in the place where the family's shrine had been, as a talisman to ward off the new dangers of the age. During these years activities tantamount to Mao worship were also visible: bowing to Mao's portrait at weddings and funerals, performing "loyalty dances" toward him, chanting his quotations in unison, and so forth.[31] Many temples and shrines were desecrated and closed in this period, and the remaining monks were in many cases required to give up monastic life and engage in manual labor, and some were pressured to marry. The graves of some Kuomintang figures, CCP "renegades," and others were also defaced during the Cultural Revolution, and a new round of confiscation of burial lands took place as well, in some cases without the notification of kin to collect remains that had occurred during the Leap. In general this phase of active hostility toward all aspects of traditional funerals continued for much of the Cultural Revolution decade.

Since Mao's death in 1976 contradictory tendencies have been visible. Increased tolerance toward tradition and religion has made it possible for some funeral specialists to reappear and acquire customers again, and for some families to gingerly take down their Mao (or Hua Kuo-feng) portraits and put up new ancestral plaques. The partial revival of traditional funeral customs is clearly being fostered by the rural responsibility systems. In part these reforms make wealth and competition for wealth "good" rather than

30. See Charles Taylor, *Reporter in Red China* (New York: Random House, 1966), p. 147.

31. In 1952 English observers had commented approvingly that, whereas under the Nationalists schoolchildren had to bow three times to portraits of Sun Yat-sen and recite his will each Monday morning, there were no such worship-like activities toward Mao under the new regime. See Ralph and Nancy Lapwood, *Through the Chinese Revolution* (London: Spalding and Levy, 1954), p. 81.

bourgeois or even reactionary. Therefore displays of wealth and success through funeral processions are no longer so clearly tabooed.[32] In addition, the rural responsibility system is altering the placement of graves. With collective fields broken up into family plots once again (with long-term leases even if not de jure ownership), graves have begun to "invade" the cultivated fields as in earlier days. William Hinton bemoans the situation in Long Bow village in the following terms: "Here and there, graves appear in the very middle of fertile plots that liberated peasants had cleared of all impediments less than a generation ago. How long will it take for the dead to reoccupy the land so recently bequeathed to the living?"[33] Not only cultivated land is affected. A report from Hunan claims that peasants in one county there dug sixty graves in the playing fields of a secondary school.[34] Access to choice burial sites is once again an issue, with several reports of pitched battles fought between kin groups over this issue.[35] Apparently, even in Peking the ban on burials within city limits has broken down, and the city fathers decry the appearance of hundreds of new graves on the grounds of the Summer Palace, Fragrant Hills, and other scenic spots. (The problem, it is said, is not only the disfiguring of the landscape, but the fire danger created by graveside burning of ritual objects.)[36] Presumably, suburban peasants are often the culprits in such cases, but there are some signs of "retrogression" in the death rituals of urbanites as well. I am not certain to what extent urbanites have been able to arrange for burials once again, rather than cremation, but a reported decline from 37 percent of all deaths handled by cremation in 1978 to 30 percent in 1983 suggests that some change along these lines has occurred.[37] Even urbanites who continue to accept cremation are lavishing care and money on fancy funeral clothes for the deceased, which newly opened shops are selling.[38] One Shanghai critic noted the following trend: "The obsolete custom of offering a beancurd dinner to mour-

---

32. The Chinese press still carries stories encouraging modest funerals, but undercuts their message by the larger number of articles praising newfound wealth and conspicuous consumption. But cadres and party members can still get into trouble for engaging in too lavish and traditional funerals. For one such case, in which more than 5,000 yuan was spent on the funeral of a county leader in Shansi province, see FBIS, Sept. 25, 1980, p. R-1. For a similar incident, involving a four-day funeral costing 4,340 yuan, see FBIS, Jan. 29, 1986, p. K-2.

33. William Hinton, Shenfan (New York: Random House, 1983), p. 764.

34. See People's Daily, June 18, 1982.

35. See, for example, FBIS, Feb. 4, 1983, p. P-1; and March 19, 1982, p. P-2; China Daily, Nov. 15, 1983.

36. See China Daily, March 23, 1984, p. 3.

37. See Beijing Review, April 1, 1985, p. 9. Some doubt about the accuracy of such statistics is raised when the same article provides numbers on cremations and burials which imply less than a 20 percent cremation rate. See also Shen Ji, "Cremation Taking Root."

38. Allen Abel, "All Sales Final at Shop for Dead," Toronto Globe and Mail, Feb. 11, 1985. Reference courtesy of Evelyn Rawski.

ners has degenerated into a sumptuous feast. Sending wreaths to pay hom-
age to the dead and express condolences has gone out of fashion. More
people have begun sending brocade quilts or cash instead. Showing off one's
wealth on such occasions serves only to detract from the memory of the
deceased."[39] So, in a number of significant ways, post-Mao trends have
allowed or fostered the revival of some aspects of traditional funeral customs and more elaborate funeral expenditures even in urban areas.

On the other hand, official efforts to encourage the new ritual forms continue. Some cities began to require cremation, thus helping to give rise to
underground corpse-smuggling rings.[40] In other cities it is only party and
Youth League members and state cadres that are obligated to accept cremation, but other state employees who opt for burial will not have their funeral
expenses paid.[41] These efforts culminated in a national set of regulations
published in February 1985. These regulations call for a step-by-step adoption of cremation in all areas that are densely populated, have a shortage of
arable land, or have ready access to transportation (to get to the nearest
crematorium). Where conditions do not allow cremation, the regulations
require either deep burial or burial in an out-of-the-way collective cemetery.
Graves that have invaded arable and public lands should be moved, and the
production and sale of paper money and other "superstitious" ritual items
are to be banned. State cadres who violate these rules will not have funeral
fees paid and may even face disciplinary action.[42] Evidently phenomena
such as the "grave invasions" and the reported decline in cremations since
1978 have led to this revived effort to enforce the new funeral customs.

At the elite level a debate has broken out, which is being expressed
through funeral behavior. The impetus seems to stem from the contrast between the way the deaths of Mao and Chou En-lai were handled in 1976,
with Mao embalmed and displayed under glass in his new mausoleum, and
Chou cremated, with his ashes scattered over the land. Although nobody
else has been mummified since Mao, still the established mode of handling
the death of a leading figure, as was already noted, is to have a paying of last
respects to the body in a hospital, cremation, a memorial meeting with
perhaps two to three thousand attending in the Great Hall of the People,
and then preservation of the ashes in Pa-pao-shan cemetery in Peking. But
some leading figures have left requests that, following Chou's example,
more simplified procedures be adopted. Sun Yeh-fang, Su Yu, and a number
of other prominent figures, for example, left dying wishes that no last re-

---

39. Letter to the editor published in *China Daily*, March 8, 1984, p. 4.
40. See Jay and Linda Mathews, *One Billion* (New York: Random House, 1983), p. 139.
41. See *FBIS*, April 9, 1981, p. P-2.
42. See *FBIS*, Feb. 28, 1985, pp. K-13–14; "Funeral Customs Experience Change," *Beijing Review*, April 1, 1985, pp. 9–10.

spects should be paid and no memorial meetings held, and that their ashes should be scattered rather than preserved.[43] By such actions they seem to criticize the hypocrisy of having lavish funerals for officials while the common people are required to mark deaths in a simple manner. Others dying in the same general time period, however, such as Soong Ch'ing-ling and Liao Ch'eng-chih, have not taken up this lead but have continued to follow the established form. It would appear, then, that in regard to funeral policy the post-Mao period cannot be characterized simply as an era of liberalization. Rather, it seems apparent that the "struggles between the old and the new in the resting places of the dead" are far from over in contemporary China.[44]

## HOW MUCH CHANGE?

To what extent have funeral rituals been transformed in post-1949 China, and what is the nature of death rituals currently? I utilize the funeral cases from interview materials here to consider this question systematically. In regard to cremation versus burial, the most important pattern to note is the rural-urban gap in contemporary customs. In the large cities cremation was already becoming accepted before the Cultural Revolution and was close to being universal by the 1970s. To be more specific, 38 percent of our pre-1965 funeral cases from large cities but only 7 percent of those from small cities, towns, and rural areas involved cremation; after 1966, 85 percent of funerals in the large cities involved cremation, but still only 13 percent of the cases from smaller cities, towns, and villages. Some informants claim that most urbanites now readily accept cremation, while others claim that many would prefer burial but find it too difficult and costly to arrange, given the general absence of coffin shops, transport difficulties, and so forth. In large cities, then, old people who fear cremation and desire a burial are faced with a dilemma. They can leave and locate in a rural native place where they can be buried after they die, but in doing so they will be distancing themselves from the high-quality urban health care that might help keep them alive. On the other side of the coin, the same concern may make peasants reluctant to accept referrals to an urban hospital when they do need care, for fear of dying there and ending up being cremated. It is also reported that rural elderly are reluctant to move into old-age homes now being established, because they fear their burial plots will be taken away

43. See *FBIS*, Aug. 7, 1980, p. L-1; Oct. 21, 1983, p. K-10; and Feb. 13, 1984, p. K-3. Actually, a large memorial meeting with 5,000 attending was held for Chou, but then his ashes were scattered, as he had requested. See *Peking Review*, January 23, 1976, pp. 3–4.

44. One letter written to a Chinese newspaper expresses hope that the new frugal official funerals will have an impact: "What a striking contrast. I believe the initiative taken by the few will ultimately lead to a radical change in funerals that are reminiscent of bygone days when superstition and ostentation prevailed." See *China Daily*, March 8, 1984, p. 4.

and they will end up being cremated.[45] In smaller cities and towns cremation is not universal, and some people arrange for burials while others accept cremation. (Here the availability of burial land nearby may be a factor.) Crematoria are not even available yet in all of China's county towns.[46]

In most parts of the Chinese countryside burial appears to be the general rule still. Only those who live in city suburbs or near county seats with crematoria really have the option of cremation in any case. So in spite of more than three decades of advocating cremation, authorities in China have not really attempted to make this a viable option for the bulk of the population. The result, according to one Chinese source, is that 90 percent of urbanites are now cremated, but only 15 percent of rural residents, yielding the nationwide estimate for 1983 of 30 percent cremations.[47] It is clear that reform programs have contributed to a sharp rural-urban gap that didn't exist before 1949.

To a considerable extent, this same sharp rural-urban gap is visible in other aspects of funeral behavior. So far as one can tell, funerals in rural China are still largely traditional in form, although somewhat simplified in comparison with the traditional scene. Our research on rural Kwangtung found the following stages nearly universal following a death: notification of kin, moving the dying person to a parlor or public hall, purchasing a coffin, donning mourning clothes, the eldest son's going to "buy water," dressing the corpse, keeping vigil and wailing through the night, encoffining, burning paper ritual offerings and lighting firecrackers, proceeding to the grave with horns and drums, graveside offerings, the burial, return for a funeral meal, later memorial rites (one a week, in some cases up until the forty-ninth day, and on later death anniversaries and at *ch'ing ming* as well), and then a second burial several years later.[48] In the early 1970s Taoist priests, hired *feng-shui* specialists, and astrologers were generally absent in rural Kwangtung funerals, although there are some indications in the Chinese press that they have reemerged to some extent in the 1980s. Some elements of the ritual process—full mourning dress and carved or substitute

45. See Hsu Ming 許明, "Nung-ts'un lao-jen pu-yuan chin ching-lao-yuan ti yi-ta ku-lu" 農村老人不願進敬老院的一大顧慮 [One major worry that makes rural elderly unwilling to enter old age homes], *She-hui* 社會, 1984, no. 3, p. 26. For a poignant example of one old couple in Honan separated by the rural-urban divide, see Mathews and Mathews, *One Billion*, p. 129.

46. One Chinese source (See Zhang Weimin, "Chinese Burial Customs") claims that there are now 2,500 crematoria in China, which might suggest that China's roughly 2,000 counties would all be covered. However, a more recent source reveals that only 85 percent of China's cities and only 40 percent of her counties have crematories available. See *Beijing Review*, April 1, 1985, p. 9.

47. See Zhang Weimin, "Chinese Burial Customs."

48. For more detail, consult Parish and Whyte, *Village and Family in Contemporary China*, pp. 261–266.

ancestral tablets, for example—were visible in some villages and families and not in others. But still almost all of the funerals recounted to us took a basically traditional form, rather than the officially approved memorial-meeting format. In other words, with minor exceptions the basic elements of funerary rituals described by James Watson in chapter 1, and most of the elements of traditional burial rites as well, were still being followed in Kwangtung villages. (The few cases of rural memorial meetings were special in some way—a commune cadre who died, a peasant killed while protecting commune property, etc.) So for most peasants in Kwangtung in the 1970s funeral customs were probably not that much different from what they had been for relatively poor families and peasants outside of dominant lineages in the period before 1949.[49] And in the period since our interviews were conducted, anecdotal evidence suggests a revival of traditional practices and also heightened differentiation in funeral elaborateness between the rural rich and poor.

In the large cities, in contrast, the memorial meeting is increasingly dominant: they occurred in 40 percent of our city funeral cases from before the Cultural Revolution, and in 69 percent of the cases afterward. Memorial meetings are not always held, in spite of Mao's blessing of this form forty years ago.[50] It is urban work units that decide whether to sponsor a memorial meeting or not. Some large and resource-rich units are said to convene such meetings for all of their personnel, and even for retired staff members, with the expenses covered by the unit. But many if not most state enterprises hold memorial meetings only for cadres, model workers, and other "special" staff members, and not for ordinary workers and retirees. In small collective enterprises, finally, memorial meetings are rare, and funeral expenditures are not even paid in many cases, so that the entire matter is left up to the family.

If no memorial meeting is being officially held, the family of the deceased may still decide to organize one themselves, and the deceased's work unit may send representatives. In these circumstances some families may decide not to hold a memorial meeting, but to have simplified versions of traditional funeral observances in the home, or to dispense with everything except the paying of last respects. Finally, there are instances in which memorial meetings are more or less tabooed, particularly for people with

49. In other words, the extremely lavish funerals of the rural elite were no longer visible, and one could say that there was more equality in the way peasants left this world. This reduced inequality may help explain the lament of a burial specialist in Kwangtung that things are not as good as they used to be, as recounted in Steven Mosher, *Broken Earth* (New York: Free Press, 1983), pp. 302–304.

50. Actually, since Mao advocated holding such meetings for those who had "done some useful work," it might be argued that he provided the basis for differential treatment.

bad class backgrounds, criminals, and those in political trouble.[51] Also, memorial meetings will not be held for those who commit suicide, particularly if the suicide was clearly politically motivated. The writer Yang Chiang observed one such case in a cadre farm in 1970. A thirty-three-year-old male sent-down cadre who had committed suicide was hurriedly buried by members of the farm's army propaganda team with no coffin and no ceremony. When the cadre farm was later moved, the field in which the unmarked grave was located was plowed under, leaving no sign that anyone had been buried there.[52]

The memorial meetings held in urban areas conform closely to the officially approved format. The body will be picked up from the hospital (where most urban deaths now occur) and delivered to the funeral parlor. If no unit sponsorship is involved, relatives and friends will convene there in one of the smaller rooms, dressed in normal clothes except for the mourning armbands or cloth flowers. One or more of those present will say a few words in memoriam, then all will bow, and then they will file past the body and leave. Occasionally, recorded music, a few wreaths, and an enlarged picture of the deceased will add to the atmosphere. The body will then be cremated and the ashes put in a box selected by the family (there are several styles with varying prices) and either placed there for storage or taken home. If the unit sponsors a memorial meeting, it will usually rent a larger hall in the funeral parlor. The activities will be much the same, but there will be more wreaths and perhaps live music, and the speakers will be leading figures in the work unit, rather than family members or friends. In addition, in such cases the body may not be present, but may be kept in an adjoining room. For prominent national leaders, as was already noted, there may be several thousand people attending a memorial meeting, necessitating that it be held in a large public auditorium, such as the Great Hall of the People.

It might seem that cremation and memorial meetings would be absolutely incompatible with holding any traditional religious observances in the home, but that is not always the case. Some urbanites (particularly older

51. This was the fate of purged individuals such as Liu Shao-ch'i, but also of humbler people who were on the political outs. For example, when Ruth Lo's professor husband died in 1969 while still under a political cloud, the only person to come to the funeral home aside from family members was one old friend, and there were no speeches and no ceremony. See Ruth Earnshaw Lo, *In the Eye of the Typhoon* (New York: Harcourt Brace Jovanovich, 1980), pp. 135–137. In the same period an intellectual living in Peking learned that individual cremation was forbidden for those in political trouble who died. Such individuals were subject to collective cremations, making it impossible for family members to retrieve identifiable individual ashes for preservation. See Yue and Wakeman, *To the Storm*, p. 190. Since 1979 the government has declared that class labels should no longer be recorded and used as the basis for discrimination, so presumably this one criterion for ineligibility no longer applies.

52. See Yang Jiang, *A Cadre School Life: Six Chapters* (Hong Kong: Joint Publications, 1982), pp. 50–53.

women, but also some recent rural migrants and poorly educated urbanites) are apparently able to figure ways in which the soul of the deceased could survive cremation. In such households there may be substitute ancestral shrines established, typically with a picture of the deceased, and regular food offerings and even the burning of incense and paper ritual objects on holidays and death anniversaries.[53] But for most urbanites postfuneral observances seem to be minimal, and to take a commemoration rather than a worship form, as is officially recommended. The mourning armband may be worn for a few weeks, relatives may be invited back for a postfuneral meal, and flowers will be put out by the ashes on subsequent ch'ing-mings and death anniversaries. But little else is involved.[54]

In the 1970s in urban areas there generally was substantial compliance with official funeral reform goals. Compliance was, to be sure, less than complete, in several respects. First, as was already noted, in small cities and towns burial was still common, and funerals continued to be closer to traditional than officially approved forms for many who died. Second, even in large cities some determined individuals managed to arrange for burial and to sustain traditional funeral rituals to some extent. Finally, there were also some cases of incongruous combinations, with, for example, hired specialists surreptitiously chanting in the home prior to cremation.[55] Still, on balance, it is fair to say that in the large cities Bodde's "sharp break with tradition" has come to pass.

## THE MEANING OF THE CHANGES

Given the substantial success of the CCP in inducing change in urban death practices, what are the implications of current customs? The first and perhaps most important point has already been stressed: Contrary to the often professed goal of reducing the gap between "town and country," post-1949 changes have actually widened the gap substantially by altering urban customs dramatically while rural funeral customs have only been altered

53. This use of pictures does conflict with the generalization offered by James Watson in chapter 1 that ancestral shrines always take a written rather than a picture form.

54. During a visit to his home town in Hunan in 1959, Mao Tse-tung made an unscheduled visit to his parents' grave site. There he placed a hastily improvised pine-bough wreath at the grave and bowed solemnly. Later, perhaps feeling he had to justify this action to an official traveling with him, he said, "We communists are thorough-going materialists who don't believe in spirits. But one must acknowledge the parents who bore one and the party, the comrades, the old teachers, and friends who instructed one." Cited in Roderick MacFarquhar, *The Origins of the Cultural Revolution*, vol. 2 (New York: Columbia University Press, 1983), p. 190.

55. Or the procession to the crematorium in Tientsin with some mourners in white hats or white headbands with a red spot in the middle of the forehead, as seen by visitors in 1972. See Hsu-Balzer et al., *China Day by Day*, p. xxxiv.

slightly. The importance of this change is to be found not simply in the fact that peasants and urbanites, who formerly knew a common ritual vocabulary, are now increasingly aliens to each other's customs. Ties between rural and urban areas before 1949 were expressed not only in common culture but in social ties and interaction, and these have also declined. Before 1949 some urbanites were buried in city and suburban cemeteries, but many sought burial in their rural native places. Graves of parents and grandparents in a rural locale then required periodic visits home by city-based descendants to take part in grave-sweeping and ancestral shrine observances. With cremation the rule, these links to rural grave sites are gone, and urbanites have their rural roots and contacts increasingly attenuated. The "native place psychology" of Chinese urban areas has been sharply eroded by post-1949 changes. In fact, the reduced rural-urban contacts involved in funeral matters are probably a reflection more than a cause of the growing rural-urban gap. Other reforms, such as the implementation of systems of migration restrictions, household registration, and rationing, as well as the fundamentally different forms structural change has taken in city and village since 1949, should probably be seen as the major sources of this gap.[56] But insofar as the reformed funeral customs have meanings and psychological implications that are in contrast with the traditional set, they not only reflect but reinforce the dramatic polarization of society in the People's Republic across the rural-urban divide.

What are the specific features of the new rituals that prompt new understandings among urbanites? Several are fundamental even if fairly obvious. Reformed urban rituals are not designed to clear the way for the deceased's journey into the afterlife, nor to help establish benevolent supernatural influences (or ward off malevolent ones) on the descendants. The atheistic creed of the CCP finds its reflection in the this-worldly emphasis of the reformed rituals. Individuals find their perpetuity in the contributions they made while they were alive and in the gratitude felt by colleagues and friends (more so than by family members).[57] Death itself is not to be feared, and death for a worthy cause is honorable. Consequently, death should be seen as nonpolluting. ("Bad deaths" may in a certain sense still be seen as polluting, however. Two cases of cremations in rural areas in our sample involved suicides by urbanites rusticated there. Local authorities went to the expense and trouble of having the bodies rushed into the county town to be

56. This issue is argued in greater detail in the author's article, "Town and Country in Contemporary China," *Comparative Urban Research* 10 (1983): 9–20.

57. In a chilling short story by Liu Pin-yen, ash urns of three formerly prominent officials carry on a conversation about whether they will be remembered now that they are dead. The former economic minister's ashes say, "They can't forget. As long as my mines and factories still exist, they won't forget me." See Liu Binyan, "Warning," in his *People or Monsters?* (Bloomington: Indiana University Press, 1983), p. 71.

cremated, apparently in part out of fear that a village burial would incite sympathy and protest.) People should not fear contact with the deceased and the family of the deceased, and the descendants do not need to withdraw into deep mourning for an extended period of time. Rather, a modest but minimal set of gestures to show respect for the dead is expected, but these should not interfere with the resumption of normal activities immediately after the cremation. One shows respect for the deceased by the same way the deceased gains honor: by making active contributions to society. Cremation itself expresses the finality of death, with no remaining bones and souls requiring perpetual care. (However, the great popular concern for preserving and caring for the remains, even if they are in ash form, shows that this finality of death is not completely accepted—see further comments on this point later.) And as one does not need to be concerned with the supernatural, so one should not consult specialists in this realm and be bound by their advice and predictions. Rather than picking a funeral time and a burial place in accord with the words of astrologers and geomancers, one should arrange things to fit the convenience of the living.

The scale and type of funeral observances also express profound changes in urban life. The reformed rituals emphasize the role of the individual, on the one hand, and of the corporate work organization, the party, and the state, on the other, while they fundamentally de-emphasize the role of kinship and descent groups. The individual is emphasized primarily through a Western import: funeral eulogies. These direct attention away from the corpse as ancestor-to-be and toward the life that preceded it, causing those present to reflect on the personality, the history, and the accomplishments of the one being honored.[58] In modest memorial meetings organized by the family the emphasis is on all of those close to the deceased, rather than on a line of descent, and work-unit representatives often attend. In the larger memorial meetings organized by work units, we have already noted that the role of kin is even more marginal. In such cases the funds come from the work unit, the eulogies are provided by its leaders, and colleagues from work swamp kin and friends in numbers attending. In general, public institutions—hospitals, funeral parlors, work organizations—have now displaced the home as the arenas for funeral observances. The immediate family is reduced to a peripheral role in the memorial meeting proceedings: those attending, and particularly the leading cadres, shake hands (another Western import) with the bereaved as they leave. Here we see symbolized the fundamental dependence of urban individuals, in death as in life, on the bureaucratized state and its grass-roots representatives, production units.

58. In imperial times the epitaphs written for prominent people did have an individual life focus, but these were prepared separately from the funeral itself. Ben Elman directed my attention to such epitaphs.

Individuals and families depend on the favor they win with work-unit authorities, rather than on the favor they may earn with departed ancestral spirits. Descendants depend on jobs, housing, and other resources controlled by the state, rather than on property inherited from the deceased. In a certain sense the 1958 slogan at the head of this chapter does apply to urban areas today—the work organization and the party provide all of the *feng-shui* you need.[59]

Kin are of course still involved even in large memorial meetings, but they are involved in different ways. No sharp distinction is made between patrilineal kin and others—in mourning dress or otherwise—and attendance should be bilateral in emphasis. Similarly, daughters should join these activities on an equal basis with sons. Furthermore, with the elimination of graded mourning costumes, near and distant kin should participate on an equal footing. Finally, the customary rule about senior generations not taking part in mourning for younger generations does not hold for memorial meetings. I do not know if the father of Wang Chieh (one of the young soldier-martyrs of the 1960s) wore an armband and wept at his son's memorial meeting, but in principle he should have.[60] So, in attendance at funerals a new egalitarian ethic is stressed. Kin related in various ways meet as rough equals (and as equals with non-kin) in paying their last respects to the deceased.

If attendance at reformed urban funerals stresses equality of status, the scale of these funerals is a quite different matter, as should already be obvious. Funeral observances range all the way from essentially nothing to elaborate gatherings with several thousand attending. The differences express fundamental features of the new social order. Individual or family wealth is no longer the main determinant of the elaborateness of an urban funeral, although family resources may have some influence on the scale of those memorial meetings that work units do not organize. A primary determinant of funeral scale is the level and resources of the work unit. As was already noted, some work units tend to everything from cradle to grave, or rather ash box, but others do not. Where one is situated in the complex system of administered control over urban resources determines how well one will fare, again in death as in life.

Within enterprises, as I have also noted, memorial meetings are not always held, or held on the same scale, for all personnel. In theory the primary criterion is the "contributions" made by the deceased. This means that

59. One unanswered question is whether changes in policies in recent years, such as allowing children to inherit jobs from their parents and allowing the revival of urban private enterprise, will foster renewed emphasis on filial bonds in urban funeral rituals.

60. I don't have information detailed enough to be certain how much these norms are actually followed in contemporary memorial meetings—an interesting topic for future research.

"model workers" are often so honored. Ordinary staff members can be catapulted into the honored category if they die in the right way, such as in a work accident, and of course many model individuals, from Chang Ssu-te to Wang Chieh, had this quality. But contributions often in practice are equated with rank: those who held high posts in the unit are assumed to have made greater contributions. So the varying scale of funerals establishes contemporary China as a rank, more than a class, society. (This feature of Chinese society is also reflected in the graded cemeteries. Normally only cadres above the rank of thirteen—the so-called high-ranking cadres—are eligible for burial in Peking's Pa-pao-shan cemetery for "heroes of the revolution." Just down the road there is a separate and less elaborate cemetery in which the ashes of "commoners" can be deposited.) Contributions, to be acknowledged, should also be recent, and the more years since an individual has retired, the less likely the unit is to hold an elaborate memorial meeting for him, other things being equal. The variations in memorial meetings thus express a modest de-emphasis on age as a status factor in urban China. To be sure, memorial meetings tend in general to be more elaborate for those with higher rank and longer work histories, who are necessarily older. But both in the elaborate memorials held for young martyrs and model workers and in the modest remembrances for retirees the ranking by age is violated, making it less of a factor than in traditional funerals.[61] Finally, also noted was the fact that some factors can disqualify one for a unit-organized memorial meeting—notably bad class background, criminal behavior, political trouble, or suicide. A "bad death" can wipe out earlier contributions, and only some individuals deserve to be honored and remembered by the new order.

It is worth noting, however, that one's status in the People's Republic of China is not immutable even after death. Given the changing political lines in the PRC, those honored at the time of their deaths may fall from grace later, and those in disgrace may be posthumously rehabilitated. As the Red Guards desecrated some graves in 1966, so after Mao's death K'ang Sheng's place in Pa-pao-shan was thrown into question.[62] On the other hand, note the T'ien-an men riots in 1976 demanding more elaborate memorials for

61. Being married is also not as important a qualifying factor for a full-scale observance. But funerals for children still seem to be very simple affairs.

62. K'ang was a leader specializing in police and security affairs who sided with the radicals during Mao's later years. K'ang's family hurried to Pa-pao-shan cemetery in 1980, five years after his death, to remove his ashes before they could be "evicted." See Mathews and Mathews, *One Billion*, p. 14. See also Liu Binyan, "The Warning." See also Frederic Wakeman's discussion in chapter 11 in this volume on the debate over whether to remove Mao's remains from his memorial hall. This practice of "posthumous purges" is not unique to the Chinese, of course. Khrushchev had Stalin's body removed from its honored place beside Lenin in his mausoleum and buried in a simple grave in the Kremlin wall.

Chou En-lai and the posthumous memorial meetings held in recent years for
Liu Shao-ch'i, Lao She, and many other victims of the Cultural Revolution.
(That posthumous rehabilitation should take the form of a memorial meeting in such cases indicates the CCP's acceptance of the great importance of
proper funeral observances.) So even after death one's standing and honor
depend upon the shifting lines and policies of the state, rather than being
under the control of descendants or of wind and water.

However, it cannot be assumed that family members are always helpless
pawns in these matters. Given both the way that the fates of family members
are interlinked, even beyond the grave, and the stress the CCP leadership
continues to give to proper (even if reformed) funeral rituals and subsequent
memorial activities, descendants often expend a great deal of time and energy trying to gain approval for the rehabilitation of a family member who
died in disgrace. If they can utilize their personal contacts and networks to
arrange for a posthumous memorial meeting, the restoration of a defaced
grave, or a commemorative article in the newspaper, then they will have
succeeded in manipulating the system instead of being simply manipulated
by it.[63] A striking example of this phenomenon occurred in Nanking in
1984–85. The director of a museum there, Yao Ch'ien, had been accused in
the press of plagiarism and other wrongs, and this drove him to commit
suicide in November 1984. In this case the manner of his death did not
disqualify him from normal funeral activities, and his body was placed in
the museum for the paying of last respects. His family, convinced he had
been unfairly defamed, then refused to move his body from the museum
until his name was cleared. Bureaucracy being what it is, it took nine
months before the central authorities in Peking formally rehabilitated him,
and all of this time his body remained in the museum, which therefore had
to remain closed. Only after he was rehabilitated was the body removed and
the museum reopened.[64]

CONCLUSIONS

In general, it should be clear that certain core messages are conveyed by the
new funeral rituals. In particular, these reformed customs emphasize the
meaning and value to be gained in society rather than beyond, and that
one's status in society during life and afterward is dependent fundamentally
on one's place and contributions in the bureaucratic pecking order, with

63. Articles in the press commemorating the eightieth, ninetieth and so forth anniversaries of the birth of a famous person are a frequent way of conveying honor to a deceased person
and his or her family.
64. See Alice Davenport and Alain Larocque, "The Fall and Rise of an Errant Museum
Curator," *Far Eastern Economic Review*, Feb. 6, 1986, pp. 43–45.

minimal mediation by family or kin. These messages contrast in very fundamental ways with those reinforced by traditional funeral rituals, with their stress on reliance on patrilineal kin, the power of the supernatural, death pollution, property transmission, and the competition of family units for status and wealth within the broader fate shared with lineage mates.

Since to a considerable extent traditional funeral rituals are still being followed in many if not most Chinese rural areas, I stress here again that contemporary funerals are one major indicator and reinforcer of the growing gap between rural and urban in post-1949 China. I have argued that this divergence in death rituals is greater than that which existed before the revolution, and it also appears greater than that which occurs in contemporary Taiwan and Hong Kong.[65] This gap in ritual forms is not based simply on rural poverty and ignorance, factors that might be eliminated in time, but instead is the product of the sharply differing organizational systems imposed on city and countryside by China's Communist rulers.

In terms of the themes of this volume, we are left with one major puzzle concerning the meaning of the changes in urban China. I have noted that urban funeral rituals have been largely transformed, so that now the combination of the paying of last respects, memorial meetings, and cremation is widely followed. Does this mean, as James Watson's provocative essay would seem to imply, that most of China's 200 million urbanites are no longer ritually Chinese? In spite of the dramatic changes that have occurred, such a conclusion would appear to be premature. In fact, the evidence for urban China raises questions about Watson's stress on orthopraxy over orthodoxy as well.

It is clear that, in the large cities at least, most urbanites no longer follow any of the nine ritual steps that Watson identifies as constituting the basic structure of Chinese funerary rites.[66] If we examine what Watson calls the ideological domain, however, more extensive continuities are visible. It is, to be sure, debatable whether a multipart soul is part of contemporary ideology, or whether the spirit of the deceased is seen as particularly volatile or dangerous. But most of the other elements identified by Watson as forming

65. For discussions of religious rituals in urban Hong Kong, see Morris Berkowitz, F. P. Brandauer, and J. H. Reed, *Folk Religion in an Urban Setting* (Hong Kong: Christian Study Center, 1969); John Myers, "Traditional Chinese Religious Practices in an Urban-Industrial Setting: The Example of Kwun Tong," in Ambrose King and Rance Lee, eds., *Social Life and Development in Hong Kong* (Hong Kong: Hong Kong Chinese University Press, 1981), pp. 275–288. An island-wide survey in Taiwan in 1970 found only modest differences between urban and rural areas in the proportion of households having altars, ancestor tablets, incense pots, and other ritual objects. See Wolfgang Grichting, *The Value System of Taiwan 1970* (Taipei, n.p.), pp. 208–209.

66. Or at least, that only glimmers of the traditional forms are still visible, as in the armbands or cloth patches that have replaced mourning gowns, and the modern records or bands that are sometimes used instead of the traditional drums and horns.

the ideological domain of funerary rites are still being stressed. Even though official atheism argues that there is no life after death, still a strong sense of the continuity between this world and the next is maintained. The physical remains of the deceased, if not the spirit, exist in a vast pecking order that mirrors the rank society that exists in contemporary China. Obligations to kin persist beyond the grave in the form of responsibility to insure a proper resting place for the ashes of the deceased as well as to safeguard or to advance the deceased's reputation. And in death the relative status of the deceased, and any defiling or repairing of his or her resting place, can have a very tangible influence on the lives and prospects of living descendants. Even the balance of the sexes in death mentioned by Watson is also visible, as the ash boxes of both parents are often preserved together, with flowers or other "modernized" offerings placed before them on death anniversaries and at *ch'ing-ming*.

One might read Watson's essay as implying that even in pre-Communist times the disposal of the remains of the deceased was a matter of much lesser concern than the funeral itself. And the atheistic creed of the CCP and the promotion of cremation might have been expected to reinforce a tendency to treat the disposal of remains as a casual and unimportant matter. It is clear, however, that urbanites view the question of disposal of the remains of a loved one as anything but casual and unimportant. In fact, considerable care and effort are expended in ensuring that remains are given "proper" treatment, even though the options available have changed so that criteria of what is proper have been redefined. The other side of the coin is that Chinese urbanites become very upset at the prospect that they might not be able to arrange such proper treatment. One of the things about the Cultural Revolution that most outrages urban Chinese today is the fact that in that period many people were not able to meet these obligations. As was noted earlier, some individuals died and were disposed of in collective or unmarked graves, and family members were not even notified until after the fact.[67] Others were subject to collective cremations, so that no individual ashes could be retrieved and cared for; still others had their remains disposed of without notification of kin. In other cases family members had to mount heroic efforts, against considerable bureaucratic and economic obstacles, to make sure that the remains of a loved one received proper treatment.

Yue Daiyun tells of such an effort in regard to her own mother. To begin with, Yue suspects that her mother's death in late 1966 was due to a

---

67. Yue Daiyun recalls going to retrieve the body of her mother from a hospital morgue in 1967 and seeing there the body of a teenage girl who had been beaten to death by Red Guards. The thought that her own children might meet the same fate—as an unclaimed corpse—sent shivers of fear through her. See Yue and Wakeman, *To the Storm*, p. 189.

botched medical procedure attributable to the chaos the Cultural Revolution created in hospitals. Then she and her brother were told they had to arrange for the transport of their mother's body from the morgue to the funeral parlor within two days, or else the body would simply be disposed of. Then she was told by the administrators at the "commoners" Pa-pao-shan cemetery that they would need a death certificate from her or her brother's work unit specifying that their mother had died of some natural cause and was not a member of "the black gang," or else the mother would be subjected to collective cremation. Her brother's bosses refused to take the risk of supplying the necessary certification, but fortunately Yue's superiors were more compassionate. But even with this certificate in hand Yue and her brother still had no easy way to arrange for the transport of the body. Finally, with time running out, they were able to perch at a truck station and, in exchange for some gifts, to get a truck driver to agree to spend his lunch break delivering their mother's body to the cemetery. There she was individually cremated, and the ashes were deposited in the one remaining niche in the wall of the ash repository. (Other grief-stricken families with ash boxes in hand were being turned away with the claim that there was no space.)

Then Yue was sent to the countryside and was not able to come back at the end of three years to reclaim the ashes. Fortunately, the payment of an additional fee made it possible to have her mother's ashes remain for a fourth year and thus to avoid the threatened disposal of them in a mass grave. At the end of four years Yue was able, using ties through a cousin and a suitable bribe, to arrange for the retrieved ash box to be buried individually on a lovely hillside spot in the Fragrant Hills. (The auspiciousness of the spot is clear when she says that it was very close to the grave of the famous Chinese opera star Mei Lan-fang.) Family members carried cement and water up the hill to mix for a simple headstone, and an old family friend inscribed it with the characters of Yue's mother and father, for he would eventually join her there. With this grave completed, the family finally felt that its obligations had been met, and Yue and her father felt great relief that the many unhappy fates that the mother's remains might have met had been avoided.[68] How typical this one case is I do not know, and of course many families were neither so resourceful nor so lucky. But this case does testify to the central importance now assigned to proper disposal of the dead, and to the anger and frustration that can be directed against "the system" when such proper disposal is made so difficult. (It should be noted, however, that in most periods China's Communist rulers have honored such sentiments and have made allowances for this sort of strong popular desire to insure a proper resting place for loved ones.)

68. Yue and Wakeman, *To the Storm*, pp. 187–193.

These final observations lead to several conclusions. First, the radical transformation of urban funerary rites has led them to convey a substantially different meaning than did the traditional rites. Second, in spite of this transformation of funerary rites and their new messages, much of the ideological domain of traditional funerals persists. Third, the persistence of the traditional ideological domain of death rituals helps to give special meaning to the disposal and care of the remains of loved ones, since it is particularly in providing such care that the obligations between generations are met. In some sense, then, the required changes in death rituals have had the effect of displacing much of the emotional meaning and force from the funerary rites to what Watson calls the rites of disposal. But disposal of the dead is only minimally ritualized. Even in terms of the treatment of remains, it is more the ideological content than the ritual forms that are important. It would appear that the flexibility of Chinese ritual behavior that Watson comments on is even greater than he allows for. In contemporary death rituals orthodoxy is more important than orthopraxy, in Watson's terms, and the rites of disposal assume greater importance than the modernized funerary rituals. But in the enduring stress on the strong links and obligations between family members which persist beyond the grave, if not in ritual structure, modern Chinese urbanites can still express their essential Chineseness.[69]

69. One might argue that if the recent innovation adopted by a few of China's leaders—of holding no memorial meeting and asking that their ashes be scattered after death—became the new official norm, this would pose a greater threat to the continuities in the ideological domain of funerals than do the customs the CCP currently tries to foster.

# CONTRIBUTORS

MYRON L. COHEN, Professor of Anthropology, Columbia University, New York, New York 10027.

ELIZABETH L. JOHNSON, Curator, Museum of Anthropology, University of British Columbia, Vancouver, Canada V6T 1W5.

EMILY MARTIN, Professor of Anthropology, Johns Hopkins University, Baltimore, Maryland 21218.

SUSAN NAQUIN, Professor of History, University of Pennsylvania, Philadelphia, Pennsylvania 19104.

EVELYN S. RAWSKI, Professor of History, University of Pittsburgh, Pittsburgh, Pennsylvania 15260.

STUART E. THOMPSON, Lecturer in Asian Anthropology, School of Oriental and African Studies, University of London, Thornhaugh Street, London WC1H OXG England.

FREDERIC WAKEMAN, JR., Professor of History, University of California, Berkeley, California 94720.

JAMES L. WATSON, Professor of Anthropology, Harvard University, Cambridge, Massachusetts 02138.

RUBIE S. WATSON, Associate Professor of Anthropology, University of Pittsburgh, Pittsburgh, Pennsylvania 15260.

MARTIN K. WHYTE, Professor of Sociology, University of Michigan, Ann Arbor, Michigan 48109.

# GLOSSARY-INDEX

Chinese terms marked (C) are in colloquial Cantonese and are romanized in the Yale system, as found in Parker P. F. Huang's *Cantonese Dictionary* (New Haven: Yale University Press, 1970). Cantonese place names marked (C) in the glossary are romanized according to the system found in *A Gazetteer of Place Names in Hong Kong, Kowloon, and the New Territories* (Hong Kong: Government Press, 1969). Terms marked (H) are in Hokkien, romanized in the Bodman system, as found in Nicholas C. Bodman's *Spoken Amoy Hokkien* (Kuala Lumpur: Grenier and Son, 1955). All other Chinese terms not so marked are in Mandarin, Wade-Giles romanization, as found in *Mathews' Chinese-English Dictionary* (Cambridge: Harvard University Press, 1963).

A-mi-t'o-fo 阿彌陀佛 (Amitahba Buddha), 61, 185, 193, 196n64, 197. *See also* Buddhism
Acrobats. *See* Rites, funeral: entertainment at
Afterlife, xiii, 8, 9, 11, 13, 24, 84, 180–202, 314. *See also* Belief
Ahern, Emily Martin. *See* Martin, Emily
Aisin Gioro, 232, 234n16
Almanacs, 25, 56, 57, 65
Altar of Earth, 228, 232, 243, 251, 253
Amiot J. J. M., 245, 246, 250
Amoy, 31, 51, 52, 53, 72, 135, 197, 291n5
*an chi-ting fang-chen pan* 按既定方鍼辦 [act according to principles laid down], 267n56, 270, 275
*an-chu* 安主 [placing the tablet on the altar], 42
*an-tsang* 安葬 [peaceful burial], 134
*Analects*, 26, 27, 30. *See also* Confucianism

Ancestor worship, xiii, 8, 23–24, 45, 180; and elites, 29–30, 32; and state religion, 30n21, 229, 251; at graves, 44, 204, 210, 226; in ancestral halls, 45, 204; and food, 73, 79; and geomancy of burial, 204n6, 207, 227; at home, 208
Ancestors: and descendants, 79, 207, 226–227; as ghosts, 188; transformation of spirit to, 204; depersonalizing of, 205; domestic cult of, 208; survival as, 209–210; imperial, and state religion, 253
Ancestral estate. *See tsu*
Ancestral halls, 76, 204, 208, 215, 218, 224, 232–233. *See also* Ancestral tablets
Ancestral tablets: ceremony of dotting the, 42, 89, 92, 102, 104, 189, 247, 250, 252; care of, 44, 45; and souls, 56, 92, 188, 201, 207, 208; inscribers of, 65; installation of, 65; and food offerings, 79, 90, 91; and